SOCIAL
THEORIES
OF RISK

SOCIAL THEORIES OF RISK

SHELDON KRIMSKY
and DOMINIC GOLDING, *Editors*

Westport, Connecticut
London

Library of Congress Cataloging-in-Publication Data

Social theories of risk / edited by Sheldon Krimsky and Dominic
  Golding.
      p.   cm.
    Includes bibliographical references and index.
    ISBN 0–275–94168–X (alk. paper). — ISBN 0–275–94317–8 (pbk. :
  alk. paper)
      1. Risk—Sociological aspects—Congresses.   I. Krimsky, Sheldon.
  II. Golding, Dominic.
  HM201.S65   1992
  302'.12—dc20   91–47739

British Library Cataloguing in Publication Data is available.

Library of Congress Catalog Card Number: 91–47739
ISBN: 0–275–94168–X
ISBN: 0–275–94317–8 (pbk.)

First published in 1992

Praeger Publishers, 88 Post Road West, Westport, CT 06881
An imprint of Greenwood Publishing Group, Inc.

Printed in the United States of America

The paper used in this book complies with the
Permanent Paper Standard issued by the National
Information Standards Organization (Z39.48–1984).

10 9 8 7 6 5 4 3 2

To Carolyn, Alyssa, and Eliot (SK)

To Claire and Heather (DG)

And to those dedicated to an understanding of the human dimension of risk.

Contents

Tables and Figures

TABLES

FIGURES

Preface

The field of risk studies grew out of the practical needs of industrialized societies to regulate technology and to protect their citizenry from natural and technological hazards. From its inception the study of risk was positioned at the intersection of academic, governmental, and industrial interests. Rising public concern about environmental hazards, in conjunction with growing corporate fears about liability, brought risk assessment and risk management to the foreground in the public and private sectors.

In large measure, the practical and theoretical approaches to risk have progressed in parallel fashion. Theory has been informed by practice, and occasionally, practice has been guided by theory. A sign that the field of risk studies has matured over the past two decades is the appearance of distinct paradigms, models, and conceptual frameworks that provide coherence to a field that abounds in scientific studies, case analyses, and empirical findings. Other indicators of the maturation of risk scholarship are the emergence of professional societies, specialized journals, and academic programs of study. Nonetheless, there are no books that trace the social and intellectual history of the dominant and emerging paradigms, their underlying assumptions, and the foundational issues they seek to address. This book is intended, therefore, to fill an important gap in the scholarship of risk studies.

To initiate the preparation of this book, the editors convened a workshop in Cambridge, Massachusetts, in January 1990. Several of the leading proponents of and adherents to the established and emerging paradigms were invited to prepare papers for discussion. The workshop was intended as a first step, and the papers were subject to a searching review and have been substantially revised since the workshop was held. Additional contributions were solicited to fill intellectual gaps and to ensure the comprehensive coverage of the principal paradigms in the field.

This book is a unique collection of papers from leading social science scholars in the field of risk. Each contributor was asked to discuss his or her theoretical perspective, or to provide a critical review of an established perspective that seeks to explain a key aspect of the social or scientific response to risk. A set of theoretical questions were prepared to guide the authors in preparation of their papers and to encourage consistency and comparability in terms of scope and content. The authors were asked to trace the intellectual origins and histories of their particular perspective on risk, outlining the principal elements and underlying assumptions of the framework. We were interested in understanding what the theories were supposed to explain, whether they bore any predictive knowledge, and what implicit or explicit presuppositions about risk, values, and rationality they carried. Another unique feature of the book is the attempt to combine personal intellectual histories of the contributors with the intellectual roots of the different perspectives on risk. Consequently, each chapter begins with a brief biographical sketch of the author(s). These personal biographies are fascinating, not only because they provide some intriguing details about the circuitous paths by which many of us come into the field of risk, but also because they highlight how these paths have crossed and what have been some of the seminal influences on individuals in particular and the field in general. Most notably, we see that Gilbert White has had a major influence on several individuals and that his early work in natural hazards paved the way for much subsequent research.

Our goal in this book is to bring together in one place a body of established and promising work that informs the largely empirical field of risk studies, that addresses the theoretical foundations of the field, and that reflects on what we know about risk as a psychological, social, and cultural phenomenon. These chapters not only inform us of the tributary ideas that spawned the social studies of risk, but they also examine the more mature paradigms of the field.

The book has four parts. Part I provides a conceptual and historical perspective on risk scholarship. In Chapter 1, Sheldon Krimsky discusses the contributions of theory to the risk literature and explores the types of contributions and their underlying assumptions, including models, ontological claims, and explanatory schemata, that have become part of the systematic treatment of risk. Dominic Golding presents a brief social and programmatic history of the field in Chapter 2. The chapter traces the growth and professionalization of risk research in the social sciences, by examining patterns of funding, the development and composition of the Society for Risk Analysis, the establishment of centers of research, and the content of the principal journal, *Risk Analysis*. In Chapter 3, Ortwin Renn develops a taxonomy that situates the major risk perspectives within the social and natural sciences according to their assumptions and methodologies, and their instrumental and social functions. Renn's classification shows that each perspective on risk fills a particular niche in a large, complex field poised for an integrative theory.

The five chapters comprising Part II present a spectrum of current theories of risk at different stages of maturation. In Chapter 4, Steve Rayner takes a comprehensive look at the development and current status of the cultural theory of risk. Rooted in anthropology, cultural theory has the broadest reach within the social sciences, covering risk selection, objectivity, science, rationality, and public perception. Rayner outlines the fundamental elements and assumptions of the theory and traces the various influences, including his own, that have molded the theory since its beginnings with Mary Douglas' work on ritual defilement. While the cultural theory of risk has generated considerable interest and even controversy, the psychometric paradigm has been perhaps the most influential in both academic and applied arenas. As such, we may see this as the dominant paradigm in the field. Paul Slovic and his colleagues at Decision Research have been the principal architects and proponents of the paradigm. In Chapter 5, Slovic discusses the origins of the paradigm and summarizes the empirical evidence that has made public perception of risk a central research program in contemporary risk studies for over two decades. In 1988, Roger Kasperson and his colleagues at the Center for Technology, Environment, and Development (CENTED), in collaboration with Paul Slovic, presented a new conceptual framework, which they called the social amplification of risk. In Chapter 6, Kasperson explains that the framework was intended to be a more holistic analysis of risk and its social meaning, drawing on elements of various competing and complementary theories, especially communications theory. Like the cultural and psychometric theories, the framework seeks to explain the apparent paradox that minor risks are often treated with great concern by the public, while other seemingly greater risks are ignored.

Chapters 7 and 8 present two emerging paradigms that have several features in common. In his "arena theory," Ortwin Renn (Chapter 7) proposes that risk controversies and conflicts are often not about risk per se but about access to resources. Risk in this context is used as a rallying point for group mobilization. Ingar Palmlund (Chapter 8) extends some of the metaphors used in arena theory (such as actors, stage, and audience). She builds an elaborate model of risk management as social drama, based on Aristotle's theory of dramatic form. Many risk events follow a pattern of exposition, complication, crisis, and dénouement similar to the structure of classical tragedy. The social drama metaphor provides us with a vivid lexicon and a powerful descriptive tool with which to examine the social dynamics of environmental hazards.

Part III examines the roles and limitations of experts, and the epistemological development and claims of science in risk assessment. In Chapter 9, Harry Otway gives a personal account of the changes he has experienced in his professional and intellectual career. Otway maps out a path that began with his belief that the key to understanding the clash between expert and public views of risk lay with cognitive psychology and that risk problems were amenable to technical solutions. He concludes with skepticism about the explanatory efficacy of the psychometric paradigm, with the realization that public responses to technological risks are intrinsically social and political in nature, and with the insight that science faces inherent limitations in seeking rational responses to risk events. William Freudenburg (Chapter 10) combines findings from cognitive psychology with themes of scientific rationality to paint an illuminating picture of the pitfalls of risk assessment. Freudenburg demonstrates that experts use simplifying heuristics and have biases similar to those held by the public, leading to systematic errors in the risk assessment process. This implies that public skepticism about expert assessments may be justified, and indeed may even be a prudent response in the light of uncertainty.

Silvio Funtowicz and Jerome Ravetz (Chapter 11) take this opportunity to lay out in detail the history, fundamental assumptions, and latest revisions of their familiar and widely cited tripartite division of risk assessment as *applied science, professional consultancy,* and *post-normal science.* They argue that in many contemporary risk problems the stakes are so high and the uncertainties so great that we need a new kind of science to provide credible and useful answers. This new science must depend on extended peer communities and extended facts. In sum, a "soft" science capable of handling "trans-scientific" problems will be necessary to make the "hard" policy decisions that lie ahead for risk management. In Chapter 12, Brian Wynne picks up on many of the themes addressed in chapters 9 through 11 when he examines the role of scientific knowledge in risk controversies and the way the social relations of technology shape the debates. Wynne offers a social constructionist interpretation of risk and is careful to dissociate himself from conspiracy theories and more populist perspectives. He believes that all bodies of knowledge, both expert and lay, can contribute to the resolution of disputes, but it must always be recognized that each body of knowledge is conditioned by social relations. The challenge for risk assessment, therefore, is to identify legitimate concerns in light of their social context and framing.

Part IV treats the problem of *setting* policy (how we ought to behave) in the face of uncertain knowledge about risks. Howard Kunreuther (Chapter 13) presents a conceptual framework that links descriptive analysis with prescriptive guidelines for managing low-probability/high-consequence events. Recognizing the limitations of traditional expected utility analysis, Kunreuther examines the roles of alternative policy tools for managing risks, including market-based incentive systems, compensation, insurance, and regulation.

A fundamental problem in policy making is the tension between the necessary reliance on experts and the democratic desire to incorporate public values and preferences. In Chapter 14, Detlof von Winterfeldt describes a tried-and-tested methodology that can help solve this problem. The method combines the multiple stakeholder approach for obtaining public value inputs with formal methods for eliciting expert judgments. These are used to construct a multi-attribute utility model for the various stakeholders. The goals of this process are to encourage the articulation of the different values held by stakeholders and to build a consensus for decision making. The process is not intended to derive estimates of the "true" risks. Chris Whipple (Chapter 15) argues that much of the disagreement and conflict about risk results from the ways in which the problems are framed. While there are cases where social conflicts over risks are due to different values among groups, Whipple argues that there is often considerable consensus on common values. Focusing on these shared values will help to reduce conflict and prevent some of the wild swings that afflict policy making.

The search for a synoptic view of societal risk taking will continue as long as the social and technical approaches to technology reach different conclusions or as long as we are impelled to understand how the management of risky technologies conforms or departs from some ideal of reason. It is our hope that both the established and exploratory theories presented in this volume will increase awareness among scholars both in the natural and social sciences of the vitality and imagination that has been characteristic of this field.

Acknowledgments

A book of this nature is clearly a cooperative effort. Not only have the individual authors produced their own contributions, but many read the early drafts of others and made helpful suggestions to their colleagues. The authors were patient and responsive to the persistent requests of the editors for refinements, and for this we are grateful. The editors are also grateful to Roger Kasperson and Howard Kunreuther, who served as an advisory committee in the early stages of the project.

We especially wish to express our appreciation to the Center for Environmental Management at Tufts University for providing the funding for this project, titled "Emerging Paradigms of Risk and Risk Communication: A Cultural Synthesis," under the assistance agreement CR813481 between the U.S. Environmental Protection Agency and the center. Some special people who provided support, vision, or guidance are Darwin Wright, EPA project officer for the Tufts-EPA cooperative agreement, Anthony Cortese, Dean of Environmental Programs, and William Moomaw, director of the Research and Policy Development at the Center for Environmental Management. Through the format of the cooperative agreement we had considerable latitude in approaching the subject matter covered in this work in as fresh and creative a way as our intellects would permit. It should be noted, however, that while the information and analysis in this book have been funded wholly or in part by the U.S. Environmental Protection Agency, they may not necessarily reflect the views of the agency, and no official endorsement should be inferred.

Others who deserve special mention for their valuable contributions are two graduate students in the Department of Urban and Environmental Policy at Tufts: Leah Steinberg, for her help in researching Chapter 2 and in organizing the 1990 symposium on theories of risk; and Peter Stott, for his highly prized editorial work, desktop graphics, and overall management of the manuscript in its final stages.

PART I

Conceptual and Historical Perspectives

CHAPTER 1

The Role of Theory in Risk Studies

Sheldon Krimsky

There were three stages to my intellectual development. I began serious academic studies in mathematics and physics. After earning a master's degree in physics, I entered the second stage of my formal education by turning my attention to philosophy and more specifically to the philosophical foundations of science. My doctoral research examined the use of thought experiments (mental models or *Gedankenexperimente*) in the development of physical theory. The issues of primary interest to me were the form and nature of scientific theory, the structure of scientific explanation, and the metaphysical foundations of science. The writers of special significance to me were Ernst Mach (*Knowledge and Error*, 1926), Thomas Kuhn (*The Structure of Scientific Revolutions*, 1962), Norwood Russell Hanson (*Patterns of Discovery*, 1963), Karl Popper (*The Logic of Scientific Discovery*, 1959), Paul Feyerabend (*Against Method*, 1975), and J. D. Bernal (*The Social Function of Science*, 1939). These and other works highlighted for me an issue that would later be the cornerstone of my investigations into the role of science in public policy: What claim can science make to objective truth, and what role does value play in the scientific enterprise?

In 1973, after teaching philosophy for three years, my attention began to turn toward the social enterprise of science, including its impact on public affairs. This transition, prompted in part by a geographical relocation, afforded me the opportunity to apply philosophical analysis to policy issues. I embarked on the third stage of my academic education with postdoctoral studies in economic theory and environmental policy. My first involvement in the field of risk studies began rather unexpectedly. I was asked by the city of Cambridge, Massachusetts, to serve on a local review board to assess the risks of the newly discovered recombinant DNA techniques in molecular biology, which were being introduced into the university research laboratories. Subsequently, I was appointed to the U.S. National Institutes of Health's Recombinant DNA Advisory Committee. Both of these experiences sharpened my interest in the role of science and politics in assessing the risks of new technologies. The works of Dorothy Nelkin, Jerry Ravetz, and Alvin Weinberg resonated with my own perspectives drawn from other philosophical traditions. I began to write about the interplay among science, values, and policy, with several recurring questions providing the thematic link. Why do experts disagree about risks? To what extent is risk assessment a science and to what extent is it metaphysics? Is there an objective basis for a science of risk? How is the technical enterprise of risk assessment reflected in the socioeconomic and political context of science? I have come to appreciate the fact that science, embedded as it is in its cultural context, can still pursue objectivity as an ideal, that rational thinking about risk is not expressed in one form, and that the impulse for expertise and the impulse for democratic process establish a constructive tension in society.

This chapter examines the contributions of theory construction in the social studies of risk. I begin by discussing the meaning of theory and theoretical activity. After distinguishing several modes of theory building, including laws, causal models, frameworks, and explanations, I give examples of how components of theory building have been applied in studies of risk.

The theoretical writings on risk emanate from many disciplines—both the mode of inquiry and the form of the explanation are reflected in the disciplinary traditions. My inquiry also examines the intellectual lineage behind two distinct paradigms of risk, one based upon the primacy of individuals (psychometric theory) and the other on the primacy of groups (cultural theory).

HIGHER-ORDER EXPLANATIONS

One of the twentieth century's leading philosophers, Alfred North Whitehead (1947, 3–4), wrote:

All the world over and at all times there have been practical men absorbed in "irreducible and stubborn facts:" all the world over and at all times there have been men of philosophic temperament who have been absorbed in the weaving of general principles. It is this union of passionate interest in the detailed facts with equal devotion to abstract generalisation which forms the novelty in our present society.

Whitehead understood that modern civilization, having emerged from the Enlightenment and the Industrial Revolution, was brought about through the confluence and cooperation of two types of temperaments, one focusing on the "here-and-now" of hard facts and practical knowledge, and the other on the lofty pursuit of abstract ideas, imagination, and philosophical reasoning. In the premodern world, the division between fact and theory, among other things, had class overtones. As philosopher of science Philipp Frank (1957, 25) observed:

We might say the "lower" strata collected facts while the "higher-ups" advanced principles. Contact between the two types of knowledge was discouraged by social custom. If a man of high social status attempted to apply his "philosophy" or "science" to technical problems, he was severely criticized. Experimental testing of general principles requires manual labor, which was regarded by the ancient Greeks as the appropriate occupation of slaves but not of free men.

The mutual reinforcement of theory building and fact gathering is a key to understanding the birth of modern science. As new disciplines develop and claim knowledge about the world, whether they begin at the empirical or theoretical pole, they are eventually balanced by the other mode of inquiry. In the language of the philosopher Immanuel Kant (N. K. Smith 1963, 93), concepts (the cognitive forms through which empirical observations are structured) without percepts (the data of observation) are empty, and percepts without concepts are blind.

The field of risk studies has strong roots in fact gathering. The collection of injury and mortality data for diseases and other natural hazards, as well as for personal and industrial accidents, provided vital information to insurance companies, health care planners, and safety engineers. Such raw empiricism, however, has its limits. Extrapolations of actuarial data are of limited use in assessing the risks of new technologies; inductive methods cannot be rationalized in the face of qualitative change.

Theory construction began in risk studies when hypothetico-deductive modeling of risk events was introduced in fields like toxicology and engineering. These theories were constructed with the expectation that predictions of future tragedies could forestall, eliminate, or greatly reduce the adverse consequences of technological innovation.

When popular attitudes and understanding about risk diverged appreciably from the predictions and explanations of experts, policy makers became attentive to the social dimensions of risk. Social scientists framed a set of questions collateral to risk assessment, such as, Why is it that lay people often fail to follow the advice of experts in responding to the risks of modern life? How can we explain the unusual and sometimes enigmatic selection and prioritization of risks within a particular culture?

Public opinion polls, attitude surveys, and case analyses are often a starting point. Early empirical studies help to frame the boundaries of the phenomena in question and highlight the growing disparity between experts and the popular culture. Public attitude data provide the grist for social scientists who search for a conceptual structure through which to interpret the broad patterns of meaning and explanation associated with risk that are the hallmark of social theory construction.

Early natural hazards researchers first identified and then tried to explain what they viewed as paradoxical behavior, that is, that people continue to live in flood-plain areas, refuse insurance, and ignore warnings. Economists, geographers, and psychologists advanced theories and hypotheses to account for the apparent irrationality of certain population groups in the 1940s and 1950s.

THE MEANINGS OF *THEORY*

Since the study of risk draws upon contributions from both the natural and social sciences, and since the term *theory* means quite different things across disciplines, there is a wide range of activities that might be termed *theory building*. Contributions to our theoretical knowledge of risk range from modeling the effects of chemical carcinogens to explaining the social response to technological or natural hazards. To appreciate fully these contributions to this field of inquiry, we must view the notion of theory with a wide-angle lens.

A useful distinction can be made between *theoretic activity* and *theory* per se. The former refers to certain methods of analysis, conceptualizations, or approaches to problems that are synthetic, abstract, and/or integrative, and apply to large domains of phenomena. The latter consists of a set of principles (axioms, empirical generalizations, laws) that provide explanatory coherence to an empirical domain. Theories may be descriptive (if they explain, predict, or account for empirical phenomena) or normative (if they stipulate a set of a priori rules of rational behavior, methodological norms, or ethical principles).

Useful theoretic activity need not always lead to theory development. This terminology allows us to appreciate the differences among conceptual clarification, the use of analogy, taxonomies, models, and a fully developed formal theoretical structure. Too often the term *theory* is loosely applied outside of the highly formalized natural sciences. Reynolds (1971) cites several examples of the shallow application of the term *theory* in the social sciences: vague conceptualizations of descriptions of events; prescriptions of desirable social behaviors; any untested hypothesis or idea.

Disciplines vary significantly in what they view as a theoretical enterprise. At one end of the spectrum, the term *theory* in physics refers to a set of formal axioms that are given an empirical interpretation (a nomological–deductive system of explanation). The theory accounts for some current body of empirical data and provides for the prediction of new observations. At the other end of the spectrum, the term *theory* is used loosely to refer to a single posited conjecture for explaining an event. In the popular lexicon, *what is your theory?* means *what is your explanation (or hypothesis) of the occurrence?* Between these extremes lies the more intermediate role theoretic activity plays in the study of risk. At the very least, we can say that a theory must offer a system of concepts and statements, models, or principles, which, in concert, make the empirical world more intelligible. According to John

Ziman (1968, 38), "A theory provides a logical ordering, a pattern, for observations."

I have been particularly careful to avoid defining *theory*. Others have found solace in Wittgenstein's view that a concept or activity can have meaning without having a clear and precise definition. As philosopher of science Wilfred Sellers (1970, 343) once wrote, "The term theory . . . covers a wide variety of explanatory frameworks resembling one another by that family resemblance which is easy to discern but most difficult to describe." Another philosopher, Dudley Shapere (1977, 556), remarked, "It is notorious that philosophers of science have provided no generally acceptable definition of 'theory' (or set of criteria for identifying theories) . . . it is easier to identify paradigm cases of theories in science than it is to formulate a general definition of 'theory' or a set of general criteria for identification of theories." In the behavioral sciences, and particularly in interdisciplinary studies, the contributions of theoretical work cover a much broader range of conceptual activities than they do in the natural sciences. Theories describing human behavior are rarely formalized (with the exception of economics and decision analysis). Some theories are not even designed to be empirically testable, but nonetheless provide a useful way of framing hypotheses or structuring empirical phenomena.

MODES OF THEORETICAL APPLICATIONS

The most salient theoretical contributions in the social studies of risk may be classified by the following categories: quantitative laws; static taxonomical frameworks; systems models; causal models; process models; functionalist explanations; cognitive explanations; and analogical models and interpretive representations. It should be noted, however, that some of these categories are vague, and several may apply to a single explanatory construct.

Quantitative Laws

Few attempts have been made to posit quantitative relationships or laws describing behavioral phenomena involving risks. Starr (1969) believed that he had discovered three such laws, although he assigned them tentative status:

1. The public is willing to accept voluntary risks about 1,000 times greater than involuntary risks.
2. The acceptability of risks appears to be roughly proportional to the third power of the benefits.
3. The acceptable level of risk is inversely related to the number of persons exposed to that risk.

While there has been minimal effort at replicating Starr's results, the putative "laws" of risk have not gained wide acceptance among risk specialists. Fischhoff, Slovic, and Lichtenstein (1979) found some agreement with Starr on the relationship between risk acceptability and benefits. Otway and Cohen (1975) replicated the analysis and found that the data do not support the quantitative formulations. Indeed, they observed that the voluntary risk lines intersect, indicating that people were willing to accept high involuntary risks with large benefits.

Subsequently, Starr, Rudman, and Whipple (1976) posited two additional quantitative laws of risk, one concerning the frequency and magnitude of risk events, and a second on the societal resilience to a given accident. They hypothesized that the probability or frequency of an event falls off as an exponential function of the magnitude: Log f = a − bM (where f = frequency, M = magnitude [e.g., fatalities], a,b = constants). According to this nomological statement, an event with 100 times the fatalities of another event will occur at a frequency much lower than one-hundredth that of the event with lesser magnitude.

Whether the putative law of association between the frequency and magnitude of event-fatalities holds up remains to be seen. Nevertheless, there are important intuitive and sociopsychological aspects to the conjecture. The public response to causes of human fatality is affected by time compression. Time-concentrated fatalities (e.g., catastrophic accidents like plane crashes) are less tolerable to the public than risk events with the same number of fatalities but distributed more widely in space and/or time. Greater societal effort is directed at reducing the frequency of catastrophic as compared to noncatastrophic fatalities. This finding is certainly consistent with the inverse nonlinear function connecting frequency and magnitude posited by Starr, Rudman, and Whipple (1976).

The second quantitative formulation posits a functional relationship between society's ability to bounce back after a catastrophic event with a set of social variables. Starr, Rudman, and Whipple (1976) hypothesized a direct relationship between societal resilience (R) and societal population (P) and average lifetime (L), and an inverse relationship to a function of the level of technology (B), average recovery times (t_r), time to discover the source of damage (t_d), time to correct mistakes (t_c), average disability per person affected (M), and the size of the population affected by the event (S).

$$R = \frac{PL}{BSt_r t_d M t_c}$$

The authors claimed that "the more technically advanced a society is, the lower its resilience," because in complex social systems, the breakdown of one critical subsystem disables the entire system (Starr, Rudman, and Whipple 1976, 656).

This hypothesis describing societal resilience is an interesting but highly suspect functional relationship. Complex technological societies may or may not be more subject than simpler societies to catastrophic breakdown, and are not necessarily less resilient once a breakdown takes place. Burton, Kates, and White (1978, 223) conclude, "Nature, technology, and society interact to generate vulnerability and resilience vis-à-vis disaster." This functional relationship bears resemblance to another hypothesis that appears in popular accounts of ecology—namely, that for natural ecosystems the stability of the system is related to its complexity. These hypotheses imply that, for stability, technological systems should be simple and natural systems complex. However, some simple agri-economies may experience wide swings as a consequence of a single catastrophic event. Alternatively, some of the world's major industrialized cities have been highly resilient in the face of major earthquakes. Much depends on the nature of the linkage between the subunits of a system, whether natural or technological, and the type of external perturbation. The two abiding metaphors are the "domino effect" and the "ballast system effect." In the former case, a small change knocks out the entire system, whereas in the latter, the damage to one ballast in a submarine is insulated from the other parts of the system, causing minimal disruption.

The third putative "law" states that as the number of people exposed to a risk increases, the acceptable level of risk is diminished; that is, people's threshold for tolerable risk is lowered. This generalization fails to account for cases in which society exerts considerable effort to save a few lives, as when Tylenol capsules were recalled from the market when it was discovered that a few capsules were laced with cyanide.

Finally, based on this analysis of current public policies, Starr, Rudman, and Whipple (1976, 630) also proposed a numerical upper bound of 10^{-2} (disease, mortality rate) and a lower bound of 10^{-6} (natural hazards) for the public's acceptance of involuntary risks.

The nomological formulations proposed by Starr, Rudman, and Whipple have not been advanced in the theoretical literature. They have been treated either as "philosophical speculations," heuristics that provide a mathematical shorthand for a qualitative description of causally related phenomena, or simply aberrant uses of quantitative reasoning. Despite the failed effort at quantitative formulations of social phenomena, certain segments of the social science community remain convinced that the model for all scientific explanation is physics.

Static Taxonomic Frameworks

The function of a taxonomy is to offer a conceptual net or template that provides order or structure to a domain of empirical phenomena. The "static taxonomical framework" (STF) makes no claim to describing a causal process. It is atemporal. In the tradition of classical biological taxonomies of plants and animals, STFs are instrumental category structures with no explanatory or ontological significance. They serve a nascent theoretic role for suggesting lines of inquiry, dividing up a field of study, making salient distinctions about modes of social behavior, or generating hypotheses. Taxonomies are not true or false, just more or less useful.

The process of classifying modes or objects of inquiry into a typology is a prerequisite for any scientific activity. Risks may be divided in many ways, including the nature of the hazard (e.g., natural vs. technological; acute vs. chronic), the route or medium of exposure (e.g., air pollution, water pollution), and the nature of the consequences (e.g., injuries vs. fatalities; carcinogens vs. noncarcinogens, etc.). Among the more formal and elaborate taxonomies that have been developed are Rowe's "factors in risk valuation" (Rowe 1977, 42); Hohenemser, Kasperson, and Kates' (1982) hazard classification; Slovic, Fischhoff, and Lichtenstein's (1985, 104, 120) risk characteristics; schematizing social phenomena, as in von Winterfeldt and Edwards' (1984, 63) "taxonomy of technological controversies"; or classifying theories (see Renn's taxonomy of risk perspectives in Chapter 3), and Burton and Kates' (1964, 415) taxonomy of natural hazards.

Systems Models

A systems model is a representation of the components of a system which exhibits the relationships among the elemental parts and expresses a direction of action and reaction. Systems models are often presented as "black boxes" (inputs and outputs) or schematics with directionality and feedback loops. These models can contain elements in quite disparate categories, representing an interface of human, ecological, and technological interactions. An example is Kates' model (Kates 1971, 443) to describe the human adjustment to natural hazards (see Figure 1.1).

While a systems model exhibits the interactive components of some dynamical process, it does not necessarily exhibit information about the causal factors underlying that process. Empirical observations may reveal causal factors in which events are temporarily located. Once those empirical associations are established, a causal model emerges. The test of effectiveness for a systems model is whether it accounts for the discrete subcomponents of a dynamical process, their interdeterminations, and feedback loops. Until the model can be guaranteed, it remains a schema with little explanatory or predictive value.

Causal Models

A set of generalized principles in the form of laws of association constitutes a causal theory of a class of phenomena. The causal laws may be deter-

Figure 1.1
Human Adjustment to Natural Hazards

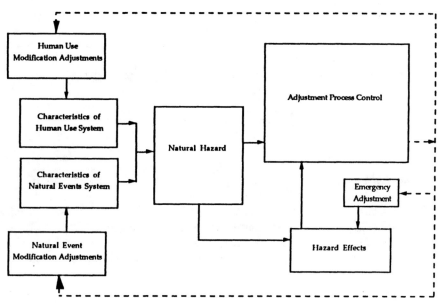

Source: Redrawn from Kates (1971, 443). Used by permission.

ministic (if A then B) or probabilistic (if A then probably B). Causal laws permit the prediction of consequent events from antecedent conditions.

Classical forms of causal law (if A then B) are not found in the social and behavioral theories of risk. However, we do see an emphasis on causal frameworks. A causal framework (or model) describes a sequence of events from the initiating condition to a final outcome. Each component in the chain is a generic type of event or activity. The function of the framework is to posit the generalized relationships between the components in a causal process. Because human behavior is involved, the framework must leave room for free will; consequently no iron law of necessity operates in the causal chain. The framework is effective if it correctly corresponds to empirical observation—for example, that processes of the type described can be deconstructed into the set of essential (necessary and sufficient) factors.

Hohenemser, Kasperson, and Kates (1982) posited a causal structure of technological hazards that is based on a seven-stage model starting with human needs and ending in biological effects (see Figure 1.2). Soderstrom et al. (1984) constructed a causal model of the psychosocial impacts on the restart of the Three Mile Island (TMI) nuclear facility. In their model, public perceptions of the TMI operation were caused by specific factors and re-

Figure 1.2
Causal Model of a Hazard

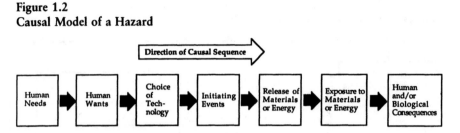

Source: Redrawn from Hohenemser et al. (1982, 134). Used by permission.

sulted in first-order (psychological and physiological) and second-order (behavioral, group, and community) impacts.

Each link in the causal chain is necessary for the final event to be realized. If the issue is groundwater contamination, the causal model directs us to a possible set of prerequisites. However, the model does not allow us to make a prediction (e.g., the Nile River is polluted) from a general schema and a set of initial conditions without causal laws.

Kasperson, Renn, et al. (1988) advanced a causal framework that is designed to integrate different dimensions of risk (technical, social, cultural, and psychological) within a single model (see Chapter 6). The model is causal, not in the sense of positing laws of causality, but rather in the sense of outlining a causal process (risk event, sources of amplification, channels of amplification, social stations of amplification, individual stations of amplification, group and individual responses, ripple effects, and impacts). An analogy is drawn with communications theory, where signals are modulated through transmission lines and transducers from a source to a final receiver. The framework sets the goals of the research agenda—namely, that "a full-fledged theory of the social amplification of risk should ultimately explain why specific risks and risk events undergo more or less amplification or attenuation" (Kasperson, Chapter 6).

Process Models

A process model consists of an ordered set of rules, procedures, or analytical tools that define a methodological approach to a problem or class of problems. In contradistinction to a causal model, which *describes* a class of phenomena, the process model sets forth in prescriptive fashion the steps that *ought* to be taken to reach a certain goal. Process models are generally quantized (there are discrete stages), and the stages are sequential (stage $n+1$ always follows stage n). These models are somewhat like roadmaps; if you wish to reach a particular destination, you must follow a certain path. In that sense, they provide an ordered structure to a technical analysis or planning exercise.

Rowe's (1977) analytical treatment of risk included a five-step process model of risk estimation. Several years later, building on the work of Rowe and others, the National Research Council (NRC 1983) produced a widely adopted process model designed for the social management of risks. The model consists of four stages: hazard identification, risk estimation, risk evaluation, and risk management. Each stage in the process is shorthand for a set of procedures that is more fully defined within specific disciplines (e.g., toxicology). Krewski and Birkwood (1987) provide a comparative view of various risk assessment/management models. Other examples of process models can be found in von Winterfeldt's explication of the steps in multiple stakeholder decision analysis (see Chapter 14), in the description by Kasperson, Kates, and Hohenemser (1985, 47) of a generalized program of hazard management, and in Crouch and Wilson's (1982, 104) idealized scheme for risk analysis.

Functionalist Explanations

The term *functionalism* refers to a class of explanations that have played a central role in the development of social anthropology, particularly the study of culture and institutions. Malinowski describes the role of functional explanation as "the explanation of anthropological facts at all levels of development by their functions, by the part which they play within the integral system of culture, by the manner in which they are related to each other within the system, and by the manner in which the system is related to the physical surroundings" (Nagel 1961, 52).

As a methodological approach to social phenomena, functionalism requires an examination of parts to wholes in a manner that explores how the former supports the survival, coherence, unity, interests, or values of the latter. It has been applied to explain the behavior of individuals in group settings, the survival of taboos, and the role of magic in preindustrial societies.

In sociological or cultural theory of risk, primacy is given to group attributes, ideology, or organizational norms that are instrumental to the lifestyles and chosen values of individuals. For example, Spangler (1982) and Plough and Krimsky (1987) distinguish between technical rationality, which supports the role of science, and cultural rationality, which serves the needs of the lay citizenry.

Functional explanation plays a central role in the writings of Douglas and Wildavsky. The authors claim that the types of risks the society selects out to address are functions of attributes of our social structures. "Each form of social life has its own typical risk portfolio" (Douglas and Wildavsky 1982b, 8). Risk selection is functional to cultural objectives. Rayner's discussion of grid/group analysis in Chapter 4 is a functional explanation of risk selection defined within certain institutional parameters. People are attentive to the risks that are more discordant with the values of their primary institutional affiliation, for example, hierarchy or egalitarianism. If different risks are selected out in a culture's "worry budget," the proper question to ask is how does attention to the selected risks serve the culture? Functional explanations of risk are not about "true" or "consistent" risk estimates; rather they are about the coherence between risk selection and a way of life.

Cognitive Explanations

Principles or laws of cognition, and categories of human thought, are sometimes used to explain or account for human attitudes or behavior. In his discussion of bounded rationality, Perrow (1984) focuses on the role of heuristics, or mental constructs, that simplify complex decisions. Cognitive explanations have played a significant role in the psychometric theory of risk (Slovic, Chapter 5; Fischhoff, Slovic, and Lichtenstein 1979; Tversky and Kahneman 1973, 1974). More recently, Bostrom, Fischhoff, and Morgan (forthcoming) used the term *mental models* to describe how people think about environmental phenomena. According to Bostrom, "People's mental models are determined by both their overall 'cognitive architecture' (i.e., how the mind works within its computational and memory constraints) and their expertise on a specific topic [sic]" (Bostrom 1990, 4).

Analogical Models and Interpretive Representations

One form of theory building involves the use of analogy in model construction. The history of science provides a rich source of examples where models from one discipline are reinterpreted and applied to another field. The discovery that similar structural relationships exist between two domains serves as a basis for theory construction.

Hesse (1966) distinguishes two senses in which analogy is used in science. *Formal analogy* applies when two physical theories share the same logical or formal structure; that is, both theories are described by the same set of differential equations. The second type of analogy is called *material analogy*. One theory is materially analagous to another when the relationships between the component elements of one can be useful for theory construction in the second. As an example, the wave theory of sound (with terms like pitch, frequency, and energy) is analogous to the wave theory of light; that is, the properties of sound are to pitch as the properties of light are to color (Hesse 1966, 68). Similarly, Kasperson, Renn, et al.'s social amplification framework draws a material analogy from signal theory. Signals can be amplified or attenuated in different media or when electronically altered, and risk messages are signals of a sort which may be carried in different media and affected by different social processes. Covello, von Winterfeldt, and Slovic (1987) build on the signal analogy for their model of risk communication. A three-part scheme consisting of a transmitter, a channel of communication, and a receiver provides a framework for identifying problems of communicating health and environmental risks to a lay audience.

Palmlund (Chapter 8) finds a useful analogy between dramatic form, particularly the classical structure of tragedy, and the social response to risk. She carries over terms like *actors, theater, drama,* and *roles* to develop a vocabulary that illuminates the social and political drama of environmental tragedy. Offenbacher and Slovic (1989) draw an analogy between the concept of heat in thermodynamics and the concept of quantitative risk.

One of the most important ways that analogy enters into theories of risk is in how we think about wholes and parts. We either draw our analogy from scientific reductionism (e.g., chemistry or physics), in which the whole is fully explainable by the parts, or from nonreductionist models (e.g., ecology) in which the whole has unique qualities that cannot be explained by the parts.

INDIVIDUALISM AND CONTEXTUALISM

One can find both individualist and contextualist modes of explanation in social theories of risk. In the former case the starting point of any analysis is the unit of recognition—the thinking, acting individual. Empirical data radiate from the study of individuals to generalizations about social groupings. In the latter case, emphasis is placed on the context (culture, affinity group, organization, lifestyle) as the starting point for analysis.

Two illustrations of the individualist paradigm are described by Wildavsky and Dake (1990) as the "knowledge theory" and the "personality theory." According to the knowledge theory, people respond to risk on the basis of the knowledge and information at their disposal. The personality theory seeks to explain risk aversive and risk tolerant choices of individuals by their personality types (which includes their propensity toward certain political ideologies). The most articulated, mature, and influential of the social science theories that build on an individualist paradigm are the cognitive theory of risk (see Chapter 5) and economic models of risk based on expected utility theory (Kunreuther, Chapter 13; Camerer and Kunreuther 1989a; Crouch and Wilson 1982; Rowe 1977).

The contextualist mode of analysis begins with the *setting,* for example, social structure, institutional form, or cultural milieu. Several chapters in this book reflect the contextualist mode of analysis. Rayner discusses a typology of social structure based on group membership and social relationships within the group (hierarchical vs. egalitarian) in Chapter 4. Renn's form of contextualism (Chapter 7) is symbolized by political arenas, which are the settings that shape the power struggles underlying risk discourse, while Palmlund's (Chapter 8) is the "theater" of social controversy. In the social amplification model, Kasperson (Chapter 6) emphasizes the context in which risk events and risk messages are embedded. Unlike other contextualists, however, Kasperson avoids making ontological claims about the primacy of social factors. His theory is more in the spirit of a framework, in that it provides the envelope within which empirical research takes place. Wynne's contextualism (Chapter 12) is expressed in his sociology of knowledge. Science in general, and its contribution to risk in particular, cannot provide objective knowledge, only a belief structure that is "intrinsically conditioned by social commitments" (Wynne 1982a, 139).

I shall now describe some of the intellectual lineage behind the cognitive theory of risk, one of the two central paradigms that builds its social theory from the analysis of individuals.

THEORY DEVELOPMENT IN RISK PERCEPTION

There are two principal tributaries to the cognitive theory of risk perception, sometimes also referred to as the psychometric theory of risk. First, there are the studies of public response to natural hazards such as floods, hurricanes, and earthquakes. Why do some people choose to live on a flood plain or choose to buy earthquake insurance? The theoretical contributions to this field of inquiry consist of applications of rational expectation theory, empirical generalizations (e.g., people underestimate the risk of low-frequency, high-consequence events), and models that sketch out the relevant factors of individual adaptation to natural hazards.

A second important tributary to the theory of risk perception comprises studies in cognitive psychology directed at how people reason under conditions of uncertain knowledge. The research program in cognitive psychology has had a formidable influence on current theories of public perception and will be the focus of this discussion.

The investigations of cognitive psychologists Amos Tversky and Daniel Kahneman (1973, 1974) provide a good starting point. They designed a series of laboratory experiments to determine how people solve complex problems involving frequency and probability. Typically, experimental subjects were asked to estimate outcomes after they were given a set of instructions and some information which was varied in different trials. For example, in one experiment, subjects were shown brief personality profiles randomly sampled from a group of 100 professional lawyers and engineers. The subjects were asked to give a probability estimate that the profile they had been given was that of an engineer. Tests were repeated with subjects being given different figures on the actual percentage of lawyers and engineers in the sample.

In another series of experiments, the investigators elicited the subjects' estimates of the letter frequency in certain words (e.g., does "r" appear more frequently as the first or third letter of five-letter words?). Tversky and Kahneman were interested in identifying the factors that influence people's probability estimates, such as sample size, prior probability, qualitative information about the sample, and frames of reference.

Although these were laboratory experiments, divorced from people's prac-' tical lives and work experience, what the investigators discovered had a significant influence on theory development in risk perception. They discovered that, when faced with complex problems involving probability estimates or estimates of the frequency of events, people apply certain discernable rules of judgment called heuristics to simplify the problem. The use of heuristics often leads to judgment bias.

As an example, when people are asked to compare the frequency of certain events, they will judge an event more likely to occur if it is easier for them to imagine or recall the so-called availability heuristic. Some events are easier to recall because of the event's intensity, because it has been reinforced by the media, or simply because of the subject's familiarity with it.

The next major advance in the theory came when the concept of heuristics was applied to the study of individual perceptions and estimates of the risk of technologies, disease, and natural hazards in modern life. Research programs, started in the early 1970s, attempted to explain people's extreme aversion to some hazards, their indifference to others, and the discrepancies between these reactions and expert opinions (see Chapters 2 and 5). The experimental methods were similar to the earlier investigations of Tversky and Kahneman. Students, members of the League of Women Voters, local business leaders, and experts were the subjects of laboratory studies where they were asked to place risk events on a scale, compare the risks of different activities and technologies, and rate certain characteristics of hazardous activities.

The most significant outcome from this generation of investigations was the discovery of a list of risk attributes that play a role in people's assessment of the probability, frequency, or outcome of natural and technological hazards. In some cases the attributes proved to be a better predictor of public response to an activity or technology than mortality or morbidity figures. For example, the investigators discovered that people often distinguish voluntary from involuntary events and are likely to rate the risks of voluntary activities lower than those of involuntary activities, *ceteris paribus*.

Although not stated explicitly in the research findings, the attributes of risk, such as voluntary/involuntary take on the role of heuristics as posited by Tversky and Kahneman. However, those who advance the cognitive theory of risk perception stop short of referring to the risk attributes as *heuristics*. They use terms like *determinants of perceived risk, concepts by which people characterize risks, taxonomy of hazards,* and *cognitive maps of risk attitudes and perceptions.* But risk attributes function like judgmental heuristics. They serve as filters or a priori categories through which individuals experience events as "risk laden" and render personal decisions. The theory predicts that an event perceived as involuntary, new, and catastrophic is more likely to be rated riskier than an event perceived as voluntary, old, and chronic.

There are at least eighteen risk attributes that have become the central theoretical underpinning to the cognitive (or psychometric) theory of risk perception (Slovic, Fischhoff, and Lichtenstein 1981). The attributes afford the theory of risk explanatory as well as predictive efficacy. It may be possible to predict an individual's response to an activity or technology on the basis of the individual's assignment of attributes.

Relatively little discussion has been devoted to the foundational assumptions of the cognitive theory. For example, what is the ontological significance of the attributes voluntary/involuntary, common/dread, new/old? Are they categories of cognition? Are they intrinsic properties of the event or of the technology? Or are they properties determined by the relationship of an event and a subject? The answer may be different for different attributes and different groups of people. To speak of a risk as voluntary or involuntary does not define a property of the event per se. On the other hand, the temporal distribution of an event (immediate/protracted) is a characteristic of the event (e.g., an explosion vs. long-term low-dose exposure to a chemical); however, the interpretation of long or short duration may vary along cultural lines.

There is an important difference between the early research on probability estimates and the later research on risk perception. In the former case, there was presumed to be an objectively determined probability against which one could measure a subject's rating. However, in studies of risk perception, in many instances, there is no objective measure of risk, although there are estimates or theoretical determinations by experts. This factor of uncertainty over the objectivity of risk estimates has prompted some investigators to study the risk estimators rather than the risk responders (Freudenburg, Chapter 10).

As previously noted, the cognitive (or psychometric) approach to risk perception has been guided by the individualist paradigm. The perceived risk is the outcome measurement (revealed or expressed preference) of the interaction of an individual and the external environment mediated through cognitive structure. The theory is ahistorical and noncontextual, and much of its development has centered on laboratory studies in contrast to *in situ* or ethnographic studies. The explanatory force of the cognitive theory has a strong intuitive and phenomenological grounding. And while it may not account for social desiderata, it has contributed an important schema that has clarified the meaning of risk, provided insight into issues of acceptable risk, and informed public policy.

CONTRIBUTIONS OF THE CONTEXTUALIST PARADIGM: CULTURAL THEORY

Cultural theories of risk have their lineage in anthropology both in method and content. The study of ritual in tribal society, a central goal of classical anthropology, has contributed insights into the social selection of and adaptation to risks. In his classic work, *Magic, Science and Religion*, Malinowski (1948) revealed the functions of ritual and religious practice in tribal cultures in response to high-risk and uncertain activities.

Those who have advanced a form of cultural theory to understand risk in modern technological society cite as a seminal work Mary Douglas' (1966, 1972) discussion of cultural "pollution," including ritual uncleanliness, defilement, food taboos, and risky behavior in ancient cultures. Douglas argues that many classes of risk-avoidance activities in ancient civilizations are explained by their role in creating order out of contradictory experiences and moral confusion. Beliefs about animal taboos, forbidden foods, or eating practices were adopted because they supported the conventional moral code and taxonomical classifications that created orderliness.

The investigation of forbidden activities in tribal societies and pretechnological civilizations prompted a set of inquiries that were neglected by those who studied risk from a pragmatic and problem-oriented perspective. For the anthropologist the key issue was: Why have various cultures selected certain risks and, in response, proscribed various practices in their belief structure? Douglas provided the bridge between classical anthropology and the application of its theoretical underpinnings to contemporary technological society, where the questions focus on risk selection across national boundaries and intranationally, among social groupings.

Cultural theorists have advanced our understanding of risk in three general areas:

1. the ontological status of risk;
2. a theory of risk selection; and
3. testable models that connect sociological variables with individual attitudes toward risk.

The *ontology of risk* refers to its metaphysical status as a property or quality in the physical world. Is the risk of something an objective measure of that thing, or is it a subjective value that varies according to context? Cultural theorists have criticized psychometric paradigms for advancing a realist ontology of risk (Wynne 1982a). "Risk, though it has some roots in nature, is inevitably subject to social processes" (Thompson and Wildavsky 1982, 148). However, Slovic, a leading figure in the psychometric school, denies that his theory embraces a realist ontology of risk (see Chapter 5). While neither the measurement nor the theory of public perception of risk logically rests on risk having an objective status or representing a property of the world, this assumption is commonly held among those in the technical risk assessment community who speak about the public's distorted perception.

A second contribution of cultural theorists to the ontological dimensions of risk is their critique of methodological individualism or the explanation of social behavior by the aggregate of individual behaviors. Group and social context, not individual cognition, plays the primary role in the selection and response to risk. According to this view, the proper scale of analysis of risk is sociological and not psychological. The order of explanation proceeds from the social context to the individual. The choice people make about risks is settled by the choices they make in the kinds of social institutions with which they associate (Douglas and Wildavsky 1982b, 187). "Risk is always a social product" (Thompson and Wildavsky 1982, 160).

Cultural theorists offer a general theory of risk selection that is based on a functionalist approach to cultural survival. People become concerned about certain risks because the practices associated with the risk taboos are useful (provide group/cultural stability). Functionalism preempts the role of a transcendent rationality. Like natural selection, an interpretation about risk is not right or wrong in some absolute sense; it survives or disappears because of its usefulness in the social system. This view is consistent with the idiom of cultural rationality where different stakeholders find that an event or activity labeled risky by some may function differently for others who do not share the same belief system (see von Winterfeldt's analysis of value elicitation in Chapter 14).

The third contribution of cultural theory is testable models or hypotheses from which we can draw causal or structural connections between social groupings and risk selectivity. Organizational and cultural affiliations define a belief structure for risk. "If individuals in different social contexts are firmly attached to contradictory convictions about how the world is, then it is only to be expected that they will have very different ideas of what risks are out there" (Thompson and Wildavsky 1982, 147).

Among cultural theorists, grid/group analysis has been the most prominent explanatory schema for connecting social context and organizational affiliation to individual risk selection (see Rayner, Chapter 4). The political and sociological variables distinguish between whether one is an individualist comforted by the market and disturbed by government intervention, a hierarchist who is most comfortable in highly structured organizations, or a sectarian who shuns hierarchy but thrives on group membership.

A meta-theoretical question arises in comparing individualist and contextualist approaches to risk selection. Does personality (including cognitive structure) precede context, or does context precede personality? Can one explain an organizational or political affiliation on personality type, or is it one's affiliation that determines the personality? This chicken or egg problem raises the dilemma of the primacy of contextualism (social or cultural unit) or individualism (personality type or cognitive structure). According to Levins and Lewontin (1985), a dialectical approach to the study of biological systems can avoid the confusions brought about by the establishment of dichotomous variables, for example, nature/nurture, or the psychosocial and physiological. Douglas and Wildavsky occasionally express the dialectical viewpoint. "The main questions posed by the current controversies over risk show the inappropriateness of dividing the problem between objectively calculated physical risks and subjectively biased individual perceptions" (1982b, 194); "Much as in biology, the cultural theory of risk perception sees the social environment, the selection principles, and the perceiving subject as all one system" (1982a, 50).

CONCLUSION

This book is the first systematic effort to highlight the contributions of the social sciences to a theory of risk. Among the perspectives represented in this work, the cognitive and cultural theories come closest to fulfilling the role of a mature paradigm. Much of the "normal science" associated with building social theory has revolved around expanding the scope and principles of these paradigms. New theories have blossomed, not as a result of a critical anomaly in the dominant paradigms but because new questions required alternative approaches. The variety of theoretical contributions in this book is a sign that social science is colonizing new domains of inquiry in the field of risk. If there is ever going to be a synoptic or unified theory of risk, it will have to take account of the issues raised in the following chapters. And since the term *risk* does not define a single discipline, a new challenge is cast upon the social sciences, namely, to discover an overarching theoretical framework that best situates risk as a field of study *among* and *beyond* traditional disciplines.

In stating that the theoretical contributions represented in these chapters are not contesting interpretations and explanations for a single domain of empirical phenomena, in the way the wave and corpuscular theories of light competed, I am not saying that there are no areas of conflict. I have tried to outline a few of these: the ontological status of risk; the nature and epistemological status of science that informs our knowledge about risk; the meaning of rationality as it applies to evaluating risk and setting standards of "acceptable risk."

The issues addressed by social theories continue to evolve from explaining risk selection, to understanding human responses, to analyzing the social function of science, to accounting for the sources and changes of societal values. As social scientists, we are seeking the fundamental level of explanation for the human response to hazardous conditions, focusing on cognition, language, emotion, reason, or cultural and social roles. The quest for theoretical coherence in our explanatory schema may be as deeply rooted in our species as the desire to understand and reduce the risks we face in daily life.

NOTE

I wish to acknowledge the invaluable contributions of my coeditor, Dominic Golding, to this chapter.

CHAPTER 2

A Social and Programmatic History of Risk Research

Dominic Golding

It may seem strange that a geographer should be involved in a volume such as this on the social science theories of risk. The relationship between humans and their environment, however, which is the essence of risk research, has been one of the dominant research themes in twentieth-century geography. The early works of the Chicago School (Gilbert White and his triumvirate of graduate students, Ian Burton, Kenneth Hewitt, and Robert Kates) on natural hazards, and floods in particular, fall squarely in this tradition. The influence of these pioneers extends beyond the boundaries of geography, as is evident from the personal testimony of several fellow contributors to this book. Gilbert White, the dean of natural hazards research, paved the way for much subsequent research that now goes under the rubric of risk analysis, but it was not until I read several of the biographical pieces in this volume that I realized the true extent of his influence.

As the youngest contributor to this book, and a relative newcomer to the field of risk, it seems somewhat presumptuous for me to trace my intellectual roots. Not surprisingly, many of the major figures whose writings have most influenced my thoughts on risk are represented in these pages. Whereas all the other contributors were trained in various traditional disciplines and later brought their skills to bear on the issues of risk, I have focused almost exclusively on risk (broadly defined) since my early graduate days. My background is therefore atypical by comparison.

As an undergraduate in Oxford, I was obliged to read the works of the Chicago School, but they seemed somewhat peripheral to my main interests at that time in more mainstream environmental issues and the geography of social segregation. My appetite for hazards research was whetted, however, when I read about the geography program at Clark University. I was especially intrigued by the work on the structure of technological hazards being done by Bob Kates, Roger Kasperson, and the other members of the Hazard Assessment Group in the Center for Technology, Environment, and Development (CENTED). The graduate program in geography at Clark University has a reputation for being unconventional and allowed me the leeway to focus my research efforts almost entirely in the area of technological hazards and risk management.

Roger Kasperson and Bob Kates shaped my nascent views on risk as a broad, multifaceted social phenomenon and introduced me to the broader social science literature on risk. As one of the premier hazards research centers in the United States, CENTED also gave me the opportunity to meet and collaborate with many of the leading risk researchers. The Hazard Assessment Group is unusual in a variety of ways, not the least of which is the success it has achieved in fostering an uncommonly open and collaborative working relationship among its diverse members. Even as a graduate student I was closely involved in all aspects of the research. Collaborative interdisciplinary research can be very frustrating, however, because it takes so long to develop the necessary rapport and cross-disciplinary communication and understanding. Nonetheless, once achieved such rapport is extremely rewarding both personally and intellectually.

It is the bane of all eclectic liberals, such as me, to see merit in the different arguments on all sides of a debate. While this magnanimity is praised in some circles (notably those comprising other eclectic liberals), it is often criticized for being weak and wishy-washy, unable to commit wholeheartedly to any theoretical approach and carry an argument to its logical end. Thus, I can sympathize with the engineer trying to define risk in "objective" fashion, although I lean toward the more "subjective" view of risk developed by the psychological, social, and cultural theorists. Each theoretical approach makes a contribution to our understanding as we see in this volume, but none alone gives a complete explanation. The psychometric studies conducted by Paul Slovic and his colleagues were a significant influence on my early thinking about risk as a multifaceted phenomenon, but I have always felt that the attributes identified need to be embedded in a broader social and cultural context. The cultural theory of risk is arguably the most elegant and comprehensive framework, although it has been criticized for its lack of empirical evidence and apparent relativism. Steve Rayner's eloquent description of risk as a polythetic concept has enormous intuitive appeal. His assertion that fairness, trust, and consent are more important than numerical estimates of risk rings true, and is amply supported by everyday experience. Thus, like many others in this volume, I believe that members of the public are not behaving irrationally when they ignore expert assessments that are based on narrow, technocratic definitions of risk. As Harry Otway and Bill Freudenburg have pointed out, the public is often wisely prudent and the experts are often mistaken. I do not, however, subscribe to conspiracy theory. I do not believe that risk scientists are generally in collusion against the public, nor do I believe that the public necessarily knows best. Rather, taking my cue from Brian Wynne, I believe that public knowledge is no less valuable than expert knowledge, and that a response that appears rational according to one perspective may be considered quite irrational from the other. In Wynne's terms, expert knowledge and public knowledge are conditional—each reflects the underlying social relations and implicit assumptions of the various actors. To derive a more complete picture of risk in the real world, it is therefore necessary to accommodate both sets of knowledge. In the same way, we can see the various theoretical perspectives as being conditional—none is necessarily better than another, and each has something to contribute to our understanding of risk. Such is the bane of the eclectic liberal!

Many academics are loathe to talk personally about themselves and their work. In part this may result from the fact that as academics we are taught to "depersonalize" our research, to write in the passive voice, and to trace our ideas to theoretical foundations, not personal influences. On the other hand, we all conjure up pictures of the major figures in our lives and are often surprised when fiction meets fact. I have always found that knowing people personally is a tremendous aid to understanding them intellectually. I was intrigued and excited when Shelly asked me to join him on this venture—a unique opportunity to try to combine intellectual and personal histories, and a wonderful opportunity to work with many of the leading lights in the field of risk. My interest in the personal, historical, and programmatic facets of the field is also evident in the following chapter.

People have engaged in risk assessment and management since time immemorial, but although its roots may be traced back beyond Greek and Roman times (Covello and Mumpower 1985), formal risk analysis is a relatively recent activity. It was not until the early part of this century that engineers, epidemiologists, actuaries, and industrial hygienists, among others, began conducting analyses of the hazards associated with technology (Kates and Kasperson 1983). At the same time, economists, geographers, geologists, hydrologists, psychologists, sociologists, and others were engaged in interdisciplinary research on natural hazards and disaster management (Burton, Kates, and White 1978; White and Haas 1975).

Legislation in the early 1970s, with the formation of federal agencies such as the Environmental Protection Agency (EPA), elevated the role of formal risk assessment in the regulatory process and led to the professionalization of risk analysis, with a burgeoning array of consulting firms to serve the private and public sectors. The increasing use of risk analysis in industry and the regulatory process lent legitimacy to this field as an academic activity (Cumming 1981; Lind 1987).

While formal risk analysis is a relatively recent activity, little has been written about its history and development. Covello and Mumpower (1985) have done an admirable job of tracing some of the "prehistory" of the field, and Dietz and Rycroft (1987) have evaluated the perspectives of a variety of "risk professionals." Most of the history, however, remains unwritten and unspoken in the minds of the small, eclectic coterie of regulators, academics, and practitioners from diverse backgrounds. This chapter traces some of this history by looking at a series of indicators of the growth and professionalization of risk research, including patterns of funding, the development of the Society for Risk Analysis, and the establishment of academic research centers. Given the nature of the book, this chapter focuses on the part played by the social sciences and does not address the development of research in the physical and life sciences, nor does it address the significant contributions made in the natural hazards and disaster research areas.

THE FUNDING OF RISK RESEARCH

Risk analysis incorporates an abundance of theoretical perspectives and methodological techniques, from models of cancer causation to probabilistic risk assessments of potentially catastrophic accidents. This research has been and continues to be funded from a variety of sources ranging from government agencies, such as the Environmental Protection Agency, the Food and Drug Administration (FDA), the Nuclear Regulatory Commission (NRC), and the Department of Energy (DOE), to private foundations. Much research is also conducted in-house by the major corporations or contracted out to consulting firms. The social sciences have traditionally received much less funding than the physical and life sciences, and it is therefore surprising that the social sciences have achieved and maintained a relatively high profile in risk research. The aim of this section, however, is not to track all sources of funding to derive some total, but rather to use the pattern of funding to illustrate the growth and direction of research in the social sciences. As such, I shall focus on the origins and development of funding for risk research at the National Science Foundation (NSF), an important barometer of the field's maturation.[1]

The National Science Foundation has funded a considerable amount of the leading research on risk in the social sciences through various programs. Natural hazards research has been funded through the Earthquake Hazards Mitigation Program and the Natural and Man-Made Hazard Mitigation Program at NSF. Much of the early work at Decision Research and at the Center for Environment, Technology, and Development was funded through the Research Applied to National Needs (RANN) Program. Risk research, however, was not an explicit program area until the formation of the Technology Assessment and Risk Analysis Program in 1979.

Technology Assessment and Risk Analysis (TARA) Program

In March 1979 the House Committee on Science and Technology encouraged the National Science Foundation to develop a program of "systematic research to improve the methods for evaluation of long-term comparative risks of alternative technological solutions, including inaction, to such national concerns as energy, materials, environmental quality, food or drugs" (U.S. Congress 1979, 28–29). The committee noted that "the ability to assess alternative policies lags well behind the need. Those who perform risk and benefit assessments recognize and deplore the weakness of available tools and methods, while, at the same time, attempting to meet the growing demand" (U.S. Congress, 1979, 29). The committee believed that universities and organizations such as the National Academy of Sciences were the "natural developers and repositories of the required skills and methods," and that the National Science Foundation had a major responsibility to "promote education in risk assessment methods and to stimulate public and professional application of comparative risk research" (U.S. Congress 1979, 29). The committee recommended setting aside approximately $1 million for these purposes.[2]

In response, the National Science Foundation initiated a program of research in August 1979, after close consultation with the National Academy of Sciences and members of other relevant committees. Program responsibility was assigned to the Division of Policy Research and Analysis (PRA) within the Directorate for Scientific, Technological, and International Affairs (STIA) at NSF. The scope of the Technology Assessment (TA) Program was broadened to encompass these new responsibilities, and the group was renamed the Technology Assessment and Risk Analysis (TARA) Group (NSF 1979). Joshua Menkes was then Group Leader of the TA Program, and agreed to head up the new TARA Program. Vincent Covello, who had been with the TA Group since 1978, became Program Manager for Risk Assessment and took over the major responsibilities for handling the risk-related activities within TARA.

The primary objectives for TARA were to:

• support extramural research on risk analysis;
• strengthen NSF's efforts in risk analysis by giving it a more prominent position within the organization; and
• recognize the complementarity between technology assessment and risk analysis.

In an early effort to set the directions for and boundaries of risk research, the TARA Program identified ten questions believed to be generic to risk analysis and management (Table 2.1). While we may each draw up a different list, it is interesting, ten years later, to reflect on these questions. How well have they stood up over time? How might they look different now? We can see reflected in these questions many of the issues that have dominated the field at different times, and indeed continue to dominate. The notions of risk perception and the determination of acceptable risk permeate throughout, beginning with the old saw, How safe is safe enough? There is an obvious concern for the separation between risk assessment and risk management, between science and policy making. Overall, the list would seem to be fairly robust, but with hindsight two notable themes appear to be absent—risk communication and the social and cultural context of risk, which have since become prominent areas of research in the social sciences.

In 1982, the Risk Analysis and Demonstration Act was proposed, and

Table 2.1
Ten Generic Questions for Risk Analysis and Management

1. How do we determine "how safe is safe enough?"

2. How good are the knowledge base and methods for estimating the risks associated with different technologies?

3. How are estimates of risk incorporated into decision making?

4. How do decision makers treat uncertainties associated with different risks and hazards?

5. How do features of the institutional context affect decision-making bodies concerned with risk and uncertainty?

6. What factors influence individual perceptions of risk and benefit?

7. How are perceptions of risk and benefit incorporated into public policies?

8. How does society cope with risks that are unacceptable to some segments of the population?

9. How are normative considerations such as equity and social justice balanced in decision making about risk?

10. What are the criteria for comparing and evaluating different management policies?

although it never passed, it acted as a stimulus for the development of the Risk Analysis Program within NSF. The act would have established a co-ordinated program of research on and demonstration of the methodologies, application, and potential limitations of risk analysis in the decision-making process. In particular, it would have required that the National Science Foundation develop a broad program of research on new and improved methods for gathering and analyzing data, and on the role of comparative risk analysis in regulatory decision making. Strengthening basic and applied research in these areas was intended to bolster the use of risk analysis in federal agencies and regulatory decision making.

In spite of the failure of this act to pass, the TARA staff organized and participated in several conferences and professional meetings with these goals in mind. Proceedings from several of these conferences were published and remain standard texts for the field (Table 2.2). The first annual meeting of the newly formed Society for Risk Analysis (SRA) was held at the National Academy of Sciences in Washington, D.C., in June 1981. The workshop focused on the provocative findings from the psychometric research that public perceptions of risk differ markedly from expert assessments. The topic was very much in vogue at that time, and, arguably, has been the most influential contribution of the social sciences to the conduct of risk analysis and management. The proceedings of this meeting were published

Table 2.2
Meetings and Conferences with TARA Input and Support, 1981–1985

Washington, DC June 1-3, 1981		International Workshop on the Analysis of Actual Versus Perceived Risk
	Published as:	V.T. Covello, W.G. Flamm, J.V. Rodricks, R.G. Tardiff, eds. (1983). *The Analysis of Actual Versus Perceived Risk.* New York, NY: Plenum Press.
Arlington, VA June 15-17, 1982		SRA International Conference on Low Probability/High Consequence Risk Analysis: Methods, Applications, and Case Studies
	Published as:	R.A Waller and V.T. Covello, eds. (1984). *Low Probability/High Consequence Risk Analysis.* New York, NY: Plenum Press.
Bonn, Germany July 1982		U.S.-Federal Republic of Germany (FGR) Risk Analysis Conference
	Published as:	L.B. Lave and J. Menkes. (1985). Managing Risk: A Joint U.S.- German Perspective. *Risk Analysis* 5(1):17-23.
Washington, DC April 25-29, 1983		U.S.-Federal Republic of Germany (FGR) Risk Analysis Conference
	Published as:	L.B. Lave and J. Menkes. (1985). Managing Risk: A Joint U.S.- German Perspective. *Risk Analysis* 5(1):17-23.
Les Arc, France August 1983		NATO Advanced Study Institute (ASI) on Environmental Impact Assessment, Technology Assessment, and Risk Analysis
	Published as:	V.T. Covello, J.L Mumpower, P.J.M. Stallen, and V.R.R. Uppulari, eds. (1985). *Environmental Impact Assessment, Technology Assessment, and Risk Analysis: Contributions from the Psychological and Decision Sciences.* Berlin: Springer-Verlag.
New York, NY July 31-August 1, 1983		Conference on Risk Assessment in the Private Sector
	Published as:	C. Whipple and V.T. Covello, eds. (1985). *Risk Analysis in the Private Sector.* New York, NY: Plenum Press.

as *The Analysis of Actual Versus Perceived Risk*, edited by Vincent Covello et al. (1983). At the request of the Nuclear Regulatory Commission the staff of the TARA Program were closely involved in the organization of the second SRA conference on low probability/high consequence events. The proceedings were published in the volume entitled *Low Probability/High Consequence Risk Analysis.*

With regard to extramural research, the ten generic questions in Table 2.1 were used to set the program direction and establish funding priorities. Complete details of funding from 1979 through 1983 were not available at the time of writing, but approximately 350 preliminary proposals were received during this period, and 105 were formally reviewed. With an operating budget of $1.3 million, the TARA Program awarded or committed over $1.2 million for a total of eighteen research projects in Fiscal Year 1982 (Table 2.3). This is an average of $68,782 per project per year. In

Table 2.3
NSF Technology Assessment and Risk Analysis (TARA) Program Awards, 1979–1983

Principal Investigator	Institution	1979	1980	1981	1982	1983	Total Award Per Project
Kates	Clark University	√					
Okrent	University of California Los Angeles	√					
Raiffa & Goslin	National Academy of Sciences	√					
Baram	Boston University		√				
MacLean	University of Maryland College Park		√				
Merkhoffer	SRI International		√				
Phillipson & Atkisson	J.H. Wiggins Company		√				
Zimmerman	New York University		√				
Bracken & Baram					49,280		
Baram & Miyares	Decision Science Consortium, Inc.				11,977		
Brown	University of California Berkeley			√	100,000		
Craik	Woodward–Clyde Consultants			√	48,826		
Keeney	Brookings Institution				162,768		
Lave	Midwest Research Institute				50,917		
Lawless & Jones	Brookings Institution				19,197		
NA	East-West Center				100,000		
NA	J.H. Wiggins Company				49,504		
NA	New York University				3,930		
NA	University of Arizona				9,288		
Edwards & von Winterfeldt	University of Southern California			√	100,000	133,657	263,035
Grobstein	University of California San Diego				118,820	118,820	341,640
Lay	Mitre Corporation				30,000	118,876	148,876
Oleinick	University of Michigan				70,940	45,726	220,000
Page & Ferejohn	California Institute of Technology				83,575	66,381	149,956
Slovic & Lichtenstein	Decision Research				129,059	64,529	193,588
Stolwijk, DeLucca & Gold	Yale University			√	100,000	217,020	475,528
Baram	Boston University					147,922	147,922
Dyer	University of Texas					56,146	56,146
Rose & Miller	Massachusetts Institute of Technology					50,000	50,000
Shrader-Frechette	University of California Santa Barbara					13,675	13,675
Wright	Council of State Governments					97,440	97,440
Total					1,238,081	1,130,192	2,157,564
Average					68,782	94,183	179,797

√ Funds awarded but amount unknown

Source: NSF Briefing Book.

1983 the TARA budget increased to $1.34 million, with $1.13 million committed to new and continuing awards for twelve research projects (an average of $94,183 per project per year). Many projects received funding over several years. From the data available, an average of $179,797 was awarded over the course of an individual project.

The findings from many of these projects were presented at a series of conferences for principal investigators between 1982 and 1985 and brought together in one volume, *Risk Evaluation and Management* (Covello, Menkes, and Mumpower 1986), which remains the best statement of the state of the art in risk analysis at that time. In the preface to this volume, the TARA triumvirate, Covello, Menkes, and Mumpower, reiterate the ten generic questions as the organizing framework, and it is instructive to look over the table of contents as an indicator of the principal topics of interest. Not surprisingly, the volume divides into three parts: public perceptions of risk, risk evaluation methods, and risk management. As such the volume illustrates the thrust of the TARA Program, with its emphasis on social science perspectives, rather than the more technical engineering and toxicological approaches to risk analysis that were funded principally through other programs and agencies. Given this thrust, the TARA Program was instrumental in drawing the distinction between "technical" risk assessment and risk evaluation and management.[3]

With the arrival of Ronald Reagan in the White House, there was growing doubt about the place of policy analysis at NSF during the early 1980s. Many felt that NSF should fund only more basic research. During the years 1983 and 1984 there was a strong effort to phase out the Division of Policy Research and Analysis and eliminate the Technology Assessment Program. The risk assessment part of the TARA Program was inevitably caught up in the struggle, but survived under a new guise. The risk program moved into the Division of Social and Economic Sciences (SES) under the Decision and Management Sciences (DMS) Program.

The majority of NSF funding for risk-related research in the social sciences has since come through this program.[4] Figure 2.1 illustrates that the total number and amount of awards under DMS has increased steadily since 1981 (although these figures are not in constant dollars). It is also evident that the proportion of total funding allotted to risk-related research increased through 1987, and has since stabilized at approximately $1 million (the level originally prescribed by the House Committee on Science and Technology). In recognition of the growing importance of risk-related research, the DMS Program changed its name in 1986, becoming the Decision, Risk, and Management Science (DRMS) Program.

The overall objective of DRMS is to build an interdisciplinary science base for decision making and management. . . . The program supports research that explores fundamental issues in management science, risk analysis, public policy decision

Figure 2.1
Annual Number and Total NSF-DRMS Awards, 1981–1989

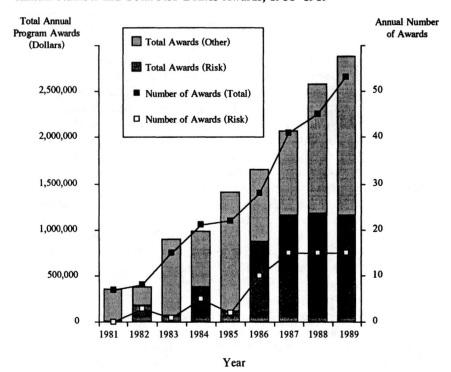

making, judgmental processes, behavioral decision making, organizational design, and decision making under uncertainty. [DRMS 1990]

Figure 2.2 indicates that the average annual award per risk project ($72,203 overall since 1982) tends to be slightly higher than the average annual award per project in other areas ($54,753).[5] While the DRMS Program has no criteria for allocating funds to the different research areas, the distribution reflects the composition of the advisory panels and their informal understanding of the need for diversity.[6]

   While much of the research funded through DRMS has practical significance, program staff were increasingly concerned that some of this research was becoming too divorced from practical application. Consequently, early in 1990, the DRMS Program began sponsoring the Joint NSF/Private Sector Research Opportunities Initiative to encourage the academic community to engage in collaborative research with the private sector. Under this initiative, DRMS matches private sector support for one or two years up to $75,000 per year. During the first eighteen months of the initiative, eight awards were made, including three in the area of risk. As with other DRMS awards,

Figure 2.2
Average Annual Project Awards from NSF-DRMS, 1980–1989

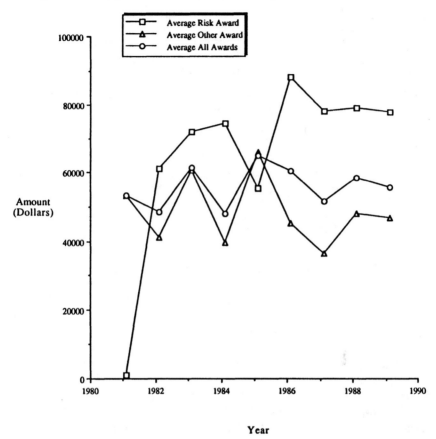

the selection panels aim to maintain a broad, representative mix of research topics, and there are no strict criteria for allocating funds to different topical areas. The DRMS staff are enthusiastic about this new initiative and hope to increase the number of funded projects in the future.[7]

EVIST/EVS Program

The Ethics and Values Studies in Science, Technology and Society (EVS) Program (formerly the Ethics and Values in Science, Technology [EVIST] Program) at NSF has also funded a significant number of risk-related projects since the mid–1970s (Hollander and Steneck 1990). Of the 172 projects funded by EVIST/EVS from 1976 to 1987 (Table 2.4), research on hazards

Table 2.4
EVIST/EVS Funded Risk Projects, 1976–1987

Project Area	1976	1977	1978	1979	1980	1981	1982	1983	1984	1985	1986	1987	Total
Risk/benefit	—	2	1	—	—	1	—	—	1	1	—	3	9
Hazards	2	1	2	—	3	5	3	2	2	3	1	1	25
All Projects	23	12	17	14	10	17	11	8	14	15	10	21	172

Source: Adapted from Hollander and Steneck (1990).

(25 projects) dominates, and additional projects were in the area of risk-benefit research (Hollander and Steneck 1990, 88).

THE SOCIETY FOR RISK ANALYSIS

The Society for Risk Analysis was founded in 1980.[8] Like most societies of its kind, the SRA owes its existence to a mixture of serendipity and the foresight of a small band of stalwarts. Early in 1979, Robert B. Cumming, a genetic toxicologist from Oak Ridge National Laboratory (ORNL), was visiting Europe. Cumming realized that much of the intellectual ferment in a variety of fields at that time focused on *risk*—a new concept that crossed disciplinary boundaries. In Stockholm, his conversations with Lars Ehrenberg, a mutation theorist, confirmed his convictions on the need for a broadly based international journal on risk. Cumming returned to the United States determined to solicit interest and support for the venture, spurred on by the encouragement of Mortimer Mendlesohn at the Lawrence Livermore National Laboratory and Alexander Hollaender at ORNL.

At the urging of Bob Tardiff, then head of the Board of Toxicology and Environmental Health Hazards at the National Academy of Sciences, a committee was formed to explore ideas. The informal committee comprised about twenty of the leading figures in the fledgling field of risk studies (including Robert Cumming, Vincent Covello, Gary Flamm, Allen Newell, Tim O'Riordan, Joseph Rodricks, and Robert Tardiff, among others) and met several times at the academy in late 1979 and early 1980. The committee was unanimous in perceiving the need for a journal to encourage interdisciplinary communication and exchange. Each of the committee members was actively involved in research on risks to health, safety, and the environment. All felt that the professional societies to which they belonged, and the journals to which they subscribed, were inadequate to address the broad questions of risk that span the traditional disciplines. At the same time, however, several leading biological and health scientists were questioning the validity of the methods of risk assessment, and many environmentalists were skeptical of the usefulness of the techniques. Risk analysis needed to develop a more respectable image, and a new journal seemed the perfect vehicle for such an endeavor. Flamm suggested that the likely success of a journal would be enhanced by the formation of a parallel society that would encourage a professional identity, promote respectability, provide a forum for the exchange of ideas, and encourage the submission of quality manuscripts for publication. Such a society would also serve as the immediate audience and peer review community.

Testing the waters, Cumming found several publishers who were keen to publish such a journal. The idea of a new journal on engineering, biology, health, or the environment had little cachet, but a new journal combining elements from each under the rubric of risk was something unique. The committee chose Plenum Publishers, who remain the official publishers for the society.

The committee also met to consider terms and definitions in this fledgling field, defining risk as a probabilistic concept and clarifying the confusion between risk and hazard. The decision was made to use the more inclusive term *risk analysis*, encompassing both risk assessment and risk management, as the title for the journal. *Risk Analysis* therefore became the official journal of the Society for Risk Analysis, which established its editorial board and policy.

As stated in its constitution, the major aims of the Society for Risk Analysis are to promote:

• knowledge and understanding of risk analysis techniques and their applications;
• communication and interaction among those engaged in risk analysis; and,
• dissemination of risk analysis information and concepts, and the advancement of the state-of-the-art in all aspects of risk analysis. [SRA 1990]

As an interdisciplinary society attempting to meet these goals, the SRA draws its membership from a variety of backgrounds and professions, including representatives from industry, government, and academia. Membership of the SRA has grown steadily from 300 in 1981 to a plateau of around 1,500 since 1987 (Figure 2.3). This steady growth is also reflected in the formation of two affiliate sections in Europe and Japan and the spawning of thirteen chapters in the United States (SRA 1990). With this impressive growth, the SRA has since met several goals set by Lester Lave in 1985, although not during his term as president (1985–86).[9] The SRA has yet to meet the most ambitious of these goals, however, that of doubling its membership to a level of 2,000 members.

Prior to 1984 representatives from state and federal government agencies comprised the single largest group of members. Since 1984, however, the membership has become more diversified.[10] In terms of disciplinary background, the biological and health sciences dominate, with engineering and

Figure 2.3
Society for Risk Analysis Membership, 1980–1989

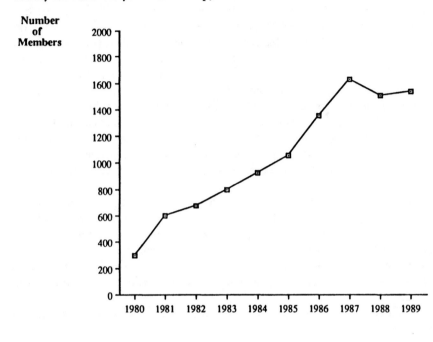

physical sciences forming a major proportion of the remaining members. Social scientists, by contrast, comprise only a minority of the total membership. Unfortunately, the SRA has not maintained easily retrievable records of members' affiliations, disciplinary backgrounds, and topical interests, although there are plans to collect such information in the future.

The affairs of the SRA are conducted through an elected council comprising four officers, the past president, and nine councilors. The council meets twice a year and the executive committee (comprising the president, president-elect, treasurer, secretary, and past president) three times a year. Table 2.5 lists the members of the executive committee since the formation of the SRA, with their affiliation and disciplinary background.

Table 2.6 shows the distribution of members of the committee by disciplinary background using the very general categories of life sciences, physical sciences and engineering, and social sciences. These categories match the three categories often used by the SRA in dividing up the program for its annual meetings, namely, biological and health issues, engineering and statistics, and social and policy issues. Recognizing that the boundaries between

Table 2.5
SRA Executive Committee Membership, 1980–1991

Year	President	President-elect	Secretary	Treasurer	Past-president
1980-81	Robert B. Cumming Oak Ridge National Laboratory (genetic toxicology)	Joseph Rodricks Clement Associates (toxicology)	Robert G. Tardiff National Academy of Sciences (toxicology)	Gordon Newell National Academy of Sciences	
1981-82	Robert B. Cumming Oak Ridge National Laboratory (genetic toxicology)	Chris Whipple Electric Power Research Institute (engineering)	Kenneth A. Solomon Rand Corporation (engineering)	V.R.R. Uppuluri Oak Ridge National Laboratory (mathematics)	
1982-83	Chris Whipple Electric Power Research Institute (engineering)	Paul Slovic Decision Research (psychology)	Kenneth A. Solomon Rand Corporation (engineering)	V.R.R. Uppuluri Oak Ridge National Laboratory (mathematics)	Robert B. Cumming Oak Ridge National Laboratory (genetic toxicology)
1983-84	Paul Slovic Decision Research (psychology)	Elizabeth Anderson Environmental Protection Agency (chemistry)	Michael Baram Boston University (law)	Howard Kunreuther Wharton School (economics)	Chris Whipple Electric Power Research Institute (engineering)
1984-85	Elizabeth Anderson Environmental Protection Agency (chemistry)	Lester Lave Carnegie Mellon (economics)	Michael Baram Boston University (law)	Howard Kunreuther Wharton School (economics)	Paul Slovic Decision Research (psychology)
1985-86	Lester Lave Carnegie Mellon (economics)	Paul F. Deisler Shell Oil Company (chemical engineering)	Michael Gough Office of Technology Assessment (biology)	Steve M. Swanson American Petroleum Institute (economics)	Elizabeth Anderson Environmental Protection Agency (chemistry)

Table 2.5 (continued)

Year	President	President-elect	Secretary	Treasurer	Past-president
1986-87	Paul F. Deisler Shell Oil Company (chemical engineering)	Vincent T. Covello NSF (social psychology)	Michael Gough Office of Technology Assessment (biology)	Steve M. Swanson American Petroleum Institute (economics)	Lester Lave Carnegie Mellon (economics)
1987-88	Vincent T. Covello NSF (social psychology)	Richard C. Schwing General Motors (chemical engineering)	Francis M. Lynn University of North Carolina (economics/health policy)	Joseph Fiksel Teknowledge (operations research)	Paul F. Deisler Shell Oil Company (chemical engineering)
1988-89	Richard C. Schwing General Motors (chemical engineering)	B. John Garrick Pickard, Lowe & Garrick (physics/applied science)	Francis M. Lynn University of North Carolina (economics/health policy)	Joseph Fiksel Teknowledge (operations research)	Vincent T. Covello NSF (social psychology)
1989-90	B. John Garrick Pickard, Lowe & Garrick (physics/applied science)	Curtis C. Travis Oak Ridge National Laboratory (engineering/applied mathematics)	Vlasta Molak National Institute for Occupational Safety and Health (biochemistry)	Raymond F. Boykin California State University, Chico (management science)	Richard C. Schwing General Motors (chemical engineering)
1990-91	Curtis C. Travis Oak Ridge National Laboratory (engineering/applied mathematics)	Warner North Decision Focus (physics, mathematics, and operations research)	Vlasta Molak National Institute for Occupational Safety and Health (biochemistry)	Raymond F. Boykin California State University, Chico (management science)	B. John Garrick Pickard, Lowe & Garrick (physics/applied science)

Note: The table indicates the disciplinary background and the affiliation of each member at the time of his or her appointment.

Table 2.6
SRA Executive Committee Membership by Disciplinary Background, 1980–1991

Discipline	Executive Committee		President
	(a)	(b)	
Life Sciences	5	9	2(c)
Physical Sciences/Engineering	10	24	6
Social Sciences	8	19	3
Unknown	1	1	

(a) counting members once even if serving for two or more years
(b) counting in terms of person/years on committee
(c) Cumming served as Interim President (1980-81) and President (1981-82)

these categories are both fuzzy and permeable, and that individuals with academic backgrounds in one area may have since shifted their interests elsewhere, it is nonetheless instructive to look at the disciplinary origins of the leading figures as a reflection of the nature of the SRA. Table 2.6 reveals that the SRA has been quite successful in maintaining a balance among the three areas. Contrary to expectations, however, engineering and physical sciences do not dominate overwhelmingly, except perhaps in terms of the number of presidents. Surprisingly, the life sciences make a poor showing in the executive positions despite their numerical dominance among the membership. More surprising still is the strong presence of the social sciences on the executive committee. Without detailed statistics on membership affiliations and disciplinary backgrounds, however, it is impossible to form a more complete picture of the profession. The strong position of the social sciences in the SRA may be related to the nature of risk problems. Important ideas contributed by the social sciences have fired the imagination of those involved in risk management. Concepts such as the public perception of risk, risk evaluation and acceptability, and risk communication have captured the limelight, to the dismay of some who see risk management as a technical problem with technical solutions. Hence, there has been a move to divide the SRA into more discrete units organized by disciplinary focus (SRA 1991).

RISK CENTERS

The Society for Risk Analysis is just one of a host of institutions that have grown to serve the needs of this diverse and expanding field. Risk assessment is now an institutionalized activity for many state and federal agencies. Many of the larger corporations have developed in-house capabilities and programs in risk assessment, communication, and management. Smaller corporations, government agencies, and citizens' groups are now able to draw on the expertise of a burgeoning array of consulting firms. Social science and scientists are very much caught up in this institutionalizing process, and the development of interest in this area is indicated by the growth in the number of research centers devoted to the study of risk.

The list in Table 2.7 is not exhaustive, but it does indicate the major academic centers conducting research on a variety of aspects of risk. The list does not include many other institutions actively engaged in basic and applied research, such as the national laboratories (e.g., ORNL), corporations (e.g., General Motors Research Laboratories), and a multiplicity of consulting firms. Rather, the list incorporates quasi-autonomous academic research centers that focus principally on risk issues. The list is also biased toward the social sciences and is intended therefore to illustrate both research trends and the major actors in the field, although the list excludes many of the centers that focus on natural hazards research.

One of the first centers of risk research was the Disaster Research Center, which was founded by sociologists Russell Dynes and Enrico Quarantelli in 1963 at Ohio State University, and moved to the University of Delaware in 1985. The center began conducting research on community responses to and recovery from natural disasters as analogues for likely responses in the event of nuclear attack. Much of the early work at the center was funded by the Federal Emergency Management Agency (FEMA). Through the use of "quick response teams," the center has been able to develop an invaluable data base of over 500 field studies of short- and long-term community response and recovery. More recently the center has shifted its focus to technological hazards with studies on sociobehavioral responses to acute chemical hazards, mass media reporting of disasters, and the problems of mass evacuation and sheltering.

While there are many centers that conduct research on environmental issues in general and natural hazards in particular, many will consider the first "real" risk center to be the Center for Technology, Environment, and Development (CENTED) at Clark University. In 1972, geographers Robert W. Kates and Roger E. Kasperson collaborated with physicist Christoph Hohenemser to extend natural hazards theory to the analysis of nuclear power. This collaboration led to the formation of the Hazard Assessment Group, which has since been the leading research group in the center. The multidisciplinary group has engaged in a diversity of projects funded by the National Science Foundation (through RANN, TARA, DRMS, and EVIST/ EVS). These focus on the scientific, social, and ethical issues of risk assessment and management, and incorporate basic theoretical work on hazard taxonomies, and comparative risk analysis, risk perception, and risk communication. The group's research has ranged over a broad array of topical areas including public opposition to nuclear power, emergency planning for

Table 2.7
Major Academic Centers of Risk Research in the Social Sciences

DATE	INSTITUTION	FOUNDERS	RESEARCH FOCUS
1963	Disaster Research Center University of Delaware Newark, Delaware 19716	Russell R. Dynes E.L. Quarantelli	Group and organizational aspects of disasters.
1975	Center for Technology, Enivironment, and Development (CENTED) Clark University Worcester, MA 01610	Christoph Hohenemser Roger E. Kasperson Robert W. Kates	Interdisciplinary research on technical, social and ethical issues of risk assessment, evaluation, and management.
1976	Decision Research 1201 Oak Street Eugene, OR 97401	Baruch Fischhoff Sarah Lichtenstein Paul Slovic	Behavioral decision theory, especially concerning probabilistic judgement, risk perception, and risk communication.
	Natural Hazards Research and Applications Information Center Institute of Behavioral Science University of Colorado Boulder, CO 80309	Gilbert F. White	National clearinghouse for research data on natural hazards and disasters. Publishes *Natural Hazards Observer*.
1977	Environment and Policy Institute East-West Center Hawaii	Kirk Smith	Interdisciplinary research on environmental policy alternatives, especially for Asia-Pacific region.
1978	Institute for Risk Analysis American University Washington, DC	William Rowe	
1970s[a]	Department of Engineering and Public Policy Carnegie-Mellon University Pittsburgh, PA 15213	Lester Lave M. Granger Morgan	Risk analysis, risk communication and public policy, especially concerning issues with significant technical complexity.
1970s[b]	Institute for Safety and Systems Management University of Southern California Los Angeles, CA 90089	John Cahoon	Research focuses in three areas: human factors; decision analysis and operations management; and safety, risk and hazard assessment.
1982	Institute for Risk Research University of Waterloo Waterloo, Ontario N2L 3G1	Neils Lind	Issues of public policy and risk in Canada. Publishes *Risk Abstracts*.
	Energy, Environment and Resources Center (EERC) University of Tennessee Knoxville, TN	William Colglazier	Operation of Waste Management Research and Education Institute and the Water Resources Research Center. Publishes *Forum for Applied Research and Public Policy*.

Table 2.7 (continued)

DATE	INSTITUTION	FOUNDERS	RESEARCH FOCUS
1984	Center for Environmental Management (CEM) Tufts University Curtis Hall 474 Boston Avenue Medford, MA 02155	Anthony D. Cortese	Research, education, and training institute. Research focuses on health effects of environmental toxins, risk assessment, and pollution prevention.
1985	Risk and Decision Processes Center Wharton School University of Pennsylvania Philadelphia, PA 19104	Howard Kunreuther	Psychological, economic, and decision-making theory. Compensation, insurance, pricing, and equity.
1986	Environmental Communication Research Program 122 Ryders Lane Cook College Rutgers University New Brunswick NJ 08903	Peter M. Sandman	Basic research on risk communication. Production of handbooks for risk communicators in industry, government, and the media.
1987	Center for Law and Technology Boston University 765 Commonwealth Avenue Boston, MA 02215	Michael Baram	Education, research and public service focusing on risk analysis, risk communication, and risk management.
	Center for Risk Management Resources for the Future 1616 P Street, NW Washington, DC 20036	Paul Portney	Research, policy analysis, education and outreach related to risk assessment and management.
	Center for Risk Management of Engineering Systems University of Virginia Thorton Hall Charlottesville, VA 22910	Yacov Y. Haimes	Cross-disciplinary approaches to risk management of engineering systems. Risk quantification, preference measurement, and decision processes.
	Western Institute for Social and Organizational Research (WISOR) Department of Psychology Western Washington University Bellingham, WA 98225	George Cvetkovich	Applied social psychology, including the role of geography in subjective perceptions of risk, role of information in the development of community hazard conflicts, cognitive and emotional aspects of risk information processing.
1988	Center for Risk Communication Division of Environmental Sciences Columbia University 60 Haven Avenue New York, NY 10032	Vincent T. Covello	Risk communication about toxins and drugs.
1989	Center for Risk Analysis Harvard School of Public Health 677 Huntington Avenue Boston, MA 02116	John Graham	Risk analysis, risk management, and public policy.

[a] Founded in 1969 but not active in the risk area until the early to mid-1970s.
[b] Founded in the 1950s but not active in the risk area until the mid to late 1970s.

nuclear power plant accidents, radioactive waste management, occupational risks, and corporate risk management. More recently the group has turned its attention to the transfer of hazardous technologies to underdeveloped countries and the risks of global environmental change. The group has always fostered interdisciplinary and interinstitutional research, and much work has been conducted collaboratively with representatives of many of the other centers listed in Table 2.7. The theoretical work on the social amplification of risk described in this volume (see Chapter 6) is a notable example of this kind of collaborative research, in this case involving Paul Slovic from Decision Research.

Decision Research was founded in 1976 by Sarah Lichtenstein, Baruch Fischhoff, and Paul Slovic, all of whom had previously been affiliated with the Oregon Research Institute. Originally a branch of the consulting/research firm Perceptronics, Decision Research became an independent nonprofit institute in 1986. Perhaps no other center has had a more profound influence on the nature of the risk debate. Slovic, Fischhoff, and Lichtenstein and their colleagues were largely responsible for developing the psychometric paradigm, which seeks to explain the discrepancy between public and expert perceptions of risk (see Chapter 5 in this volume for a more complete discussion of the development, underlying assumptions, and principal findings of this work). The group was largely responsible for introducing the notion of perceived risk, which has been a powerful, provocative, and recurring theme since before the first SRA conference, entitled "The Analysis of Actual Versus Perceived Risk." This work on perceived risk has spawned several other themes that have dominated the field at different times, most notably the notion of acceptable risk and the more recent interest in risk communication.

Both the public and private sectors have been exceedingly interested in risk communication. Like so many new ideas, risk communication was seen as the answer to many thorny problems—most notably as a means to bridge the gulf between expert views and public perceptions of risk. Of course, it is never that easy, and while the focus on risk communication has clarified some problems, it has not been a universal panacea. Nonetheless, the surge of interest in risk communication was responsible for the establishment of the next generation of risk centers. The first of these was the Environment Communication Research Program at Rutgers University. The program was founded in 1986 by journalism professor Peter M. Sandman, who has gathered together a small group of some of the most able practitioners in the field. The group specializes in providing handbooks (e.g., Hance, Chess, and Sandman 1988) and practical advice for risk communicators in industry, government, and the media. Several other centers were established in 1987–88 and conduct basic and applied research in risk communication. These include the Center for Law and Technology at Boston University, the Center for Risk Communication at Columbia University, and the Western Institute for Social and Organizational Research at Western Washington University.

Several risk centers may be loosely grouped together in terms of a common focus on decision making. Decision analysis was first applied to risk problems in the 1970s (Renn 1985, 118), and the techniques have since been enhanced by researchers at these centers. In particular, Detlof von Winterfeldt, at the Institute of Safety and Systems Management, along with his colleagues Ward Edwards and Ralph Keeney, has been a leading proponent of the decision analytical techniques of multi-attribute utility analysis and expert elicitation (see Chapter 14 for a full account of the development and assumptions of this approach). Under the directorship of Howard Kunreuther, the Wharton Risk and Decision Processes Center has focused on low probability/high consequence events and the way these events affect the decisions of individuals, businesses, and government under different regulatory and market conditions. The center's research is both descriptive and prescriptive, and draws on psychological, decision-making, and economic theory (see Chapter 13 in this volume for further details of this approach). In 1986 the center was the recipient of a major three-year award from DRMS for a project on "The Role of Insurance, Compensation, Regulation, and Protective Behavior in Decision Making About Risk and Misfortune."

The diverse faculty at the Department of Social and Decision Sciences, Carnegie-Mellon University, have focused their research activities on the development of empirically based behavioral theories of decision making. The faculty include sociologists, economists, decision scientists, statisticians, and other social scientists. Baruch Fischhoff joined the faculty in 1987, after twelve years with Decision Research. The department is closely allied with the Department of Engineering and Public Policy, which has been active in risk assessment since the early 1970s. In 1987, Granger Morgan, Lester Lave, and Baruch Fischhoff were awarded a major three-year grant from DRMS for a project entitled "Improving Risk Management Through Improving Theory and Practice in Risk Perception and Risk Communication."

The Center for Risk Management, at Resources for the Future, and the Center for Risk Analysis, at the Harvard School of Public Health, are two relatively new centers with similar research goals and agendas. The Center for Risk Management was founded in 1987 by Paul Portney, at the urging of William Ruckelshaus, former EPA Administrator. The center has drawn together an interdisciplinary team to conduct research, policy analysis, and educational and outreach activities related to risk assessment and management. The center has received substantial funding through a cooperative agreement with EPA, and much of the research has focused on issues of special interest to this agency. The Center for Risk Analysis was founded in 1989 by John Graham and has been aggressively successful in establishing a niche in an increasingly crowded research environment. The center's research has focused on the public health aspects of risk analysis and management.

Finally, there are several centers that tend to focus on the life science or physical science and engineering aspects of risk analysis. These include the Center for Risk Management of Engineering Systems, University of Virginia; the Institute for Risk Research, University of Waterloo; the Risk Sciences Research Center, University of Arkansas; and the Energy, Environment and Resources Center, University of Tennessee.

PUBLICATIONS

The growing interest in all aspects of risk has generated a veritable mountain of published and unpublished literature, ranging from newsletters, journals, and how-to (as well as how-not-to) manuals to more scholarly tomes. In 1981 the field had only one journal, *Risk Analysis*. Now the field boasts three additional journals dedicated exclusively to risk as it is broadly defined: *Risk Abstracts*, the *Journal of Risk and Uncertainty*, and *Risk: Issues in Health and Safety*. In the area of natural hazards, there are several journals (e.g., *Disasters, International Journal of Mass Emergencies and Disasters*) and a newsletter (*Natural Hazards Observer*). There are also numerous other journals in very specialized areas related to risk (e.g., toxicology, operations research, decision making, policy sciences).

The Society for Risk Analysis has two official publications, *RISK Newsletter* and *Risk Analysis*. *RISK Newsletter* began in March 1981 as a quarterly publication, although it had some teething problems and the early issues were a little erratic at times. Since 1988 *RISK Newsletter* has been issued three times a year. SRA president and founding member Robert Cumming was the first editor through 1981, when George Flanagan took over until 1986. Lorraine Abbott was assistant editor from 1981 to 1986 and editor from 1986 to the present. During this time *RISK Newsletter* grew into a sizable publication with regular columns and short, informative articles about current events and activities in the realm of risk. Robert Cumming was also first editor of *Risk Analysis* from 1981 to 1983, and senior editor from 1983 to the present. Curtis Travis has been editor since 1983. During this time the journal has doubled in size, although it accepts less than 50 percent of the articles submitted.

Since the journal *Risk Analysis* is the official publication of the SRA and in many ways the flagship of the field, it merits closer scrutiny, although this does not deny the importance of the other risk journals. Figures 2.4 through 2.8, therefore, show the results of a content analysis of the articles (excluding letters, notes and comments, book reviews, and the like) published in the journal between 1980 and 1990. (It should be noted that the boundaries between these classificatory categories are fuzzy, and any one

Figure 2.4
Number of Articles in *Risk Analysis* by Discipline, 1981–1990

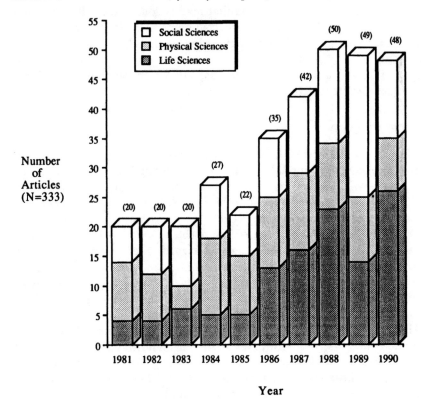

article may not easily fit a particular category. Assuming consistency of analysis, however, the general trends over time should be suitably illustrative.)

Following the convention adopted by the society at its annual meeting, Figure 2.4 shows the distribution by three disciplinary categories: life sciences (including toxicology and epidemiology); physical sciences and engineering; and social sciences (including economics, psychology, and law). Evidently, the total number of articles increased dramatically in 1986, but, surprisingly, the number of articles from the physical sciences and engineering remained roughly constant, while the number of social science and life science articles increased substantially. This relative change is more obvious in Figure 2.5. Through 1985 the physical sciences and engineering averaged about seven articles per year, and this has almost doubled to thirteen articles per year since 1986. The social sciences doubled from eight per year prior to 1986 to fifteen per year since, and the life sciences more than trebled the number of contributions from less than five per year to

Figure 2.5
Distribution of Articles in *Risk Analysis* by Discipline, 1981–1990

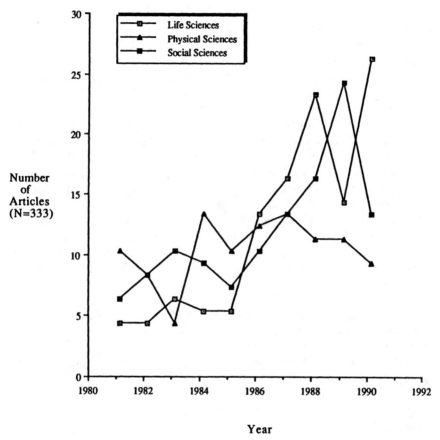

over eighteen per year. Curiously, the life sciences and social sciences alternate dominance, with the former favoring even years and the latter odd. Assuming a similar pattern continues in 1991, the life and social sciences will come more closely into line, with around seventeen or eighteen articles per year. Given the interdisciplinary nature of the journal, the editors try to achieve a balance by topic and disciplinary emphasis, but the final mix will also reflect the quantity and quality of articles submitted and the prevailing topical interests in the field. It is impossible to say if these trends reflect the membership of the society without more detailed membership statistics. The small number of articles from the physical sciences and engineering may be a cause for concern, especially the downward trend since 1987. It may be that researchers in these disciplines are preferring to publish in more narrowly defined disciplinary journals than the broader interdisciplinary outlets such as *Risk Analysis.*

Classifying topical areas in risk studies is highly problematic, given the fuzzy boundaries and overlapping areas of interest and expertise. Following the conventions established elsewhere (Kates 1978; NRC 1983; Royal Society 1983), I distinguish between risk estimation (including risk identification), risk evaluation (including risk perception), and risk management (including risk communication). Risk estimation and identification includes toxicological and epidemiological studies and structural and statistical analyses. Risk evaluation includes methods of comparing risks and determining "acceptability" (e.g., cost-benefit analysis). Risk management includes options for controlling or mitigating risks. (See Krewski and Birkwood [1987] for a more extensive discussion of these distinctions.) Bearing in mind the difficulties in making clear distinctions, all the articles from 1981 through 1990 were classified according to their principal emphasis. Each article was classified in only one category. The results of the analysis are shown in Figures 2.6 and 2.7. Evidently, articles on risk estimation dominate in *Risk Analysis*, and this dominance has been growing. Articles dealing with issues of risk management are less numerous, but have also been growing consistently. Only the category of risk evaluation has remained relatively constant, in spite of the increase in the overall number of articles in the journal.

Finally, Figure 2.8 illustrates the relative popularity of three topics: risk perception, risk acceptability, and risk communication. Given the very small number of articles represented here, any conclusions should be drawn very carefully. With such small numbers the patterns are very susceptible to differences in coding and classification, especially since any particular article may address more than one topic. These caveats aside, the arrival of risk communication as a focus of study in 1986 is perhaps the most striking pattern.

CONCLUSIONS

The goal of this chapter was to provide a broad-brush picture of the development of risk research for the social sciences in the United States. There are places where the paint is a little thin, and significant gaps remain to be filled. Nonetheless, from the indicators identified, we can see that the social sciences have been intimately involved in the growth and professionalization of risk research. Indeed, one might argue that the social sciences appear to have an influence beyond expectations, given the relatively small number of researchers in the social sciences and the relatively low level of funding. This influence is manifest in the makeup of the executive committee of the Society for Risk Analysis and from the results of a content analysis of one of the leading risk journals, *Risk Analysis*. The National Science Foundation provided approximately $1 million per year for risk research

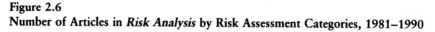

Figure 2.6
Number of Articles in *Risk Analysis* by Risk Assessment Categories, 1981–1990

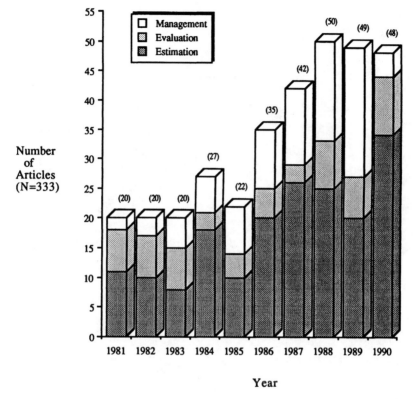

in the social sciences through the 1980s. Originally, this funding came through the Technology Assessment and Risk Analysis Program, and later through the Decision, Risk, and Management Science Program. In real terms, therefore, the levels of funding have actually declined, while the research output has increased.

The Society for Risk Analysis is the principal professional organization representing academics and practitioners in the field. Membership has grown more diversified since its foundation in 1980, but the society is still dominated by the physical and life sciences. The social sciences, however, have achieved a stronger presence on the society's executive committee than one would expect. A parallel pattern emerges from an analysis of the society's official journal, *Risk Analysis*. The social sciences have maintained a strong representation in the journal, although the life sciences remain dominant. The greatest surprise is the relatively weak showing by the physical sciences and engineering. In terms of topical interest, risk estimation remains the

Figure 2.7
Distribution of Articles in *Risk Analysis* by Risk Assessment Categories, 1981–
1990

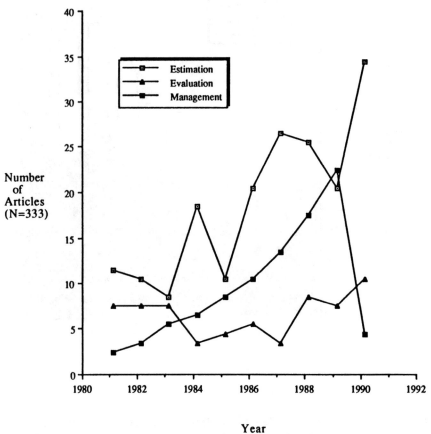

dominant focus, although there has been a growing interest in risk management, and especially risk communication.

Additional work will need to be done to fill in several gaps and paint a
more complete picture of the social science contributions to risk research.
First, the levels of funding described here need to be put in context by
comparing them with the levels of funding in the physical and life sciences,
and by estimating the amounts of funding from various sources other than
NSF, such as government agencies, corporations, and private foundations.
Second, it would be interesting to conduct a more detailed content analysis
of *Risk Analysis* and the other principal journals in the field. Kates and
Kasperson (1983) conducted a very useful review of the major books published in the field from 1970 to 1983, and it would be very helpful to extend

Figure 2.8
Number of Articles in *Risk Analysis* by Selected Topics, 1981–1990

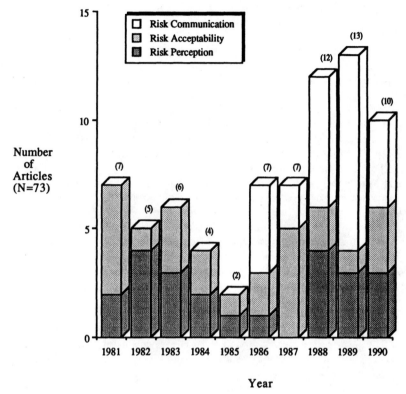

this analysis to include books published since then. Third, the list of institutions involved in risk research needs to be expanded beyond the limited perspective here that focuses on those academic centers loosely within the realm of the social sciences. The expanded list should include centers outside academia and beyond the social sciences, such as government and corporate laboratories and even consulting groups. Surprisingly, there is no thorough listing of such centers. Fourth, it would be fascinating to conduct similar analyses of funding sources, publications, and institutions in Western Europe and other parts of the world. Finally, there is a great need for a work that explores the historical and intellectual links between the natural hazards and technological hazards research areas—something that many people talk about, but which has yet to be written.

NOTES

I should like to thank Robert Bordley, Vincent Covello, Robert Cumming, Gary Flamm, Jeanne X. Kasperson, Robin Keller, Sheldon Krimsky, Howard Kunreuther,

Granger Morgan, Jeryl Mumpower, Paul Slovic, Peter Stott, and Curtis Travis for
the invaluable information they provided for this chapter and for their comments
on previous drafts. I should also like to thank Leah Steinberg for her help in conducting the content analysis and collecting much of the information on centers of
research.

1. The information in this section is based on a series of conversations with a
number of individuals who were closely involved with the various research programs.
I am particularly indebted to Robert F. Bordley, Vincent Covello, Robin Keller,
Howard Kunreuther, Jeryl Mumpower, and Paul Slovic. In terms of documentation,
the NSF *Briefing Book on the PRA Risk Analysis Program and Its Relationship to
Other Government Agencies* was particularly useful for background information.

2. Vincent Covello, personal communication, August 13, 1990.

3. Jeryl Mumpower, personal communication, August 22, 1990.

4. This discussion does not attempt to address funding sources and patterns for
natural hazards research. Suffice it to say that natural hazards research has been
funded by a variety of agencies and NSF programs including the Earthquake Hazards
Mitigation Program and the Natural and Man-Made Hazard Mitigation Program.

5. Please note that many projects may receive funding over several years. These
figures indicate the average award per project per year and not the average project
award in total. The average awards are slightly inflated from 1986 to 1989 due to
the award of two major collaborative grants to Carnegie-Mellon and the Wharton
Risk and Decision Processes Center.

6. Robin Keller, personal communication, July 25, 1990.

7. Personal communication with Robert F. Bordley (September 3, 1991), John
Castellan (August 30, 1991), and Howard Kunreuther (August 8, 1991).

8. The information in this section is based on various official publications of
the society, and personal communications with Robert B. Cumming (August 13,
1990) and Gary Flamm (November 28, 1990).

9. The three major goals set by Lester Lave were to double the membership; to
establish related organizations in Europe and Japan; and to establish at least ten
additional local chapters in the United States (SRA 1985).

10. Gary Flamm, personal communication, November 28, 1990.

CHAPTER 3.

Concepts of Risk: A Classification

Ortwin Renn

During my studies at the School of Social Sciences at Cologne University, I earned some extra income by doing survey work for a German polling institute. Every week I drove out to meet preselected people to ask them questions ranging from sexual preferences to attitudes toward government. Meeting hundreds of strangers over the long period of my undergraduate and graduate studies changed my attitudes toward people as well as my appreciation for the social sciences. I found in many of my respondents much wisdom and curiosity, both of which were largely ignored by my research instruments. I was bound to my prestructured, standardized questionnaire and forced to use categories that my respondents felt inappropriately described their opinions and values. Remote from the actual field work, the social scientists of the polling institute used the numerical data to draw conclusions about people's feelings and behavior. Often these conclusions appeared superficial or inadequate, since I had been exposed to the social context in which the responses were given.

This experience had a lasting effect on my academic career. First, it brought me closer to the "rational actor paradigm," which was very unpopular in the early 1970s in sociology circles at German universities. The dominant sociological paradigms in those days were either Marxist or systems theories (particularly Parsons and Merton), both of which emphasized structural factors for social behavior rather than individual or group actions. Second, it encouraged my interest in communication. I observed that many individual as well as group decisions were made without adequate information about potential consequences of the selected actions. This appeared to be particularly true for decisions or actions with respect to technological risks. Translating the results of scientific studies into everyday language and expressing the interests and values of the affected social groups to decision makers was, in my eyes, a prerequisite for rational decision and policy making. Third, it provided me with the incentive to experiment with novel social research methods that would capture the "hidden" wisdom of many people and be more appropriate to decipher the preferences of the respondents. In the course of this pursuit, I became an ardent proponent of citizen participation. Together with other colleagues, in particular Peter Dienel from the University of Wuppertal, I conducted participation-oriented social research aimed at measuring public preferences in a social context, in which all participants had the opportunity to learn more about their options and expected consequences prior to the elicitation of their preferences.

My experiences with public participation, particularly the times when the process failed to accomplish its goals, encouraged me to think again about the structural variables and their influence on people's behavior and collective decision making. I have become convinced that the complexity of social life cannot be adequately addressed by one perspective alone. The major goal of this chapter, therefore, is to argue in favor of an integration of inter- and intradisciplinary perspectives. The chapter compares the various perspectives and determines the functions and limitations of individual versus structural and objective versus constructivist concepts in risk analysis.

A major function of all social systems is to reduce complexity and select those areas of concern for which it appears worthwhile to spend scarce resources. This is also true with regard to risk. Social systems need to define criteria that allow them to prioritize their actions and to neglect those risks that appear trivial.

What criteria are appropriate for dealing with risks? How safe is safe enough? Should society adopt a set of uniform criteria for all types of risk regardless of context? Who should be involved in designing these criteria? Who should be held accountable if the criteria prove inadequate? These questions are at the core of the present risk debate. The responses to these questions depend on the perspectives of the different actors in society (Bradbury 1989). If risk is seen as an objective property of an event or activity and measured as the probability of well-defined adverse effects, the policy implications are obvious. Order risks according to "objective" measures of probability and magnitude of harm, and allocate resources to reduce the greatest risks first. If, on the other hand, risk is seen as a cultural or social construction, risk management activities would be set according to different criteria, and priorities should reflect social values and lifestyle preferences. These two positions represent extremes in a spectrum of risk perspectives.

As with most extreme positions, the positivistic view of risk and the social constructivist view are poor descriptions of reality (Short 1989; Dietz, Frey and Rosa, forthcoming). To my knowledge, there is not a single society in which uniform criteria for all risk types have been established. Graham and Vaupel (1981) calculated that, depending on risk type and content, risk policies in the United States reflect implicit values of life ranging from several thousand to several million U.S. dollars. Similarly, the relativistic view of social constructivism is difficult to justify upon observing that many nations have adopted very similar standards and risk reduction priorities in spite of major cultural and social differences (Coppock 1985; Jasanoff 1986;

Bauman and Renn 1989). A theoretical framework somewhere between these two extremes should be able to provide a more adequate approach to explain social responses to risk.

This chapter reviews the major candidates for risk perspectives that fall within the spectrum of the two extremes and explains the rationale behind each perspective. My goal is to describe, analyze, and evaluate the various risk concepts in order to match the appropriate tool to the problem. In the first sections, I explain the perspectives, discuss the prospects and limitations of each perspective, and describe their realm of application. Based on this comparison, in the final section I deduce the need and potential for an integrative perspective.

OVERVIEW OF RISK PERSPECTIVES

There can be no theory or scientific investigation without classification (Blumer 1931). Classification defines the conceptual tools necessary to select and order the phenomena a researcher attempts to study. The literature provides an array of classifications. Some are based on hazard types (Lowrance 1976; Hohenemser, Kates, and Slovic 1983, 1985), others on definitions of risks (Vlek and Stallen 1980; Fischhoff, Watson, and Hope 1984), others on risk characteristics (Starr 1969; Slovic, Fischhoff, and Lichtenstein 1981; Slovic 1987), others on risk conflicts (von Winterfeldt and Edwards 1984), and some on semantic images revealed through risk perception studies (Renn 1989a). All of these classifications have specific merits but provide little insight into the philosophies and mind-sets that underpin different concepts of risk.

Few attempts have been made to develop a transdisciplinary taxonomy of risk perspectives. Bradbury distinguished two types of risk concepts: risk as a physical attribute and risk as a social construct (Bradbury 1989; see also Wynne 1984a and Rayner 1987b). From a sociological point of view, May lists three perspectives on risks: cultural, individual choice, and systems approaches (May 1989). Several other sociological classifications have been proposed, but they focus exclusively on sociological or cultural concepts (see discussion below). A broader classification has been developed by Dietz, Frey, and Rosa (forthcoming) that distinguishes between technical (subdivided into assessment, evaluation, and management), psychological, sociological (subdivided into contextual and organizational), anthropological, and geographical perspectives. Their classification is more descriptive than analytical. In a recent review on the risk communication literature, Markowitz (1991, 2) concludes, "All these risk strategies [for conceptualizing risks and risk communication] cannot deny the fact that, although the growing risks of societal development have been the central focus of modern society, there is no approach in sight that could integrate the variety of

definitions and concepts and offer a common conceptual denominator"
(translation by author).

A classification may not offer one common conceptual denominator, but
it may provide a framework for comparison and analysis of the different
risk concepts and thus help to define common elements and distinctions
between different concepts. Based on earlier work (Renn 1991c; Häfele,
Renn, and Erdmann 1990), there appear to be seven approaches to the
conception and assessment of risk, largely grounded in the various academic
disciplines:

• the actuarial approach (using statistical predictions);
• the toxicological and epidemiological approach (including ecotoxicology);
• the engineering approach (including probabilistic risk assessment, PRA);
• the economic approach (including risk-benefit comparisons);
• the psychological approach (including psychometric analysis);
• social theories of risk; and
• cultural theory of risk (using grid-group analysis).

All these concepts vary in the selection of the underlying base unit (i.e.,
operational definition), the choice of methodologies, the complexity of risk
measures, and the instrumental and social function of the risk perspective.
Figure 3.1 illustrates the seven different risk perspectives and lists the characteristics of each perspective. In addition, the figure includes the basic
problems and applications of each perspective.

All risk concepts have one element in common: the distinction between
reality and possibility (Markowitz 1991; Evers and Nowotny 1987). If the
future is either predetermined or independent of present human activities,
the term *risk* makes no sense. This may seem obvious, but only in the context
of fairly recent developments in our own culture; it contrasts sharply with
more fatalistic views of nature and society. For example, a recent tunnel
collapse in Saudi Arabia was considered inevitable, and it was assumed that
the victims of this accident would have died in some other way if the accident
had been prevented by human activities. If one's fate is predetermined, there
is no need for anticipating future outcomes other than to please one's curiosity, because negative consequences cannot be avoided.

If the distinction between reality and possibility is accepted, the term *risk*
denotes the possibility that an undesirable state of reality (adverse effects)
may occur as a result of natural events or human activities (see NRC 1983;
Fischhoff, Watson and Hope 1984; Luhmann 1990). This definition implies
that humans can and will make causal connections between actions (or
events) and their effects, and that undesirable effects can be avoided or
mitigated if the causal events or actions are avoided or modified. Risk is
therefore both a descriptive and a normative concept. It includes the analysis

Figure 3.1
A Systematic Classification of Risk Perspectives

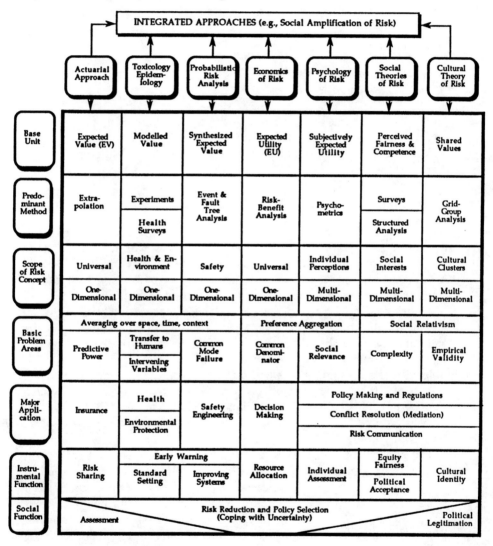

of cause-effect relationships, which may be scientific, anecdotal, religious, or magical (Douglas 1966); but it also carries the implicit message to reduce undesirable effects through appropriate modification of the causes or, though less desirable, mitigation of the consequences.

The definition of risk contains three elements: undesirable outcomes, possibility of occurrence, and state of reality. All risk perspectives provide different conceptualizations of these three elements. They are paraphrased in the following three questions:

1. How can we specify or measure uncertainties?
2. What are undesirable outcomes?
3. What is the underlying concept of reality?

In this chapter, these three questions—the conceptualization of uncertainty, the scope of negative effects, and the degree to which human knowledge reflects reality—serve as guidelines for distinguishing the different perspectives.

TECHNICAL RISK ANALYSES

The actuarial approach (first column in Figure 3.1) provides a straightforward answer to these questions. The base unit is expected value, that is, the relative frequency of an event averaged over time. The undesirable events are confined to physical harm to humans or ecosystems, which can be objectively observed or measured by appropriate scientific methods. An application of this approach may be the prediction of fatalities in car accidents for the coming year. The expected value can be extrapolated from the statistical data about fatal accidents in previous years. This perspective of risk relies on two conditions. First, enough statistical data must be available to make meaningful predictions. Second, the causal agents that are responsible for the negative effects must remain stable over the predicted time period (Häfele, Renn, and Erdmann 1990). The resulting risk assessment is reduced to a single dimension representing an average over space, time, and context.

The assessment of health and environmental risks (second column in Figure 3.1) is similar to the actuarial analysis but differs in the method of calculating the possibility of undesirable effects. In risk assessments, causal relationships have to be explored and modeled explicitly. Based on toxicological (animal experiments) or epidemiological studies (comparison of a population exposed to a risk agent with a population not exposed to the risk agent), researchers try to identify and quantify the relationship between a potential risk agent (such as dioxin or ionizing radiation) and physical harm observed in humans or other living organisms (Lave 1987; Renn 1985). Modeling is used to isolate a causal agent from among several intervening variables. These risk assessments can serve as early warning signals to inform society that a specific substance may cause harm to humans or the environment.

Probabilistic risk assessments (third column in Figure 3.1) attempt to predict the probability of safety failures of complex technological systems even in the absence of sufficient data for the system as a whole (Lowrance 1976; Hauptmanns, Herttrich, and Werner 1987; Morgan 1990). Using fault-tree or event-tree analyses, the failure probabilities for each component of the system are systematically assessed and then linked to the system structure. All probabilities of such a logical tree are then synthesized in order to model the overall failure rate of the system. A probabilistic risk assessment provides the same product as the actuarial analysis, that is, an average estimate of how many undesirable events one can expect over time as a result of a human activity or a technological failure. Its major problems lie in the modeling of common mode failures, that is, the simultaneous breakdown of technical components, and of human-machine interactions. Probabilistic risk assessments have been specifically valuable in detecting deficiencies in complex technical systems and in improving the safety performance of the technical system under consideration (see Figure 3.1).

These three perspectives have much in common and can be grouped together as technical perspectives. They anticipate potential physical harm to human beings or ecosystems, average these events over time and space, and use relative frequencies (observed or modeled) as a means to specify probabilities. The normative implication is obvious: since physical harm is perceived as an undesirable effect (at least for most people and society as a whole), technical risk analyses can be used to reveal, avoid, or modify the causes that lead to these unwanted effects. They can also be used to mitigate consequences, if causes are yet unknown, remote from human intervention or too complex to modify. Their instrumental functions in society are, therefore, oriented to risk sharing and risk reduction, through mitigation of consequences, standard setting, and improvements in the reliability and safety of technological systems (see Figure 3.1).

The technical analyses of risk have drawn much criticism from the social sciences (Hoos 1980; Douglas 1985; Mazur 1985; Beck 1986; Freudenburg 1988; Clarke 1989; Meyer-Abich 1989). First, what people perceive as an undesirable effect depends on their values and preferences. Second, the interactions between human activities and consequences are more complex and unique than the average probabilities used in technical risk analyses are able to capture. Third, the institutional structure of managing and controlling risks is prone to organizational failures and deficits which may increase the actual risk. The interaction between organizational malfunctions and risk is usually excluded from technical risk analyses. Fourth, the numerical combination of magnitude and probabilities assumes equal weight for both components. The implication is indifference between high-consequence/low-probability and low-consequence/high-probability events with identical expected values. However, people show distinct preferences for one or the other (Fischhoff, Goitein, and Shapiro 1982; Slovic 1987; Renn 1990).

From the normative perspective, the practice of risk minimization implies a clear distinction between experts and laypersons. Risk reduction or mitigation is based on the assumption that risk should be reduced in proportion to the expected or modeled harm to humans or ecosystems (Morgan 1990). This assumption is highly contested: social actions to cope with risk are not confined to the single goal of risk minimization but include other objectives such as equity, fairness, flexibility, or resilience (Short 1984; Nowotny and Eisikovic 1990). The inclusion of these complementary objectives requires participation by interest groups and the affected public. Furthermore, technical risk analyses can provide only aggregate data over large segments of the population and long time duration. Each individual, however, may face different degrees of risk depending on the variance of the probability distribution (Beck 1986). A person who is exposed to a larger risk than the average person may legitimately object to a risk policy based on aggregate calculations. The extent to which a person is exposed to a specific risk also rests on lifestyle factors and anecdotal knowledge, both of which are mostly unknown to scientists performing risk analyses. Brian Wynne (1991a) documented the failure of risk experts to recognize the extensive knowledge of local farmers about sheep habits and the physical environment when they conducted a risk analysis of the Chernobyl fallout in Scotland (see Chapter 12 for further details). Finally, some critics argue that the dominance of science in risk policy making provides too much power to an elite that is neither qualified nor politically legitimated to impose risks or risk management policies on a population (Jasanoff 1982).

How valid are the criticisms by social scientists? In my opinion, all the critical remarks are well taken and point to the problem that technical risk analyses represent a narrow framework that should not be the single criterion for risk identification, evaluation, and management. In contrast to many risk analysts, most notably the National Academy of Sciences (National Research Council 1983; see also Lowrance 1976; Rowe 1977), I believe that the above limitations of technical risk analyses apply not only to risk evaluation and management, but also to identification and quantification (see Hattis and Kennedy 1990; Brown and Goble 1990). Technical risk analyses rest on many "trans-scientific" assumptions (Weinberg 1972), such as the selection rules for identifying undesirable effects, the choice of a probability concept, and the equal weighting of probability and magnitude (Renn and Kals 1990). All of these conventions in risk analyses can be defended through logical reasoning, but they represent only parts of what individuals and society experience as risk (Renn and Swaton 1984; Jasanoff 1986; Kasperson, Renn, et al. 1988). Complementary risk analyses by the social sciences are necessary to capture the areas of risk experience that are either ignored or dismissed by technical risk analyses.

This does not mean, however, that technical risk analyses are unnecessary or less relevant than broader concepts of risk. They do serve a major purpose. After all, people are getting hurt or killed in accidents, in natural disasters, or through pollution. I agree with Short (1989), who insists that risk cannot be confined to perceptions and social constructions alone, but that objective outcomes are an integral part of the social processing of risk. Technical risk analyses help decision makers to estimate the expected physical harm. They provide the best knowledge about actual damage that is logically or empirically linked with each possibility of action. In terms of the three guiding questions stated above, technical analyses rely on relative frequencies as a means to express probabilities. This definition excludes unexpected events and aggregates data over space, populations, and time. The undesired effects are confined to physical harm to humans and ecosystems, thus excluding social and cultural impacts. Technical analyses assume a mirror relationship between observation and reality and do not consider that causes of harm and the magnitude of consequences are both mediated through social experience and interaction.

The narrowness of this approach contains both its weakness and its strength. Abstracting a single variable from the context of risk taking makes the concept of risk one-dimensional but also universal. Confining undesirable consequences to physical harm excludes other consequences that people might also regard as undesirable, but physical harm may be the only consequence that (almost) all social groups and cultures agree is undesirable. The evaluation of consequences differs considerably among groups when undesirable effects include value violations, inequities, or social interests. All these additional effects may or may not be more relevant than physical harm to different actors in society, but they always rely on subjective preferences. Physical harm on the other side appears to be universally accepted as a negative effect, which should be avoided. The exclusion of social context and meaning from technical risk analyses provides an abstraction that enhances the intersubjective validity of the results but at the price of neglecting the social processing of risk (see Brehmer 1987).

ECONOMIC PERSPECTIVES ON RISK

All risk concepts of the social sciences have in common the principle that the causes and consequences of risks are mediated through social processes. The concept closest to the technical approach is the economic concept of risk (fourth column in Figure 3.1). The major difference here is the transformation of physical harm or other undesired effects into subjective utilities (Just, Heuth, and Schmitz 1982; V. K. Smith 1986). The base unit of utilities describes the degree of satisfaction or dissatisfaction associated with a possible action or transaction. Whether physical harm is evaluated as pleasure or disaster remains irrelevant in the technical understanding of risk. Not so in economics: the relevant criterion is the subjective satisfaction with the potential consequences rather than a predefined list of undesirable effects.

The shift from expected harm to expected utility serves two major purposes. First, subjective (dis)satisfaction can be measured for all consequences, including psychological or social effects that are deemed undesirable. Second, and more important, the common denominator "personal satisfaction" allows a direct comparison between risks and benefits across different options (Merkhofer 1987). The question, How safe is safe enough?, cannot be answered by the three technical concepts unless there is a threshold of exposure between zero risk and some risk or unless the benefit of each option is identical (if so, you should choose the one with the lowest risk). Using utilities instead of physical harm provides a common denominator that enables each individual to compare options with different benefit profiles according to overall satisfaction (see Derby and Keeney 1981; Shrader-Frechette 1984). Utility is universal and one-dimensional (see Figure 3.1).

If risks can be expressed in terms of utilities, which some authors contest (see the debate between Kelman 1981a and Butters, Califee, and Ippolito 1981), they can be integrated into a decision process in which costs and benefits are assessed and compared. Since risks denote possible costs rather than actual costs, they have to be weighted by the probability of their occurrence. Furthermore, since risks and benefits may not materialize until years after implementing the desired option, the consequences have to be discounted (Hyman and Stiftel 1988). Economic theory perceives risk analysis as part of a larger cost-benefit consideration in which risks are the expected utility losses resulting from an event or an activity. The ultimate goal is to allocate resources so as to maximize their utility for society (V. K. Smith 1986).

The economic risk concept constitutes a consistent and coherent logical framework for situations in which decisions are being made by individuals and in which decision consequences are confined to the decision maker. In the risk area both conditions are rarely met (Coase 1960; Hyman and Stiftel 1988). First, most decisions on risks are collective decisions (public or meritocratic goods), which require the aggregation of individual utilities. How to measure the welfare of society, however, remains a major problem, since the subjective nature of utility does not provide a logically valid method to aggregate individual utilities into a single societal welfare function (see Figure 3.1). Averaging over expressed preferences is a common but unsatisfactory method for determining the utility of collective goods. Second, many transactions between individuals imply the imposition of risks on third parties, who may not benefit or benefit only marginally from the transaction itself (social costs or external effects).

Another major issue of critique is the underlying philosophy of the economic approach. The two basic foundations of economics are the rational actor paradigm and the reliance on utilitarian ethics (Freeman 1986; see Sen 1977 for a thorough critique of these foundations). People, for example, do smoke or drink, buy foolish things, or engage in activities that do not provide any utility to them. At the same time, people show compassion for others and may seek to increase the utility of other people even at their own expense. This behavior is contrary to the naive version of the rational actor paradigm, which postulates that people with full information will act in accordance with their own interests. Economic theory is, however, compatible with a modified and more realistic version of the rational actor paradigm, which assumes that people have subjective motives for performing an action and that they try to assess consequences of their action in the light of these motives (Jungermann 1986).

The reliance on utilitarian or contractual ethics is a more serious problem. This can be highlighted by the example of siting a hazardous waste facility. Economic theory would suggest an auction among potential host communities for determining the site for a hazardous waste facility. The lowest bidder in such an auction is likely to be the community with the highest marginal utility for increased revenues, that is, the poorest community in the pool. As a result of this difference in marginal utility, all the poor communities will end up having all the nasty facilities. From a utilitarian viewpoint, this is not a problem, because the poor community increases its utility by accepting a risk in exchange for money, and the rich community also wins by spending money for not being exposed to the risk. Other ethical perspectives, especially deontological ethics (normative values derived from introspection rather than evaluation of consequences), would postulate that a fair distribution of risks and benefits is a value in itself and should not be subject to bargaining (MacLean 1986).

Although the economic perspective promises a one-dimensional risk measure that is supposed to make benefits and risks commensurable, the problems of aggregating individual utilities, the existence of individual preferences for probabilities, the problem of finding an appropriate discount rate for risk consequences in the future, the effects of transactions on third parties, and the reliance on the rational actor model and utilitarian ethics impede the application of this concept in risk policies (see Baram 1980). This is aggravated by the fact that utilities are often measured in monetary units, which are perceived as incommensurable with the risk of serious health impediments or even death. In spite of these criticisms, the economic approach serves several vital functions in risk policies:

1. It provides techniques and instruments to measure and compare utility losses or gains from different decision options, thus enabling decision makers to make more informed choices (not necessarily better choices).

2. It enhances technical risk analyses by providing a broader definition of undesirable events, which include nonphysical aspects of risk.

3. Under the assumption that market prices (or shadow prices) represent social utilities, it provides techniques to measure distinctly different types of benefits and risks with the same unit.

4. It includes a model for rational decision making, provided that the decision makers can reach agreement about the utilities associated with each option.

In terms of the three guiding questions, the economic concept of risk is based on probabilities, a social definition of undesirable effects based on individual utilities, and the treatment of these effects as real gains or losses. In contrast to the technical approaches, probabilities are not only conceptualized as relative frequencies but also as strength of beliefs (Fischhoff, Lichtenstein, et al. 1981).

PSYCHOLOGICAL PERSPECTIVES ON RISK

The psychological perspective on risk expands the realm of subjective judgment about the nature and magnitude of risks in three ways (Column 5 in Figure 3.1). First, it focuses on personal preferences for probabilities and attempts to explain why individuals do not base their risk judgments on expected values (Pollatsek and Tversky 1970; Lopes 1983; Luce and Weber 1986). One of the interesting results of these investigations was the discovery of consistent patterns of probabilistic reasoning that are well suited for most everyday situations. People are risk averse if the stakes of losses are high and risk prone if the stakes for gains are high (Kahneman and Tversky 1979). Furthermore, many people balance their risk-taking behavior by pursuing an optimal risk strategy which does not maximize their benefits but assures both a satisfactory payoff and the avoidance of major disasters (Tversky 1972; Simon 1976; Luce and Weber 1986). Portfolio theory is one example of this kind of strategy. According to this theory, investors should select a portfolio of stocks in which the risk of losing money on one share is balanced by the probability of gaining money on another share. This example and many others show that deviations from the rule of maximizing one's utility are less a product of ignorance or irrationality than an indication of one or several intervening contextual variables, which often make perfect sense when seen in the light of the particular context and the individual decision maker's values (Lee 1981; Brehmer 1987).

Second, more specific studies on the perception of probabilities in decision making identified several biases in people's ability to draw inferences from probabilistic information (Festinger 1957; Kahneman and Tversky 1974, 1979; Ross 1977). These biases refer to the intuitive processing of uncertainty. For example, events that come to people's mind immediately are rated as more probable than events that are less mentally available. Although these biases constitute clear violations of logical rules, their implications might have been overrated in the literature (Fischhoff, Lichtenstein, et al. 1981). A major reason for this is that many laboratory situations provide insufficient contextual information to provide enough cues for people on which they can base their judgments (Lopes 1983). Relying on predominantly numerical information and being unfamiliar with the subject, many subjects in these experiments revert to "rules of thumb" in drawing inferences. In many real life situations, familiarity with the context provides additional information to calibrate individual judgments, particularly for nontrivial decisions (see Heimer 1988).

Third, the importance of contextual variables for shaping individual risk estimations and evaluations has been documented in many studies on risk perception (Jungermann 1986; Slovic 1987; Renn 1990). Psychometric methods have been employed to explore these qualitative characteristics of risks. The following contextual variables of risk have been found to affect the perceived seriousness of risks (Slovic, Fischhoff, and Lichtenstein 1981; Vlek and Stallen 1981; Renn 1983, 1990; Covello 1983; Gould et al. 1988; Jungermann and Slovic, in press):

- *the expected number of fatalities or losses:* Although the perceived average number of fatalities correlates with the perceived riskiness of a technology or activity, the relationship is weak and generally explains less than 20 percent of the declared variance (Renn 1983; Jungermann and Slovic, in press).

- *the catastrophic potential:* Most people show distinctive preferences among choices with identical expected values (average risk). Low-probability/high-consequence risks are usually perceived as more threatening than more probable risks with low or medium consequences (von Winterfeldt, John, and Borcherding 1981).

- *qualitative risk characteristics:* Surveys and experiments have revealed that perception of risks is influenced by a series of perceived properties of the risk source or the risk situation (Slovic, Fischhoff, and Lichtenstein 1981; E. J. Johnson and Tversky 1984). Among the most influential factors are the perception of dread with respect to the possible consequences; the conviction of having personal control over the magnitude or probability of the risk; the familiarity with the risk; the perception of equitable sharing of both benefits and risks; and the potential to blame a person or institution responsible for the creation of a risky situation. In addition, equity issues play a major role in risk perception.

- *the beliefs associated with the cause of risk:* The perception of risk is often part of an attitude that a person holds about the cause of the risk, that is, a technology, human activity, or natural event. Attitudes encompass a series of beliefs about the nature, consequences, history, and justifiability of a risk cause (Otway 1980; Thomas, Maurer, et al. 1980; Otway and Thomas 1982; Renn and Swaton 1984). Often risk perception is a product of these underlying beliefs rather than the cause for these beliefs (Clarke 1989). In a recent cross-cultural comparison of risk perceptions, environmental versus technical beliefs of the respondents were better predictors for perceived seriousness of risk than national differences or other explanatory variables (Rohrmann 1991).

This list of factors demonstrates that the intuitive understanding of risk is a multidimensional concept and cannot be reduced to the product of probabilities and consequences (Allen 1987b). Risk perceptions differ considerably among social and cultural groups. However, it appears to be a common characteristic in almost all countries in which perception studies have been performed that most people perceive risk as a multidimensional phenomenon and integrate their beliefs with respect to the nature of the risk, the cause of the risk, the associated benefits, and the circumstances of risk taking into one consistent belief system (Renn 1989a).

In terms of the three guiding questions listed above, the psychological perspective on risk includes all undesirable effects that people associate with a specific cause. Whether these cause-effect relationships reflect reality or not is irrelevant. Individuals respond according to their perception of risk and not according to an objective risk level or the scientific assessment of risk. Scientific assessments are part of the individual response to risk only to the degree that they are integrated in the individual perceptions. Furthermore, relative frequencies or other (scientific) forms of defining probabilities are substituted by the strength of belief that people have about the likelihood that any undesirable effect will occur.

The focus on the individual and his/her subjective estimates is also the major weakness of the psychological perspective (Mazur 1987; Plough and Krimsky 1987). The broadness of the dimensions that people use to make judgments and the reliance on intuitive heuristics and anecdotal knowledge make it hard, if not impossible, to aggregate individual preferences and to find a common denominator for comparing individual risk perceptions. Furthermore, these physical studies fail to explain why individuals select certain characteristics of risks and ignore others (Dietz, Frey, and Rosa forthcoming).

From a normative perspective, knowledge about individual perceptions of risk cannot be translated directly into policies (Renn 1990). If perceptions are partially based on biases or ignorance, it does not seem wise to use them as yardsticks for risk reduction. In addition, risk perceptions vary among individuals and groups. Whose perceptions should be used to make decisions on risk? At the same time, however, these perceptions reflect the real concerns of people and include the undesirable effects that the technical analysis of risk often miss. Facing this dilemma, how can risk perception studies contribute to improving risk policies? They can

- reveal public concerns and values;
- serve as indicators for public preferences;
- document desired lifestyles;
- help to design risk communication strategies; and
- represent personal experiences in ways that may not be possible in the scientific assessment of risk.

In essence, the psychological studies can help to create a more comprehensive set of decision options and to provide additional knowledge and normative criteria to evaluate them (Fischhoff 1985). Similar to the other perspectives, the psychological perspective on risk contributes valuable information for understanding risk responses and for designing risk policies, but it is limited in its comprehensiveness and applicability.

SOCIOLOGICAL PERSPECTIVES ON RISK

Classifications in sociology face the insurmountable problem that there are as many perspectives within sociology as there are sociologists. Since the demise of the structural-functionalist school in sociology, no dominant camp has evolved, which leaves the field open to an array of competing approaches ranging from an adaptation of the rational actor approach to Marxist and structural analyses. All sociological and anthropological concepts of risk, however, do have in common the notion that "humans do not perceive the world with pristine eyes, but through perceptual lenses filtered by social and cultural meanings transmitted via primary influences such as the family, friends, superordinates, and fellow workers" (Dietz, Frey, and Rosa forthcoming). The social sciences present a patchwork of different concepts focused on special aspects of risk or the circumstances of the risk situation. Some examples are

- studies on organizational aspects of risk (Perrow 1984; Clarke 1989);
- studies in the sociology of disasters (see the edited volume by Dynes, De Marchi, and Pelanda 1987);
- analyses of media coverage and communication (Mazur 1981, 1984; Raymond 1985; Lichtenberg and MacLean 1988; Peltu 1988; Stallings 1990; Peters 1990);
- investigations of risk conflicts and their causes (O'Riordan 1983; von Winterfeldt and Edwards 1984; Edwards and von Winterfeldt 1986; Dietz, Stern, and Rycroft 1989);
- analyses of equity and fairness (Kasperson and Kasperson 1983; MacLean 1986; Rosa 1988; Brion 1988);
- analysis of risk distribution among classes and populations (Schnaiberg 1986; Beck 1986, 1990);
- studies on the epistemology or legitimation of risk knowledge (Rip 1985; Jasanoff 1986; Dietz and Rycroft 1987; Evers and Nowotny 1987).

Any attempt to classify these studies and link them to underlying theoretical concepts is like trying to find order in chaos. Notwithstanding the frustrations that are likely to evolve when sociologists try to classify sociological schools of thought, the literature offers a wide variety of taxonomies, even in the narrow field of risk and disaster research (see Stallings

Figure 3.2
Major Sociological Perspectives on Risk

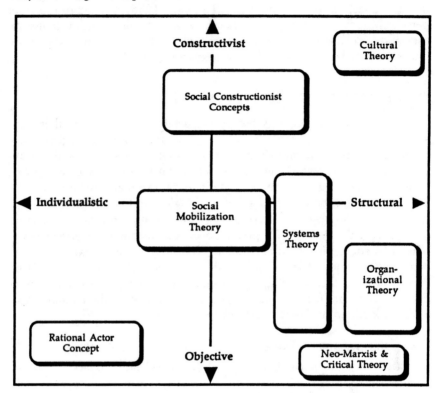

1987; Kreps 1987; May 1989; Bradbury 1989; Short 1989; Dietz, Frey, and Rosa forthcoming). However, they all use different frameworks and classification criteria.

Rather than reviewing the reviews, I venture to add an additional taxonomy, which is shown in Figure 3.2. This taxonomy orders the sociological approaches with respect to two dimensions: (1) individualistic versus structural and (2) objective versus constructivist. The major reasons for this classification are as follows:

- The classification is simple and straightforward (hence open to critique).
- The classification fits the overall framework of risk perspectives developed above.
- All sociological studies fall within the boundaries of these two dimensions.
- The two dimensions appear to be sufficient to separate concepts that are clearly distinct from each other.

What are the meanings of the two dimensions? The two attributes *individualistic* and *structural* indicate the base unit of the analysis. It is either the individual or a social aggregate such as an institution, a social group, a subculture, or a society. Structural concepts emphasize that complex social phenomena cannot be explained by individual behavior alone but that they rest on interactive, often unintentional effects among individuals and between these larger units. *Objective* and *constructivist* concepts differ in their view of the nature of risk and its manifestations. Whereas the objective concept implies that risks and their manifestations are real, observable events, the constructivist concept claims that risks and their manifestations are *social artifacts* fabricated by social groups or institutions. Figure 3.2 indicates the location of some major theoretical approaches to the social processing of risk. Not included are case studies, problem-oriented studies without reference to a theoretical concept, purely normative or ethical approaches, and (the ever popular) conspiracy ideologies. Given these limitations, the dominant approaches are the rational actor concept, social mobilization theory, organizational theory, systems theory, neo-Marxist and critical theory, and social constructionist concepts.

Rational actor concept. This concept is widely used in economical analyses of social behavior and in a variety of social science applications (Dawes 1988). Social actions are seen as a result of deliberate intentions by individual or social actors to promote their interests. Social groups and institutions experience a social conflict if the interests of one group conflict with the interests of another group. The stakes of social actions are real, and the actors are individuals who may also represent groups and institutions. If members of one party perceive risks as a threat to their interests, they will mobilize political actions to reduce or mitigate the risk. This protective behavior may contrast with the interests of another party who benefits from the risk source. Institutional and individual behavior is governed by strategies to select the best means for accomplishing a predefined goal (Stallings 1987).

Social mobilization theory. Social mobilization theory focuses on two questions: Under which circumstances are individuals motivated to take actions (McCarthy and Zald 1977; Watts 1987), and what are the structural conditions necessary for social groups to succeed, that is, to accomplish their goals (Gamson 1990)? The relevance to the risk problem is obvious. The first question refers to the elements of the social experience of risk that trigger actions by individuals; the second to the results of social processing of risk among different social actors (McAdam, McCarthy, and Zald 1988). In the early development of social mobilization theories, most studies were based on the objective-individualistic approach and the rational actor concept, but later researchers favored a structural analysis of motivation and group performance (Klandermanns 1984; McCarthy and Zald 1977). Joining social movements such as environmental groups cannot be fully explained by comparing payoff and participation costs (regardless of whether benefits are expressed in monetary units or other terms). Being attracted to a movement may be the result of relative deprivation, imitation of peer group behavior, socially held convictions, or other structural factors (Marx-Ferree and Miller 1985). The same is true for performance of social groups and institutions. Success and failure may be less related to effort or strategies of each social actor than to arena rules and interactive (unintended) consequences of all actors' communication and behavior in the arena (see my Chapter 7 in this volume).

Organizational theory. Organizational theory emphasizes two structural aspects of institutions: the routinization of tasks and the diffusion of responsibility. Since risk management of complex technologies requires institutional operation and control, routinization and diffusion of control impact the performance of risk managers (Perrow 1984; Clarke 1989). For example, a technological risk situation, which includes organizational factors such as complacency of operators or inadequate control, may produce a much higher risk for the public than the risk measure calculated by technical risk assessment. As a result, the technological risk assessment may underestimate the "real" risk because routinization of tasks and diffusion of responsibility are both factors that are likely to increase the probability of operational errors or inadequate control (Freudenburg 1989).

Systems theory. Systems analysis regards risks as an element of a larger social or institutional unit. It focuses on structural factors and spans *real* and *constructed* realities. Risk issues evolve in an evolutionary process in which groups and institutions organize their knowledge about their natural and social environment and share this knowledge with other social systems through communication (Luhmann 1986, 1990; Stallings 1987). Various systems of knowledge compete in a society and are subject to a selection and adaptation process that is governed by structurally determined criteria. These criteria indicate and provide a basis to evaluate perceived advantages for the macrosystem in order to sustain its basic biological, social, and cultural functions. Advantages can be *real* in the sense that they promote evolutionary adaptation, or *constructed* in the sense that they promote self-confidence and reassurance within a given social system. This approach, after one of its derivations, functional-structural analysis, dominated the discipline of sociology in the 1950s and 1960s, is almost absent from U.S. literature on risk, but remains very prominent in the European sociological literature (Luhmann 1990).

Neo-Marxist and critical theory. These concepts share the objective component of the rational actor approach but rely on structural analysis for determining institutional interests and social group behavior (Habermas 1984–87; Forester 1985; Dombrowski 1987). The focus is on the normative aspect of emancipation rather than explanation of risk experience or policies for risk reduction. Emancipation in this context involves the empowerment of groups and communities to enable them to determine their own acceptable risk level. According to this perspective, present risk policies suffer a legitimation crisis because they are based on the imposition of risks by one social group on another (reproduction of class structure) and are often not in the interest of those who have to bear them (lack of social integration). The risk experiences by different social groups reflect the class structure of society and indicate the inequities in the distribution of power and social influence.

Social constructionist concepts. These concepts treat risks as social constructs that are determined by structural forces in society. Issues such as health threats, inequities, fairness, control, and others cannot be determined by *objective* scientific analysis but only reconstructed from the beliefs and rationalities of the various actors in society (Johnson and Covello 1987; Bradbury, 1989; Gamson and Modigliani 1989). The fabric and texture of these constructions reflect both the interests/values of each group or institution in the various risk arenas and the shared meaning of terms, cultural artifacts, and natural phenomena among groups (Wynne 1983; Rayner 1987b). Risk policies result from a constant struggle of all participating actors to place their meaning of risk on the public agenda and impose it on others. The need to compromise between self-interest, that is, constructing one's own group-specific reality, and the necessity to communicate, that is, constructing a socially meaningful reality, determines the range and limitations of possible constructs of reality. Technical risk analyses are not necessarily superior to any other construct of risk because they are also based on group conventions, specific interests of elites, and implicit value judgments (Appelbaum 1977; Dietz, Stern, and Rycroft 1989).

In addition to an emphasis on social processing of risk, all six approaches, though the organizational concept to a lesser extent, appear to have a common interest in explaining or predicting the experience of social injustice and unfairness in relation to distributional inequities (see column 6 in Figure 3.1). The individualistic concepts regard inequities as potential violations of group interests, whereas the structural concepts treat them either as a reflection of the "real" inequities in the distribution of power and social resources or as a dysfunctional result of inadequate balancing of social interests and values. In the social constructivist perspective, perceived violations of fairness constitute a powerful social construct that can be used in the respective risk arena to demand corrective actions, provided that the group's claim of unfair treatment can be made plausible to the other groups. In the objective perspective, inequities are reflections of class structure and domination. The power elites provide justifications for these "real" inequities by creating or referring to social constructions such as religions or ideologies.

From a normative point of view, the sociological perspectives illuminate the need to base risk policies on the experience of inequities, unfairness, and—to a lesser degree—perceived social incompetence (see Figure 3.1). These three experiences are not the only social consequences that people may perceive as undesirable effects, but they are probably the most important in conjunction with perceived health impairments. Many of the perception variables, such as personal control and voluntariness, reflect the same concern. As a consequence, sociological studies can help to address the issues of fairness and competence and provide normative conclusions for legitimizing risk policies. However, these conclusions will vary considerably depending on which of the six perspectives is being employed. One example is the contrast between the neo-Marxist and the rational actor perspective. The neo-Marxist perspective implies that capitalist societies can only mask inequities by offering compensation or participation, because an equitable solution would necessitate a fundamental change in the basic power structure of society. The rational actor approach suggests that compensation of risks is the right tool to balance the interests of risk creators and risk bearers.

In terms of the three guiding questions noted above, the sociological perspectives include undesirable events that are socially defined and (in some cases) socially constructed. *Real* consequences are always mediated through social interpretation and linked with group values and interests. Possibilities for future events are not confined to the calculation of probabilities but encompass group-specific knowledge and vision. Furthermore, possibilities are shaped by human interventions, social organizations, and technological developments. Ignoring the connections between social organizations and technological performance may seriously underestimate the likelihood of failures. Lastly, reality is seen as a system of both physical occurrences (independent of human observations) and constructed meanings (with respect to these events and to abstract notions, such as fairness, vulnerability, and justice).

The broad scope of sociological perspectives and the inclusion of social experience of risk close the gap that is left open by the other perspectives on risk. This accomplishment, however, has its price. The necessity to reduce the complexity of the social world and to model the major influential factors opens the door for subjective selection and ideological reasoning. The outcome of a sociological analysis is at least partially predetermined by the theoretical concept on which the analysis is based. Furthermore, the complex reality offers empirical proof for almost any perspective (it may, however, falsify theories within a perspective). As a result, social actors in society often select the perspective that best serves their interests (legitimation function) and ignore those perspectives that are antagonistic to their interests.

THE CULTURAL PERSPECTIVE ON RISK

In recent years, anthropologists and cultural sociologists have suggested that social responses to risks are determined by prototypes of cultural belief patterns, that is, clusters of related convictions and perceptions of reality (see column 7 in Figure 3.1). Based on studies of early organizational principles in tribal communities, one school of anthropologists identified several generic patterns of value clusters that distinguish different cultural groups from each other (Douglas 1966; Thompson 1980a; Douglas and Wildavsky 1982b; Rayner, 1987b; Schwarz and Thompson 1990). These different groups form specific positions on risk topics and develop corresponding attitudes and strategies. This approach is both structural and constructivist (Figure 3.2). Most proponents of this theory agree that it does not apply to individual attitudes or convictions but to larger social aggregates such as organized groups or institutions (Rayner 1984; opposite view in Wildavsky and Dake 1990). However, cultural prototypes can be used to predict individual responses, particularly responses of individuals in their social roles as representatives of agencies, industries, or private organizations. In addition, the cultural approach perceives environment and risk as social constructs (Wildavsky 1979).

Whereas the sociological analysis of risk links social judgments about risks to individual or social interests and values, the cultural perspective assumes that cultural patterns structure the mind-set of individuals and social organizations to adopt certain values and reject others. These selected values determine the perception of risks and benefits (see column 7 in Figure 3.1). The number and types of such cultural patterns are not always consistent in the literature. Douglas and Wildavsky distinguish between center and periphery (1982b); Rayner uses four prototypes (Rayner 1987b; Rayner and Cantor 1987) and Thompson five (Thompson 1980a). I shall address the latter classification, which is more inclusive. (See Chapter 4 for a longer discussion of the origins and development of cultural theory.) Figure 3.3 illustrates the five prototypes. The types differ in the degree of *group* cohesiveness (the extent to which individuals take on a group mind-set and find identity in a social group) and the degree of *grid* (the extent to which someone accepts and respects a formal system of hierarchy and procedural rules).

Organizations or social groups belonging to the *entrepreneurial* prototype perceive risk taking as an opportunity to succeed in a competitive market and to pursue their personal goals (Rayner 1987b). They are less concerned about equity issues and would like the government to refrain from extensive regulation or risk management efforts. This group contrasts most with organizations or groups belonging to the *egalitarian* prototype, which emphasizes cooperation and equality rather than competition and freedom. Egalitarians focus on long-term effects of human activities and are more likely to abandon an activity (even if they perceive it as beneficial to them) than to take chances. They are particularly concerned about equity. The third prototype, the *bureaucrat*, relies on rules and procedures to cope with uncertainty. As long as risks are managed by a capable institution and coping strategies have been provided for all eventualities, there is no need to worry

Figure 3.3
Risk Taking in the Context of Cultural Prototypes

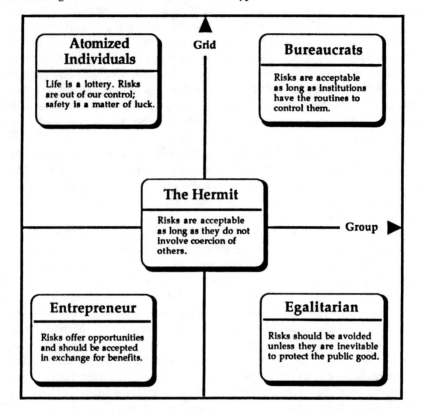

about risks. Bureaucrats believe in the effectiveness of organizational skills and practices and regard a problem as solved when a procedure to deal with its institutional management is in place. The fourth prototype, the group of *atomized* or *stratified individuals*, principally believes in hierarchy, but its members do not identify with the hierarchy to which they belong. These people trust only themselves, are often confused about risk issues, and are likely to take high risks for themselves, but oppose any risk that they feel is imposed on them. At the same time, however, they see life as a lottery and are often unable to link harm to a concrete cause (Thompson 1980a). The last group is the group of *autonomous individuals* in the center of the group-grid coordinates. Thompson describes autonomous individuals as self-centered hermits and short-term risk evaluators. I like to refer to them as potential mediators in risk conflicts, since they build multiple alliances to the four other groups and believe in hierarchy only if they can relate the authority to superior performance or knowledge (Renn 1992).

In terms of the three guiding questions, cultural analysis implies that the definition of undesirable events, the generation and estimation of possibilities, as well as the constructions of reality depend on the cultural affiliation of the respective social group. If this were true, cultural theory would qualify as an exclusive and comprehensive theory of risk since all risk experience is seen as a reflection of cultural affiliations.

The premise that cultural theory can serve as an umbrella for all other risk perspectives is doubtful at best, if not unsubstantiated. First, most authors within the cultural theory emphasize that cultural prototypes do not characterize individuals but social aggregates. The reason for this is obvious. Anecdotal evidence tells us that individuals may belong to different organizations and groups having different cultural profiles. An owner of a business (entrepreneurial prototype) may belong to a fundamentalist church (egalitarian prototype) and serve as treasurer in a volunteer charity organization (bureaucratic prototype). But role differentiation and segmentation of individuals are mirrored in the functional differentiation of social aggregates (see B. B. Johnson 1987). Environmentalists and industrialists may be easy to classify, but what about the League of Women Voters, the American Association of Retired People, the American Automobile Association, and others? If groups are mixtures of prototypes, the cultural perspective loses much of its explanatory power.

Second, the relationship between cultural prototype and organizational interest is unclear and problematic. If cultural affiliation precedes interest, then what determines to which cultural prototype groups or organizations belong? Are we born as entrepreneurs or egalitarians? Are social institutions formed because cultural prototypes desire to express themselves? If cultural affiliations are social acquisitions learned through interaction with others, then they must be linked with personal or institutional tasks or interests. For example, an interest in preserving the environment may lead to the adoption of an egalitarian viewpoint, or vice versa.

Third, the selection of the five prototypes as the only relevant cultural patterns in modern society needs more evidence than the reference to tribal organizations. Many social groups seem to have agendas and worldviews that cannot be captured by the five prototypes. For example, many religious groups are very hierarchical in structure but egalitarian in doctrine. It is also unclear why only hierarchy and openness matter in cultural prototypes. Why not other characteristics such as spirituality or vulnerability? The inherently reductionist view of partitioning culture into four or five segments appears to be too simplistic (see Funtowicz and Ravetz 1985).

Lastly, the cultural perspective has not provided sufficient empirical evidence of its validity. This is partly due to the problem of measurement (see Rayner 1990). Organizational philosophies are often hidden and cannot be revealed by interviewing representatives of these organizations. Furthermore, if prototypes are mixed in organizations, then the perspective (similar to many sociological concepts) is not falsifiable. Any observed behavior is compatible with some mix of prototypes. Some attempts have been made to collect or reinterpret empirical data about individual values and attitudes in the light of cultural theory (Buss, Craik, and Dake 1986; Wildavsky and Dake 1990). However, the empirical data suggest that beliefs representing various cultural prototypes are related to individual attitudes toward risks. This phenomenon can well be explained in terms of underlying individual values or worldviews.

Similar to the other perspectives, the cultural theory of risk has its shortcomings and its merits. My critical remarks about the perspective are meant to reject the claim that cultural theory is sufficient to explain the social processing of risk. It is the "cultural imperialism" (Kasperson, Chapter 6) or the "cultural determinism" (Nelkin 1982) to which I (and others) object. The reduction of cultural clusters to basically three important prototypes (entrepreneurial, egalitarian, and bureaucratic) may be a valid and intuitively plausible hypothesis in analyzing risk responses, but it should be treated as a hypothesis rather than the exclusive explanation. The emphasis on values and worldviews rather than interests and utilities (which in themselves are reflections of one worldview) is a major accomplishment of this theory. People are not motivated by payoffs only. Neither are organizations. To understand organizational behavior, interests, norms, values, and self-images have to be taken into account. Furthermore, what people and organizations perceive as undesirable events reflects their perception and evaluation of the cultural definition of the social context and its relevance for their worldview.

Based on the constructivist concept, the cultural theory of risk offers an interpretation of the social experience of risk without falling prey to the trap of arbitrariness that characterizes many of the sociological analyses inspired by the same philosophy (Rayner 1987b). It can offer additional evidence for the importance of cultural factors in risk perception and risk policies. It also provides better explanations for social actions that seem to be in conflict with either the technical risk analyses or the obvious interests of the initiating group.

CONCLUSION

What is the major lesson to be learned from the classification of risk perspectives? Figure 3.1 shows that all these perspectives have their specific niche in the analysis of risk. Technical analysis provides society with a narrow definition of undesirable effects and confines possibilities to numerical probabilities based on relative frequencies. However, this narrowness is a virtue as much as it is a shortcoming. Focused on "real" health effects or ecological damage, technical analyses are based on a societal consensus of undesirability and a (positivistic) methodology that assures equal treatment for all risks under consideration. The price we pay for this methodological rigor is the simplicity of an abstraction we make from the culture and context of risk-taking behavior.

The other perspectives on risk broaden the scope of undesirable effects, include other ways to express possibilities and likelihood, and expand the understanding of reality to include the interpretations of undesirable events and "socially constructed" realities. The social experience of risk includes the perception of actual damage, but it is more focused on the evaluation of the risk context and the associations between the risk and social or cultural artifacts.

Cultural reason does not deny the role of technical reason; it simply extends it. The former branches out, while the latter branches in. Cultural rationality does not separate the context from the content of risk analysis. Technical rationality operates as if it can act independently of popular culture in constructing the risk analysis, whereas cultural rationality seeks technical knowledge but incorporates it within a broader decision framework. [Plough and Krimsky 1987, 8–9]

Integrating all these perspectives in order to do justice to the phenomenon of risk in our society appears to be necessary for both the analysis of risk experience and the prescription of risk policies. While few would dispute that the observed risk behavior of individuals and groups is puzzling enough to get the social and cultural sciences involved, many feel that risk policies should be based solely on technical and economic considerations.

This would indeed be appropriate if society were only concerned about risk minimization. If all society cared about was reducing the amount of physical harm done to its members, technical analyses and economic balancing would suffice for effective risk management. Included could be the perspective of organizational sociology to make sure that technical safety measures are paralleled by institutional control and monitoring. The social sciences would only be needed to sell the risk management packages to the "misinformed" public via risk communication.

However, society is not only concerned about risk minimization. People are willing to suffer harm if they feel it is justified or if it serves other goals. At the same time, they may reject even the slightest chance of being hurt if they feel the risk is imposed on them or violates their other attitudes and values (Otway and von Winterfeldt 1982). Context matters. So does procedure of decision making independent of outcome. Responsive risk management needs to take these aspects into account. The social science perspectives on risk can help to enrich risk management. They can

- identify and explain public concerns associated with the risk source;
- explain the context of risk-taking situations;
- identify cultural meanings and associations linked with special risk arenas;
- help to articulate objectives of risk policies in addition to risk minimization, such

as enhancing fairness and institutional trust and reducing inequities and vulnerability;
- design procedures or policies to incorporate these cultural values into the decision-
making process;
- design programs for participation and joint decision making; and
- design programs for evaluating risk management performance and organizational
structures for identifying, monitoring, and controlling risks.

The above discussion, however, demonstrates that the inclusion of the
social science perspectives for normative use in policy making faces two
major drawbacks. First, the advice of social scientists will vary considerably
depending on the worldview and disciplinary background of the individuals
asked. Second, unlike the technical or economic perspective, the social science concepts offer no common denominator for measuring cultural or
social acceptability (Douglas 1985). What constitutes a value violation for
one group may be perfectly in line with the values of another group. Who
is going to decide which social construction of reality has more validity than
another competing construction?

Risk policies can cope with the first problem by employing different
perspectives in analyzing the situation and by knowing the relative advantages and disadvantages of each perspective. The second problem creates
more difficulties. It is obvious that a simple or even complex algorithm of
multidimensional decision making would not resolve the potential conflicts
between competing social constructions (although formal multi-attribute
decision analysis may provide an excellent framework for structuring problems and decision options). There is also no impartial referee available to
judge the appropriateness of cultural constructions. The only viable resolution of these conflicts in democratic societies is by initiating a discourse
among the major parties involved in the decision-making process or affected
by the decision outcomes (Habermas 1971). Such a dialogue can be organized in the form of advisory committees, citizen panels, formal hearings,
and others (Fiorino 1989). Democratic values can provide the means by
which to construct this dialogue, and the social science perspectives can
help to make these forms of dialogue work, that is, to make sure that each
group can bring their own interest and values to the process and yet reach
a common understanding of the problem and the potential solutions (Renn,
Webler, and Johnson 1991).

The need for social science perspectives in risk analysis and risk management is impeded by the fragmentation of the social sciences and the claim
of exclusiveness or incompatibility with competing perspectives. This analysis has demonstrated that such a competition is neither theoretically compelling nor helpful. It has become evident that a novel and integrative
framework is necessary to capture the full extent of the social experience
of risk and to study the dynamic processing of risks by the various partic-

ipants in a pluralistic society. Such a novel approach cannot and should not replace the existing perspectives, but should instead offer a meta-perspective that assigns each perspective an appropriate place and function. The major objective of such a meta-perspective is to make the various perspectives compatible with each other and to provide a semantic framework that allows comparative analysis across the various perspectives. A potential candidate for such an integrated framework is the concept of social amplification, which is described in this volume (see Chapter 6). Whether the social amplification framework can meet this challenge remains to be seen.

PART II _____

Social, Cultural, and Psychological
Paradigms

CHAPTER 4 _____

Cultural Theory and Risk Analysis

Steve Rayner

The development of cultural theory in the field of risk analysis has been a sustained collaborative effort among several individuals and institutions. To separate my particular contribution from others, particularly Michael Thompson and Mary Douglas, is unthinkable for me. However, the editors of this volume have requested that I begin with a short autobiographical preface that tells how I personally came to be involved in cultural theory and risk analysis.

Undergraduate studies at the University of Kent at Canterbury in philosophy and theology reflected my consuming interest in the way people throughout history and in all cultures have used ideas about nature to support their moral and political arguments. Graduate studies in anthropology at University College London confirmed the universality of this phenomenon, even in the seemingly unlikely subject of my Ph.D. dissertation on the proliferation of extreme Marxist sects inhabiting the British political byways of the 1970s (Rayner 1979). My studies of political organizations and their views of nature (in those days I was mostly concerned with grand themes of time and space, and millenarian prophesies) led me to the Russell Sage Foundation in 1980 to join Mary Douglas in the study of American environmental groups and their inclination to catastrophist views of technological risk. My perspectives on risk perception and personal risk management were strongly influenced by fieldwork among medical users of ionizing radiation (Rayner 1986a). This remains one of a very few firsthand empirical studies of risk behavior that has been executed explicitly from a cultural perspective.

Another formative influence around this time was my work with a Columbia University mathematician, Jonathan Gross, on methodological refinement for measuring the grid and group dimensions (Gross and Rayner 1985). Although the measurement paradigm we created is too demanding for most empirical applications, working out the principles for measuring multiple hierarchies (grid) and social networks (group) helped to clarify the principles of cultural analysis in risk behavior.

During this same period, my attention shifted from a preoccupation with the cultural dynamics of social movements per se to issues of risk management and technology acceptance. In 1984, I suggested that the definition of risk employed by engineers and psychologists was too narrow for the purposes of public policy. Rather than asking "How safe is safe enough?," I suggested that we need to address the issue of "How fair is safe enough?" Instead of the conventional narrow definition of risk as probability × consequences, I suggested a Wittgensteinian *family resemblance* category of risk (Rayner 1987a).

These influences helped to formulate a study of the market and societal acceptance of advanced reactor concepts conducted at Oak Ridge National Laboratory (ORNL), where I had moved in 1983. Robin Cantor and Robert B. Braid were my collaborators in this research. In the reactor concepts study, we developed the cultural focus on issues of trust, liability, and consent (TLC) in risk management as expressed by utility commissions, power companies, and public interest groups to improve our understanding of how these groups might treat technological and investment risks in the year 2010 (Rayner and Cantor 1987).

My interest in perception of risk over long time frames expanded, as did the geographical scale of my work. Since 1988 I have focused almost exclusively on global environmental risk analysis and problems of risk management across jurisdictional boundaries within and among nation states.

Cultural theory argues that risks are defined, perceived, and managed according to principles that inhere in particular forms of social organization. The cultural theory of risk perception first entered public policy debates a decade ago with the publication of Michael Thompson's paper "Aesthetics of Risk: Culture or Context" in Schwing and Albers' (1980) landmark volume *Societal Risk Assessment: How Safe Is Safe Enough?* Since that time, the theory has been the focus of widespread debate in both scholarly and policy communities. Despite this attention, cultural theory seldom has been applied in risk analyses for technological decision making. Cultural theorists have made few systematic empirical studies of risk perception and management. The studies that do exist tend to be scholarly analyses of past debates and decision making about technology rather than contributions to the solution of current problems.

It appears that while the principles of cultural theory have been enormously influential, its practical application has been very limited. In this chapter I will explore some of the origins of this disparity between the influence and practice of cultural theory. In doing so, I will reiterate the principles and history of cultural theory, highlighting some significant differences among its proponents. Finally, I will respond to some of the objections to cultural risk analysis that I have encountered repeatedly over the past ten years.

CONVENTIONAL THEORIES AND CULTURAL THEORY

A useful place to begin such a review of cultural theory is to identify the important ways in which it differs from other approaches with respect to risk perception, risk communication, and risk management.

Almost without exception, attempts to understand human behavior related to technological risk begin with an event, an activity, or a statement of the probability and consequences of an activity that is assumed to be the stimulus for human responses. The conventional order of risk events is assumed to be as follows: The external risk stimulus causes an individual risk perception, which may be the subject of attempts at risk communication, leading to risk management efforts to prevent the unwanted event or to ameliorate its consequences.

This ordering is implicit or explicit in both the natural hazards research tradition and in psychometric risk studies, although the histories of these two approaches are quite separate (cf. other chapters in this volume). The model of perception here is that of vision or hearing rather than that of touch or taste. The perceiver essentially is the passive recipient of an independent stimulus, rather than an active agent, like a baby, groping with or sucking on the world in the search for information. The risk perception problem in these approaches is to account for the discrepancy between some people's estimates of the risks or potential consequences of certain events and actuarial data or expert assessments.

The dominant model of risk communication essentially is one of information transmission with the goal of educating the recipient. The main concern is how to pass quantitative information about the probabilities and consequences of events from one information bearer (the transmitter) to another (the receiver) through a medium (the channel) with the minimum of distortion (Kasperson, Renn, et al. 1988). But information transmission is only one part of communication, which also involves developing shared meaning among individuals, institutions, and communities and establishing relationships of trust (Rayner 1988a).

The concept of management implicit in the conventional conceptualization of risk is both directive and reactive. It is directive in that it actively seeks to achieve specifiable goals of prevention or limitation through explicit procedures. Piecemeal coping, development of tolerance, and implicit avoidance behaviors usually are not considered management strategies in this framework.[1] Conventional risk management also is reactive in that it is the final step in the process. Its role is to solve problems that have been perceived and made the subject of communication, either as a precursor or a management response, rather than to seek out issues for attention.

Cultural theory differs from conventional approaches to risk perception in that it assumes an active, rather than passive, perceiver. Furthermore, this perceiver is not an individual, but an institution or organization that is driven by organizational imperatives to select risks for management attention or to suppress them from view (Douglas 1985). According to cultural theory, institutional structure is the ultimate cause of risk perception; risk management is the proximate stimulus rather than its outcome. In addition to being proactive, management strategies in cultural theory include various coping and adaptive behaviors that tend to be discounted in conventional approaches. Finally, risk communication in cultural theory emphasizes creation of shared meaning and trust over the transfer of quantitative information (Rayner 1988a).

Thus, cultural theory is fundamentally a social theory concerned first with relationships among human beings and second with societal relationships with nature. Methodological individualism that extrapolates from individual behavior to social action has no place in cultural analysis. The sociological basis of the cultural theory of risk was established fourteen years before the publication of Thompson's "Aesthetics of Risk."

ORIGINS OF CULTURAL ANALYSIS

The cultural theory of risk did not originate from concern with technological or natural hazards, but in the anthropological study of ritual defilement. Mary Douglas' *Purity and Danger* (1966) is a modern classic of anthropology. Douglas' concern in this work was with moral rather than environmental pollution. A principal focus of the book is on the relationship between dietary restrictions and the social order. For example, she dismisses medical explanations for the dietary restrictions of Leviticus, such as the prohibition of pork, as later rationalizations dating from the time of Maimonides (twelfth century). Why would only the Israelites have made an empirical connection between pork and diseases such as trichinosis? Why was pork prized by other societies, such as China, which had much more sophisticated medical technologies than the ancient Israelites? Economic explanations she finds equally uncompelling. If, as Marvin Harris (1974) claims, pork was expensive to rear in the Middle East, why did it not become a prized luxury rather than subject to abomination?

Douglas insists that we should take seriously the explanation given in Leviticus. Foods prohibited to the Israelites are all taxonomic anomalies. Pigs have cloven hooves but do not chew the cud like other clove-hoofed animals. Snakes are prohibited because they live on land but have no legs, as land animals generally do. Shellfish live in the water, yet lack the fins and scales characteristic of true fish, which are the prototypical water creatures. Prohibited items straddle classificatory boundaries. They are monsters abominated by the Lord and by his chosen people.

This explanation is intuitively satisfying. It works, and it conforms to the justifications given by the authors of Leviticus. But why should the Israelites uniquely care about classificatory anomalies? In fact, Douglas finds that such concerns are not unique to the Israelites but thrive today in support of the social structure of many tribal societies. The particular emphasis placed on unambiguous classificatory boundaries by the Israelite lawmakers seems perfectly consistent for a monotheistic society anxious to distinguish itself from the multitude of racially identical polytheistic nomads who inhabited the Middle East at the time.

Cultural theory does not deny the realities of trichinosis or tapeworm. However, Jewish dietary restrictions illustrate a basic principle of cultural theory. Whatever objective dangers may exist in the world, social organizations will emphasize those that reinforce the moral, political, or religious order that holds the group together.

GRID AND GROUP

While *Purity and Danger* won widespread acclaim, Douglas' next book, *Natural Symbols* (1970), was more controversial. In this work, Douglas began to systematize her insights from *Purity and Danger* to develop a typology of social structure and views of nature. This was the origin of *grid/ group analysis*, which, at least implicitly, informs all cultural risk analysis (Table 4.1).

The *group* variable represents the degree of social incorporation of the individual in a social unit. Where group is weak, social networks are open-ended, while interactions with the same people tend to be infrequent and limited to various specific activities in each case. Weak-group individuals fend for themselves and therefore tend to be competitive. By way of contrast, where the group variable is strong, groups interact frequently and in a wide range of activities. Strong-group people depend on each other, which promotes values of solidarity rather than the competitiveness of weak group.

Whereas the group variable describes the range of social interactions within a social unit, the *grid* variable describes the nature of those interactions. *Grid* is defined as a measure of the constraining classifications that bear upon members of any social grouping. Such classifications may be functions of hierarchy, kinship, race, gender, age, and so forth. Low grid indicates an egalitarian state of affairs in which no one is prevented from participating in any social role because he or she is the wrong sex, or is too old, or does not have the right family connections. A high-grid state of affairs is one where access to all social activities depends on one or another of these kinds of discriminations. These constraints may be imposed on people from without or within their personal social networks. Indeed, they may devote a great deal of attention to maintaining or reducing them in accordance with their own position and interests. Hence, these grid constraints are measured without regard to the strength of the group dimension.

As independent variables, grid and group may be represented as a pair

Table 4.1
Characteristics of Grid and Group

	Group	
	Low	**High**
Networks	Radical	Interconnected
Interactions	Rare	Frequent
Boundaries	Open	Closed
Shared activities	Few	Many
	Grid	
	Low	**High**
Accountability	Horizontal	Vertical
Specialization	Little	Great
Allocation of roles	Achievement	Ascription
Resource allocation	Egalitarian	Hierarchical

of orthogonal dimensions. Assessing each variable as high- or low-strength gives rise to four prototype visions of social life as illustrated in Figure 4.1.

The absence of restrictions on social behavior arising from rules or from the prior claims of others gives rise to a competitive individualist social environment, to be found at the extreme bottom left of the diagram. American entrepreneurs are a familiar example of this type, while the highly competitive pig exchanges of the New Guinea Highlands (Strathern 1971) exemplify this social context in nontechnological societies.

As social institutions make increasing demands of incorporation and regulation, society moves from sector A (low group/low grid) to C (high group/high grid). Individualism and competition may not be entirely absent, but the further into C we go, the more control will be vested in formal systems until, at the extreme top right corner, all aspects of social life are strictly controlled by hierarchical authority. That authority may be a church, a state bureaucracy, or, on a smaller scale, a patriarchal family head.

To the bottom right of this continuum between competition and bureaucracy we find a collectivist egalitarian framework, sector D (high group/low

Figure 4.1
Grid/Group Typology

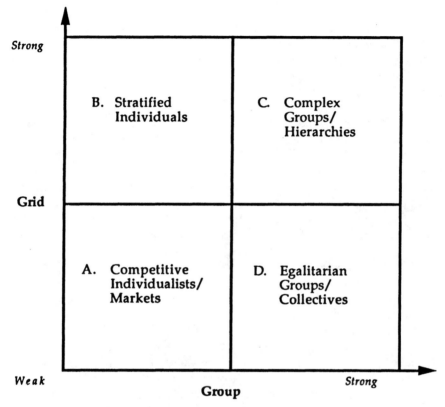

Strong

B. Stratified
   Individuals

C. Complex
   Groups/
   Hierarchies

Grid

A. Competitive
   Individualists/
   Markets

D. Egalitarian
   Groups/
   Collectives

Weak

Strong

Group

grid), such as that which is maintained within many religious sects, revolutionary political groups (Rayner 1982, 1986b, 1988b), and some segments of the antinuclear energy movement and other environmentalists (Rayner and Cantor 1987). In the absence of strong individual leaders or established bureaucratic procedures to resolve disputes, the reality of egalitarian groups frequently is characterized by infighting between covert factions.

Finally, sector B (low group/high grid) is the category of stratified, often alienated, individuals. In competitive organization, there are people who, having no goods or services to exchange, get driven out of the market. In hierarchical systems, there are people who are excluded from the ladders of power. These are not hermits, withdrawn from society, but those who occupy institutional niches where choices tend to be highly restricted by limited resources or by constraining rules. Very often, these are people who have the fewest or the least socially valued skills in a wider arena. They tend to be the most vulnerable in any social system. In other cases they may be the silent majority that does not become actively involved in public debates through apathy as much as inability to participate.

The two-dimensional diagram presents a set of limits within which the individual can move around or within which a social organization may develop and change. Between the lowest and the highest conceivable group strengths, there is a continuum of possibilities for grid strengths. The diagram is useful both for indicating the combination of grid and group at a fixed time, and for charting social change over a period of time (Gross and Rayner 1985; Rayner 1986b).

The objective of considering grid and group simultaneously is not merely to describe patterns of solidarity rules and social classifications governing the allocation of roles. The fundamental purpose of grid/group analysis is to provide a framework within which a cultural analyst may consistently relate differences in organizational structures to the strength of arguments that sustain them.

Grid-group analysis treats arguments as both reflecting and constituting the experience both of belonging to a social organization and of social differentiation within and between organizations. In this, it follows the notion that individuals negotiating their way through the organizational constraints of actively interpreting, challenging, accepting, and recreating their social environment are limited to a style of discourse consistent with the constitutive premises of that environment.

At low grid, where there is little classificatory distinction between individuals and roles are not ascribed but achieved, there is the advantage that it makes no sense to argue that a person should be denied a job "because she is black" or "because it's not women's work." On the other hand, at high grid there is less ambiguity about roles and status. A benefit of a strongly regulated society is that people know how they are expected to behave at work, at home, in church, in the street, and when introduced to strangers.

The degree of collectivity experienced by people also constrains the legitimacy of the arguments to which they may resort to justify their actions. Where the collective pressures are weak, at low group, one would expect expression of individualistic values of originality and self-reliance, in contrast with the collectivist ideology of mutual aid and responsibility which legitimates a high-group social experience. Cultural theorists use the term *cosmology* to describe this framework of ultimate justifications that are invoked to support the social order.

The cosmological focus of *Natural Symbols* was much broader than environmental, technological, or human health risks. Douglas had demonstrated her interest in the cultural aspects of emerging environmentalism in a short paper entitled "Environments at Risk" (1972). However, it was not until 1978 that Michael Thompson authored the first papers explicitly linking grid/group to risk preferences in the West German debate about nuclear energy (Thompson 1982a) and among Sherpa Buddhists in the Himalayas

(1982b). By 1980, when I joined Douglas' staff at the Russell Sage Foundation in New York, she was poised to make the cultural study of risk her first priority. In 1982, the same year that Thompson's papers were published in the open literature, Douglas and her collaborator, political scientist Aaron Wildavsky, released *Risk and Culture* (Douglas and Wildavsky 1982b).

RISK AND CULTURAL THEORY

Cultural analysis of risk looks behind the perception of physical risks to the social norms or policies that are being attacked or defended. Built on Douglas' earlier work, *Risk and Culture* argues that health and environmental concerns cannot be taken only at face value. Of all the things people can worry about, they will be inclined to select for particular attention those risks that help to reinforce the social solidarity of their institutions. By way of illustration, Douglas and Wildavsky describe the belief of the Hima, a Ugandan pastoralist people, that cattle will die as a result of contact with women or if someone eats arable produce while drinking cow's milk. These beliefs reinforce both the traditional sexual division of labor among the Hima and their distinct identity from neighboring farming people.

In the United States, Douglas and Wildavsky viewed high concern with cancer risks from industrial pollution as a consequence in the growth of the environmentalist movement. However, while Thompson's cultural analysis of risk controversies expanded the categories of the grid/group typology to five,[2] *Risk and Culture* reduced the societal debate about risk to a simple dichotomy between center and border. The continuum between market and hierarchy was portrayed, not merely as an important dichotomy in the history of social thought, but reified as the central axis of modern society. Other social forms were compressed into the category of egalitarian collectivism which Douglas and Wildavsky characterized as *sectarian*. While markets and hierarchies were portrayed as making rational tradeoffs among the benefits and costs of difficult technological choices, so-called sectarians were taken to task for employing irrational fears about nature and technology to resolve their own organizational problems.

This oversimplified polemic detracted from the central message of the book, which is that all segments of society actively select their risks for attention. *Risk and Culture* instantly proved controversial. The rich cultural diversity encompassed by the grid-group typology as a model of social possibilities was, in effect, reduced by the authors and critics alike to a traditional conflict of interests between a conservative industrial rationality and a radical rural-idealist opposition.

The characterization of the entire environmental movement as sectarian, or low grid/high group, was unconvincing to social scientists with field experience of the environmental movement (Nelkin 1982). While the radical grassroots wing of environmentalism, such as the Clamshell Alliance, does seem to fit the egalitarian description, old, established organizations, such as the Sierra Club, seem to be high grid/low group. Whereas the Clams deliberately modeled themselves organizationally on the Anarchist Federations of Civil War Spain, the modern Sierra Club is largely a mail network whose leaders reflect high social status outside of the group. Further contrast is provided by some of the Washington environmental nongovernmental organizations (NGOs), such as the Natural Resources Defense Council, that operate in a decidedly entrepreneurial mode, more characteristic of market low-grid/low-group institutions. NIMBY (not-in-my-backyard) organizations, focusing only on locational issues, seem to fit better in the high-grid/low-group category (Gross and Rayner 1985; Rayner and Rickert 1988).

Douglas' response to the difficult reception given *Risk and Culture* was a slim volume entitled *Risk Acceptability According to the Social Sciences* (Douglas 1985). Although it was not directly a reply to critics, Douglas acknowledges in her introduction that the controversy over *Risk and Culture* provided much of the impetus for the later work. The reception of *Risk and Culture* surely would have been much smoother had that book been preceded by such a scholarly assembly of sociological arguments and research to support its case.

The argument commences with the identification of how divergent moral principles may affect the perception of risk, a topic generally neglected by philosophers in favor of determining proper distributional principles for gains and liabilities. It is frequently observed that where one stands depends on where one sits. Douglas suggests that what one sees depends on where one stands. Douglas' perceiver is an active choice maker, but not the kind of choice maker presented in rational choice theory. Rather, she recognizes the inability of rational choice theory to deal with moral ends and presents an alternative theory to explain why we select for attention the risks that we do. If the cultural processes by which societies select certain kinds of dangers for attention are based on institutional procedures for allocating responsibility, for self-justification, or for calling others to account, it follows that public moral judgments will advertise certain risks powerfully, while the well-advertised risk will turn out to be connected with legitimating moral principles.

Those familiar with her earlier works on the relationship between institutional structures and value systems will not be surprised at Douglas' insistence that reflection on this general problem requires a basis for comparing human societies that will not be distorted by differences of scale, technology, literacy, and so on, but will work as well in a factory or office as it will in a primitive village.

As in *Risk and Culture*, Douglas initially uses two kinds of societies to illustrate her case about the selection of risks by active perceivers. These are the competitive, market-type society, based on contract, and the hierarchical society in which social relationships are constrained by status. While markets and hierarchies together comprise Douglas and Wildavsky's *center* of modern society, here there is more exploration of the differences between them. Rather than a dichotomy between center and border, Douglas creates a triangular space for societal disagreement about risk that includes a third kind of institution, the egalitarian-collectivist type that is frequently represented in industrial society by voluntary groups.[3]

Each of these types corresponds to a cell of the grid/group typology. Markets are low grid/low group. Hierarchies are high grid/high group. Egalitarian collectivists are low grid/high group.[4] Thus Douglas suggests a solution to the question of the social origins of societal disagreements about which risks to fear, and the apparent inconsistency of public judgments. At the very least, three fundamentally different value frameworks coexist in complex societies and lead to very different ways of seeing risks. For example, it often has been suggested that nuclear energy requires a healthily bureaucratic management system to ensure operational safety and nonproliferation of nuclear materials. Market institutions that operate power plants in the United States are likely to resist a bureaucratic approach to safety through regulation. But, in any case, the technology is unlikely to prove amenable to those concerned to safeguard strict egalitarian institutional values.

A POLYTHETIC CONCEPT OF RISK

However and wherever it is discussed, it seems that there is a consensus that the essence of risk consists of the probability of an adverse event and the magnitude of its consequences. Other considerations, such as those of societal risk management, may be recognized as important, but are viewed as deriving from this Aristotelian definition. I have argued (Rayner 1987a) that this set of unique necessary or sufficient conditions (*essence*) may be adequate to define risk at the level of engineering-type calculations, but is quite misleading at the broader, more intractable level of risk management. This requires a little more consideration of the epistemological problem raised by the type of definition that we can give to the concept of risk.

Wittgenstein offered the first serious critique of Aristotelian essentialism in modern times. In rejecting the principle of substitution, Wittgenstein asked the question, "What is a game?" The traditional response would be to enunciate the necessary and sufficient conditions for a game, but Wittgenstein demonstrated the impossibility of this approach: "For if you look at them [games], you will not see something that is common to *all*, but similarities, relationships, and a whole series of them at that" (1953, 31ᵉ.66).

For example, let us try to derive the essence of a game from the list of cricket, soccer, chess, and solitaire. Soccer and cricket are both played on a field by two teams of eleven players with a ball. However, each game has different constitutive rules, aims, and strategies. The only similarity that this pair has with chess is that all three are competitive; but solitaire is not. Solitaire does have in common with chess that it is played with pieces on a board. So there is a series of links which connect soccer, cricket, chess, and solitaire, but there is no single feature or set of necessary and sufficient conditions which is characteristic of and common to all. It may be objected that solitaire is a puzzle, but since we have failed to detect an essence of games, any attempt to distinguish puzzles and anything but a set of close relatives in the wider family-resemblance category of games would seem to be fruitless.

Wittgenstein described this state of affairs by the celebrated analogy of a thread which does not take its strength from any single strand running the whole length, but from the overlapping of many strands. The category of games is an open concept in Wittgenstein. We can recognize games as a form of characteristic human activity, and it can be shown that individual games are similar sorts of things, but no single universal feature common to all games can be stated. Wittgenstein claimed that there were many concepts similar to the category of games in this respect. Indeed, he sometimes seems to imply that all categories are like this, for even if we do discover a single strand running the whole length of the thread, we would not be justified in regarding this as the source of the thread's strength.

Similarly, the occurrence of a single feature in every member of a category is not sufficient to justify any claim that this is the essence of the category. For example, the fact that all games are goal-oriented activities (beating the opposition, solving the puzzle, or completing a number of rounds) cannot establish goal orientation as an essence. Although goal orientation may be a necessary but insufficient condition of a game, it is also a consistent feature of activities that are not games.

In all of these systems of concept formation, items at one end of the chain that constitutes a category need not have any conditions in common with those at the other end. This is the case with the category of *risk*. For example, commonsense definitions frequently do not depend on probabilities of loss. My own father used to puzzle me by insisting that he occasionally liked to bet, but he never gambled. His definition of risk was not dependent on probability of loss, but on the prospect of losing more than one can afford. On the other hand, economists sometimes like to talk of upside risk, where no losses are involved. Like the "six men of Indostan" in J. G. Saxe's celebrated poem (1868), risk analysts of different scientific disciplines grasp a different part of the beast and characterize the whole by the parts.

THE FAIRNESS HYPOTHESIS

My experience has been that the public does not care much about probabilities in choosing between two courses of action when the differences in probability are as small as they are in most of the risk management decisions that policy makers currently face. These are not situations where the probabilities and magnitudes are indisputably high, but unclear cases involving very low probabilities, such as occupational radiation-exposure levels in medicine and industry or permissible levels of possible carcinogens in food or the environment.

Contrary to the common complaint of risk managers, I have found that only a tiny minority of the public expects that life ought to be entirely free of involuntary danger. So, what do most of the policy makers' constituencies care about? I suggest TLC: trust, liability, and consent.

a. Are the institutions that make the decisions that manage and regulate the technology worthy of fiduciary trust?
b. Is the principle that will be used to apportion liabilities for an undesired consequence acceptable to those affected?
c. Is the procedure by which collective consent is obtained for a course of action acceptable to those who must bear its consequences?

This gives us a polythetic definition of risk as probability (P) × magnitude (M) of consequences + TLC ($R = PM + TLC$) where at the engineering end of the conceptual chain $R = PM$ and at the societal end $R = TLC$. Principles of trust, liability, and consent are themselves subject to institutional preferences that will vary as part of the cultural context.

These influences helped to formulate the study of market and societal acceptance of advanced reactor concepts at Oak Ridge National Laboratory (Rayner and Cantor 1987). Our concept of risk management required that the analysis explicitly recognize the social issues of trust equity. Consequently, we focused on questions about the preferred principles different parties hold with respect to obtaining consent from those affected by risks, distributing the liabilities, and justifying trust in the relevant institutions. For the purpose of this pilot study, we limited the scope of the analysis to three constituencies: (1) the utilities, (2) state public utility commissions (PUCs), and (3) public interest groups critical of nuclear power.

Examining the perspectives of the major constituencies on the basis of the *technology choice*, and not the *probability of harm*, indicated that their predominant concerns about risks were fundamentally different. For the utilities, the risk from the decision is investment risk (i.e., the risk that the cost of plants will not be fully recovered from ratepayers). This is not to say that utilities are unconcerned with health and safety risks. However, they view them as part of the technical design that is licensed by regulators. State PUCs are concerned with economic risks that might arise either because costs are incurred that were not anticipated, utilities fail to perform as expected, or demand fails to grow at a rate that warrants new capacity. Their concern for health and safety risks is incorporated into their general concern that, from the public's point of view, a plant's costs will outweigh the benefits.

In contrast, the public interest groups focus almost entirely on health and safety risks, pointing out that because these risks are imposed by one group and inevitably fall unevenly on others, they cannot be treated as acceptable under any circumstances. For them, a risk that threatens an individual's health is a risk that cannot be spread equitably. Such incompatibilities in the type of risk being addressed by each constituency make the search for solutions considerably more difficult.

The analysis revealed that each constituency conceptualized basic nuclear issues differently. The ways in which they differ suggest that they propose an implicit agenda of interest that makes it difficult to understand the concerns of others. The different ways of conceptualizing problems are indicated in three critical regulatory concerns: (1) the need for the plant (consent); (2) who pays for the plant (liability); and (3) the management of the technology (trust).

CULTURE AND REGIMES

At the same time that we were conducting this research in the United States, Michael Thompson was ploughing his own furrow for cultural risk analysis in Europe. His International Institute for Applied Systems Analysis (IIASA) working papers on energy policy and technology choice were eagerly sought after and became widely circulated classics of the gray literature. Many of these pieces were incorporated into *Divided We Stand*, which he coauthored with Michiel Schwarz (Schwarz and Thompson 1990).

Divided We Stand marks a major contribution to cultural theory by refocusing attention away from accounting for the perceptual biases of individual cultural constituencies and toward the dynamic interactions among diverse cultural factions to create (often implicitly) risk management regimes. Thus, Schwarz and Thompson raise the possibility of recasting cultural bias in risk perception not as constraints but as particular forms of expertise that together and in competition contribute to resilient solutions to risk management problems. Such frameworks may be formal, such as a hospital or a large, complex corporation, or informal, such as the interaction among environmentalists, corporations, and regulators. In either case, Schwarz and Thompson (1990) borrow from political science the term *regimes* to describe them. At the international level of global risk management, Gerlach and Rayner (1988) have applied a similar approach to the problems of coordinating international action in response to the threat of climatic change.

Indeed, it was in the context of international studies that the term *regime* was coined to describe a level of international cooperation that is more specific than a loose-knit international *order*, such as a regional or the world

Table 4.2
A Typology of Social States Defined by Institutions

	Organization	No organization
Regime	Civil Society	Anarchy
No regime	Freestanding organization	State of nature

economic order, but institutionally less formal than an *organization*, defined by Young (1989) as a "material entity with physical locations." Young uses these distinctions to propose a provocative matrix based on the presence or absence of regimes and organizations in an international order (Table 4.2).

Interestingly, there is nothing unique to international affairs in the four categories that Young's typology generates. Indeed, he states explicitly that regimes and organizations are both subsets of institutions and that regime theory should be located in the broader context of the interdisciplinary study of institutions. It is all the more ironic, therefore, that regime theorists in political science have practically ignored anthropological perspectives on governance and the role of culture in knowledge creation, communication, and consensus formation.

From the standpoint of cultural theory, Young's typology is nested within itself, like a Russian doll, from the largest scale of social interaction at the level of the global community (a regime without organization) through the United Nations (a regime with organization), through regional relationships (with or without organizations), to national communities (with organizations), ethnic groups (often spanning national boundaries without organizations), to local communities and voluntary organizations. At each level, down to the very simplest face-to-face community, we can expect what appears to be a freestanding organization at one level, for example, a hospital, to be a complex regime encompassing elements of civil society, anarchy, and the state of nature at another level. International anarchy (defined as a social state without central organizations) at one level may be revealed to consist of a regime. incorporating elements of civil society and organizations that from another perspective appear to be freestanding. For example, although zonal arrangements for fisheries are not sanctioned by international organizations, they closely follow existing territorial distributions, presided over by freestanding national governments, and could be interpreted as an extension of the existing regime of international civil society. Cultural theory, as it is applicable to formal organizations and informal networks of interaction, is an obvious partner for regime theory in developing new levels of understanding about institutional behavior at all levels from global to local.

CONTROVERSIES IN CULTURAL THEORY

Now that cultural theory has existed as a theory about technology and environmental risk for a decade, it seems appropriate to review some of the persistent objections to the theory that I have encountered over that time.

Specifically, I propose to discuss six major objections to cultural theory: that it

1. leads to cultural relativism and solipsism;
2. is no more than stereotyping;
3. cannot accommodate differences of scale;
4. is deterministic;
5. ignores issues of power and self-interest; and
6. is inherently conservative.

Relativism and Solipsism

The problem of the epistemological status of relativism in scientific knowledge is rooted in the process by which that knowledge is created, and the relationship between that process and the particular variety of relativism that is being advocated. It is interesting that critics often characterize the relativist position by the extreme argument that knowledge created in one set of social circumstances is entirely self-validating and incommunicable to members of another culture or subculture. On this basis, it is objected, any one person's version of the world has as valid a claim to be scientific truth as any other, and any ludicrous proposition is believable (Agassi 1984).

However, this final solipsism is actually the very antithesis of cultural, as opposed to individual, relativism. Cultural relativism emphasizes that the validity of public knowledge depends on its relation to the context of its creation through social activities such as science, technology, religion, and even magic. By denying the possibility of directly comparing knowledge to nature, except through the culturally created categories of human thought, cultural theorists are emphatically not denying the existence of any basis for validating public knowledge, of which scientific knowledge is one sort. On the contrary, we argue that public knowledge always must be evaluated as part of the social system, the laboratory, workshop, community, or sect, that creates and sustains it (Douglas 1978). The socially determined rules for establishing claims to knowledge, testing them, and evaluating them therefore become part of that knowledge, as do the rules that interdict certain kinds of inquiry (Ravetz 1986), for example, the boundary rules of academic disciplines (Douglas 1984). The point is that public knowledge can be evaluated only as a whole system, a process of production and use, and not as an artifact to be compared against nature's pattern (Bloor 1976).

To reduce this argument to the personal solipsism that our critics ascribe to us is a travesty of the cultural theorists' position. However, such a reductionism enables naive realists to attack cultural relativism on yet another front. Accepting solipsism would oblige cultural theorists to deny that knowledge created in different contexts may refer to one thing. Yet it is clear that at least some culturally created concepts may refer to phenomena that exist independently of those concepts, although they may be knowable only through one or another version of them. That is to say that socially created categories and modes of reasoning are not the only constraints on human knowledge. Much of human knowledge is obtained through experience with forces that would continue to exist in the absence of human agency (Barnes 1974; Bloor 1976). This practical experience is interpreted through cultural categories but, in some useful sense, may be said to exist independently of those categories. It may, therefore, be described as *natural feedback* into the knowledge process.

Even the exponents of philosophical idealism have been obliged to confront the phenomenon of natural feedback in order to escape solipsism. Bishop Berkeley (1710) identified this experience as human perception of the ideas of the supreme spirit that were irresistible to lesser spirits who could not perceive them as their own. The good bishop's dean misunderstood the accommodation with natural feedback that was achieved even in Berkeley's fanciful idealism. The dean refused to open the front door to his superior on the basis that Berkeley argued that objects exist only insofar as they are conceived of by spirits. It should therefore have been possible for Berkeley to pass through by a simple act of thought. However, in attempting to expose the absurdity of Berkeley's position by invoking natural feedback, the dean neglected to note that Berkeley had already incorporated the concept into his own system. The door was conceived of by the same God who attends to sycamore trees in quadrangles when no one else is about,[5] and Berkeley was obliged to acknowledge that input.

Nature, of course, seldom presents such clearly defined signals as the door that God presented to Berkeley. Natural feedback into the knowledge process is, therefore, always subjected to the conceptual massaging imposed by existing categories of thought. The combination of natural feedback with cultural constraints on the organization of information forms a total knowledge system, parts of which (to use the jargon of systems analysis) may be *overdetermined* by either cultural or natural constraints at different times and places. However, both types of constraints are always present in the knowledge process and profoundly shape our most fundamental ordering concepts, such as space and time (Rayner 1982). Traditional empiricism has tended to reify the feedback process, according the artifactual status of objective knowledge to the information that it is seen to provide, while seeking to separate the culturally determined components of knowledge and reducing them to the status of subjective values. The convenience of the fact/value dichotomy is clearly attractive to exponents of science for policy who seek clear and simple solutions to complex problems (Cohen 1985). Alas, it does grievous violence to our ability to find real solutions.

It should be noted that there is nothing in this argument to preclude the transferability of knowledge from one context to another, although such arguments have been made by cultural relativists such as Wittgenstein (1953), who insisted that if lions could speak we could not understand them because they would speak *lion*. Such a transfer of knowledge, however, would itself transform the recipient culture and in some way, trivial or significant, inevitably alter the social relations within it. In these cases, the interesting question for the risk analyst is not whether different social systems can converge on common definitions of problems at some useful level. Modern world history has indisputably demonstrated that this is possible, though often difficult. Rather we should start by asking what is at stake for those involved in developing a cross-cultural consensus, and how flexible is the particular knowledge process to enable it to accept or resist the change?

Fortunately, the field of risk analysis has already produced a model of the production of scientific knowledge that enables us to address these questions. Funtowicz and Ravetz (1985) have described three kinds of science predicated by two variables, *systems uncertainty* and *decision stakes*. Whereas systems uncertainty contains the elements of inexactness, uncertainty, and ignorance encountered in technical studies, decision stakes involves the cost or benefits of the various policy options to all interested parties. This model generates three kinds of science, each with its own style of risk assessment (Figure 4.2).[6]

Low systems uncertainty and decision stakes describe situations in which data bases are large and reliable, and the technical community largely agrees on appropriate methods of investigation. Funtowicz and Ravetz called this *applied science*. I prefer the term *consensual science* because the adjective *applied* is commonly used to describe scientific activities that are designed to produce information for practical technical purposes, even where decision stakes and systems uncertainty are higher. The consensus referred to here is achieved, in part, by the low decision stakes. Controversies about scientific facts are unlikely to be heated where the symbolic loads that such facts carry are either well established or unimportant. Knowledge is likely to have a very strong component of natural feedback based on long-term practical interaction between the social systems represented here and the nonhuman universe. The variations in perspective on risk emphasized by cultural theory are likely to be minor within this framework.

When both systems uncertainty and decision stakes are considerable, but professional expertise is still a useful guide to action, Funtowicz and Ravetz

Figure 4.2
Funtowicz and Ravetz's Three Kinds of Science

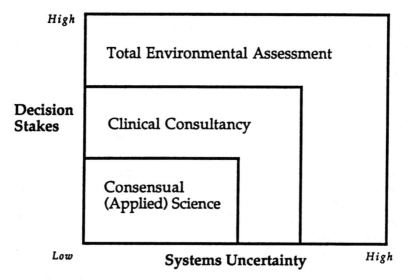

Source: Redrawn from Rayner (1988b, 171).

defined a different style of activity, the *clinical* mode of technical consultancy. This kind of activity involves the use of quantitative tools, supplemented explicitly by experienced qualitative judgment. The exercise of this
judgment increases the decision stakes for the consulting scientists and begins to bring to the fore differences of interpretation rooted in perhaps
competing institutional, educational, and disciplinary cultures. There is
some kind of unstable balance or alternation of overdetermination between
natural feedback and cultural constraints on the knowledge process throughout this kind of activity.

Finally, when decision stakes and systems uncertainty are very high, Funtowicz and Ravetz present us with a scientific style they term *total environment assessment*. This kind of activity is permeated by qualitative
judgments and value commitments. Inquiry, even into technical questions,
takes the form largely of a dialogue, which may be in an advocacy or even
an adversary mode. Although the number of risk assessments that fall into
this category is only a tiny proportion of the whole, they often are those of
greatest political significance. As Ravetz and Funtowicz note, total environmental assessment provides the most plausible opportunity for the application of a cultural relativism perspective, for here the social constraints
on the knowledge process are clearly dominant over natural feedback.

Given the compatibility of this framework with cultural theory, as I have
described it, it is unfortunate that Funtowicz and Ravetz initially presented

their model as a critique of the cultural perspective, which they disparagingly termed *social reductionism*. Although not naive realists themselves, they share the realists' concern that recognizing the cultural construction of risk will lead to social irresponsibility in facing threats to life and limb arising out of technology and the environment. I have argued above that this concern is misplaced (except insofar as any theory can be abused by the unscrupulous). However, Funtowicz and Ravetz described their model as a solution to "the difficulty created by the contradiction between the ideal of public-knowledge science and the characteristics of the problems encountered in risk assessment, without falling into sectarian relativism or social reductionism."

Rather than being an antidote to cultural theory, the distinction of three kinds of science more properly defines those instances where the role of cultural variation in knowledge is, respectively, trivial, integral, and dominant as we move from consensual science, through clinical consultancy, to total environmental assessment. The role of natural feedback varies inversely to that of cultural constraints through the same progression.

Stereotyping

It has been objected that cultural theory, both in general and in its particular application to risk analysis, is no more than stereotyping. In its simplest form, this criticism may be a gut-level objection to categorizing people. Cultural analysis unambiguously highlights the fact that risk management is people management. Both social classification and social management are uncomfortable concepts for a society that places such a high value on individualism as the United States of America. Yet, techniques of risk analysis that claim to be socially and morally neutral can be demonstrated to serve particular interests. For example, Morone and Woodhouse (1986) observe that risk managers tend to resort to formal risk assessment techniques, such as PRA, as a substitute for political and value judgment to provide an unambiguous technical basis for what are inherently contentious decisions. It is precisely because cultural analysis systematically exposes the ambiguity of existing ideological hegemonies and makes it possible to compare them that it is so threatening to some observers.

Grid/group analysis enables us to analyze cultural values and beliefs as carefully maintained regulators of social organization, rather than as mere reflections of the economic or political order. Through cultural theory analysis, we are able to see how symbols are invoked by people in order to convince and coerce each other to behave in a certain way, as well as to justify their own actions. Cultural theory shows how culture works as a social control mechanism and a means of accounting for actions. It explicitly classifies the strategies of disputants in familiar types of debates by showing how various arguments in families, churches, political parties, and sports clubs involve the fundamental issues of where the institution should draw its group boundary and how it should regulate itself internally. Such endless debates about admission, penalties and remission, leadership styles, and allocation of resources all draw upon the protagonists' conceptions of the cosmos, of what is fair, what is possible, and above all, what is natural or even holy. The task for cultural theory is to identify the moral bias that arises in each kind of social organization.

All anthropologists make the sorts of comparisons we are describing here. However, they usually make them at lower levels of formality. Although there are those who would be reluctant to associate their work with any typological approach, and especially one that uses numerical scales, their own generalizations from synchronic or diachronic comparison involve, at the very least, an implicit informal typology.

Explicit comparisons are better because they are more readily accessible to the scrutiny of others than implicit assumptions tucked away in the corners of an ethnographer's undeclared viewpoint. I prefer devising explicit typologies, subject to the risk that they can be criticized and improved by others, to preserving some misguided sense of humanistic integrity by side-stepping the problem of the relation between thought and society.

A more detailed argument is that cultural theorists have compounded the general sin of stereotyping by getting the types wrong. In particular, several reviewers (Nelkin 1982; Kaprow 1985) have objected that many environmental organizations do not fit the egalitarian collectivist mold (see above). It seems to me that this is a valid objection to errors in the execution of some cultural analysis as well as to the specific theory within cultural analysis that seeks to explain environmental and health concerns simply as a function of egalitarian collectivism.

Having studied egalitarian social organization for considerably longer than risk and technology issues (Rayner 1979, 1982, 1986b, 1988c), I am bound to say that I see no *necessary* connection between the two. I suggest that the predominance of egalitarian elements in the environmental movement observed by Douglas and Wildavsky in *Risk and Culture* is due to the fact that most emerging social movements start as voluntary organizations with the organizational problems that Douglas and Wildavsky, and other scholars (e.g., Olson 1965), have described.

Whereas egalitarianism continues to prevail among the deep ecologists, it has never been a feature of long-established conservationist groups like the Sierra Club, whose original appeal was to high-grid/high-group social elites, and subsequently became high-grid/low-group mail-order, mass-membership organizations. Furthermore, modern organic farmers and service companies selling energy efficiency clearly are making market-style investment decisions in a mode characteristic of low-grid/low-group entrepreneurs.

The environmental movement is itself a regime consisting of a variety of perspectives, at least partially shaped by cultural variation. The challenge to cultural theorists in the second decade of cultural risk analysis is to understand the dynamics of these regimes and their interaction with other social institutions and movements. I will expand on this point below in the discussion of self-interest.

Scale

The issue of the diversity of cultural types within the broad framework of the environmental movement raises the problem of the scale at which cultural analysis can be applied. In *Cultural Bias*, Douglas (1978) describes the typology in terms of face-to-face interactions of the "negotiating individual." The method outlined in *Measuring Culture* (Gross and Rayner 1985) also focuses on the transitivity, proximity, and closure of social network interactions to measure *group*, and upon the specialization, symmetry, and accountability of roles within the network. My early fieldwork among egalitarian organizations and later work with medical personnel (Rayner 1986a) was based on face-to-face *social units* (Gross and Rayner 1985).

Clearly, face-to-face interaction is the level at which grid/group analysis is empirically most persuasive. However, the fieldwork required is extensive and meticulous, which may partially account for just how little rigorous empirical work has been performed at this scale. The study of radiation hazards in hospitals indicates how even large face-to-face institutions may have to be broken down into smaller social units for the purpose of cultural analysis. The existence of plural rationalities in a single institution, such as the hospital, indicates that the larger unit is understood better as a *regime*, consisting of competing and cooperating cultures, than as a single culture.

There are important implications here for the various theories of corporate culture that have appeared in recent years. The hospital study showed common cultures in similar occupational niches across all of the hospitals studies. Surgeons tended to behave like entrepreneurial big men, administrators were hierarchical, and janitors and junior nurses were stratified individuals. At the same time there was little evidence of a distinctive culture differentiating each hospital from the others.

This insight can be applied even at the international scale where horizontal and vertical axes of social affiliation can be identified (Rayner 1988b). For participants in global environmental decision making, nation states constitute the vertical dimension of social affiliation. Participants reside in, and may officially represent, nation states or other territorial units. However, the participants also arrive playing particular roles as members of various, often competing, interest groups in negotiations and disputes. These roles constitute the horizontal dimensions of social affiliation. Each role has its own particular perspective that joins its members across vertical linkages (Figure 4.3). For some purposes, horizontally affiliated populations (just

Figure 4.3
Vertical and Horizontal Axes of Cultural Affiliation

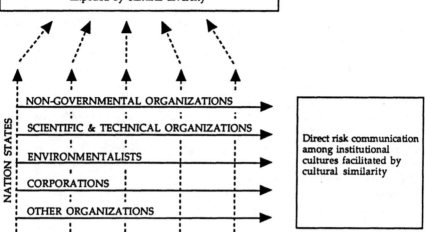

Source: Redrawn from Rayner (1988b, 173).

like the hospital occupations) will be quite similar in their actions and beliefs and will more likely communicate successfully with each other than with those with whom they simply share a national heritage. At the level of experience of cultural regimes, antinuclear protesters in the United States are much like those in the United Kingdom or West Germany, and they have a common basis on which to act. Likewise, personnel in the nuclear power industry in the United States share experience of a cultural regime with their counterparts in Germany or the United Kingdom (Gerlach and Rayner 1988).

No matter how much the various constituencies in a process of environmental decision making are shaped by their particular adaptive strategies and tasks, they also are operating in and from a larger cultural context. They are products of their larger society and its culture—what Goodenough (1971) calls a "public culture." In our terms, British corporate regimes may tend to be more hierarchical than American ones (which may also account for the differences in acceptance of nuclear energy in these countries). Until recently, the entrepreneurial spirit has not been admired in cultural hierarchies like the Soviet Union. However, the theory is not deterministic. America has bureaucracies, egalitarian champions trumpet their causes in Europe, while Soviets and Chinese attempt, in different ways, to harness entrepreneurial talents to their cause of economic development. It is the particular mixture of institutional cultures that gives each country its characteristic cultural regime, a particular preference for the German, British, French, or American way of doing things.

Existing research on the topic of national differences in institutional arrangements for making and implementing environment and technology policy is somewhat fragmented. Some comparative studies have been made of national debates over certain technologies. For example, Nelkin and Pollack (1981) have compared French and German controversies over nuclear energy. Sweden and the United States have been compared with regard to air quality (Lundqvist 1980) and occupational safety and health policies (Kelman 1981b; Golding 1990). An IIASA study of liquified natural gas terminal siting in Europe and the United States (Kunreuther, Lathrop, and Linnerooth 1982) focuses on different institutional arrangements for managing technology and potential environmental disaster.

Many of these studies tend to emphasize contrasts between the essentially cooperative regimes for environmental protection in Europe and the more confrontational approach that predominates in the United States. As Jasanoff (1986) points out, the cultural determination of scientific issues has played a relatively small part in these studies. Their emphasis has been on the demands of interest groups and the responsiveness of political and legal institutions to rival claims about nature and technology. But scientific and technical knowledge about health and the environment also is dominated by cultural interpretations. Furthermore, Gerlach and I have suggested (Gerlach and Rayner 1988; Rayner 1988b, 1991) that the existence of cultural commonalities across national boundaries may hold the keys to resolving difficult issues such as those of coordinating global action to combat the risks of global climate change.

However, at any level of analysis, that of face-to-face groups, centralized institutional corporate or national regimes, or polycentric national or international regimes, it is absolutely necessary to hold scale variables constant in making comparisons. Comparing, say, a local NIMBY with the Intergovernmental Panel on Climate Change would violate this principle and would not result in a valid cultural comparison.

Douglas' "negotiating individual" notwithstanding, *Measuring Culture* explicitly rejects attempts to classify individuals by grid and group variables. Certainly, it would violate the principle of keeping constant scale variables to compare an individual with a social unit, although some cultural theorists have attempted it. It is these attempts that give some basis to the objection that cultural theory is deterministic.

Determinism

Cultural theorists are taken to task for cultural determinism: the view that culture locks individuals into a particular worldview. The objection here is the obvious one that we all know individuals we would classify as hierarchical, entrepreneurial, or egalitarian who behave quite at odds with the predictions of cultural theory. Also, even fairly homogeneous institutions do not always conform consistently with cultural expectations.

In response to such objections, I reiterate that cultural theory is not a psychological theory of personality types. It is a social theory that views social organization as presenting patterns of opportunities and constraints for what can be said in a particular social context.

This is not cultural determinism. It does not mean that individuals can see the world only one particular way according to their experiences of grid/ group pressures. The grid/group model does not preclude psychological theories of how different personality types might gravitate toward one kind of social context or another. It does not tell us what economic inducements or deprivations dispose persons to change their social organization and adapt their cosmological outlook accordingly. What grid/group analysis does assume, however, is, first, that cultural bias is unavoidable and, second, that there is a limited number of cultural packages from which people are free to choose when they settle for any particular style of social organization.

We do not claim that every member of a social unit in a particular grid/ group category will exhibit a predictable attitude to any single issue, such as nuclear power. We are, rather, attempting to predict statistical trends in the patterns of arguments associated with particular forms of organization. As such, statistical variation is to be expected. For this reason I am unenthusiastic about attempts to argue back from written texts that their authors must have belonged to one or another cultural type unless there is independent evidence about their experience of social structure.

However, there are differences among cultural theorists on this point. Some, including Douglas, subscribe to a *stability hypothesis* (Figure 4.4). This states that individuals will seek to homogenize their experience of social structure in different areas of their lives. According to this view, individuals from hierarchical families will seek hierarchical jobs and join hierarchical organizations, while egalitarians and entrepreneurs also will seek to reproduce the same cultural context in all their activities. The stratified individualists are invested with so little capacity for action in this schema that they simply have to put up with others defining all aspects of their lives for them.

According to the stability hypothesis, it is possible to argue that individuals will tend actually to think exclusively in terms constrained by one of the four possible cultural types. An alternative view, the *mobility hypothesis* (see Figure 4.4), posits that cultural theory is limited only to predicting how things can be said in a particular context. For example, it is not possible to appeal to authority in arguing among egalitarians. Appeals to the common good are unlikely to carry much weight in the competitive marketplace, but arguments about opportunities for individual advancement might do well. According to this view, individuals may flit like butterflies from context to

Figure 4.4
Comparison of Stability and Mobility Hypotheses

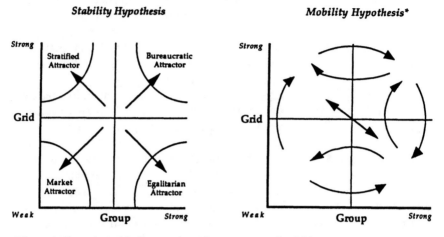

*Theoretically and empirically, certain paths seem not to be viable.

context, changing the nature of their arguments as they do so. Of course, some individuals will be more successful than others in moving from context to context, while others may find their personal rhetorical skills better suited to one context than others and concentrate their activity in that kind of arena. However, this view does not compromise the position that within any context the arguments that can be used with credibility will be limited by the social organization.

For my own taste, the stability hypothesis veers too closely toward cultural determinism. Furthermore, it does not conform to my empirical field experience as a grid/group analyst. The mobility hypothesis allows for greater creative mobility and the development of a dynamic model of risk behavior that includes other important influences on behavior, in particular the logic of self-interest.

Self-Interest

The most widely accepted paradigm in social science for the explanation of human behavior is that of self-interest (Lasswell 1958; March and Simon 1958; Easton 1965). This concept dominates the economists' account of the search for profit and the political scientists' analysis of the quest for power. Not only have cultural theorists been accused of ignoring self-interest, Schwarz and Thompson (1990) explicitly reject the concept as having any systematic explanatory power. Yet, the diversity of cultural types embracing environmental issues indicates that self-interest may be critical for some. This particularly seems to be the case with modern organic farmers and energy service companies.

Because the functions of organizations do not differ systematically on a single dimension, and because organizational interests tend to be specific to the issues being debated, a general framework to predict institutional responses to risk may prove elusive. However, I am prepared to venture a preliminary attempt, using the case of climate change.

Most institutions concerned with the threat of global climate change urge prudence. However, there are at least two very different interpretations of what is prudent under circumstances of high uncertainty. These interpretations are well represented by the positions of EPA Administrator William Reilly and former White House Chief of Staff John Sununu. Faced with the same data and similar information on the state of scientific consensus on climate change and its impacts, Reilly has advocated an activist stance and endorsed the notion that society should take out a fairly extensive insurance policy against the uncertain, but potentially disastrous, outcomes by pursuing greenhouse gas emission reductions. However, Sununu is convinced that the prudent course of action, based on the same uncertain information, is to avoid the potentially high opportunity costs of prophylactic emissions reductions that later may prove to have been either unnecessary or ineffective. The first position, supporting extensive investments against the possibility of a significant negative outcome, has been enunciated, especially in Europe, as the *precautionary principle*. The strategy of avoiding unnecessary opportunity costs I shall refer to as the *proof-first principle*.

The different interpretations of prudence by the EPA and the White House cannot be explained simply by cultural differences. Although the EPA is more egalitarian than many other government agencies, it remains essentially a bureaucracy and an integral part of the federal executive branch. Other parts of the administration also are divided. For example, the Department of Energy is itself split, along fairly obvious functional lines, with the Office of Fossil Energy following in the footsteps of the Tobacco Institute by insisting that there is no compelling evidence of cause and effect. Clearly, the functional self-interest of institutions is an important variable in shaping risk discourse. The question is whether there is any systematic relationship between function (self-interest) and structure (culture).

The rows of Table 4.3 consist of the cultural types in declining order of organizational formality from hierarchy to equality. The columns indicate broadly defined organizational functions ordered in increasing levels of generality from the specific goal of environmental protection to the broadest issues of economic and societal development. The table is completed by the inclusion of examples of the type of organization that corresponds to each of the nine cells, a prediction of its reasoning style (reductionist, pragmatic, or holistic), and of its interpretation of prudence (its choice of the precautionary principle or the proof-first principle).

Table 4.3
Interaction of Organizational Function and Structure in Framing Uncertainty

Structure	Function		
	Environmental Protection	*Social/political Regulation*	*Economic Development*
Hierarchy	• Reductionist style • Precautionary principle e.g., federal and state environmental regulators	• Reductionist style • Proof-first principle e.g., courts, public utility commissions	• Reductionist style • Proof-first principle e.g., federal and state energy and commerce departments
Market	• Pragmatic style • Precautionary principle e.g., environmental entrepreneurs, energy service companies	• Pragmatic style • Mixed prudence e.g., federal and state legislators	• Pragmatic style • Proof-first principle e.g., utilities, manufacturing companies
Collective	• Holistic style • Precautionary principle e.g., grassroots environmental groups	• Holistic style • Precautionary principle e.g., town meetings	• Holistic style • Mixed prudence e.g., alternative economic think tanks

The prediction of reasoning style varies consistently with culture and is unaffected by function. Since we know that hierarchies like to routinize decision making, often combining incompatible agendas without acknowledging differences, we anticipate a tendency to reductionist reasoning that renders parts of a problem susceptible to a decision rule and is unlikely to expose contradictions in the institution's utterances or actions. Hence the attractiveness of benefit-cost analysis or probabilistic risk analysis to these institutions. By way of contrast, success in the market depends on judgment skills and flexibility to recognize and exploit opportunities. Resort to rules is likely to give way to pragmatic assessments of gain or loss. Finally, egalitarian collectivists seek to marshal the fullest range of arguments in favor of their position. They are likely to be adept at connecting technical, ethical, and socioeconomic arguments in a holistic fashion.

Unlike variation in reasoning styles, the interpretation of prudence seems to depend on the interaction of culture and the extent to which the goals of the organization are dominated by the specific function of environmental protection. The institutions charged with environmental protection consistently advocate precaution. Even the hierarchical environmental protection agencies, which might be organizationally disposed to proof-first, are aware that the constituency to which they must ultimately answer and that will lobby most effectively for their funding comprises precautionary environmental activists. Institutions charged with nurturing economic growth tend to want proof before agreeing to environmental investment that may constrain economic growth. However, the NGO think tanks can afford the luxury of open speculation about the down side of uncertainties that for political and economic reasons, respectively, the commerce agencies and utilities cannot. Finally, the institutions whose goals require them to mediate between the demands of environmental protection and economic growth tend to find their approach to prudence heavily modified by their institutional structure, courts favoring proof, legislatures favoring some balance of prior proof and precaution, and participatory structures favoring precaution.

Hence, the relationship between cultural orientation based on social organization and the strategic attitude of an institution toward uncertainty in debates about environmental and technological risk is not a simple one of risk-loving markets, risk-averse collectives, and risk-managing hierarchies. Rather, the constraints upon discourse and the credibility of arguments within various institutions interact with functional preferences based on self-interest to shape the style and content of intervention in the wider debate.

Whereas science for public policy in the United States is dominated by the bottom left half of Table 4.3, its British and European equivalents tend to be dominated by the top right. There can be little wonder that, in 1985, nations of the European Community took a proof-first approach to international proposals to ban chlorofluorocarbons (CFCs) in aerosols, while the United States, emphasizing precautionary principles, was a strong supporter of such a ban. A similar contrasting pattern of policy formation between Europe and the United States occurred with the issue of lead in gasoline.

Yet for carbon dioxide (CO_2) emission reductions the approaches seem to be reversed, with the United States dragging behind the Europeans. Self-interest appears to be at the root of U.S. reluctance to commit to emission reductions. As the highest absolute and per capita emitter of CO_2, with abundant coal supplies, a vast road transportation infrastructure, and multibillion dollar investments in clean-coal technology, powerful interests are likely to demand prior proof before commitment to action. Banning the production or use of an individual manufactured substance is much easier to monitor and enforce than reducing emissions of CO_2, which come from almost innumerable types of sources. Hence, the pragmatic reasoners may swing toward the proof-first principle in this case.

The focus of this table on the decision-making strategies of each cultural type also helps us to address the accusation of inherent conservatism.

Conservatism

Some commentators have suggested that cultural theory is inherently politically conservative. For example, Kaprow (1985) fears that cultural theory will allow industry to reject liability claims on the basis that risk is only in the nose of the beholder, has no objective existence in nature, and therefore cannot justify expensive compensatory or corrective action. Industry as well might fear that acceptance of cultural theory may strengthen the legal actions of community and labor activists who currently have to prove *probable cause* of injury according to quite stringent scientific and legal criteria (Rayner 1987b).

Other commentators claim that cultural theory portrays environmental fears as irrational. Although some of the rhetorical flourishes of *Risk and Culture* may give such an impression, cultural theory, taken as a whole, clearly recognizes the existence of plural rationalities coexisting in complex societies and specifically rejects the notions of irrational risk perceptions presented in much of the psychological literature (Lopes 1987).

The systematic deconstruction of one's worldview by an analytic device, such as cultural theory, is threatening to almost everyone (including some of us cultural theorists). We cherish our individuality and prefer to think of ourselves as independent thinkers who have arrived at a worldview that in a significant sense is a truer reflection of reality than competing ideas. However, the specific accusation of inherent conservatism and support of industry against labor and the environment has a characteristically egalitarian ring. It certainly appears that egalitarians are more threatened by such deconstruction than markets or hierarchies, such that they see cultural theory as an instrument of market and bureaucratic power.

While I have argued that cultural analysis is as potentially subversive of market interests as of labor and community interests, supporters of business have not proved sensitive to this fact. Similarly, bureaucratic agencies involved in regulating hazardous technologies have not risen up against cultural theory, despite the fact that it exposes much of their risk assessment technique as legitimatory ritual (Wynne 1982b) rather than the neutral science they pretend it to be.

I suggest that market cultures are pragmatic problem solvers. Until cultural theory makes serious inroads into the conduct of their risk management practices, they are unlikely to pay much attention. Their response to the "threat" of cultural deconstruction so far has been to ignore it. Conversely, the reductionist decision mode of hierarchists enables them to disconnect cultural theory from its wider societal implications, including its implications for the legitimacy of risk management, and embrace cultural theory as yet another technique of analysis, albeit a rather minor one with an undeveloped empirical content. In this way the "threat" of cultural theory is defused. However, for holistic problem solvers, such as egalitarians, the options of ignoring or co-opting cultural analysis are not available. Just as their holistic worldview enables egalitarians to function as early warning systems of threats to environmental systems, they are equally sensitive to challenges to social systems, including the adversarial risk management regime of which they are a major part.

This final consideration brings us back to the issue broached at the start of this chapter, of the disproportionate influence of cultural analysis at the rhetorical level, relative to the extent of its empirical practice in risk management and public policy. I suggest that cultural analysis itself is the object of cultural interpretation and rhetorical discourse in which its interpretation depends on the culture and the self-interest of the user. While cultural theory has achieved prominence as a useful ideological weapon, the methodological vigor required for empirical cultural analysis has discouraged its practice.

FUTURE DIRECTIONS

I see two linked imperatives currently facing cultural analysis. First, largely within the cultural paradigm is the development of a systematic theory of regimes along the lines discussed in this chapter. However, that process will require cultural theory simultaneously to become more outward looking. Particularly as the focus of risk analysis moves from risks with single types of source (such as accidental releases from chemical plants) with local consequences to multiple source types with regional or global consequences (such as greenhouse gas accumulations), interdisciplinary analysis will grow in importance (Figure 4.5). A systematic approach to risk management regimes may present an opportunity to overcome the vast gaps that presently exist between various social science paradigms for risk analysis.

Each of the existing behavioral-science paradigms offers a plausible explanation for a different aspect of the problem. Psychologists and decision theorists have identified the use of heuristics and biases by individuals in their risk behavior. This seems quite compatible with the anthropological claim that not all of these biases are universally distributed and that different institutional arrangements shape their selection. The whole point of identifying cultural biases in risk behavior is to understand their role in stakeholder interactions.

Perhaps I am optimistic in interpreting current competition among the behavioral paradigms of risk analysis. All share the view that risk behavior is a function of how human beings, individually and in groups, perceive their place in the world and the things that threaten it. As truly interdisciplinary research in risk behavior develops, psychologists, decision theorists, anthropologists, sociologists, economists, and political scientists will converge on explanatory concepts and terminologies that grow out of their collective interaction with the field of study. The emergence of a *regime* of risk analysis from the current *state of nature* will not be a particularly painless or orderly process, but it is a necessary one.

Figure 4.5
The Changing Challenge for Risk Analysis

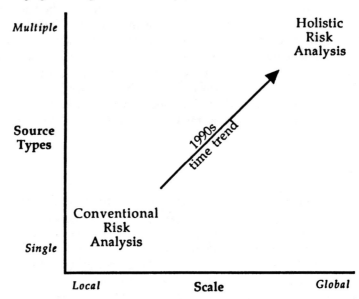

NOTES

1. Of course there are important expectations to this generalization. Natural hazards research has addressed piecemeal adaptation, and risk avoidance is addressed in economics, for example, G. Calabresi, *The Cost of Accidents* (New Haven: Yale University Press, 1977).

2. Thompson (1982a) describes how the combination of grid/group analysis with topological catastrophe theory can yield a three-dimensional diagram that includes a withdrawn cosmology of independent hermits. However, this approach has not been more widely exploited by cultural theorists.

3. Both markets and collectives espouse equality, but whereas the market institution focuses on equality of opportunity among individuals, the collectivist institution emphasizes strict equality of condition among members (Rayner 1988c).

4. However, even in *Risk Acceptability*, Douglas acknowledges only three of the four social categories generated by the grid/group typology. Although the residual category of social organization is omitted, rather than forced into the sectarian designation, the NIMBY organizations that Gross and Rayner (1985) identified as high grid/low group are still consigned to the egalitarian collectivist category.

5. I refer to the famous limerick by Monsignor Ronald Knox and the anonymous reply:

> There once was a man who said 'God
> Must think it exceedingly odd
> If he finds that this tree

Continues to be
When there's no one about in the quad.'

'Dear Sir, Your astonishment's odd:
I am always about in the Quad.
And that's why the tree
Will continue to be,
Since observed by Yours faithfully, God.'

6. In Chapter 11, Funtowicz and Ravetz present a revised version of this figure (Figure 11.1). The region originally labeled "total environmental assessment" is renamed "post-normal science," and the authors clarify further the distinctions between the three kinds of science.

CHAPTER 5 _____

Perception of Risk: Reflections on the Psychometric Paradigm

Paul Slovic

My interest in psychometrics began during my undergraduate years at Stanford University, where I was fortunate to be exposed to stimulating courses in psychological measurement and personality assessment taught by Quinn McNemar and Lewis Goldberg. My interest in risk developed "by chance," when I was assigned as a research assistant to Clyde Coombs during my first year as a graduate student in psychology at the University of Michigan. I was fascinated by a study Coombs was doing in which he examined people's preferences among gambles. I replicated and extended this study as a first-year project. The following year I began to work with Ward Edwards, who was doing experimental studies of risk taking and decision making. In Edwards' laboratory I met Sarah Lichtenstein and Amos Tversky, who were also students of Edwards. Lichtenstein, Edwards, and I teamed up in a study of boredom-induced changes in preference among bets (Slovic, Lichtenstein, and Edwards 1965). Lichtenstein and I went our separate ways but were reunited in Eugene, Oregon, in 1966 and have worked together since then.

About 1975, Sarah Lichtenstein, Baruch Fischhoff, and I began a research program designed to study what we referred to as "cognitive processes and societal risk taking" (Slovic, Fischhoff, and Lichtenstein 1976). This initiative was a natural evolution of the laboratory studies on decision making under risk that Lichtenstein and I had been doing since 1960. In 1970, we were introduced to Gilbert White, who asked if our research could provide insight into some of the puzzling behaviors he had observed in the domain of human response to natural hazards. Much to our embarrassment, we realized that our laboratory studies had been too narrowly focused on choices among simple gambles to tell us much about risk-taking behavior outside the laboratory.

White's questions were intriguing, and, with Howard Kunreuther, we turned our attention to natural hazards, attempting to relate behavior on flood plains and earthquake faults to principles that had been emerging from psychological studies of probabilistic judgments and risky choice (Slovic, Kunreuther, and White 1974). We found the work that Amos Tversky and Danny Kahneman had been doing on heuristics and biases in probabilistic thinking (Tversky and

Kahneman 1974) to be particularly valuable in explaining people's responses to the threats posed by natural hazards. The mid–1970s were a time in which concerns about pesticides and nuclear power were rapidly increasing, and we soon found our attention drawn to technological hazards. Discovery of Chauncey Starr's stimulating article titled "Social Benefit Versus Technological Risk" (Starr 1969) set us on a course that my colleagues and I continue to explore today.

THE PSYCHOMETRIC PARADIGM AND ITS ORIGINS

Starr's paper sought to develop a method for weighing technological risks against benefits to answer the fundamental question, "How safe is safe enough?" His *revealed preference* approach assumed that, by trial and error, society arrives at an essentially optimum balance between the risks and benefits associated with any activity. Under this assumption, one may use historical or current risk and benefit data to reveal patterns of "acceptable" risk/benefit tradeoffs. Examining such data for eight industries and activities, Starr concluded that (a) acceptability of risk from an activity is roughly proportional to the third power of the benefits from that activity; (b) the public will accept risks from voluntary activities (such as skiing) that are roughly 1,000 times as great as it would tolerate from involuntary activities (such as food preservatives) that provide the same level of benefits; and (c) the acceptable level of risk is inversely related to the number of persons exposed to the risk.

The merits and deficiencies of Starr's revealed preference approach have been debated at length (e.g., Fischhoff, Slovic, and Lichtenstein 1979; Otway and Cohen 1975). We were particularly concerned about its assumptions. It is politically conservative in that it enshrines current economic and social arrangements, assuming that *accepted risks* are *acceptable risks*. It ignores distributional questions (who assumes what risks and who gets what benefits). It makes strong assumptions about the rationality of people's decision making in the marketplace and about the freedom of choice that the marketplace provides. It assumes not only that people have full information but also that they can use that information optimally. Finally, from a technical standpoint, it is no simple matter to develop the measures of risks and benefits needed for the implementation of this approach.

Concerns about these assumptions and the difficulties of data collection motivated us to conduct an analogous study using questionnaires to ask people directly about their perceptions[1] of risks and benefits and their *expressed preferences* for various kinds of risk/benefit tradeoffs. This approach appealed to us for several reasons: it elicits current preferences; it allows consideration of many aspects of risks and benefits besides dollars and body counts; and it permits data to be gathered for large numbers of activities and technologies, allowing the use of statistical methods to disentangle multiple influences on the results. Over the years, many studies of risk perception have been carried out using this approach (Slovic 1987).

In our replication of Starr's study, and in much of our subsequent work, we went beyond merely asking about risk and benefit. Borrowing from personality theory, we also asked people to characterize the "personality of hazards" by rating them on various qualities or characteristics (e.g., voluntariness, catastrophic potential, controllability, dread) that had been hypothesized to influence risk perception and acceptance (Starr 1969; Lowrance 1976).

Another distinguishing feature of our studies has been the use of a variety of psychometric scaling methods to produce *quantitative* measures of perceived risk, perceived benefit, and other aspects of perceptions (e.g., estimated fatalities resulting from an activity). First we used magnitude estimation techniques (Stevens 1958) to assess risks and benefits and perceived frequencies of fatal events (Fischhoff, Slovic, et al. 1978; Lichtenstein, Slovic, et al. 1978). Later we moved to numerical rating scales. In subsequent studies, we have supplemented these measures with traditional attitude questions and nontraditional word association and scenario generation methods. We have referred to this general approach and the theoretical framework in which it is embedded as the *psychometric paradigm.*

Of course, the psychometric paradigm, with its elicitation of perceptions and expressed preferences, has its own assumptions and limitations. It assumes that people can provide meaningful answers to difficult, if not impossible, questions ("What is the risk of death in the United States from nuclear power?"). The results are dependent upon the set of hazards studied, the questions asked about these hazards, the types of persons questioned and the data analysis methods. The questions typically assess cognitions— not actual behavior. Despite these and other limitations, the studies using this approach have invariably produced coherent and interesting results that have motivated further use of the paradigm.

One of the most important assumptions in our approach is that risk is inherently subjective. Risk does not exist "out there," independent of our minds and cultures, waiting to be measured. Human beings have invented the concept "risk" to help them understand and cope with the dangers and uncertainties of life. There is no such thing as "real risk" or "objective risk." The nuclear engineer's probabilistic risk estimate for a reactor accident or the toxicologist's quantitative estimate of a chemical's carcinogenic risk are both based on theoretical models, whose structure is subjective and assumption-laden, and whose inputs are dependent upon judgment. Nonscientists have their own models, assumptions, and subjective assessment techniques (intuitive risk assessments), which are sometimes very different from the scientist's methods. It was no accident that our studies asking people (and experts) to judge risk left risk undefined. This was done to allow the inherent subjectivity of risk to be expressed.

In sum, the psychometric paradigm encompasses a theoretical framework that assumes that risk is subjectively defined by individuals who may be influenced by a wide array of psychological, social, institutional, and cultural factors. The paradigm assumes that, with appropriate design of survey instruments, many of these factors and their interrelationships can be quantified and modeled in order to illuminate the responses of individuals and their societies to the hazards that confront them.

EARLY RESULTS

The early results from psychometric studies of perceived risk have been reviewed by Slovic (1987) and will be referred to only briefly in this section.

One of the most exciting findings, to those of us who drafted the first questionnaires (and who realized their difficulty), was that people could, and would, answer them, making hundreds of judgments per person in sessions lasting up to several hours. Equally surprising to us was that the results seemed to make sense and provide insight into many of the puzzling phenomena evident in societal risk management and its controversies. Perceived and acceptable risk appeared systematic and predictable. Psychometric techniques seemed well suited for identifying similarities and differences among groups with regard to risk perceptions and attitudes. Our results also showed that the concept "risk" meant different things to different people. When experts judged risk, their responses correlated highly with technical estimates of annual fatalities. Laypeople could assess annual fatalities if they were asked to (and they produced estimates somewhat like the technical estimates). However, their judgments of "risk" were sensitive to other factors as well (e.g., catastrophic potential, controllability, threat to future generations) and, as a result, differed considerably from their own (and experts') estimates of annual fatalities.

Another consistent result from psychometric studies of expressed preferences was that people tended to view current risk levels as unacceptably high for most activities. The gap between perceived and desired risk levels suggested that, contrary to the assumptions of the revealed preference approach, our respondents were not satisfied with the way that market and other regulatory mechanisms had balanced risks and benefits. Across the domain of hazards, there seemed to be little systematic relationship between perceptions of current risks and benefits. However, studies of expressed preferences did seem to support Starr's conclusion that people are willing to tolerate higher risks from activities seen as highly beneficial. But whereas Starr concluded that voluntariness of exposure was the key mediator of risk acceptance, studies of expressed preference have shown that other characteristics, such as familiarity, control, catastrophic potential, equity, and level of knowledge, also seem to influence the relationship between perceived risk, perceived benefit, and risk acceptance.

Various models have been advanced to represent the relationships between perceptions, behavior, and these qualitative characteristics of hazards. As we shall see, the picture that emerges from this work is both orderly and complex.

Factor-Analytic Representations

The "personality profiles" that emerged from psychometric studies showed that every hazard had a unique pattern of qualities that appeared to be related to its perceived risk. Figure 5.1 shows the mean profiles that emerged for nuclear power and medical X-rays in one of our early studies (Fischhoff, Slovic et al. 1978). Nuclear power was judged to have much higher risk than X-rays and to need much greater reduction in risk before it would become "safe enough." As the figure illustrates, nuclear power also had a much more negative profile across the various risk characteristics.

We observed that many of the qualitative risk characteristics that made up a hazard's profile were highly correlated with each other, across a wide range of hazards. For example, hazards rated as "voluntary" tended also to be rated as "controllable" and "well-known;" hazards that appeared to threaten future generations tended also to be seen as having catastrophic potential, and so on. Investigation of these interrelationships by means of factor analysis indicated that the broader domain of characteristics could be condensed to a small set of higher-order characteristics or factors. Figure 5.2 presents a spatial representation of hazards within a factor space derived from more than 40,000 individual ratings (34 respondents × 81 hazards × 15 characteristics per hazard).

The factor space presented in Figure 5.2 has been replicated across numerous groups of laypeople and experts judging large and diverse sets of hazards.[2] The factors in this space reflect the degree to which a risk is understood and the degree to which it evokes a feeling of dread.

Research has shown that laypeople's risk perceptions and attitudes are closely related to the position of a hazard within the factor space. Most important is the factor "Dread Risk." The higher a hazard's score on this factor (i.e., the further to the right it appears in the space), the higher its perceived risk, the more people want to see its current risks reduced, and the more they want to see strict regulation employed to achieve the desired reduction in risk. In contrast, experts' perceptions of risk are not closely related to any of the various risk characteristics or factors derived from these characteristics. Instead, experts appear to see riskiness as synonymous with expected annual mortality (Slovic, Fischhoff, and Lichtenstein 1979). As a result, many conflicts about "risk" may result from experts and laypeople having different definitions of the concept. In such cases, expert recitations of "risk statistics" will do little to change people's attitudes and perceptions.

Figure 5.1
Profiles for Nuclear Power and X-Rays Across Nine Risk Characteristics

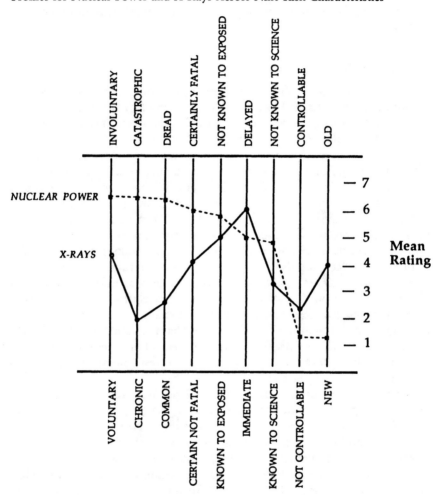

Source: Redrawn from Fischhoff et al. (1978, 147). Used by permission.

Perceptions Have Impacts

Another direction taken by early work within the psychometric paradigm was to examine the role of perceptions in determining the degree of impact resulting from the occurrence of an "unfortunate event" (e.g., an accident, a discovery of pollution, sabotage, product tampering, etc.).

Risk analyses typically model the impacts of such events in terms of direct harm to victims—deaths, injuries, and damages. The impacts of an unfor-

Figure 5.2
Location of 81 Hazards on Factors 1 and 2 Derived from the Interrelationships Among 15 Risk Characteristics

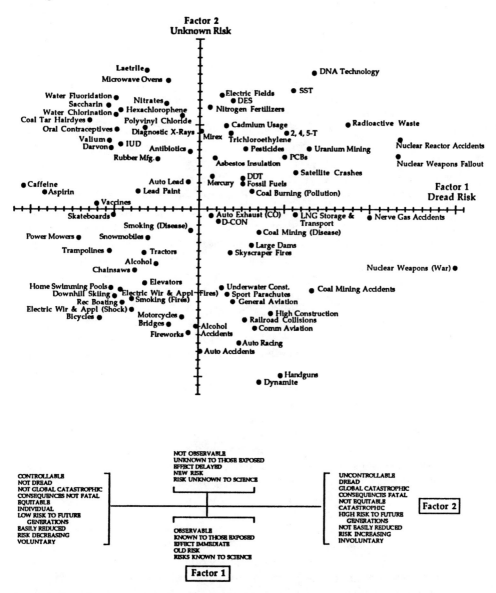

Note: Each factor is made up of a combination of characteristics, as indicated by the lower diagram.

Source: Redrawn from Slovic, "Perception of Risk," *Science* vol. 236 (17 April 1987): 282, copyright 1987 by AAAS. Used by permission.

tunate event, however, sometimes extend far beyond these direct harmful effects, and may include indirect costs to the responsible government agency or private company that far exceed direct costs. In some cases, all companies in an industry are affected, regardless of which company was responsible for the mishap. In extreme cases, the indirect costs of a mishap may even extend past industry boundaries, affecting companies, industries, and agencies whose business is minimally related to the initial event. Thus, an unfortunate event can be thought of as a stone dropped in a pond. The ripples spread outward, encompassing first the directly affected victims, then the responsible company or agency, and, in the extreme, reaching other companies, agencies, and industries.

Some events make only small ripples; others make big ones. Early theories equated the magnitude of impact to the number of people killed or injured, or to the amount of property damaged. However, the accident at the Three Mile Island (TMI) nuclear reactor in 1979 provided a dramatic demonstration that factors besides injury, death, and property damage can impose serious costs. Despite the fact that not a single person died at TMI and few if any latent cancer fatalities are expected, no other accident in our history has produced such costly societal impacts. In addition to its impact on the utility that owned and operated the plant, this accident also imposed enormous costs on the nuclear industry and on society. These came from stricter regulation, reduced operation of reactors worldwide, greater public opposition to nuclear power, reliance on more expensive energy sources, and increased costs of reactor construction and operation. The point is that traditional economic and risk analyses tend to neglect these higher-order impacts; hence they greatly underestimate the costs associated with certain kinds of mishaps.

A conceptual framework aimed at describing how psychological, social, cultural, and political factors interact to "amplify risk" and produce ripple effects has been presented by Kasperson, Renn, Slovic, et al. (1988). An important element of this framework is the assumption that the perceived seriousness of an accident or other unfortunate event, the media coverage it gets, and the long-range costs and other higher-order impacts on the responsible company, industry, or agency are determined, in part, by what that event signals or portends. *Signal value* reflects the perception that the event provides new information about the likelihood of similar or more destructive future mishaps (Slovic, Lichtenstein, and Fischhoff 1984).

The informativeness or *signal potential* of an event, and thus its potential social impact, appears to be systematically related to the characteristics of the hazard and the location of the event within the factor space (see Figure 5.3). An accident that takes many lives may produce relatively little social disturbance (beyond that caused the victims' families and friends) if it occurs as part of a familiar and well-understood system (e.g., a train wreck). However, a small accident in an unfamiliar system (or one perceived as poorly

Figure 5.3
Accidents as Signals: The Relation Between Signal Potential and Risk
Characterization for 30 Hazards Selected from Figure 5.2

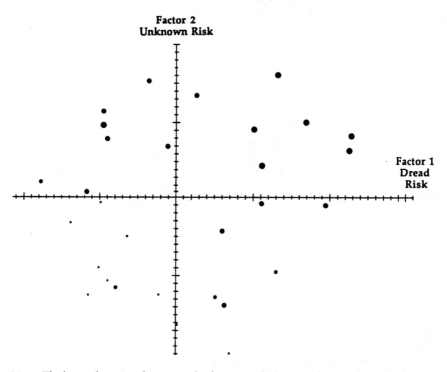

Note: The larger the point, the greater the degree to which an accident involving that hazard
was judged to "serve as a warning signal for society, providing new information about
the probability that similar or even more destructive mishaps might occur within this type
of activity." The higher-order costs of a mishap are likely to be correlated with signal
potential.

Source: Redrawn from Slovic, Lichtenstein, and Fischhoff (1984, 472). Used by permission.

understood), such as a nuclear reactor or a recombinant DNA laboratory,
may have immense social consequences if it is perceived as a harbinger of
further (and possibly catastrophic) mishaps.

One implication of the signal concept is that effort and expense beyond
that indicated by a cost-benefit analysis might be warranted to reduce the
possibility of "high-signal accidents." Unfortunate events involving hazards
in the upper right quadrant of Figure 5.2 appear likely to have the potential
to produce particularly large ripples. As a result, risk analyses and risk
management decisions regarding these hazards need to be sensitive to these
possible higher-order impacts.

RECENT DEVELOPMENTS

The pace of psychometric research has accelerated in recent years. The early work has been replicated and extended with new and more interesting kinds of respondents and with very different sets of hazards and characteristics. Important concepts from other domains, such as stigma, have been brought to bear upon risk perception and risk-impact analysis.

New Respondents

Our early studies were limited, by financial constraints, to local populations of students and citizen groups (League of Women Voters; business clubs). In recent years, the paradigm has been applied internationally, sometimes with local groups and sometimes with representative national samples. International studies have contrasted perceptions of college students in the United States, Hungary (Engländer et al. 1986), Norway (Teigen, Brun, and Slovic 1988), Hong Kong (Keown 1989), Japan (Rosa and Kleinhesselink 1989), Poland (Goszczynska, Tyszka, and Slovic 1991), and the Soviet Union (Mechitov and Rebrik 1990). Some of the largest discrepancies have been found between American and Hungarian students. The Hungarians perceived much lower risks from eighty-four of ninety activities. Within each country, the relative ordering of concerns was also much different. Hungarians saw relatively greater risks from hazards in the lower left quadrant of the factor space—railroads, boating, home appliances, and mushroom hunting—whereas the Americans were relatively more concerned with hazards in the upper right quadrant pertaining to radiation and chemical technologies. Turning to nonstudent populations, Gould et al. (1988) studied representative samples of 1,320 individuals living in New England and the southwestern United States in a replication of our earlier studies. Morgan et al. (1985) surveyed 116 alumni of Carnegie-Mellon University regarding perception of risks from electric and magnetic fields. Kunreuther, Desvousges, and Slovic conducted a national telephone survey in the United States, focusing on perceptions of nuclear power and nuclear waste. We have also conducted two large psychometric surveys of the general public in Sweden (Slovic, Kraus, Lappe, Letzel, and Malmfors 1989) and Canada (Slovic, Kraus, Lappe, and Major 1991). Kraus and Slovic (1988) surveyed a large sample of consumers in six different regions of the United States regarding their perceived risks from household products.

These large-scale studies have produced numerous interesting results, of which I shall mention only a few. One intriguing finding by Morgan et al. (1985) was that perceived risks associated with electric and magnetic fields from power lines and electric blankets were relatively low. However, when the respondents were given a supposedly nonalarming briefing about research on health effects of fields (which said that many studies had been done, but no adverse human health effects had yet been reliably demonstrated), their perceptions on subsequent retest shifted toward greater perceived risk. They also saw risks of electric fields from transmission lines and electric blankets as less well known, more dread, more likely to be fatal, less equitable, and less adequately controlled after receiving this information. Today, as research studying health effects of exposure to electric fields remains inconclusive but is discussed frequently in the news, perception of risk from these fields is rapidly increasing (Coy 1989).

A second finding of interest comes from the national surveys we have conducted in Sweden and Canada. Figure 5.4 shows mean risk/benefit perceptions in Canada for thirty-three items, more than half of which pertain to medicines and other medical devices and treatments. Careful examination of the figure illustrates some findings that have appeared in a number of surveys. Nuclear power, an industrial radiation technology, has very high perceived risk and low perceived benefit, whereas diagnostic X-rays, a medical radiation technology, have the opposite pattern (relatively low perceived risk, very high perceived benefit). A parallel finding occurs with chemicals. Nonmedical sources of exposure to chemicals (e.g., pesticides, food additives, alcohol, cigarettes) are seen as very low benefit and high risk; medical chemicals (e.g., prescription drugs, antibiotics, vaccines, vitamins) are generally seen as high benefit and low risk, despite the fact that they can be very toxic substances and human exposure to them is quite great. The favorable perceptions and acceptance of risks from X-rays and most medicines suggests that acceptance of risk is conditioned by perceptions of direct benefits and by trust in the managers of technology, in this case the medical and pharmaceutical professions. It is also clear that there is no general or universal pattern of perceptions for radiation and chemicals. Further demonstration of this point comes from studies of radon, which, like X-rays, is a hazard of little concern to most people (Sandman, Weinstein, and Klotz 1987). In contrast, food irradiation, like nuclear power, generates enough concern to block the application of that technology. In the domain of radiation and chemical technologies there appears to be little relationship between the magnitude of risk assessed by experts (health physicists, epidemiologists, and toxicologists) and the magnitude of perceived risks. This state of affairs, and the opposition to many technologies that accompanies it, is a source of great frustration and concern to many (e.g., Whelan 1985; Wildavsky 1979). We shall return to this issue later.

Psychometric surveys provide a wealth of quantitative data that permit one to monitor perceptions over time. In 1987 we replicated a study that we had first conducted in 1979, using the same population (University of Oregon students). Across the eight-year period there was remarkable stability for some items (e.g., nonnuclear electric power, bicycles, tractors, cosmetics, food preservatives). Some items showed sizable increases in perceived benefits (e.g., commercial aviation, satellites, microwave ovens, ra-

Figure 5.4
Mean Perceived Risk and Perceived Benefit for 33 Activities, Substances, and Technologies Based on a National Survey in Canada

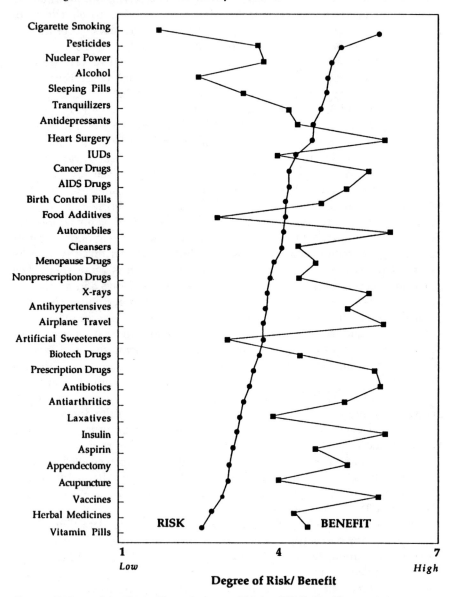

Source: Redrawn from Slovic, Kraus, Lappe, and Major (1991). Used by permission.

diation therapy, heart surgery, lasers), and some showed large decreases in perceived risk (e.g., microwave ovens, lasers, oral contraceptives). By far the greatest change in perception occurred with marijuana, whose perceived benefit decreased from a mean of 53.3 (on a 100-point scale) to 21.2 and whose perceived risk increased from 25.4 to 41.0.

The large national surveys have uncovered numerous strong subgroup differences in perceptions. In Canada, perceptions of risk and benefit were strongly related to region of residence (Quebec, a French culture, stood out), age, sex, education, and degree of political activism. The sex differences were quite interesting. Close to two dozen studies have found that women have higher perceived risk for nuclear power than men (see results from Sweden in Figure 5.5). In Canada, women's perceptions of risk were equal to or greater than men's for every one of the thirty-three items studied (see Figure 5.6), and nuclear power was not exceptional in this regard.

New Hazard Domains

The earliest psychometric studies were distinguished by their comparisons of large hazard sets containing items as diverse as bicycles and nuclear power plants. Factor analysis of relationships among these items produced what might be called a "global space," as shown in Figure 5.2. A question of both theoretical and practical significance is whether the global structure would also pertain to a "local" set of hazards, all falling within the same general category. For example, one point in Figure 5.2 represents "railroad collisions." But all railroad collisions may not be the same. Would a taxonomy consisting solely of different types of railroad collisions have the same factor structure as Figure 5.2?[3]

To answer this question, Kraus and Slovic (1988) put the railroad point "under a microscope" to examine its structure. We constructed forty-nine railroad accident scenarios based on combinations of the following components:

- Type of train: traditional, high speed, rapid transit;
- Type of cargo: passengers, benign cargo (e.g., grain), chemicals;
- Type of accident: two-train collision, train-car collision, derailment;
- Location of accident: tunnel, open ground, bridge, grade crossing, mountain pass;
- Cause of accident: human error, sabotage, earthquake, mechanical failure.

Each railroad scenario was rated by fifty subjects on perceived riskiness as well as on ten additional characteristics prominent in previous taxonomies of perceived risk. Several other hazards, such as nuclear reactors, fire fighting, bicycles, and DNA research, were also rated to help calibrate the railroad data.

Figure 5.5
Risk Perceptions of Swedish Men and Women

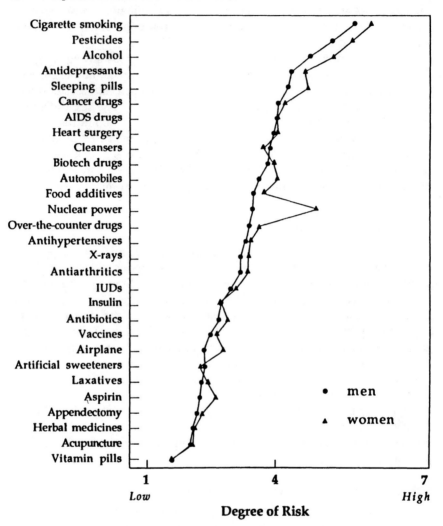

Source: Previously unpublished results from a study by Slovic, Kraus, Lappe, Letzel, and
    Malmfors (1989). Used by permission.

Psychometric analysis of these data showed considerable similarity between the railroad space and previous representations based on diverse
hazards. The railroad space was well represented by two factors in which
knowledge and catastrophic potential played defining roles. The results also
demonstrated that not all rail hazards are well represented by the point

Figure 5.6
Risk Perceptions of Canadian Men and Women

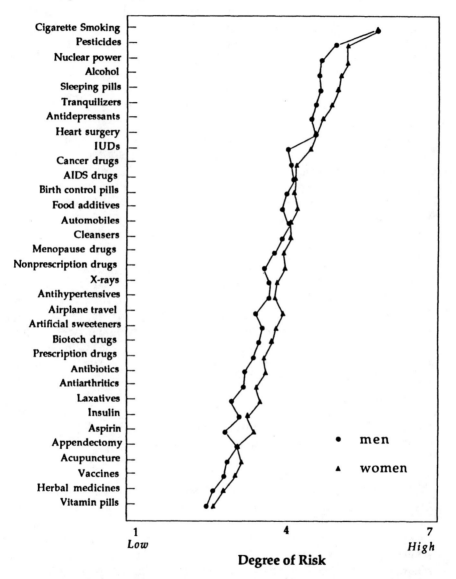

Cigarette Smoking
Pesticides
Nuclear power
Alcohol
Sleeping pills
Tranquilizers
Antidepressants
Heart surgery
IUDs
Cancer drugs
AIDS drugs
Birth control pills
Food additives
Automobiles
Cleansers
Menopause drugs
Nonprescription drugs
X-rays
Antihypertensives
Airplane travel
Artificial sweeteners
Biotech drugs
Prescription drugs
Antibiotics
Antiarthritics
Laxatives
Insulin
Aspirin
Appendectomy
Acupuncture
Vaccines
Herbal medicines
Vitamin pills

● men

▲ women

1   4   7
Low   *High*
Degree of Risk

Source: Previously unpublished results from a study by Slovic, Kraus, Lappe, and Major (1991). Used by permission.

labeled "railroad collisions" in Figure 5.2. A train carrying explosive chemicals near a city was perceived to be more like a nuclear reactor than like other rail hazards. A train carrying nontoxic freight evoked little concern. The heterogeneity of railroad hazards has important practical implications linked with our discussion earlier of signal value and impact. It may be important for policy makers and system designers to know that there are substantial differences between the degree of concern people show for an ordinary freight train derailment and the enhanced concern (and social disruption) likely to be associated with the derailment of a train carrying toxic chemicals. Thus, representing railroads as a single, homogeneous category may be quite misleading as a predictor of societal response to specific railroad hazards and accidents.

This latter point was made again in a follow-up study by Slovic, MacGregor, and Kraus (1987), which examined perceptions of risk and signal value for forty structural defects in automobiles of the kind that compel manufacturers to initiate a recall campaign. The defects were diverse, ranging from faulty defrosters to gasoline fumes that enter the passenger compartment and problems that reduce the effectiveness of steering or braking systems. Each defect was rated on a set of risk-characteristic scales that included overall vehicle riskiness, manufacturer's ability to anticipate the defect, severity of possible consequences, observability, and likelihood that the rater would comply with the recall notice (bring the car in for repair) if the defect occurred in the rater's automobile. A factor analysis indicated that these judgments could be summarized in terms of two composite factors, one representing the possibility of severe, uncontrollable damage and the other representing the foreseeability of the defect by the manufacturer. Within this two-dimensional representation, the defects were perceived quite differently, as shown in Figure 5.7. Perceived risk, rated personal compliance with a recall notice, and actual compliance rates for the defects were all highly predictable from location within the factor space (R = .89, .81, and .55, respectively). One defect stood out much as nuclear hazards do in Figure 5.2. It was a fuel-tank rupture upon impact (labeled FUELRPTR), creating the possibility of fire and burn injuries. This, of course, is similar to the notorious design problem that plagued the Ford Pinto and that Ford allegedly declined to correct because a cost-benefit analysis indicated that the correction costs greatly exceeded the expected benefits from increased safety (*Grimshaw v. Ford Motor Co.* 1978). Had Ford done a psychometric study, the analysis might have highlighted this particular defect as one whose seriousness and higher-order costs (lawsuits, damaged company reputation) were likely to be greatly underestimated by their cost-benefit analysis.

MacGregor and Slovic (1989) subsequently applied a similar analysis to thirty automobile subsystems, including braking, steering, suspension, engine, signaling, electrical, and fuel systems. Comparisons between perceptions of risk and data on accident causes showed that drivers appropriately

Figure 5.7
Location of 40 Automobile Defects Within a Two-Factor Space Derived from
Interrelationships Among Five Characteristics

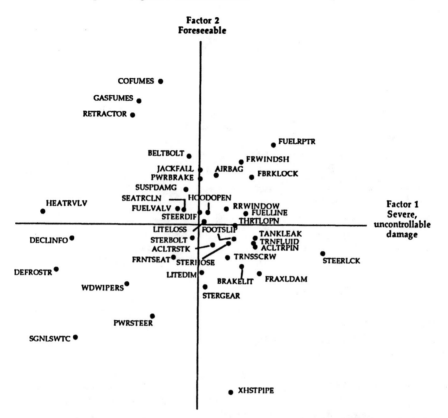

Source: Redrawn from Slovic, MacGregor, and Kraus, "Perception of Risk from Automobile
Safety Defects," *Accident Analysis and Prevention* 19 (1987), Pergamon Press. Used by
permission.

recognized the importance of brakes but underestimated the risks posed by
faulty communication and signaling systems such as headlights, brake lights,
marker lights, turn signals, and horn.

Several additional studies have focused on specific classes of hazards.
Representative samples of the general public in Sweden and Canada rated
a hazard set that primarily consisted of medicines. The two-factor repre-
sentation resulting from the study in Sweden is shown in Figure 5.8 (Slovic,
Kraus, Lappe, Letzel, and Malmfors 1989). Factor I, which was labeled
"Risk," consisted of three scales: perceived risk, the likelihood of harm,
and the seriousness of harm given a mishap. Factor II, which was called
"Warning," consisted of scales measuring newness, knowledge of risk, and

Figure 5.8
Perceptual Map of Pharmaceutical Products, Medical Treatments, and Other Hazards in the Swedish Study

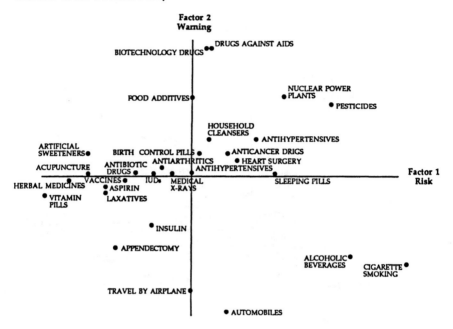

Source: Redrawn from Slovic, Kraus, Lappe, Letzel, and Malmfors (1989). Used by permission.

degree of warning signal, given a mishap. As one goes from left to right in the space, perceived risk increases. As one goes from the bottom to the top, the items are judged to have risks that are judged to be newer and less precisely known, and a mishap is judged as providing a stronger warning about the possibility that the risk is greater than was previously believed. Two features of this space stand out. First, all medicines are not alike, perceptually. Vaccines, antibiotics, and antiarthritic drugs, each of which can have significant risks, are perceived as rather benign (close to aspirin and laxatives). Antidepressant drugs and sleeping pills stand out as the pharmaceutical drugs of greatest concern, a fact that we have traced to concerns about addiction, abuse, and overdosing. Second, all of the medicines cluster near the midpoint of the warning dimension, suggesting a moderate but not extremely high potential for ripple effects in the event of adverse reactions or other problems. Of course, under certain conditions, it is clear that medicine failures can have immense repercussions, as happened with Thalidomide.

Another special domain that we have studied only with college student subjects consisted of thirty-seven LULUs (locally unwanted land uses) and

Table 5.1
Environmental Features Studied

1.	Heavy smog	20.	Large dam
2.	Heavy traffic	21.	Sewage treatment plant
3.	High crime rate	22.	Recombinant DNA laboratory
4.	Industrial waste disposal problem	23.	A main route for transport of LNG
5.	Severe water problem	24.	Active volcano (100 miles away)
6.	Nuclear power plant	25.	Large prison facility
7.	Nuclear waste storage site (100 miles away)	26.	Institution for the criminally insane
8.	Earthquake-prone area	27.	Coal-fired power plant
9.	Hurricane/tornado-prone area	28.	Hydro-electric power plant
10.	Acid rain	29.	Overpopulation/ overcrowding
11.	Strip mining	30.	Water shortages
12.	High levels of radon gas	31.	Chemical manufacturing plant
13.	Heavy use of pesticides	32.	High noise level
14.	Heavy use of herbicides to control weed and grass growth	33.	High alcohol consumption rate
15.	Asbestos-insulated buildings	34.	Legalized gambling
16.	Plutonium plant	35.	Legalized prostitution
17.	A main route for transporting high-level radioactive waste	36.	Ku Klux Klan headquarters
18.	Military weapons manufacturing facility	37.	Nuclear weapons test site (100 miles away)
19.	Extensive landfills		

other noxious environmental features such as smog, crime, air pollution, prisons, earthquake proneness, chemical and nuclear waste storage facilities, and so on (see Table 5.1). A large sample of students rated each of these items on each of seven risk-characteristic scales, resulting in the factor space shown in Figure 5.9. It is significant that a nuclear waste repository (said to be located 100 miles away) was perceived more negatively across the scales than a nuclear power plant, a high crime rate, an industrial waste disposal problem, and most other noxious features. Perceived personal risk was highly correlated with Factor 1 ($r = .72$) and was not significantly related to Factor 2.

A study by Benthin, Slovic, and Severson (in press) examined perceptions of risk and benefit from thirty activities that put young people at risk, including problem behaviors such as excessive drinking, smoking cigarettes, taking drugs, having unprotected sex, and socially approved risk taking such as playing contact sports, skiing, and riding motorcycles. Each of the

Figure 5.9
Spatial Representation of Perceptions Among 37 Unwanted Environmental
Features

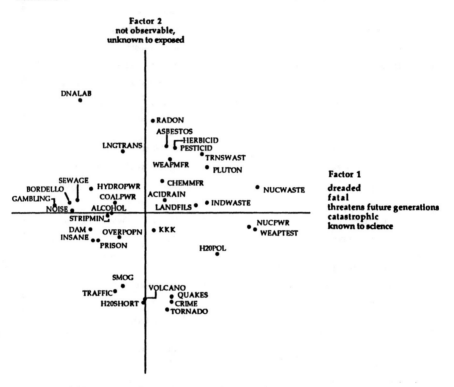

thirty activities was rated (by high school students—mean age 15.5 years) on fourteen characteristics, some taken from our previous risk perception studies (knowledge of risk, old/new, perceived risk and benefit, control) and some taken from the literature on adolescent behavior (perceived peer influence, admiration).[4] In addition, the respondents (who were anonymous) were asked to indicate whether they had participated in these activities during the past six months. The results indicated that participation in risk activities was related to very distinct cognitive and social perceptions. From a cognitive perspective, young people who engaged in a risky activity reported greater knowledge of its risks, less fear of the risks, less personal risk, more personal control over risk, less ability to avoid the activity, and higher participation in the activity by others. From a social viewpoint, participants in risky activities reported greater peer influence, less desire for regulation of the activity by authorities, and greater benefits relative to risks.

Of particular interest was the indication in these data that some highly dangerous activities are also greatly admired. A factor space was derived from these data. However, as we shall see in the next section, this data set contains important differences among individuals that can be best analyzed and described by techniques somewhat different than factor analysis.

New Methods of Analysis

The fact that we seem to learn something new about risk perceptions whenever we conduct one of these studies does not indicate, however, that our methodology has been optimal. In a knowledge vacuum, any reasonable empirical study is likely to provide useful insights. Over the years, a number of methodologically sophisticated researchers have criticized this work for (a) providing the characteristics of perceived risk to respondents, rather than letting the respondents provide them (see, e.g., Earle and Lindell 1984; Perusse 1980; Vlek and Stallen 1981); and (b) relying exclusively on principal components factor analysis to examine the dimensionality of the data (Arabie and Maschmeyer 1988). Vlek and Stallen (1981) used a "vector model" called PRINCALS (de Leeuw and van Rijckevorsal 1980) to show that individuals differed in their cognitive representations of hazards, thus demonstrating that aggregate representations masked important information. Kraus and Slovic (1988), using a "policy-capturing methodology," also found significant individual differences in subjects' models for perceived risk. Johnson and Tversky (1984) collected data on hazards in several different ways, permitting them to apply principal components factor analysis, multidimensional scaling methods, and discrete clustering models to the results. They found that each approach provided different perspectives and insights regarding the representation of perceived risk.

Arabie and Maschmeyer (1988) provided an extensive overview and critique of risk perception methodologies, arguing for greater use of methods permitting individual differences to be represented spatially and greater use of methods based on discrete clustering models. Specifically, they suggest the use of three-dimensional factor analysis (e.g., Kroonenberg 1983; Tucker 1964) and multidimensional scaling techniques such as INDSCAL (Carroll and Chang 1970) to assess individual differences and the use of models such as ADDTREE (Sattath and Tversky 1977) or ADDCLUS (Shepard and Arabie 1979) to represent hazards within discrete clusters.

In light of these criticisms, we and others have begun to reanalyze our data sets, using some of these alternative exploratory multivariate techniques. Easterling (1989) has recently applied the INDSCAL method to our data on adolescent risk perception. INDSCAL simultaneously creates a spatial mapping of perceptions and assesses individual differences with reference to the space. Recall that each high school student rated thirty hazards on fourteen characteristics, producing a fourteen-element profile for each haz-

Figure 5.10
Derived Stimulus Configuration: Hazard Space Derived from INDSCAL Analysis

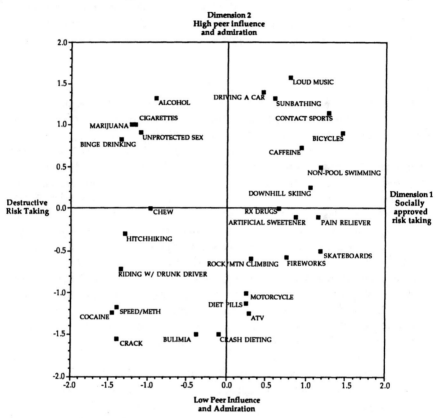

Source: Redrawn from Easterling (1989). Used by permission.

ard. All pairs of profiles (e.g., driving a car vs. rock climbing) are compared, and a Euclidian distance measure is computed as a measure of profile similarity for each pair. Analysis of these distance measures by means of INDS-CAL produces a group space of hazards and places each individual subject within that space according to the degree to which he or she weights the dimensions of that space (as inferred from the profile similarity matrix for each subject). Figure 5.10 shows the two major group dimensions that emerged from Easterling's analysis of the adolescent sample. Dimension 1 (horizontal axis) clearly separates the activities, with socially approved activities falling toward the high (right-hand) end of the dimension and socially disapproved activities falling toward the low (left) end. Dimension 2 (vertical axis) appears to reflect aspects of peer influence and admiration, anchored by socially influenced behaviors such as drinking alcoholic beverages, driving a car, listening to loud music, playing sports, and sunbathing at the high end of peer influence and admiration, and by crash dieting, bulimia, diet pills, and drug abuse at the low end.

The INDSCAL analysis produces weights for each dimension for each respondent. The weights given Dimensions 1 and 2 for each of the thirty subjects are plotted in Figure 5.11. Each single-digit number in the space represents an individual respondent, and the number indicates the number of different kinds of destructive risk-taking activities that person had reported engaging in. Each individual is scaled in terms of a vector or arrow emanating from the origin of the space. The number is located at the tip or endpoint of the vector—the line is not shown. The position of the tip is determined by the angle of the vector, which, in turn, reflects the relative weight given each of the dimensions. The distance of the number from the origin reflects the degree to which this model fits the subject's responses. If both dimensions are of equal importance, then the person's point will fall on a straight line bisecting the angle (45 degrees) between the dimensions. Individuals below that line weight Dimension 1 more heavily, and those above the line weight Dimension 2 more heavily.

The intriguing result shown in Figure 5.11 is that adolescents who participated in one or more types of destructive risk taking weighted Dimension 2 more heavily (and Dimension 1 less heavily) than did nonparticipants in dangerous activities. The line shown in the figure is slightly greater than 45 degrees above the horizontal axis. Prediction based on this line would correctly classify twenty-seven of the thirty young people as either participants or nonparticipants (zero scorers) in destructive risk taking. These results suggest that adolescents who engage in the dangerous activities located toward the left-hand side of Figure 5.10 do not perceive a great deal of difference between those activities and the safer activities toward the right-hand side of the space. In other words, some may find these dangerous activities acceptable because they are not perceived to be true risks or outliers within the realm of possible adolescent behaviors. The analysis also indicates that those who engage in destructive risk taking exaggerate the differences between activities on Dimension 2, suggesting that they are relatively more sensitive than nonparticipants to elements of peer influence.

It is important to add that the analysis depicted in Figures 5.10 and 5.11 represents prediction of recent or ongoing behaviors from current perceptions. The challenge for future research is to determine, by means of longitudinal studies, whether individual differences in perceptions develop in advance of engagement in harmful risk taking. If so, this methodology may be able to depict those perceptions in a way that signals or forecasts a change in risk-taking behavior.

This INDSCAL analysis indicates that our previous studies, relying on

Figure 5.11
Subject Weights for Dimensions in the Group Hazard Space

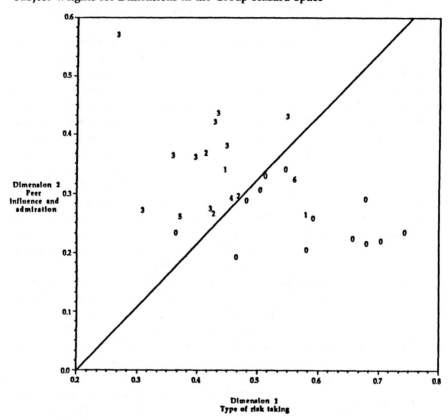

Note: Each number represents a respondent, coded according to the number of destructive
   risk-taking activities in which that person participated.
Source: Redrawn from Easterling (1989). Used by permission.

factor analysis of group means, may have missed important individual differences in perceptions. Wider use of scaling methods that take individual
differences into account seems warranted.

New Theories and Conceptual Frameworks

Confirmatory Modeling

Psychometric studies of perceived risk have been relatively theoretical,
and the methods of data collection and analysis have reflected this orientation. Principal components factor analysis and INDSCAL, which have
been illustrated above, along with the other methodologies described by

Arabie and Maschmeyer (1988), all fall into the general class of *exploratory* multivariate methods. The data analysis tends to precede conceptual analysis. As useful as these methods may be, they do not allow explicit specification and testing of theory.

We are now at a stage where we can begin to piece together theories and frameworks. Fortunately, there are analytic methods appropriate for this stage. In particular, a variety of techniques known as *confirmatory* multivariate methods have been developed for the express purpose of theory testing. Examples of methods that fall within this class are covariance structure analysis (LISREL) and partial least squares (PLS) analysis (Bentler 1980; Fornell 1982).

In testing theories, confirmatory approaches are able to analyze multiple criteria and predictor variables, unobservable theoretical variables, and errors in measurement. In contrast, many exploratory procedures can address only one or two of these aspects, and none can cope with them all. For example, factor analysis handles unobservable variables but is not confirmatory. Multiple regression allows for tests of significance regarding parameter estimates and the regression equation, and thus in a weak sense is confirmatory. However, such analysis is limited to a single observable criterion variable. In addition, multiple regression assumes that all explanatory variables have the same status and have a direct effect on the criterion variable.

Burns et al. (1990) used confirmatory methods to test the theoretical framework that Kasperson, Renn, Slovic, et al. (1988) developed to explain social impacts of risk events. This theory, labeled "the social amplification of risk," addresses the fact that the adverse effects of a risk event sometimes extend far beyond the direct damages to victims, property, and environment and may result in massive indirect impacts (see discussion in Chapter 6). Models based on analysis of 108 accident events were consistent with the theory in the sense that the social and economic impacts of an adverse event were determined not only by the direct biological and physical consequences of the event, but by elements of perceived risk, media coverage, and signal value. A particularly important signal was the perception that the event was caused by managerial incompetence.

New Forms of Risk Impact—Stigma

In 1986 we were afforded the opportunity to work with an interdisciplinary team of social scientists in what was the largest social impact assessment project ever attempted. The task was in some sense an impossible one—to forecast the social and economic impacts on residents and communities in southern Nevada in the event that the nation's high-level nuclear waste repository was sited, built, and put into operation at Yucca Mountain. As we sought to find some way to approach this daunting task, we came upon the concept of *stigma*. As we examined this concept, it became evident that stigmatization is closely associated with perception of risk.

Goffman (1963) noted that the word *stigma* was used by the ancient Greeks to refer to bodily marks or brands that were designed to expose infamy or disgrace—for example, to indicate that the bearer of the mark was a slave or a criminal. As it is used today, the word denotes a victim "marked" as deviant, flawed, limited, spoiled, or generally undesirable in the view of some observer. When the stigmatizing characteristic is observed, perception of the victim changes in a negative way. Prime targets for stigmatization are members of minority groups, the aged, persons afflicted with physical or mental disabilities and deformities, and behavioral deviants such as criminals, drug addicts, homosexuals, and alcoholics. Individuals in these categories have attributes that do not accord with prevailing standards of the normal and the good. They are denigrated and avoided.

Jones et al. (1984) attempted to characterize the key dimensions of social stigma. The six dimensions or factors they proposed were as follows:

1. *Concealability.* Is the condition hidden or obvious? To what extent is its visibility controllable?

2. *Course.* What pattern of change over time is usually shown by the condition? What is its ultimate outcome?

3. *Disruptiveness.* Does the condition block or hamper interaction and communi cation?

4. *Aesthetic qualities.* To what extent does the mark make the possessor repellent ugly, or upsetting?

5. *Origin.* Under what circumstances did the condition originate? Was anyone responsible for it, and what was he or she trying to do?

6. *Peril.* What kind of danger is posed by the mark and how imminent and serious is it?

Peril, Dimension 6, is the key link between stigma and perceived risk, but other dimensions may also come into play in the stigmatization of hazards. It seems evident that stigmatization can be generalized from persons to products, technologies, and environments. For example, nuclear and chemical waste disposal sites may be perceived as repellent, ugly, and upsetting (Dimension 4) to the extent that they become visible (Dimension 11). Such waste sites may also be perceived as disruptive (Dimension 3). They are certainly perceived as dangerous (Dimension 6).

A stigma resulting from pollution by a toxic substance is described by Edelstein (1986), who analyzed a case in which a dairy's cows became contaminated with PCBs for a short period of time. Once this contamination became known (a visible mark) the reputation of the dairy was discredited and its products became undesirable, even though the level of PCBs was never sufficiently high to prohibit sale of those products. Edelstein shows, step by step, how this incident meets the various criteria of stigmatization put forth by Jones et al.

Although Edelstein's case of stigma involved dairy products, only a short leap is required to extend the concept to environments that have been contaminated by toxic substances (Edelstein 1988). Times Beach, Missouri, and Love Canal, New York, come quickly to mind.

We have recently been exploring ways to measure environmental stigma. One method that seems quite promising uses a word-association technique to evoke the imagery, knowledge, attitudes, beliefs, and affective states associated with specific environments. Word associations have a long history in psychology, going back to Galton (1880), Wundt (1883), and Freud (1924). More recently, Szalay and Deese (1978) have employed the *method of continued associations* to assess people's subjective representation systems for a wide range of concepts. This method requires the subject to make repeated associations to the same stimulus; for example:

war: soldier;

war: fight;

war: killing;

war: etc.

Szalay and Deese argue that this technique is an efficient way of determining the contents and representational systems of human minds without requiring those contents to be expressed in the full discursive structure of language. In fact, we may reveal ourselves through associations in ways we might find difficult to do if we were required to spell out the full propositions behind these associations through answers to questions.

We conducted a study in which we asked University of Oregon students to produce continued associations to four states: New Jersey, Nevada, Colorado, and California. Subjects answered anonymously and without time pressure, to allow full expression of their thoughts. The results of this study clearly demonstrated environmental stigmatization in the minds of our sample of Oregon students. The image of New Jersey was dominated by pollution, including toxic waste, filth, and garbage as members of the most common associative category. New Jersey was also seen as overcrowded, ugly, and associated with crime. Its farms and beaches were very infrequent images. Nevada's imagery was dominated by its desert landscape, along with entertainment, gambling, and prostitution. It is also becoming associated with things nuclear (fifth most frequent category). Its scenic beauty, outdoor recreation, and ranches are secondary to these other images. Images of Colorado and California are far more positive than images of New Jersey and Nevada.

Returning to the issue of Yucca Mountain, we conducted a series of studies

Table 5.2
Hierarchy of Images Associated with an "Underground Nuclear Waste Storage Facility"

	Category	Frequency	Images Included in Category
1.	Dangerous	179	dangerous, danger, hazardous, toxic, unsafe, harmful, disaster
2.	Death	107	death, sickness, dying. destruction
3.	Negative	99	negative, wrong, bad, unpleasant, terrible, gross, undesirable, awful, dislike, ugly, horrible
4.	Pollution	97	pollution, contamination, leakage, spills, Love Canal
5.	War	62	war, bombs, nuclear war, holocaust
6.	Radiation	59	radiation, nuclear, radioactive, glowing
7.	Scary	55	scary, frightening, concern, worried, fear, horror
8.	Somewhere else	49	wouldn't want to live near one, not where I live, far away as possible
9.	Unnecessary	44	unnecessary, bad idea, waste of land
10.	Problems	39	problems, trouble
11.	Desert	37	desert, barren, desolate
12.	Non-Nevada location	35	Utah, Arizona, Denver
13.	Storage location	32	caverns, underground salt mine
14.	Government/industry	23	government, politics, big business

using the method of continued association to document the relationship between images, risk, preferences, and economically important behaviors (Slovic, Layman, Kraus, et al. 1991). First we demonstrated that cities and states had diverse positive and negative images, as noted above. Second, we showed that by rating the degree of positive and negative affective content and summing these ratings across a person's set of images for each stimulus city or stimulus state, we could accurately predict a person's expressed preferences for future vacation sites, places to retire, and places to locate new businesses. Imagery was also predictive of previous visits to a place. Third, we asked people to associate to the concept of an "underground nuclear waste storage facility." The results, shown in Table 5.2 for a representative sample of residents in Phoenix, Arizona, could not have been more negative or more representative of a stigmatized environmental facility. Fourth, we showed that nuclear imagery had already infiltrated the minds of about 10 percent of our respondents when they associated to the state

"Nevada." We traced this nuclear imagery to knowledge of the nuclear weapons test site located near Yucca Mountain. We also found that nuclear imagery, when present, was associated with much lower preference for Nevada as a place to vacation.

We concluded that, were development and operation of the Yucca Mountain site to proceed, any problems associated with the repository would have the potential to link the repository, things nuclear, and many other highly negative images with the state of Nevada and the city of Las Vegas. Increased negativity of imagery, as we had demonstrated, could possibly lead to serious impacts on tourism, migration, and economic development in the southern Nevada region. Through the mechanisms of social amplification, even minor problems could increase stigmatization, due to heavy media coverage and the attention drawn to these problems by special interest groups. Although precise specification of the probability, magnitude, and duration of such impacts is beyond the state of the art in social science prediction, it is clear that such impacts cannot be ignored in decisions about the siting and management of the repository. The state of Nevada has cited the findings from these studies as instrumental in the state's decision to prevent the federal government from performing any further investigation of the Yucca Mountain site (McKay 1990).

The stigmatization of environments has several important implications for hazardous waste management in general. First, it implies that, whatever the health risks associated with waste products, there are likely to be significant social and economic impacts on regions perceived as polluted, or as dumps. Second, it also gives additional importance to managing wastes effectively so that stigmatizing incidents (even ones without significant health consequences) will not occur.

Just as environments can become stigmatized by risk problems, so can products (the IUD, the Pinto) and their manufacturers (A. H. Robbins, Ford Motor Company). Union Carbide has undoubtedly become stigmatized because of the Bhopal accident, and Exxon as well because of the oil spill at Valdez.

Technologies become stigmatized by risk, too. The image of most chemical technologies is so negative that when we asked college students and members of the general public to tell us what comes to mind when they hear or read the word "chemicals," by far the most frequent response was "dangerous" or some closely related term (e.g., toxic, hazardous, poison, deadly); beneficial uses of chemicals were rarely mentioned (see Table 5.3).

Toward Deeper Levels of Analysis: Intuitive Toxicology

The power of factor analysis and multidimensional scaling lies in their ability to synthesize tens of thousands of judgments into a few visual displays. This broad descriptive capability carries with it, of necessity, a weak-

Table 5.3
College Students' Word Associations to the Stimulus Term "Chemicals"

	Category	Frequency	Images Included in Category
1.	Dangerous	59	toxic, hazardous, deadly, destruction, accidents, poisonous, explosive, kill, harmful, Bhopal, cancer, bad, noxious
2.	Chemical names and elements	45	H_2SO_4, ozone, carbon, dioxin, gas, DDT, cyanide, methane, hydrogen, monoxide, oxygen, uranium, acid
3.	Pollution	29	Love Canal, greenhouse effect, smelly, Teledyne, Wah Chang, air pollution
4.	Laboratory	30	experiments, science
5.	Chemical types	21	herbicides, pesticides, preservatives, vitamins, fertilizer, drugs, medicines
6.	Chemistry*	16	
7.	Useful	14	beneficial, jobs, benefits, valuable, products, helpful
8.	Wastes*	10	
9.	Food*	9	
10.	"Paraphernalia"	11	beaker, bottles, flasks, litmus, test tubes, hood, stockroom
11.	Burn	12	burner, bunsen-burner, burning
12.	Dow*	6	
13.	War	11	warfare
14.	Technology	7	industry

* The category name is the exact response.

ness. The analyses lack depth. They provide only a surface level of description that leaves many questions unanswered. Why do we not dread auto accidents? Why have perceptions of marijuana changed so drastically among college students over the past eight years? Why do adolescents who engage in dangerous activities believe that they cannot avoid doing so, but once engaged in them, believe that they can control the risks? Why are chemical risks of such great concern?

Answers to these sorts of questions require different methods of analysis—methods that may afford deeper understanding of specific issues, rather than broad, but shallow, representations.

We have begun to reach for a deeper understanding of perceived risks from chemicals. Given the importance of chemical technologies in our daily lives, the extremely negative perceptions of chemical risks held by so many people is nothing short of astounding. This negativity of perceptions is especially significant in light of the immense scientific and regulatory efforts that have been designed to reduce public exposure to, and harm from, chemicals. Billions of dollars have been spent on risk assessment studies by toxicologists and epidemiologists. Massive regulatory bureaucracies have been formed to oversee the use of these risk assessments for standard setting and risk management.

Yet, despite this enormous effort, people in the United States and many other industrialized nations see themselves as increasingly vulnerable to the risks from chemical technologies and believe that the worst is yet to come. Regulatory agencies have become embroiled in rancorous conflicts, caught between a fearful and dissatisfied public on the one side, and frustrated industrialists and technologists on the other. Industry sees an urgent need to communicate with the public but does not know how to do so.

Nancy Kraus, Torbjorn Malmfors, and I have approached this problem from a perspective that we have labeled "intuitive toxicology" (Kraus, Malmfors, and Slovic 1992). Humans have always been intuitive toxicologists, relying on their senses of sight, taste, and smell to detect unsafe food, water, and air. The science of toxicology has been developed to supplement, and in many cases replace, our sensory systems. However, as a report by the National Academy of Sciences has indicated (NRC 1983), toxicological risk assessment itself is inherently subjective, relying heavily on assumptions and judgment.

The objective of our current research is to explore the cognitive models, assumptions, and inference methods that comprise laypeople's "intuitive toxicological theories" and to compare these theories with the cognitive models, assumptions, and inference methods of scientific toxicology and risk assessment. We hope that such comparisons will expose the specific similarities and differences within expert communities as well as the similarities and differences between lay perceptions and expert views. We also hope that the knowledge gained from these comparisons will provide a valuable starting point around which to structure discussion, education, and communication about toxicological risk assessment.

We have begun this effort by identifying several fundamental principles and judgmental components within the science of toxicological risk assessment. Questions were developed based on these fundamentals in order to determine the extent to which laypeople and experts share the same knowledge base and conceptual framework. Our questions addressed the following topics:

- conceptions of toxicity;
- conceptions of the relationship between chemical dose and exposure and risk to human health;
- trust in use of animal and bacterial studies to determine risk to humans;
- attitudes toward chemicals and their risks;

Table 5.4
Statements Designed to Assess Sensitivity to Degree of Exposure

---

- If you are exposed to a toxic chemical substance, then you are likely to suffer adverse health effects.

- If you are exposed to a carcinogen, then you are likely to get cancer.

- For pesticides, it's not how much of the chemical you are exposed to that should worry you, but whether or not you are exposed to it at all.

- A chemical was found in a city's supply of drinking water in a concentration of 30 parts per million. Because scientists believed that there might be harmful effects from this level of exposure to the chemical, the water was filtered by a process that was able to reduce, but not eliminate, the chemical concentration in the water. Under most circumstances this means that the danger associated with drinking the water has also been reduced.

- There is no safe level of exposure to a cancer-causing agent.

- interpretation of evidence regarding cause-effect relationships between exposure to chemicals and human health.

Questions on these topics were incorporated into a single questionnaire, designed for both experts and the public. This questionnaire asks a series of questions about chemicals and their risks, using an agree/disagree answer format. The term *chemicals* was defined to include "all chemical elements and compounds, including pesticides, food additives, industrial chemicals, household cleaning agents, prescription and nonprescription drugs, etc." Table 5.4 presents five of the specific statements used to assess conceptions of toxicity and beliefs about the link between dose and exposure and possible harm.

The questions were designed, whenever possible, according to a guiding hypothesis about how experts and "lay toxicologists" might respond. For example, perhaps the most important principle in toxicology is the fact that "the dose makes the poison" (Ottoboni 1984). Any substance can cause a toxic effect if the dose is great enough. Thus we expected experts to exhibit considerable sensitivity to consideration of exposure and dose when responding to the five items in Table 5.4. In contrast, the concerns of the public regarding very small exposures or doses of chemicals led us to hypothesize that the public would have more of an "all or none" view of toxicity and would be rather insensitive to concentration, dose, and exposure when responding to these items.

The questions in Table 5.4 comprise a small part of a lengthy survey that we administered to 180 members of the Society of Toxicology and 262 members of the general public. The data showed substantial differences in the attitudes and beliefs of experts and laypeople. Laypeople tended to believe that any exposure to a toxic substance or carcinogen, no matter how small, was likely to prove harmful. Toxicologists had, as expected, a much more differentiated sense of the relationship between dose and degree of exposure and harm. Perhaps most important was the divergence of opinion among toxicologists themselves on questions pertaining to the reliability and validity of animal tests for assessing the risks that chemicals pose for humans. This lack of confidence in the science may be a significant cause of the public's anxiety and distrust. We also observed a strong "affiliation bias," indicating that toxicologists working for industry see chemicals as more benign than do their counterparts in academia and government. Industrial toxicologists were somewhat more confident than other experts in the general validity of animal tests—except when those tests were said to provide evidence for carcinogenicity, in which case many of the industrial experts changed their opinions that the tests were valid. Similar results have been found by Lynn (1987); together, these data clearly show the influence of personal and organizational values on risk assessment.

Detailed assessments of a person's knowledge, attitudes, beliefs, values, perceptions, and inference mechanisms make up what cognitive psychologists refer to as a "mental model." Our study of intuitive toxicology attempts to describe the mental models of experts and laypersons regarding the effects of chemicals on human health. Mental models of risk from radon and from electrical fields are currently being developed at Carnegie-Mellon University. I expect that this paradigm will be increasingly relied on to describe perceived risk and to facilitate communication about risk.

CONCLUDING REMARKS

The Need for a Multidisciplinary Perspective

Although the psychometric approach has been oriented toward cognitive psychology and behavioral decision theory, I believe that societal response to hazards is multidetermined and thus needs to be studied in a multidisciplinary way.

Occasionally one sees attempts to test "rival disciplinary theories" of risk perception, as though one approach—social, cultural, psychological, or economic—could be the right way to conceptualize things (e.g., Wildavsky and Dake 1990). This makes little sense to me. It is most certainly the case that information processing (cognition), personality, social factors, economic factors, and cultural factors interact to determine individual and societal response to risk. The mix may be difficult, if not impossible, to separate—witness the endless debates about nature versus nurture.

Consider, for example, the quality "dread." Most people in our culture would judge sudden death from heart disease as less dreaded than death from cancer. I am told that in some Eastern cultures the opposite is true— a lingering death from cancer is preferred because it gives one the opportunity to put one's affairs in order and say goodbye. Thus dread appears to be both psychological and cultural, and it does not seem worthwhile to me to attempt to disentangle these various aspects.

Fortunately, the psychometric approach is not inherently psychological, as shown by the inclusion of social variables in the study of adolescent risk taking, the inclusion of institutional and economic variables in the social amplification study, and the inclusion of political and ideological variables in other studies (Buss, Craik, and Dake 1986).

Risk Perception and Rationality

Are public perceptions of risk irrational? Many technologists believe that they are. For example, public perceptions of nuclear power risks have evoked harsh reactions from experts. One noted psychiatrist wrote that "the irrational fear of nuclear plants is based on a mistaken assessment of the risks" (Dupont 1981, 8). A nuclear physicist and leading advocate of nuclear power (Cohen 1983, 13) contended that "the public has been driven *insane* over fear of radiation [from nuclear power]. I use the word "insane" purposefully since one of its definitions is loss of contact with reality. The public's understanding of radiation dangers has virtually lost all contact with the actual dangers as understood by scientists."

Risk perception research paints a different picture, demonstrating that people's deep anxieties about nuclear power and its wastes are linked to numerous realities. For example, one reality for the public consists of innumerable news stories about poorly sequestered radioactive wastes from the nation's military reactors contaminating the environment and threatening human health at Hanford, Washington; Savannah River, South Carolina; Rocky Flats, Colorado; Fernald, Ohio; and other sites. Another reality for the public is witnessing the Department of Energy declare that it has no confidence in its two-year, $500 million attempt to evaluate the safety of the proposed waste repository site at Yucca Mountain, Nevada (Wald 1989). Well-publicized conflicts among scientists about the ability of animal tests to predict human health effects from chemicals (Associated Press 1990) form yet another "reality." Thus, although one may legitimately disagree with public perceptions of risk, they are clearly not irrational.

More generally, psychometric research demonstrates that, whereas experts define risk in a narrow, technical way, the public has a richer, more complex view that incorporates value-laden considerations such as equity, catastrophic potential, and controllability. The issue is not whether these are legitimate, rational considerations, but how to integrate them into risk analyses and policy decisions.

Risk Perception and Risk Analysis

Risk perception studies indicate that public views about risky technologies need to be taken seriously. The problem is that it is not obvious how to incorporate public perceptions and preferences into risk analysis and decision making. A risk manager who wants to include public perceptions will probably not know how to do so.

Some risk analysts have attempted to provide guidance about how to weigh and combine social and technical considerations. For example, Starr (1969) distinguished between voluntary and involuntary activities in assessing risk-benefit balances, and Wilson (1975) and Griesemeyer and Okrent (1981) proposed that large accidents needed to be given proportionally more weight than numerous small accidents totaling the same amount of damage. Rowe (1977) and Litai, Lanning, and Rasmussen (1983) have explored the possibility of adjusting risk estimates to take into account the importance of various risk perception characteristics; however, their work treats highly interdependent characteristics as though they were independent; thus their analyses are prone to serious "double counting" effects. Fischhoff, Watson, and Hope (1984) have suggested that multiattribute utility theory be employed to insure that social and psychological factors are incorporated into technical and economic analyses. To my knowledge, none of these various proposals has been developed to the point of application in actual risk analyses.

I know of only one method of risk analysis that has integrated technical, economic, and social (perception) factors in a formal way and done so in real applications. This approach has been developed by two Swiss analysts to aid decisions about the safety of ammunition storage depots and transportation systems, including the design of the proposed high-speed railway in Germany (Bohnenblust and Schneider 1984). The method is essentially a cost-effectiveness approach that allocates more money for risk reduction to hazards that are involuntary, poorly understood, and hard to control. Although this "Swiss model" has been successfully applied in a number of important decision problems, there is a need to align the model more closely with the research that has been done on risk perception and its impacts (e.g., signals, ripples, social amplification). A recent effort in this direction has been initiated by Burns (1990). More generally, there is need for research that determines how the public feels about incorporating risk perception characteristics as explicit criteria that are traded against cost and more traditional criteria (e.g., lives and health effects).

Risk Perception and Trust

As I contemplate the current problems most in need of research, the issue of trust leaps to the top of the list. The massive discrepancies between expert risk assessments and public perceptions and the acrimonious conflicts over risk management issues can be seen as reflecting a "crisis in confidence," a profound breakdown of trust in the scientific, governmental, and industrial managers of radiation and chemical technologies. There is a great need to understand the nature of trust in order to develop social and institutional processes for decision making that restore and maintain this vital but fragile quality. Many different methods of analysis can contribute such knowledge, but, considering the multidimensional nature of trust (ethics, intentions, competence, etc.), it appears to be a natural candidate for the psychometric paradigm.

NOTES

The preparation of this chapter was supported by National Science Foundation Grants SES 8915711 and SES 8722109 to Decision Research.

1. The word *perception* is used here and in the literature to refer to various kinds of attitudes and judgments.

2. As we shall see later, smaller and more homogeneous hazard sets can produce different spaces.

3. The answer is not intuitively obvious. Local and global representations have the same dimensions for some objects (e.g., rectangles are always defined by height and width no matter how similar or dissimilar they are), whereas the dimensions needed to represent diverse emotions such as love, pride, worry, or anger differ from the local dimensions needed to characterize the various aspects of a single emotion such as love—puppy love, maternal love, and so on (Gerrig, Maloney, and Tversky 1985).

4. The psychometric paradigm is not restricted to the study of psychological variables, as the inclusion of these social variables illustrates.

CHAPTER 6

The Social Amplification of Risk: Progress in Developing an Integrative Framework

Roger E. Kasperson

Like many others, I came to risk research through the back door. My graduate studies were in geography at the University of Chicago, where Gilbert F. White was training the first generation of hazard researchers. I worked primarily in political geography, however, under the tutelage of Norton Ginsburg and Marvin Mikesell, and my early publications focused on the geography of urban politics, political conflict over natural resource uses, and citizen participation. When I came to Clark University in 1969, my base department was government, and my teaching responsibilities largely addressed empirical political theory.

In 1971, Robert Kates and I joined with a physicist, Christoph Hohenemser, to consider what common interests geographers and physicists might have in environmental issues. Hohenemser viewed with interest the decade of work by Kates and others on natural hazards but wondered whether this approach could contribute to a complex technological problem such as nuclear power. At that time, coincidentally, the Ford Foundation was holding a "contest" for innovative approaches to technology problems; we responded with a proposal to conduct an integrated study of the technical and social risks of nuclear power and won the contest. That led to a succession of studies aimed at building a set of conceptual and analytic approaches to technological hazards and to Jeanne X. Kasperson's joining this effort. This work was eventually summarized in *Perilous Progress: Managing the Hazards of Technology* (Kates, Hohenemser, and Kasperson 1985) and *Equity Issues in Radioactive Waste Management* (Kasperson 1983b).

By the middle of the 1980s, it was apparent both that social analyses of risk had earned widespread recognition throughout the community of risk scholars and practitioners (in no small part due to the pioneering work of Slovic, Fischhoff, and Lichtenstein) and that current approaches were badly fragmented. We were engaged in collaborative research with Paul Slovic and Howard Kunreuther on the risks associated with the proposed siting of a radioactive waste facility in Nevada. The novel problems associated with such a development put into stark relief the limitations, or (put differently) the partial insights, associated with existing risk concepts and paradigms. With the generosity of the state of Nevada, and subsequently the National Science Foundation, we initiated an effort not only to evaluate the meaning of such a first-time development for the people of Nevada and their distant heirs, but to create a broader, more integrative way of thinking about risk and its experience by society. Several years later the social amplification of risk concept emerged.

In June 1988, researchers at Clark University and Decision Research proposed a new framework called the "social amplification of risk" (Kasperson, Renn, et al. 1988) for the analysis of risk. Thoughtful accompanying commentaries by the anthropologists Roy Rappaport (1988) and Steve Rayner (1988a), the sociologist of science Arie Rip (1988), and the psychologist Ola Svenson (1988) raised a variety of questions and issues while generally welcoming the search for a broader and more integrative treatment of risk. Since that time, the framework has been widely shared in the risk community as well as with other social scientists. The authors have undertaken a series of empirical investigations aimed at developing, elaborating, and applying the framework to a large and diverse data base of some 128 hazard events and to in-depth case studies of community experience with risk. Other analyses have applied the framework to a class of hazards "hidden" from societal awareness and scrutiny, to the specific problems associated with communicating risks to publics, and to why some people seek out "desired" risks. Nearly three years into this venture in empirical theory building, it is timely to assess what we have learned from the scholarly reception of this analytical framework and from the various follow-up empirical and conceptual studies that have followed.

RISK AND DISJUNCTURES

The social amplification of risk arose in response to a continuing series of disjunctures in the intellectual history of hazards and risks. The early work on natural hazards by White (1961), Kates (1962, 1971), Burton and Kates (1964), and Burton, Kates, and White (1968) envisioned hazards as the outcome of the interaction between natural processes and human activities, including their associated social and economic vulnerabilities. This, and the more recent definition of "hazards" as "threats to people and the things they value" (Kates and Kasperson 1983, 7029; Kates, Hohenemser, and Kasperson 1985, 21) and risk as "the probability of experiencing harm," would seem to hold promise for broadly defined and far-ranging conceptions of hazards and risks, their social causes, and their linkages with the environments, historical contexts, and social settings in which they occur (a need emphasized in J. K. Mitchell 1990). Yet, the way in which risk studies have developed reveals a series of disjunctures that have thwarted the development of an integrated and powerful analysis of environmental hazards. Instead, a mosaic of concepts and approaches has emerged, each of which has illuminated some "faces" of risk causation and experience while concealing others. Meanwhile, disciplinary and theoretical squabbles over the correctness of particular viewpoints have diverted energies from seeking out the meeting points of theory, from appreciating the particular contributions of alternative interpretations, and from fashioning more holistic analyses of hazard experience and its social meaning.

The most striking disjuncture has been that between the "technical" and the "social or perceptual" analysis of hazards (Freudenburg 1988). The technical concept of risk focuses narrowly on the *probability of events* (a volcanic eruption, a nuclear plant accident, an automobile collision) and the *magnitude of the consequences* (number of deaths, injuries, illnesses) that follow. "Risk" is then usually defined by the multiplication of the two terms—probability of events and consequences—with the assumption that society is indifferent toward low-consequence/high-probability hazards and high-consequence/low-probability hazards. Under the impact of numerous psychological studies that have delineated qualitative properties (newness, involuntary nature, catastrophic potential) of hazards that shape social experience and reactions (Slovic 1987), some analysts have sought to modify the calculation (as by weighting consequences) when it is the inadequacy of the underlying conception that fatally flaws the approach. Accordingly, social scientists have delighted in detailing the inadequacies of the technical concept: consequences can be satisfactorily identified only through analysis of human activity and values; "damage" is socially dependent; social processes and setting influence the incidence of hazard events; human "factors" are major contributors in hazard causation; management is rooted in social institutions and relationships. Yet, while discrediting the narrow technical conception of risk and the limitations of "mandated" science, the social science critics have offered no coherent framework or approach for integrating the technical and social aspects of risk. Meanwhile, an unsuccessful effort by a special committee of the Society of Risk Analysis to construct a consensual definition of risk has driven home what many already understood—that the defining of risk is essentially a political act.

The second disjuncture has been within the social sciences themselves. Most centrally involved in empirical studies of risk over the past two decades have been the psychologists who have explored the bases of human judgments in a world constructed from social concepts. These studies have explicitly joined risk perception and behavioral decision theory, with results that have challenged the theory of rational behavior espoused by the engineers and economists who have formed the core (some would prefer "dominant" paradigm) of technical risk analysis. In particular, this research has laid bare the heuristics that ordinary people utilize to cope with the complex array of risk information available as they wend their way through a potentially hazardous world. Cultural theorists, by contrast, beginning with Mary Douglas' *Purity and Danger* (1966), have in recent years criticized both the technical and psychological conceptualization of risk, proposing that individuals *select* what and how much to fear largely as the product of a particular cultural bias or to support a particular way of life (Douglas and Wildavsky 1982b; Douglas 1985; Thompson, Ellis, and Wildavsky 1990). Those risks selected for concern and worry are functional in that they strengthen one way of life while weakening others. Thus these critics have often claimed (on scant empirical evidence) the preferability of cultural theory over other competing explanations.

This paradigm imperialism is quite apparent in a recent study (Wildavsky and Dake 1990) that champions cultural theory over psychological approaches and manages to overlook those concepts and findings in alternative theories that elucidate different parts of the risk experience and that would form the base of a more powerful interpretation (although Duke has gone on to more ecumenical analyses). Meanwhile, sociologists and policy analysts have seen risk as an element in social movements or dynamics of social controversy (Mazur 1981; Krimsky and Plough 1988) and disasters as a phenomenon for studying critical problems of social structures and processes (Kreps 1984, 1989), whereas economists tend to see hazards as market externalities requiring social intervention (Viscusi 1983). Ironically, the social scientists among risk analysts are the ones who have failed to incorporate the important insights generated by alternative approaches to risk and to harness the full power of the social sciences in enriching the analysis of risk.

The third disjuncture lies in the largely separate confluences that have marked the intellectual history and sociology of what should be the integrated subject matter of risk. Natural hazards research, risk analysis, and disaster sociology have tended to have their own professional conferences, journals, networks of informal contacts, and bodies of accumulated empirical findings. Personal observation suggests that no more than a handful of scholars regularly attends both the annual meetings of the Society for Risk Analysis and the annual Natural Hazards Workshop in Boulder, cross-references the three domains in published articles and books, and routinely integrates the predominant conceptual structures. Recent years have witnessed more crossover between the two oldest research areas, disaster sociology and natural hazards research (see, for example, Drabek 1986 and Comfort 1988), but both fields remain quite isolated from risk analysis, which has been largely focused on technological impacts. This disjuncture is paradoxical insofar as no clear dividing line separates natural and technological hazards or disaster sociology, and the capacity for these different schools of scholars to learn from one another is high (Short 1984).

The final disjuncture lies in the nature of knowing and science. Although it is generally well appreciated that science and formal analysis are sharply constrained in what they can know, risk analysis often proceeds in blissful isolation from that recognition. Alvin Weinberg (1972) early on blew the whistle on this hubris, pointing out that most of the truly difficult social risk issues were *trans-scientific*—that is, they could be raised but not answered by science. Von Winterfeldt and Edwards (1984) argue that the most difficult risk controversies are the "technological mysteries" over which debates oscillate between issues of fact and issues of values.

But the roots of disjuncture are deeper. O'Riordan and Rayner (1990) have argued that concepts such as *risk* and *sustainable development* are fundamentally limited in two respects: scientific knowledge confronts huge chasms of chaos (unpredictable uncertainty) that lie at the boundaries of current knowledge, and scientific knowledge moves along pathways that strip away essential interconnections and thereby unavoidably distorts the character of the phenomenon under study. The early hazard analysts appreciated that comprehension of human experience of risk cannot proceed by science alone but requires infusion from indigenous or "folk" knowledge and analogical reasoning, a requirement often overlooked in contemporary risk analysis. Brian Wynne (1989c, 1991a) points out in his revealing study of the responses of sheep farmers to the Chernobyl accident the failure of scientific experts to recognize that farmers possessed extensive knowledge about sheep habits and the local physical environment. Thus, an adequate characterization of the risk required that abstract and formal scientific knowledge be integrated with knowledge about sheep and sheep-farming practices (see also Chapter 12). N. S. Jodha's (1987, 1990) studies of common property degradation in the Himalayas also strikingly illustrate the importance of indigenous risk knowledge. Funtowicz and Ravetz (1990a) argue that a new kind of science is needed to understand problems that lie in the domain of high uncertainty (and human ignorance) and high value resonance (see Chapter 11 for further discussion). This new science—which they term "second order" or "post-normal" science—will not be merely new fields of expertise but "a new conception of the objects, methods, and social functions of knowledge about the material world, and its interactions with structures of power and authority" (Funtowicz and Ravetz 1990a, 74).

In 1988, it was apparent that these disjunctures sharply limited significant gains in improving our understanding of risk, its social causes and meaning, and its embedment in the fabric of society. New approaches were needed that were more holistic, that specifically fused the technical and social conceptions of risk, that appreciated and internalized the contributions of differing social theory, that joined the fragmented body of emerging empirical knowledge, and that recognized the different ways of knowing.

THE SOCIAL AMPLIFICATION OF RISK FRAMEWORK

The concept of social amplification of risk is based on the thesis that events pertaining to hazards interact with psychological, social, institutional,

158   Social, Cultural, and Psychological Paradigms

Figure 6.1
Highly Simplified Representation of the Social Amplification of Risk and Potential
Impacts on a Corporation

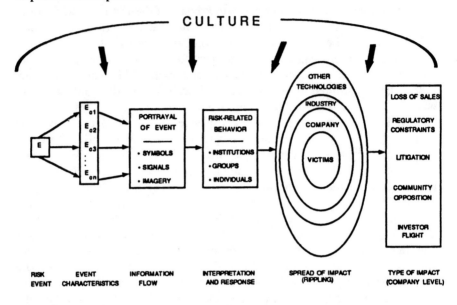

and cultural processes in ways that can heighten or attenuate perceptions
of risk and shape risk behavior (Figure 6.1). Behavioral responses, in turn,
generate secondary social or economic consequences. These consequences
extend far beyond direct harms to human health or the environment to
include significant indirect impacts such as liability, insurance costs, loss of
confidence in institutions, stigmatization, or alienation from community
affairs (Kasperson, Renn, et al. 1988).

Such secondary effects often (in the case of risk amplification) trigger
demands for additional institutional responses and protective actions, or,
conversely (in the case of risk attenuation), place impediments in the path
of needed protective actions. In our usage, "amplification" includes both
intensifying and attenuating signals about risk. Thus, alleged "overreac-
tions" of people and organizations receive the same attention as alleged
"down-playing."

Some terms used in this concept need further explanation. Risk, in our
view, is in part an objective threat of harm to people and in part a product
of culture and social experience. Hence, hazardous events are "real": they
involve transformations of the physical environment or human health as a
result of continuous or sudden (accidental) releases of energy, matter, or
information or involve perturbations in social and value structures. These
events remain limited in the social context unless they are observed by human
beings and communicated to others (Luhmann 1986, 63). The consequences

of this communication and other social interactions may lead to other physical transformations, such as changes in technologies, changes in methods of land cultivation, or changes in the composition of water, soil, and air. The experience of risk is therefore both an experience of physical harm and the result of culture and social processes by which individuals or groups acquire or create interpretations of hazards. These interpretations provide rules of how to select, order, and explain signals from the physical world. Additionally, each cultural or social group selects certain risks and adds them to its strand of worry-beads to rub and burnish even as it selects out other risks as not meriting immediate concern.

The amplification process, as we conceive it, starts with either a physical event (such as an accident) or a report on environmental or technological events, releases, exposures, or consequences. Some groups and individuals also, of course, actively monitor the experiential world, searching for hazard events related to their agenda of concern. In both cases, individuals or groups select specific characteristics of these events or aspects of the associated depictions and interpret them according to their perceptions and mental schemes. They also communicate these interpretations to other individuals and groups and receive interpretations in return. Social groups and individuals process the information, locate it in their agenda of concerns, and may feel compelled to respond. Some may change their previously held beliefs, gain additional knowledge and insights, and be motivated to take action; others may use the opportunity to compose new interpretations that they send to the original sources or other interested parties; and still others find the added information as confirming long-held views of the world and its order.

The individuals or groups who collect information about risks communicate with others, and through behavioral responses act, in our terminology, as *amplification stations*. Amplification stations can be individuals, groups, or institutions. It is obvious that social groups or institutions can amplify or attenuate signals only by working in social aggregates and participating in social processes. But individuals in groups and institutions do not act or react merely in their roles as private persons, but rather according to the role specification associated with their positions. Amplification may therefore differ among individuals in their roles as private citizens and in their roles as employees or members of social groups and organizations.

Role-related considerations and membership in social groups shape the selection of information that the individual regards as significant. Interpretations or signals that are inconsistent with previous beliefs or that contradict the person's values are often ignored or attenuated. They are intensified if the opposite is true. The process of receiving and processing risk-related information by individuals is well researched in the risk perception literature (Slovic 1987; Freudenburg 1988). But this is not sufficient: individuals act also as members of cultural groups and larger social units which codetermine the dynamics and social processing of risk. In this framework, we term these larger social units *social stations of amplification*. Individuals in their roles as members or employees of social groups or institutions do not only follow their personal values and interpretative patterns; they also perceive risk information and construct the risk "problem" according to cultural biases and the rules of their organization or group (Johnson and Covello 1987).

Cultural biases and role-specific factors are internalized and reinforced through education and training, identification with the goals and functions of institutions, beliefs in the importance and justification of social outcomes, and rewards (promotions, salary increases, symbolic honors) and punishments (demotions, salary cuts, disgrace). Meanwhile, conflicts between personal convictions and institutional obligations evoke psychological stress, potentially leading to alienation or anomie.

Both the information flow depicting the risk or risk event and the associated behavioral responses by individual and social amplification stations generate secondary effects that extend beyond the people directly affected by the original hazard event or report. Secondary impacts include such effects as

- enduring mental perceptions, images, and attitudes (e.g., antitechnology attitudes, alienation from physical environment, social apathy, or distrust of risk management institutions);
- impacts on the local or regional economy (e.g., reduced business sales, declines in residential property values, and drops in tourism);
- political and social pressure (e.g., political demands, changes in political climate and culture);
- social disorder (e.g., protesting, rioting, sabotage, terrorism);
- changes in risk monitoring and regulation;
- increased liability and insurance costs;
- repercussions on other technologies (e.g., lower levels of public acceptance) and on social institutions (e.g., erosion of public trust).

Secondary impacts are, in turn, perceived by social groups and individuals so that additional stages of amplification may occur to produce higher-order impacts. The impacts thereby may spread, or "ripple," to other parties, distant locations, or future generations. Each order of impact will not only disseminate social and political impacts but may also trigger (in risk amplification) or hinder (in risk attenuation) positive changes for risk reduction. The concept of social amplification of risk is hence dynamic, taking into account the continuing learning and social interactions resulting from social experience with risk.

The analogy of dropping a stone into a pond (see Figure 6.1) illustrates the spread of these higher-order impacts associated with the social amplification of risk. The ripples spread outward, first encompassing the directly affected victims or the first group to be notified, then touching the next higher institutional level (a company or an agency), and, in more extreme cases, reaching other parts of the industry or other social arenas with similar problems. This rippling of impacts is an important element of risk amplification since it suggests that the processes can extend (in risk amplification) or constrain (in risk attenuation) the temporal and geographical scale of impacts.

CLARIFICATIONS AND CRITICISMS

Before proceeding to the empirical studies, it may be useful to clarify certain issues that appear to have been confusing to readers of the original 1988 article and then to respond to the key criticisms that have emerged.

Clarifications

Several areas are in need of clarification. First, the *social amplification of risk* refers to the cultural, social, and individual structures and processes that shape the societal experience with risk. This shaping can enlarge (amplify) or reduce (attenuate) the risk burden to society. Although the various social structures and processes that interact with risks can be disaggregated for purposes of such analysis, such disaggregation severs key interactions and interdependencies, resulting in information loss and potential misinterpretation. Accordingly, the social amplification of risk concept specifically seeks a more holistic analysis of risk.

Second, *risk*, as treated in the amplification framework, is in part the threat of direct harm that happens to people and their environments regardless of their social constructs, and in part the threat associated with the social conceptions and structures that shape the nature of other harms (to people, corporations, social institutions, communities, and values). Thus, the *consequences* associated with a particular risk or risk event are (a) the direct effects that are normally treated in technical risk analysis, such as health effects, property damage, medical costs, and emergency response costs; and (b) the effects associated with the interaction of such harms with the social processing of the risk events, such as social stigmatization, group conflict, loss of sense of community, and social disruption. Although it is often argued that the former tend to be quantitative and the latter qualitative, both in fact usually require some combination of quantitative and qualitative assessment. What is considered a "harm," of course, is socially mediated and culturally determined. The nature of the risks and characteristics of the social amplification process will determine which category of consequences will pose the largest burden to society.

Third, the term *risk events*, as used in the conceptual discussion and in subsequent empirical analyses, refers to *manifestations of the risk*, the flow of discrete events that actualize the risk. Such events may relate to any stage of the causal model of hazard used by the Clark group (Kates, Hohenemser, and Kasperson 1985), that is: initiating events (e.g., mishaps); releases of energy, materials, or information; outcomes; exposure; or consequences. Such events need not be extreme but may comprise the bits of hazard incidence that we think of as continuing processes (such as soil erosion or routine release of pollutants to the atmosphere).

Fourth, what is *amplified* or *attenuated*, then, are primarily the *consequences* of the risk or risk event, and usually the *secondary or tertiary consequences*. Where heightened consequences occur, they may be either enlarged effects or entirely different types of effects. The amplification or attenuation of secondary consequences will further have, as noted above, direct implications for risk management and the tolerability of the risk. It is exactly this phenomenon that has so perplexed the U.S. Environmental Protection Agency in its *Unfinished Business* (1987) and *Reducing Risk* (1990) reports, in which it contrasts its lists of agency-gauged priorities (calculated from primary consequences) and public concerns (which embrace primary and secondary consequences associated with the social amplification of risk).

Fifth, under special circumstances, social amplification processes may increase the *probabilities* of all stages of risk (initiating events through consequences) by changing the culture or social setting in which the risk is embedded. Thus, an act of terrorism against an airline or a consumer product may, through extensive mass media coverage, spawn imitators, thereby producing risk contagion. Also, attenuation of the risk may, paradoxically, enlarge risk probabilities by eroding risk management resolve or diverting efforts to other risk domains, with heightened human and environmental harm the result.

Sixth, two primary stages of risk amplification and attenuation—information flow and behavioral responses—are posited. Of course, in any given case a highly interactive system is almost certain to prevail, with complex feedbacks and feedforwards. We have presented a number of components of such interactive systems in our more detailed model of the social amplification process (Kasperson, Renn, et al. 1988, Figure 2, 183). The nature of discourse about risk that characterizes the social processing of the risk will be important, with political competition to control language, symbols, imagery (Nelkin 1985), and definition of the risk problem.

Seventh, *behavioral response* in the framework refers to the complex actions (currently imperfectly understood) undertaken by formal organizations, social institutions, cultural and social groups, and individuals in reference to the risk. We see the sociological and individual interactions as inherently inseparable, with the particular social mechanisms that shape particular societal responses functioning in kaleidoscopic manner.

Eighth, *culture* in the framework occupies the position of a "super-variable," a critical variable that shapes characteristics of all stages, components, and processes in the framework, and even the risk or risk event itself. Indeed, much of the cultural theorizing about risk has addressed how culture fashions or affects various components of the social amplification of risk framework. Culture is likely to be particularly important in amplification and attenuation of risk events that trigger associations with dominant cultural values that shape institutional, group, and individual behavior. But as Rappaport (1988) points out, culture is not enough to explain the social processes that emerge; the various social sciences need to address individual differences and to analyze such elements as economic factors, social status, political position, ethnicity, and education.

Criticisms

Critical commentaries accompanied the 1988 article on social amplification of risk, and discussants at conferences and symposia since then have raised various issues. The primary issues raised and our response to them follow.

One concern has been that the social amplification of risk suggests, despite our clear intent, a "true" or "objective" risk and a "subjective" or "distorted" risk. We cannot agree. The *Risk Analysis* article makes painfully clear our view that risk is a composite of physically and socially induced effects. Many, perhaps even most, of the "direct" or "primary" effects are heavily dependent on social structures and processes. This is particularly true because of an oft-forgotten truism of risk analysis—that damage to people and what they value is the product of environmental or technological threat, human vulnerability to such threats, and values. These three terms, but perhaps especially the latter two, are socially and economically dependent. Thus, we concur fully with Rappaport (1988, 191) when he argues that "traditional risk analysis may not be able to provide realistic assessments (products of probability and gravity of consequences) in more than a very limited number of cases." On the other hand, not all risks are products of social constructs—people can be hurt whether or not they recognize or are concerned about the consequences. We recognize that, as with all models, the linear structure of our model carries the price of oversimplification. Over time we seek more complex ways of representing the dynamics of the interconnections and feedbacks that occur and in which we are deeply interested.

A second concern centers on the metaphor of "amplification." Arie Rip (1988, 193) argues, for example, that although we are correct and neutral in our definitions, "the focus as well as the concern is about intensification and the additional social costs accompanying 'exaggerated' responses. The aftermath of Three Mile Island is given as a paradigmatic example of social amplification, while there is no complementary example of the social costs of attenuation of risk." The latter point is fairly taken. Indeed, it is the case that the amplification concept first arose in our studies of radioactive waste siting where we sought to explain the potentially high consequences associated with relatively "minor" mishaps in the handling or disposal of radioactive materials. We quickly recognized, however, that both "attenuation" and "amplification" of consequences are possible and that "risk amplification" is a generic phenomenon. We are still uncertain whether the processes involved in amplification and attenuation will be mirror images or quite different. It is also entirely possible, we appreciate, that social processes may transform, reconfigure, or (in Arie Rip's term) "reinvent" the risk or risk event without substantially altering the magnitude of the overall consequences. Rip is also correct to point out that a lack of scrupulous evenhandedness carries the danger that some may misunderstand, or choose to misinterpret, the social amplification concept as a tool to handle "exaggerated" or "irrational" fears of the public. This is clearly not our intent, and in subsequent work we have gone to great lengths to emphasize equally risk amplification and attenuation. We also welcome current work, such as that of the sociologist Freudenburg, on organizational and social attenuation of risk (Chapter 10).

Related to the foregoing discussion is a third criticism that amplification as cast in our framework unduly emphasizes the electronic analogy. Rayner (1988a, 202) raises several concerns. He first argues that the electronic imagery is "too passive" to cope with the complexity of human behavior; that the addition of tuner, filters, and other devices is needed to capture the richness of human behavior. He also points out, and appropriately so, that how the receiver is tuned to receive signals on one frequency and not another and how it selects a particular signal subset from the total number of signals coming in are essential. We agree with these cautions. Although it is likely that most individuals are largely reactive to the continuing information flow on the myriad dangers that beset modern life, it is also apparent that some individuals and many organizations actively seek out and order risks. An important contribution of Rayner and other cultural theorists has been to clarify the selection of some risks and the avoidance of others according to social attributes of the cultural group (Rayner and Cantor 1987; Douglas and Wildavsky 1982b; Thompson, Ellis, and Wildavsky 1990; Wynne 1989c). A metaphor has its uses as long as it is not overworked. It is certainly not our intent to reduce social complexity to a particular communications theory or to a gross electronic metaphor. Again, we are taking additional care to tailor our use of the metaphor and related terminology so as to emphasize the integrative nature of the framework and the positive (but certainly limited) contributions that communications theory has to offer.

The fourth criticism concerns the degree of balance between individual and social processes in our treatment of amplification processes in the 1988

Risk Analysis article. Svenson (1988, 200) notes that future developments of the framework might benefit from "a more articulated system and social psychological approach" that would place findings "even more firmly in the societal context." "Although the concept features the term social," Arie Rip (1988, 195) argues, "the focus of the paper is on the individual. There is discussion of social alignments, of networks, of mass media, but the central mechanism is seen as the reception by an individual, its processing and further transmittance." Svenson and Rip are correct to note that we should have treated more fully the social interactions and processes that we identify, but Rip is incorrect to infer from that that we see individual behavior as more central than the behavior of institutions and social groups. Indeed, Figure 2 of the 1988 article provides equal attention to "social stations" and "individual stations" in shaping overall "group and individual responses." Since 1988, we have sought to emphasize social processes and have also added and highlighted culture as a pervasive determinant of the entire social processing of risk. Throughout we emphasize the holistic nature of risk experience and the embedment of individual behavior within social groups and contexts. We accept the need to continue to seek an appropriate balance and to emphasize the interconnections and interdependencies among various components of the framework.

Fifth, some respondents have questioned whether the framework is "testable" or whether it is capable of generating hypotheses. Because of the integrative nature of the framework, its overall "validity" cannot be tested (in the positivist sense) by empirical analysis. This limitation is shared with other broad social constructs, such as the cultural theory of risk or interpretation based in political economy. Thus, the social amplification concept must prove its usefulness by demonstrating its analytic strength and insights in interpreting social responses to risk difficult to explain by competing and often narrower approaches. If it proves to be a more powerful explanatory framework and if it sheds new insights, then it will find use. If not, it will be ignored, as it should be. We also seek a number of other desired properties for the conception: that it be parsimonious, that it be composed of clearly defined elements, that it be free of internal contradictions, and that it specify major relationships capable of falsification.

Related to this is the issue of predictive hypotheses. Steve Rayner (1988a, 201) has "difficulty envisaging what distinctive predictions could be offered by such a theory (i.e., social amplification) that are not available from the existing paradigms." It certainly is true that many of the hypotheses of interest in the social amplification construct will arise from components of the framework and existing theory in the social sciences. An integrative conceptualization, such as social amplification of risk, has three potential contributions: to bring competing theories and hypotheses out of their "terrain" and into direct conjunction (or confrontation) with each other; to provide an overall framework in which a large array of fragmented empirical findings can be located; and to generate new hypotheses, particularly hypotheses geared to the interconnections and interdependencies among particular concepts or components. We believe that the empirical studies applying the framework are demonstrating that the conception is proving quite robust in this respect (see below).

The criticisms from our peers have been extraordinarily valuable in enhancing the basic conception and prompting needed clarifications. But we have also specifically sought to develop the conception and to examine its usefulness in a number of empirical studies.

EMPIRICAL STUDIES OF RISK AMPLIFICATION AND ATTENUATION: MAJOR FINDINGS

The most ambitious of these studies has been a statistical comparative analysis of 128 hazard events. This work has included a doctoral dissertation by William Burns (1990), who has worked closely with Paul Slovic to apply LISREL causal modeling to a large data base of hazard events (see Table 6.1). In addition, the authors have also conducted field studies in which we examined social amplification processes in detail in their historical and community context. Ortwin Renn has applied the social amplification framework to problems of risk communication (Renn 1991b). Roger and Jeanne Kasperson (1991) have argued that one class of "hidden hazards" is associated with undiagnosed or underestimated socially amplified hazards. In addition, Machlis and Rosa (1990) have analyzed "desired risk" in terms of the framework. Here we briefly review what has been learned from these studies.

The 128 Hazard Events Study

Upon publication of our conceptual framework, it was apparent to the authors that an ambitious comparative study of social amplification experience should be undertaken to provide a richness of empirical investigations. Accordingly, a large data base of hazard events was created, composed of a wide variety of "events" chosen using the Clark University taxonomy of technological hazards (Hohenemser, Kasperson, and Kates 1983; Hohenemser, Kates, and Slovic 1983) and supplemented by a selection of natural hazards and radiological events. Individual hazard events were identified from the *New York Times Index*, largely over the past ten years. Table 6.1 provides an overview of the composition of the data base. Several examples of typical hazard events are as follows:

Abnormally high levels of mercury are found in eighteen of twenty-three children whose parents work at Staco Inc. Thermometer Plant in Putney, VT. These findings in the summer of 1984 resulted in the plant's being shut down.

Table 6.1
128 Hazard Events Data Base

---

*Biocidal Hazards (18)**

    Vaccines: adverse health effects (3)
    Chain saws: injury and/or death (3)
    Handguns: injury and/or death (4)
    Bacterial contaminations: morbidity and/or mortality (4)
    Pesticide use: adverse environmental effects (4)

Persistent/Delay Hazards (16)

    Mercury releases: toxic effects (3)
    Benzene releases: toxic effects (3)
    Radon emission: toxic effects (3)
    Chemical waste disposal: adverse health effects (4)
    Lead emissions: chronic health effects (3)

Rare Catastrophes (19)

    Airplane crashes: injury and/or death (3)
    Dam failures: injury and/or death (4)
    Chemical releases: toxic effects (4)
    Explosions: injury and/or death (5)
    Building collapses: injury and/or death (3)

Threats to Life ("Common Killers") (19)

    Smoking: chronic effects/death (3)
    Asbestos use: chronic effects/lung cancer (5)
    Automobile accidents: injury and/or death (3)
    Household/hotel fires: injury and/or death (5)
    Falls: injury and/or death (3)

Global Diffuse Hazards (17)

    CO emissions: climatic change (3)
    Dioxin release: toxic effects (4)
    Nuclear weapons testing/fallout: injury and/or chronic effects (3)
    Ozone depletion: chronic effects/deaths (3)
    Acid rain: environmental effects (4)

Natural Hazards (20)

    Lightning: injury and/or death (4)
    Floods: injury and/or death (4)
    Blizzards/snowstorms: injury and/or death (3)
    Drought: injury and/or death (3)
    Mud slides: injury and/or death (2)
    Earthquakes: injury and/or death (4)

Radiological Hazards (19)

---

*Number in parentheses indicates number of events for each type of hazard.

Dioxin is found in fish taken from Passaic River in New Jersey. Governor Kean orders ban on consumption of all fish and crabs taken from river.

Study by scientists from Environmental Defense Fund directly links, for the first time, changes in pollution emissions hundreds of miles away to changes in acidity of rainfall.

For each of the hazard events, four "pools" of data were collected. First, the authors searched the News file of the NEXIS data base of media reporting for information about the event and its characteristics, social group and public reaction, and even consequences, as well as for patterns of media coverage. Using these data and the results of risk assessments of such hazards, three experts in risk assessment rated all the events in terms of direct physical consequences. Psychometric procedures were used by Paul Slovic, Nancy Kraus, and William Burns at Decision Research to elicit public perceptions of the events, treating a large number of familiar individual assessments (such as familiarity, dread) but also attributes such as blame and perceived managerial incompetence not examined in previous perception studies. Individual behavioral intentions for each event were estimated through psychometric procedures. A fourth data pool consisted of estimates of the "social-group-mobilization potential" of each event provided through a Delphi process by a panel of social science experts. Finally, two large panels of citizens with special knowledge of social amplification (e.g., journalists, lawyers, etc.), using a summary of media information, independently scaled all 128 hazard events in terms of their estimated socioeconomic and political effects. Figure 6.2 shows these data pools and their placement in a hypothetical model of causal relationships. This is not the place for a detailed treatment of this complex study. For that, the reader should consult other sources (Renn, Burns, et al., forthcoming; Burns 1990; Burns et al. 1990) or the authors directly. Suffice it to note here that various statistical procedures were employed, including factor analysis, regression analysis, and covariance-structural analysis, to examine the relationships among these components.

From our various analyses of these data over the past several years, a number of tentative observations have emerged:

1. A high degree of "rationality" is apparent in how society responds to hazard events. The amount of press coverage is roughly proportional to the magnitude of direct, physical consequences; risk perception appears to incorporate extent of human exposure as well as risk management performance; and extent of exposure, media coverage, and characteristics of risk perception all appear to enter into social group and individual responses.

2. The extent of human exposure to the adverse direct consequences of a hazardous event appears to have more effect on risk perception and social group mobilization than does the magnitude of human injuries and fatalities. Should this finding stand up in further studies, it could be a significant element in explaining the disjuncture between technical and perceived risk.

3. The processing of risk events by the media, cultural and social groups, institutions, and individuals profoundly shapes the societal experience with risk and plays a crucial role in determining the overall societal impacts of particular hazard events.

4. The contention in many risk studies that public perceptions largely mirror media

Figure 6.2
Hypothetical Model of Causal Relationships

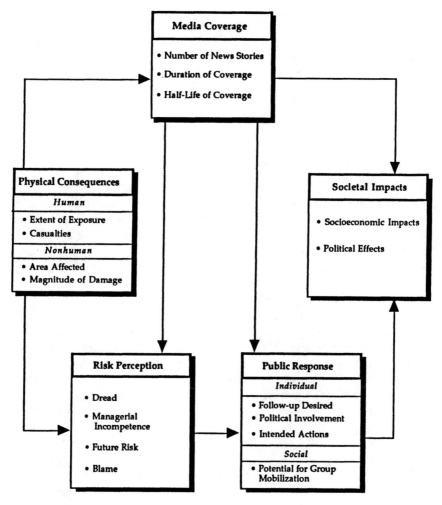

coverage needs further careful empirical confirmation. In our studies, no perception variable except dread significantly correlated with extent of media coverage once the physical consequences of the event were controlled. Generally, quantity of media coverage was a weak predictor of individual concern. Since our subjects were not actually exposed to the media coverage, however, we cannot reach any firm conclusions about this relationship. But media coverage effects on group and individual perceptions need further attention.

5. Social group mobilization appears to be highly intertwined with both media coverage and eventual social impacts of the hazard events. Heavy media reporting

appears to stimulate social mobilization, and vice versa, and that activism is a "downstream" variable in shaping eventual economic and social impacts of hazard events.

6. Finally, the role of risk signals and blame may be important contributors to social group concerns and individual responses. Certain events appear to suggest larger messages or inferences about the social meaning of the occurrence. Some events, for example, appear to suggest that managers did not really understand or were careless about the risk. Blame attributable to a corporation or governmental agency seems particularly important. This appears to be a particularly promising direction for future risk research.

Field Studies

To complement the 128-hazard-event statistical analysis, researchers undertook a number of field studies to provide an in-depth treatment of community experience with a hazard event. Four such studies were undertaken by Clark University researchers who examined social experience with a 1986 transportation accident involving low-level radioactive materials in Queens, New York, a serious 1982 nuclear plant accident in upstate (Ginna) New York, a brine seepage controversy at a planned nuclear waste facility in Carlsbad, New Mexico, and the closure of a hazardous waste site on Long Island (Glen Cove, New York). In addition, the Clark group solicited a study developed by Hans Peter Peters et al. (1987) of a construction accident at a planned nuclear waste disposal facility in Gorleben, Germany. Finally, a well-documented field study of a radioactive accident in Goiania, Brazil, by Peterson (1988) provided sufficient richness of detail to allow it to be included in this comparison. Only the four Clark field studies, however, explicitly used a common research design and procedure, although all addressed common questions.

The six cases reveal a number of interesting contrasts in seriousness and in the social processing of risk (Table 6.2). The 1986 transportation accident with low-level radioactive wastes occurred when the driver of a tractor-trailer missed a turn on the Queensborough Bridge, tried to pass under another bridge that was too low, and crashed into the underside of an elevated subway viaduct. A quick emergency response verified that none of the transported drums had been damaged, and the wastes were reloaded on a new vehicle. Nonetheless, considerable local political response resulted, including calls for federal and city investigations, city council committee hearings, and two city council resolutions.

On January 25, 1982, a leak was discovered in a pipe carrying radioactive water through a steam generator at the Ginna nuclear power plant in upstate New York. Within an hour, a tank diaphragm ruptured, and 1,700 gallons of radioactive water spilled onto the reactor floor. Plant officials declared a site emergency, the first such and most serious nuclear plant emergency

Table 6.2
Overview of Six Field Studies

	BIOPHYSICAL IMPACTS	INFORMATION FLOW	SOCIAL GROUP MOBILIZATION	SOCIOECONOMIC IMPACTS (RIPPLING EFFECTS)
QUEENS TRANSPORT ACCIDENT (1986)	Damaged truck and subway track; no radioactive release.	Mostly local media coverage; factual, accurate, reassuring.	Advocacy by local citizens against nuclear trucking; statement by Mayor Koch; City Council resolutions.	Limited emergency response costs; no broader social impacts apparent
GINNA NUCLEAR PLANT ACCIDENT (1982)	5 workers exposed, site emergency declared	Extensive local and national media coverage; locally reassuring, nationally more alarmist. Plant officials proactive in providing information.	Several local groups sponsored a protest march; national nuclear opponents came to area and made public statements.	Costs in excess of $30 million to plant, effects on industry safety systems. Little evident local concern or loss of social trust.
GLEN COVE TOXIC WASTE CONTROVERSY (1983-88)	Soil and water con-tamination on site; limited offsite contamination.	Little coverage in local media; more dramatization in N.Y. Times.	No apparent organized opposition until 1986 N.Y. Times coverage; most opposition from neighboring communities; limited local concern.	Closure of polluting plant and $3 million clean-up costs, loss of local jobs; no apparent effects on property values, some limited local worry.
GOIANIA RADIOACTIVE ACCIDENT (1987)	4 fatalities, 3-5 more expected, 64 hospitalizations, 249 suspected exposures, contamination of property and soil.	Extensive and highly alarmist media coverage, exaggeration, widespread local rumor, alarmist pronouncements by public officials.	Widespread community and local official concern, substantial political activism. Intense public concern.	Over 100,000 people tested for contamination, thousands of cases of psychogenic illness, widespread stigmatization of Goiania residents, decline in local tourism, repercussions for national nuclear program.
GORLEBEN SHAFT ACCIDENT (1987)	1 fatality, 6 injuries (3 serious).	Extensive national media coverage; more limited national coverage, little dramatization or alarm at either level but some information and inferences disputed.	Little local activism; polarized national responses conforming to pre-existing pattern in nuclear debate.	Facility project delayed, with high costs; national nuclear debate rekindled, government hearings at state and national level; little apparent local concern.
WIPP BRINE LEAK (1987-88)	No injuries, repository safety questioned.	Moderate local and regional media coverage; some national coverage, including McNeil-Lehrer, N.Y. Times, and CNN reports. Coverage factual and low-key.	Active advocacy by state-level Southwest Research and Information Center and critical scientists; little evident local concern or advocacy.	Reviews by U.S. National Academy of Sciences and General Accounting Office. WIPP opening delayed. Few apparent local or rippling effects.

since the 1979 Three Mile Island accident. Five workers were found to have been contaminated. Nonetheless, the emergency response and information dissemination were rapid, ten news conferences were held in the first day alone, and the emergency broadcast system provided rapid warning to local officials and residents. Yet the accident generated much more national attention and reaction than local community concern.

The Glen Cove case differed from the other cases in that no simple hazardous event was involved. Rather, this case involved the discovery of toxic leaks, spills, and illegal dumping that had occurred over a number of years at a local industrial plant. Eventually it was revealed that stormwaters, soils, and a local creek had been contaminated. Nonetheless, the immediate community response was restrained, tending to downplay the seriousness of the problems. Generally, local politicians were reassuring as to their efforts to control the problems.

As with Glen Cove, the leakage of brine water into the planned Nuclear Waste Isolation Pilot Plant (WIPP) near Carlsbad, New Mexico, was not a single hazard event with clear adverse consequences. Rather, the seepage of brine water into the planned repository raised concerns over the potential integrity and safety of storage of transuranic radioactive wastes at the site. Testimony presented at congressional hearings in December 1987 focused public attention on the issues. The National Academy of Sciences and the U.S. General Accounting Office both undertook reviews. In 1988, Congress postponed the opening of the facility pending the completion of further tests. Yet, again, little local community concern was apparent.

In May 1987, an accident occurred during feasibility studies of a proposed high-level radioactive waste disposal facility in Gorleben, Germany. One of the iron rings used to support the walls of a test shaft fell to the floor, one miner was killed, and two others were seriously injured. Although the accident was a "conventional" construction mishap and did not directly involve radioactive wastes, it aroused intense public and media attention. Official inquiries sought to pinpoint responsibility, and the incident rekindled the national debate over radioactive wastes and nuclear power more generally.

Finally, the most remarkable of these cases occurred in Goiania, Brazil, in 1987. Two men searching for scrap metal at a junkyard broke open a cylinder containing cesium–137 and removed 100 grams, which subsequently were widely disseminated in the city. By the end of 1987, in what emerged as a very serious nuclear accident, 249 suspected cases of contamination, 64 hospitalizations, and 4 fatalities (with another 3–5 expected over time) had been recorded. The emergency response was both delayed and highly confused. Widespread and highly alarmist media coverage led over 10 percent of the city's 1 million people to seek testing for possible contamination. The people of Goiania became stigmatized, with hotels in other parts of Brazil refusing to register Goiania residents and stonings of automobiles carrying Goiania license plates reported. Eventually, the entire Brazilian nuclear energy program was called into question as a result of the event.

These six cases reveal a number of interesting facets of the social amplification process (Table 6.2), particularly regarding information flow and processing, social group mobilization, and the nature of "rippling" effects. Kasperson, Tuler, and Himmelberger (1990) provide details of the comparative findings. Here it is possible only to summarize several of the more noteworthy results.

The amplification or attenuation of risk events through information flow is clearly complex and depends on a number of attributes of the societal processing of the events. In particular, and consistent with the results of the 128-hazard-event study, it is apparent that heavy and sustained media coverage of an event does not in itself ensure that substantial public concerns will emerge or that significant amplification of the risk through enlargement of secondary consequences will occur. Although the Goiania experience clearly documents the potentially powerful role of both the media and interpersonal flow of rumors in driving risk-related consequences, other cases point to a more complex pattern of effects. At Gorleben, for example, press reporting, though extensive at the local level, had few apparent impacts on either local public attitudes or social impacts. Similarly, the Ginna nuclear plant accident was the most extensively covered nuclear accident in the media since Three Mile Island, including front page coverage in national and local newspapers, close attention by the major television networks, and extensive local reporting. Although ripple effects were apparent at the national level, the effective emergency response by plant officials, the relatively high level of existing trust, and the active communication by plant officials with local residents were effective in blunting the creation of major adverse local impacts or loss of confidence by residents.

Indeed, the Ginna, Gorleben, Glen Cove, and WIPP cases all point to potential *layering* in social amplification of risk processes. In each of these cases, information coverage and social group mobilization produced more rippling of effects at the regional or national level than at the local level. General considerations involved in this divergence appear to be associated with scale. In the Gorleben case, the accident linked with other national or transnational events, particularly the Chernobyl accident and the Transnuclear radioactive waste scandal in Germany, to stimulate or rekindle an ongoing national debate. In the Ginna case, local community residents had generally positive prior attitudes to the nuclear plant, and the plant was an important contributor to the local tax base. At Glen Cove, a working-class community, no local groups took up the issue of toxic waste contamination, and local residents had relatively little economic stake in how the issue was resolved. At WIPP near Carlsbad, New Mexico, the brine leak controversy stimulated nuclear opponents at the state and national level, whereas the local community remained relatively unperturbed and supportive of the project. Indeed, our interviews with social group leaders at Gorleben, Ginna, and WIPP all suggested that economic benefits associated with the risky activity acted as a significant impediment to the emergence of negative responses and activism at the local level.

This scale divergence, with risk attenuation at the local level and risk amplification at higher levels, affords one additional insight. The hazardous events at Glen Cove, Queens, WIPP, and Ginna all appeared to have sufficient ingredients to produce a major local controversy that never occurred. Why? One hypothesis worth pursuing may relate to the dynamics or "take off" of the social-amplification-of-risk process. Elsewhere, Luther Gerlach (1987) has discussed the notion of "take off" in relation to social movements and the construction of risk. Our cases all had at least one of the elements—a concerned public, active media coverage, a feared risk, active opposition groups—that contribute to the social amplification of risk. Peters (personal communication) has also found in his media studies in Germany that topics become public issues only when the media report about them *and* a social group or institution takes up the subject. Can it be that individual components of social amplification processes have a "necessary but not sufficient" quality, that multiple elements of social amplification must be present if the process is to "take off" and to be sustained?

Then, too, it is apparent that two other variables may matter greatly. Preexisting levels of trust and credibility may allow risk managers to sustain an accident or event by "drawing down" the reservoir of trust that has been built up over time. Are the hazardous events that generate greatest amplification of risk primarily those that occur in contexts of distrust or low reservoirs of existing trust? Finally, it is also apparent that the effectiveness of managerial response, and particularly the emergency response and accountability during the event aftermath, are very important. Our respondents at Glen Cove, Queens, WIPP, and Ginna generally believed that the management response was timely and effective. Perhaps this is another significant ingredient in the genesis of blame, a factor we found of considerable importance in the study of 128 hazard events.

Other Related Studies

Beyond these empirical studies directly mounted to apply, test, and develop the social-amplification-of-risk framework, several other studies have utilized the framework in exploring hazard problems. The studies have treated the deliberate seeking of risk, the domain of hazards "hidden" from the public view, and the applicability of the framework to risk communication processes.

Pointing out that studies of hazards and risks have virtually overlooked a range of human activity involving the *deliberate seeking of risk* (e.g., hang gliding, rock climbing, dirt biking, etc.), the sociologists Machlis and Rosa (1990) ask whether the social amplification of risk framework can be effectively applied to this domain of "desired risk."

Evaluating key propositions in terms of current knowledge about desired risks, Machlis and Rosa reach a number of conclusions. First, they find that the social amplification concept is quite suitable for incorporating desired risk, although some terminology (e.g., "victims") may need to be recast. Second, the key variables defined in the framework are appropriate but may need to be broadened to treat such issues as benefits as part of consequences and mass culture (subsequently incorporated in the framework). Generally the application of the social amplification conception led the authors to conclude that "the framework has promise, since it generally performed well against the evidence examined" (Machlis and Rosa 1990, 167).

A recent essay (Kasperson and Kasperson 1991) examines the phenomenon of "hidden hazards." How is it, the authors query, that certain hazards pass unnoticed or are unattended by society until a serious toll is upon us? The exploration of this question treats a number of considerations directly relevant to the social amplification framework, such as the dispersed, global extent of some environmental hazards, the incidence of hazards in marginal populations, the presence of hazards hidden from view due to ideological differences, and the presence of value-threatening hazards. But one of the major types of hidden hazards, in the authors' view, is that representing the outcomes of social amplification processes.

Amplified hazards emerge as a problem in environmental and health management, the authors argue, because of the inability of existing environmental assessment methodologies to internalize such hazards. They remain "hidden" to the professional assessors until the consequences become highly visible to society, which heaps acrimonious blame on the institutions that "missed" the hazards or failed to respond in timely ways. But even improved assessment techniques, the authors argue, will run into difficulties in securing societal acceptance for its findings, for making such hazards visible threatens established regulatory and decision processes and alters the ground rules of whose values shall prevail, which impacts are legitimate, and what evidence shall count. The possible "stigma," generated by the extraordinarily negative imagery associated with the presence of a radioactive waste facility and likely to prevail in a host community, tellingly exemplifies this type of hazard. Current environmental impact methodologies and regulatory structures are unable to deal effectively with hazards involving strong technical-social interaction.

In a detailed treatment of risk communication, Renn (1991b) utilizes the social amplification framework to explore relationships among individual, social, and political responses to risk. In particular, attention is given to how the competing perspectives of individualistic (risk perception), structuralistic (cultural theory of risk, some sociological and Marxist approaches), and constructivist (social-construct theories) concepts can be brought into the integrated approach of the social amplification framework. Renn argues that this framework is a dynamic model that does not fit the traditional communication models of information transfer between sources, transmitters, and final receivers. Accordingly, he emphasizes the major amplification mechanisms that can produce changes in messages as they are socially processed through various social and individual "stations." These concepts then serve to examine eight basic hypotheses or perspectives: the media as *mirrors* of real-world occurrences, the *power hypothesis* of media coverage, the *agenda-setting hypothesis*, the *issue-creation hypothesis*, the *gate-keeping hypothesis*, the *mediating hypothesis*, the *social-construction hypothesis*, and the *symbolic-interactionist* perspective. Locating these in the social amplification framework suggests clearly, Renn argues, that the approaches have substantial overlap and can be accommodated in a broad notion of signal processing and transformation. Finally, the author applies the various components and stages of the social amplification framework to problems of risk communication.

These various empirical and conceptual studies have provided valuable applications and extensions of the initial exposition of the framework in the 1988 *Risk Analysis* article (see Table 6.3). We cannot improve on the conclusion by Machlis and Rosa that the social amplification framework, "like a net, is useful for catching the accumulated empirical findings and ...like a beacon, can point the way to disciplined inquiry" (Machlis and Rosa 1990, 164).

NEXT STEPS

Despite important follow-up studies since 1988, the social amplification of risk is still "a fledgling conceptual framework that may serve to guide ongoing efforts to develop, test, and apply such a [more fully developed] theory to a broad array of pressing risk problems" (Kasperson, Renn, et al. 1988, 180). Many different initiatives would contribute to that goal. Here we note several next steps that after more than three years of further inquiry seem most likely to produce important near-term insights.

First, there is a need for in-depth case studies in which social amplification and attenuation processes are carefully reconstructed *in their social and historical context*. Our limited case studies suggest the value of treating the breadth of amplification components and processes that shape the social experience of risk. In particular, new studies need to explore the interaction between contexts and social processing of risk and the differing types of social and individual dynamics that characterize differing human experience.

Second, cultural studies are essential. We explicitly note culture as a "super-variable" that shapes both framework components and amplification/attenuation processes. But we need greater insights derived from careful

Table 6.3
Recent Studies and Commentaries on the Social Amplification of Risk, 1987–1992

Date	Authors	Title
1987	Roger E. Kasperson, Jacque Emel, Robert Goble, Christoph Hohenemser, Jeanne X. Kasperson, and Ortwin Renn	Radioactive Wastes and the Social Amplification of Risk
1988	Roger E. Kasperson, Ortwin Renn, Paul Slovic, Halina Brown, Jacque Emel, Robert Goble, Jeanne X. Kasperson, and Samuel Ratick	The Social Amplification of Risk: A Conceptual Framework
	Roy A. Rappaport	Toward Postmodern Risk Analysis
	Arie Rip	Should Social Amplification of Risk be Counteracted?
	Ola Svenson	Mental Models of Risk, Communication, and Action: Reflections on Social Amplification of Risk
	Steve Rayner	Muddling through Metaphors to Maturity: A Commentary on Kasperson et al., The Social Amplification of Risk
1989	Roger E. Kasperson, Ortwin Renn, Paul Slovic, Jeanne X. Kasperson, and Srinivas Emani	The Social Amplification of Risk: Media and Public Response
1990	Roger E. Kasperson	Social Realities in High-Level Radioactive Waste Management and Their Policy Implications
	Gary E. Machlis and Eugene A. Rosa	Desired Risk: Broadening the Social Amplification of Risk Framework
	William Burns	Introducing Structural Models and Influence Diagrams into Risk Perception Research: Their Value for Theory Construction and Decision Making
	Roger E. Kasperson, Seth Tuler, and Jeffery Himmelberger	Field Studies of the Social Amplification of Risk
1991	Roger E. Kasperson and Jeanne X. Kasperson	Hidden Hazards
	Ortwin Renn	Risk Communication and the Social Amplification of Risk
1992	Ortwin Renn, William Burns, Jeanne X. Kasperson, Roger E. Kasperson, and Paul Slovic.	The Social Amplification of Risk: Theoretical Foundations and Empirical Applications

empirical field work of how this occurs, the differing interactions between culture and social processes, the presence of cultural prototypes in different cultures, and the types and range of effects that result. Accordingly, the need exists to examine cultural affiliations within one national culture and to determine the influence of these affiliations across different cultures.

Third, future studies need to address the sources and nature of knowledge by which society can assess the broad meaning of risk experience. Such knowledge is indispensable for an adequate conceptualization of "hazard" or "risk" and for divergences and convergences in the emergence of social meaning. These studies should provide a risk beacon into deeper questions of social organization and processes and into the nature of democracy, individual dignity, and social justice. Societal coping with threats in contexts of scientific ignorance and chaotic relationships should be part of this inquiry. Only to the extent that risk research seeks such larger ends will it prove satisfying as a domain of intellectual inquiry.

A concrete result of the first round of social-amplification-of-risk studies has been the potential importance of the notion of "risk signals." The presence of signals concerning risk and risk events, the social and individual processing of such signals, and their incorporation into social movements and agenda may provide insights quite different from those afforded by current approaches to risk. Efforts are now under way to explore the role of such signals in societal experience of risk.

Finally, the social amplification and attenuation of risk conception arose in reaction to the progressive fragmentation of knowledge, the disciplinary structuring of inquiry, and the abstraction of analytic concepts from human experience and meaning. The search for integration avowedly seeks reintegration of knowledge, inquiry, and results. To that end, studies that unabashedly seek more holistic understandings of risk are a high priority. In this sense, we do indeed seek to foster, in Rappaport's (1988, 191) terms, a postmodern risk analysis of the human world:

The human world, the world inhabited by humans, is not constituted by physical, chemical, and biological processes alone. It is also constituted culturally. As such it is not simply made of trees and rocks and water and organisms, but also furnished with and by such conceptions as truth, honor, democracy, ancestors, and gods. These conceptions figure as largely in the motives of individuals and in the ordering and governance of societies as do trees and rocks and life itself. Threats to them are not simply figments of ill-informed people who will use such understandings to resist the realistic calculations of dispassionate experts (although they may so use them). They are real. Their consideration may be beyond the scope of Kasperson et al.'s initial program but not beyond the possibilities of the postmodern risk analysis toward which they point.

NOTE

The empirical results reported in this chapter reflect collaborative research with Jeanne X. Kasperson, Ortwin Renn, and Paul Slovic. I also acknowledge, with gratitude, the support of the Nevada Nuclear Waste Project Office and the National Science Foundation. The author is solely responsible for the opinions expressed in this chapter.

CHAPTER 7

The Social Arena Concept of Risk Debates

Ortwin Renn

In Chapter 3, I reviewed the sociological and cultural perspectives on risk and discussed the strengths and the weaknesses of each framework. Whereas the rational actor approach cannot explain social situations in which incentives are not the driving forces of social action, structural approaches have difficulties in explaining the variance of individual behavior within the same structural context. The objective concepts, which focus on real consequences of action, fail to include the symbolic meanings and interpretations of events and consequently miss the variety of social constructions associated with the same "real" event. Constructivist approaches, on the other hand, are likely to be drawn into the maelstrom of total relativism with no anchor for a baseline comparison.

These observations led me to conclude in Chapter 3 that one approach alone cannot provide a thorough and valid understanding of the social experience of risk. Knowledge of physical consequences, the handling of risk information by individuals and social groups, the social and cultural meanings of risk causes and effects, as well as structural and organizational factors, shape the social experience of risk. Integrating these various perspectives is a necessary and difficult task, but it would be futile to mix them together in a soup without specifying each concept's specific contribution and creating a common network of linkages between them.

This chapter is not meant to provide such an integrative framework. Rather it illuminates one aspect of the complex risk issue that needs more theoretical grounding before it can become part of a synoptic framework. At this time, we have fairly good knowledge of the prospects and limitations of technical risk analyses; a fairly good understanding of individual risk perception; case study data about institutional management and organizational constraints; a fair amount of data from investigations into the media coverage of risk and its impacts on individual perception; interesting and often challenging essays on social constructions of risk issues; and many studies about social mobilization for political purposes. What appears to be missing, however, is a better understanding of the structural factors that shape interactions among social groups and influence the outcome of social conflicts over risk.

Social mobilization theory, a natural candidate for such an approach, addresses the questions of why individuals feel attracted to certain movements and what kind of structural conditions are likely to initiate social protest (McCarthy and Zald 1977; Walsh 1981; Klandermanns 1984). The conditions for success or failure of social movements are hardly ever discussed (McAdam, McCarthy, and Zald 1988). Neo-Marxist and critical theories tend to focus on power distribution and the inequitable sharing of resources that result from the antagonism between socially produced wealth and private ownership or management of production (Habermas 1975; Kemp 1980; Schumm 1986). This approach is inadequate to account for other important aspects of the risk debate such as evidence and value commitment. The cultural approach offers a simple and comprehensive framework for analyzing group responses, but cultural prototypes are mixed within social groups, and it is unclear how the interests and missions of groups are intertwined with their cultural affiliations (B. B. Johnson 1987). In addition, cultural theory may account for the difficulties of communication between different cultural groups, but it does not provide information that explains how these conflicts are addressed or resolved in a multicultural society.

In addition to theoretical approaches, psychologists and sociologists have used inductive empirical research to investigate social group responses to risk (for example, von Winterfeldt and Edwards 1984; Wynne 1984a; Dietz, Stern, and Rycroft 1989). These studies provide a wealth of interesting data and ideas, but do not provide a framework in which these elements are embedded.

In this chapter, I describe a possible candidate for such a theoretical framework. It is based on the political concept of arena policies (Lowi 1964, 1975; Kitschelt 1980, 1986; Hilgartner and Bosk 1988) and the basic structure of resource mobilization theory (Lipsky 1968; McCarthy and Zald 1973; Zald 1988). It is also inspired by the classic writings of Parsons (1951), Coser (1956), Easton (1965), Giddens (1985), and Gamson (1990). This modified arena theory is not an integrative framework that combines scientific, individual, social and institutional responses to risks. Its strength (and weakness) is its focus on political debates about risk issues and the behavior of each actor in such debates.

The basic claim of this theory is that social groups in a political arena try to maximize their opportunity to influence the outcome of the collective decision process by mobilizing social resources. In this respect they act according to the rational actor framework. The outcome of this struggle, however, is determined not only by individual or group actions, but also by the structural arena rules and the interaction effects among the competing groups. This theory is based on the assumption that individuals and organizations can influence the policy process only if they have sufficient resources available to pursue their goals. The political organization of an arena and the external effects of each group's action on another group's actions constitute structural constraints that make the outcome of an arena struggle often incompatible with the evidence and/or the values of any participating group.

THE BASIC STRUCTURE OF THE ARENA METAPHOR

Constitutive Elements

A social arena is a metaphor to describe the symbolic location of political actions that influence collective decisions or policies (Kitschelt 1980). Symbolic location means that arenas are neither geographical entities nor organizational systems. They describe the political actions of all social actors involved in a specific issue. Issues can be pending political decisions such as siting of facilities or increased property taxes; social problems such as crime or education; or ideas such as civil liberties, or evolution versus creationism. The arena concept attempts to explain the process of policy formulation and enforcement in a specific policy field. Its focus is on the meso-level of society rather than on the individual (micro-level) or societal behavior as a whole (macro-level). It reflects the segmentation of society into different policy systems that interact with each other but still preserve their autonomy (Hilgartner and Bosk 1988).

The arena model incorporates only those actions of individuals or social groups that are intended to influence collective decisions or policies. Somebody who merely believes in deep ecology and communicates the idea of equal rights of animals and humans to others is irrelevant in the social arena unless this person attempts to change environmental policies, reform hunting laws, or restrict current practices in agriculture and animal laboratories. Such intentional behavior is certainly not the only way that policies are affected by public input (for example, public opinion polls or media coverage may influence policy indirectly), but these external effects are conceptualized as inputs into the arena rather than as elements of the arena.

Within a policy field several arenas may exist in which actors have to be present in order to influence the policy process. Peters (1990) distinguishes among the legislative, administrative, judicial, scientific, and mass media arenas. Since these arenas are closely intertwined and share actors, I refer to them as different (theater) stages within a single arena. Stages are manifestations of the same arena within different institutional contexts, such as litigation or policy making. The number of actors and the type of public institutions involved may differ from one stage to another, but all these stages have the same functional goal of providing social input to the policy process.

That social groups in an arena intend to influence policies is the only assumption in terms of making inferences about intentions, motivations, goals, purposes, or hidden or overt motives of social actors. This assumption is very important because it provides the yardstick for evaluating social constructs that groups may use to define their cause and to pursue their goals. Under this assumption, success and failure of group activities can be measured (intersubjectively) by the amount of influence that the specific group has been able to exert on the resulting decision(s) or policies. The reasons explaining why people feel motivated to become active or why they invest time and effort to become players in the arena are not the focus of the arena concept. The study of reasons and motivations may be better served by the traditional resource mobilization theory or phenomenological approaches. To refrain from motivational analysis of the actors involved in an arena does not mean that these motivations are irrelevant for political success or failure. Within the arena theory, however, they are only of interest if they are part of the resource mobilization effort, that is, if motivations are used to generate support.

Description of the Arena Metaphor

Figure 7.1 illustrates the arena metaphor. The center stage of the arena is occupied by the principal actors, that is, those groups in society that seek to influence policies. Some groups focus on several issues at once and are hence involved in different arenas; others focus only on one issue in a single arena. Each arena is characterized by a set of rules: formal rules that are coded and monitored by a rule enforcement agency, and informal rules that are learned and developed in the process of interactions among the actors. Among the formal rules are laws, acts, and mandated procedures; among the informal rules are regulatory styles, political climate of group interactions, and role expectations. In most cases the rules are external constraints for each single actor. Formal rule changes require institutional actions; informal changes occur as a result of trial and error and may change according to whether or not rule bending is penalized. Several actors may join forces to change the rules even if they disagree on the substance of the issue.

The rule enforcement agency ensures that the actors abide by the formal rules and often coordinates the process of interaction and negotiation. In many arenas the rule enforcement agency is also the ultimate decision maker. In this case, all actors try to make their claims known to the decision makers and to convince them by arguments or through public pressure to adopt their viewpoint. In an adversarial policy style, which is typical for the United States (O'Riordan and Wynne 1987; Renn 1989b), rule enforcement agen-

Figure 7.1
Graphical Representation of the Arena Metaphor

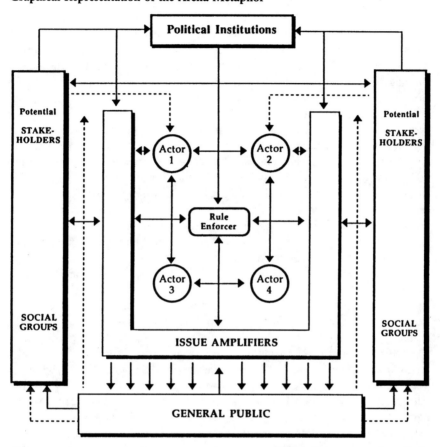

Note: Solid arrows show communication flow; dotted arrows the direction of social mobilization.

cies regard themselves more as brokers or mediators than as sovereign administrators who are consulted by various social actors, which tends to be the European policy model (Coppock 1985).

Issue amplifiers are the professional "theater critics" who observe the actions on stage, communicate with the principal actors, interpret their findings, and report them to the audience. Through this communication process they influence the allocation of resources and the effectiveness of each resource to mobilize public support within the arena. The audience consists of other social groups who may be enticed to enter the arena and individuals who process the information and may feel motivated to show their support or displeasure with one or several actors or the arena as a whole. Part of the political process is to mobilize social support by other social actors and to influence public opinion.

In contrast to traditional role theory or the theater stage metaphor (Goffman 1959; Palmlund, Chapter 8), the arena concept does not picture the actions on stage as a play with a script or actors performing role assignments. Arenas are more like medieval courtyards in which knights have fought for honor and royal recognition according to specified arena rules that determine the conditions for the fight, but leave it to the actors to choose their own strategies. Accordingly, modern arenas provide actors with the opportunity to direct their claims to the decision makers and thus to influence the policy process. Their behavior is not necessarily defined by behavioral roles and routines; actors may use innovative approaches to policy making or use traditional channels of lobbying. Arenas are regulated by norms and rules, however, which limit the range of potential options. Actors may decide to ignore some of the rules if they feel that public support will not suffer and if the rule enforcement agency is not powerful enough to impose sanctions on actors who violate the rules.

The outcome of the arena process is undetermined. On one hand, various actors may play out different strategies that interact with each other and produce synergistic effects (*game theoretical indeterminacy*). Strategic maneuvering can even result in an undesired outcome that does not reflect the stated goal of any actor and may indeed be suboptimal for all participants. On the other hand, interactions in the arena may change the arena rules (*structural indeterminacy*). Novel forms of political actions may evolve as actors experience the boundaries of tolerance for limited rule violations. Therefore, arenas often behave like indeterministic or nonlinear systems; small changes in strategies or rules are capable of producing major changes in conflict outcomes. It is also difficult to predict who is going to benefit from potential rule changes induced by trial and error. Both characteristics of arenas limit the use of arena theory for predictions, but do not compromise its value for explanation and policy analysis.

Social Resources

To be successful in a social arena, it is necessary to mobilize social resources. These resources can be used to gain the attention and support of the general public, to influence the arena rules, and to "score" in competition with the other actors. In arena theory, resources help actors to be more influential. Resources may be the ultimate goals of an actor, but more likely they are the means by which actors can accomplish their specific intentions. Whether these intentions are egoistic or altruistic, overtly stated or hidden, is irrelevant for the success of resource mobilization unless the goals themselves are used in a debate to improve one's opportunities to gain resources.

Which are the social resources that social groups need in order to be influential in society? The early functionalist school of sociology referred to social resources as "all persons or organizations, which can be of help to an individual or a social-work agency in solving problems" (Fairchild 1955, 291). As a means to mobilize resources, different functional segments of society use generalized media, that is, instruments to mobilize support (Parsons 1951; Parsons and Smelser 1956; Etzioni 1961). The medium for the economic sector is money; for the political sector, power; for the social sector, prestige; and for the cultural sector, value commitment (Parsons 1963). More recent literature suggests that these media are actually the resources that groups want to mobilize, whereas the term *media* should be confined to the currency (exchange value) within each resource type (Luhmann 1982; Münch 1982). Based on this understanding of resources, the following five resources appear to be of major relevance in describing risk arenas:

- *Money* provides incentives (or compensation) in exchange for support or at least tolerance;
- *Power* is the legally attributed right to impose a decision on others; conformity is established by the threat of punishment;
- *Social influence* produces a social commitment to find support through trust and prestige;
- *Value commitment* induces support through persuasion, solidarity, and cultural meaning; and
- *Evidence* can be used to convince persons about the likely consequences of social actions.

Table 7.1 lists these resources and describes their range of application, the medium through which they operate, and the motivator on which they are built. *Money* is most frequently used in the economic sector, but, like all other resources, it is also instrumental in other sectors such as the social system. Its medium of expression is the transfer of capital, which in turn provides incentives for other actors to show loyalty to the donor. Money usually buys compliance rather than convictions (except over long time periods).

The same is true for power. *Power* operates through coercion and requires compliance with rules and commands independent of the subjugated group's convictions or personal values. Authority and force are the two media through which power is expressed and are the bases on which power relationships are established. The motivation to comply stems from the threat of punishment, which may include physical force, although the threat alone is often sufficient to produce conformity without formal sanctions being imposed. It should be noted that I use the term *power* in the classical Weberian sense, rather than in the modern system-analytic concept of power

Table 7.1
Social Resources: Sectors, Media, and Motivators

Resources	Dominant Sector	Generalized Medium	Motivator
Money	Economy	Transfer of Capital	Economic Incentives
Power	Politics	Force	Punishment
		Authority	Compliance
Social Influence	Social System	Reputation	Trust
		Reward	Prestige
Value Committment	Culture	Persuasion	Solidarity
		Meaning	Cultural Unity
Evidence	Sciences	Methodology	Expected Impacts
		Rhetoric	

as "any type of influence to make others comply with one's intentions" (Coser 1956) or as "exclusive possession of information" (Münch 1982). Otherwise, power is difficult to distinguish from social influence or value commitment.

Social influence is a resource that operates through the media of reputation and social reward. Reputation generates trust in the specific actor even if the meanings of the actions are not understood by others. For example, asking Nobel Prize laureates to defend nuclear power or asking prominent actors to endorse toxics legislation does not mean that people are convinced that nuclear power is beneficial for them or that a new initiative restricting chemical use is desirable. People believe these actors because they are convinced of their sincerity, accept them as role models, or identify them as experts on this issue. The second medium, social rewards, constitutes symbolic reinforcements of behavior and generates social prestige. By analogy with money, social rewards can increase conformity and evoke support. Social influence is not based on shared values or meaning with respect to the issue in question, but on socially accepted incentives for assigning credibility to others and receiving social status through others.

Value commitment is a cultural phenomenon of finding meaning and sense in the behavior of social actors and society as a whole. The two dominant media of expression are persuasion and meaning. If social actors are able to persuade other actors that their behavior is in accordance with their commonly shared values, interests, and worldviews, they can count on the solidarity based on this communality. Shared meaning conveys a sense of purpose in life and creates a cultural unity that also extends into solidarity and a feeling of community. Value commitment has become one of the most powerful organizing principles in political debates as societal pluralism provides opportunities for individuals to be selective in choosing worldviews and to change alliances if this is deemed appropriate.

Evidence, the last resource, is not identical with truth. Truth is an ideal that has validity for all people at all times, whereas evidence is the claim of truth that social groups or special subsystems of society (in particular science) make based on methodological rules and accepted theoretical knowledge. Evidence is not divorced from the truth, however, as social constructivists and literary deconstructionists would like us to believe. Evidence is continuously being tested against reality. If reality shows that the evidence does not match the collective experience of reality, new knowledge is required and new evidence is sought in order to match knowledge and collective experience. Illusions, psychological and cultural denial, and reinterpretation of observations can obscure or color the experience of reality, but in a society in which pluralistic claims are permanently challenged by counterclaims and in which specialized subsystems are paid to "falsify" wrong evidence, illusions cannot be sustained forever. Unless reality is seen as the ultimate illusion (a philosophy of solipsism), it operates as a powerful yardstick to shape and redirect evidence. For example, if a group claims that a particular hazard is actually benign, repetitive occurrences of accidents with negative consequences will finally trigger a revision of this claim and may evoke a substantial loss of social influence for this specific group. Evidence is not arbitrary in spite of the fact that it is relative and pluralistic (cf. the model of graduated rationality in Renn 1981).

Evidence in the arena concept serves as a powerful social resource to convince people that the expected factual impacts of one group's claims are in their best interest, whereas the potential impacts of the competing groups' claims are not. Policy options are empirically testable. Supporting evidence can be based on past experience, logical reasoning, empirical tests, theoretical plausibility, or a combination thereof. The claim to provide the truth is supported by adhering to methodological rules of inquiry or rhetorical rules of argumentation.

In modern democratic and pluralistic societies actors need more than one resource to be successful in an arena. Neither money nor power is sufficient to shape policies. The exclusive focus on these two resources has blinded Marxist theorists to the power of persuasion and cultural meaning. At the same time, however, the exclusive focus on social influence and value commitment, as often exercised by cultural theorists, has underestimated the relevance of structural factors on the experience of reality and the shaping of policies. All actors, including the rule enforcement agency, need a minimal reservoir of each resource in order to be successful in a given arena.

The rule enforcement agency is a particularly interesting example. It may sound paradoxical, but the formal power of decision making is not sufficient to make decisions in modern democratic countries (Gale 1986). As many cases have demonstrated, citizen protests have successfully blocked the siting of unwanted facilities, although the responsible agencies had the power to override such opposition. If the agency has no resource other than power (or money), that is, if it cannot demonstrate that the impacts are benign, that the operation of a facility is in the interest of or consistent with the values of the community, or that the facility may increase the social status of this community, then the project will fail. If situations arise in which rule enforcement agencies have nothing but power, they are more willing to share this power in exchange for other resources, such as evidence or value commitment. This is probably the most powerful motivation for rule enforcement agencies to initiate citizen participation projects.

The need to collect all five types of resources creates an exchange market for resources via the generalized media of expression. Social actors with lots of money try to purchase social influence by paying highly reputable persons to join their cause. Groups that offer meaning and values use these resources for fund raising. High-prestige groups may use rewards to honor charismatic leaders, who in turn will provide value commitments. Other groups may use their power or money to hire experts in exchange for receiving evidence. Resources are partially convertible, and it depends on the context and the availability of other resources whether one resource can be exchanged for another. The exchange of resources is not a zero-sum game; they *can* be generated without subtracting resources from other groups. The generation and distribution of resources may result, however, in inflationary or deflationary developments (Parsons and Shils 1951). Too many medals, for example, diminish the social value of each medal.

Another limitation of resource exchange is the problem of legitimizing the use of resources outside their dominant application. The extensive use of one resource (such as money) outside its "home sector" is likely to come at a cost to the existing reservoir of other resources. For example, the use of money for compensation may lead to a decline in social influence and value commitment because the transaction is perceived as bribery. Similarly, the appeal to common values and convictions may be seen as a signal of weakness in the economic market, and potential investors may be more cautious to supply the respective actor with money. Gaining resources in an arena is a balancing act in which the need to exchange resources has to be weighed against the probability of losing both the resources one is willing to sacrifice and the resources one hopes to gain.

Another strategy to gain additional resources is to use one's influence in other established arenas to generate resources and to transfer them to a novel arena. At the same time, groups may enter an arena only for the sake of receiving resources that they can use for another political issue. Although arenas in modern societies tend to be structurally segmented and autonomous, the success of resource mobilization tends to depend on the perception of overall performance in several arenas. A company that wants to sell its products may enter an environmental arena in order to gain social reputation and value commitment even though the issue of this arena is of low interest to its managers. Actors also like to use "hot" issues to piggyback their own claims to the targeted audience. This is one way to gain attention and social recognition. This strategic behavior of groups is one of the reasons that arena theory makes no assumptions about the substantive goals of the actors, but limits itself to the resources that actors try to mobilize as a means to influence the policy outcomes.

Conflict Resolution in a Political Arena

Social actors will enter a risk arena if they expect that doing so will provide them with an opportunity to gain enough resources to influence the policy process (Kitschelt 1986). Beyond their reservoir of current resources, social actors can generate more resources by exchanging one resource for another and by communicating to other actors and issue amplifiers. The objective of communication is to receive public support and to mobilize other groups for one's own cause. The more resources a group can mobilize in an arena, the more likely it will succeed in pushing its interests or goals through the conflict resolution process and getting its point of view incorporated in the final decision.

At the beginning of a conflict, social resources are not equally distributed among the actors and potential actors. Since resource mobilization is not a zero-sum game, the outcome of a mobilization campaign is open and not necessarily linked with the performance of other principal actors. Conflicts are resolved either if one of the actors is powerful enough to dominate the policy outcome (this could be the legitimate decision makers, but it could also be one of the other actors) or if all relevant actors feel that their cause is better served by pursuing a compromise solution. A conflict remains unresolved if none of the actors is able to dominate the process and at the same time one or more relevant actors are convinced that they can generate or sustain more social resources by avoiding a compromise solution.

In the process of the conflict, actors communicate with each other, the rule enforcement agency, other potential actors, and the issue amplifiers. This communication serves the purpose of defining the stakes of each actor in the arena and of gaining or exchanging resources. Two feedback mechanisms are crucial for the resource mobilization purpose. First, communication may entice other groups to join or at least support the claim of one of the actors. Second, public opinion is revealed through opinion polls and other relevant public behavior. Both inputs into the arena, the mobilization of organized support and the assurance of public sympathy, help the actors increase their reservoirs of social resources (see Figure 7.1).

If all groups have a sufficient reservoir of resources, they may also opt to initiate a constructive discourse in which all participating groups can bring in their own interests and values, but orient their efforts to facilitate common understanding and to explore the range of shared interests. The personal capacity for empathy and the capability of social actors to envision the "common good" are two of the most powerful drivers for reaching agreements beyond the utilitarian approach of balancing individual interests (through mutual giving and taking and compensation). This idea of a rational and fair discourse depends on many conditions, one of which is the procurement of sufficient resources for each participating group (see Habermas 1984–87; Renn 1992, for more details). Arena theory is not only an explanatory tool for improving our understanding of risk debates, it can also be used as a normative instrument for designing discourses that help to resolve conflicts in a fair and competent manner.

APPLICATION OF ARENA THEORY TO RISK

The Mobilization Potential of the Risk Issue

Risk arenas operate under structural rules and constraints like any other arena. Risk debates focus on two issues: What is an acceptable level of risk, and how are risks and benefits distributed in society? All social groups that feel that their interests or values are affected by a specific risk source may be compelled to enter the arena. Success in the risk arena relies on the social actors' ability to mobilize resources. Beyond these communalities that risk arenas share with all other arenas, there are some specific characteristics of risk arenas that are worth mentioning.

The evidence trap. Finding a viable compromise in conflicts requires an agreement on evidence. If each group provides conflicting evidence about factual impacts, it is hard to reach a consensus. The less maneuverability groups have in making factual claims without being "falsified," the more likely it is that they will reach similar conclusions in terms of evidence. This increases the value of evidence for social mobilization. In risk issues, this normalizing effect of evidence-through-reality checks is less powerful than in other arenas, because the stochastic nature of the potential consequences (uncertainty) does not allow any inference with respect to a single facility or event. Consequently, there are competing and rationally defendable strategies for coping with risk, such as using the expected value as an orientation for risk acceptability or taking the minimax approach (minimize your maximum regret). Choosing one strategy over another obviously makes a major difference in the evaluation of risks. Furthermore, the time horizon for falsifying claims about risks is longer (in theory infinite) than any decision maker can wait. Any highly improbable event can occur today or tomorrow. Its early occurrence does not necessarily invalidate its assessment as a low-

probability event. Single events cannot be predicted by probability statements. As a consequence, social actors have a wide range of evidence options
that cannot be falsified at face value. They do not risk losing credibility by
using "self-serving" evidence to substantiate their claims. The broad range
of acceptable evidence not only makes it difficult for all groups to reach a
compromise, it also promotes inflationary tendencies for the effectiveness
of evidence. Although all groups provide reams of evidence, the value of
evidence as a resource declines in relation to the other resources. For example, the more the U.S. Environmental Protection Agency (EPA) uses scientific advisory councils or buys expertise, the less resource mobilization
potential it gains for each unit of evidence. The law of diminishing returns
is also true for social resources.

The symbolic nature of risk issues for distributional conflicts. Risk arenas
attract social groups that demand legitimation of existing distributional
practices. The risk as such may not be the trigger for entering the stage but
rather its symbolic meaning for decision-making processes in society and
for existing power structures. Such groups use the risk arena to mobilize
social resources to influence policies in other arenas. They may oppose big
business or favor deregulation. Regardless of their motives or goals, actors
in risk arenas are not always interested in the risk issue per se, especially if
it has become a symbol for other issues. The best example of such sym-
bolization is the struggle over nuclear power. Groups in this arena are not
only concerned about risks of nuclear power, but view the debate over
nuclear power as a surrogate for larger policy questions about desired lifestyles, political structure (e.g., centralization vs. decentralization), and institutional power (R. C. Mitchell 1980; Freudenburg and Baxter 1985;
Rosa, Machlis, and Keating 1988). Fighting against nuclear power gives the
protagonists social resources they need to fight their "real" battle. In highly
symbolized arenas, evidence about actual impacts is almost meaningless for
the actors, but is still a desired resource to mobilize support.

Social desirability. The tendency to use a risk arena for other purposes
is also reinforced by the saliency of the risk issue for the audience. Affluent
societies show strong concerns for health, safety, and environment (Dunlap
1989). Mobilization strategies that build on common concerns can be very
effective in generating value commitment and social influence. "Hot" risk
issues are therefore excellent vehicles on which to piggyback one's own
claims.

Structural weakness of risk management agencies. Risk management
agencies face the dilemma of dealing with ambiguities and thus often do
not succeed in exchanging power for other desired resources. In particular,
they have difficulties exchanging evidence from institutional sources for
trust, since the evidence is so often contested. As a result, they are unable
to mobilize social resources beyond their power reservoir. Because of the
weak position of the rule enforcement agencies, risk arenas tend to expe-

rience more rule innovations than other arenas where strong enforcement agencies are present. At the same time, agencies in risk arenas have less influence in resolving conflicts and persuading the actors to participate in negotiations.

The experience of confusion and distrust. Most people are confused about the competing claims of evidence by different social groups. In order to cope with this confusion, they have developed several strategies. In general, they tend to amplify the risks of collective risk sources ("better safe than sorry") and to attenuate the risks of individualized risk sources ("Why change? Even the experts can't agree on the risk"). Examples of collective risk sources are centralized technologies or chemicals in drinking water; examples of individualized risk sources are obesity, indoor radon, and other lifestyle factors (Renn 1990). Furthermore, the spectators of risk debates experience frustration and anger over the inability of the social actors to provide unambiguous evidence. As they lack immediate experience to judge the seriousness of modern risks, they tend to moralize the issue, a common resolution of factual confusion (Scheuch 1986). Moralization is a mechanism that allows spectators to form attitudes or opinions about an issue even if the beliefs about the factual outcomes indicate uncertainty or ambiguity. Moralization polarizes positions on risk policies. One position assumes that all risks are morally unjustified as long as they are capable of killing a single individual ("no compromise"); the opposite position claims that risks are inevitable side products of the desired and morally justified progress of society ("no free lunch"). Which of the two sides the spectators take may indeed be a function of cultural preferences (Douglas and Wildavsky 1982b). Social actors in risk arenas use moralization and polarization because both processes provide them with value commitment and social prestige.

Political paralysis. The plurality of evidence, the weak role of rule enforcement agencies, the tendency of the risk debate to attract symbolic connotations, and the public responses of moralization and polarization have all contributed to political paralysis: None of the actors is able to mobilize sufficient resources to force others to accept their viewpoint or to invest in a compromise. Evidence is contested, so that it cannot play a more integrative role in forging compromises; value commitment is polarized; social prestige is distributed among various adversarial camps; money experiences problems of legitimation in the risk arena; and power is insufficient. Sometimes power can triumph if the issue cools off over time and the actors become disenchanted with the issue or less vigilant. Many risk arenas, however, end in political paralysis. Some groups may benefit from paralysis, but in many cases all groups fail to reach their desired goals.

In arenas with highly ambiguous evidence presented by different actors, weak rule enforcement agencies, and a lack of immediate personal experience about the potential consequences of political decisions, the generation and distribution of resources relies almost entirely on the success of communication efforts (Gale 1986). Social prestige and value commitment become powerful resources because evidence is inflated and power or money are insufficient to dominate the debate. The recent emphasis on risk communication as a means to generate trust and commitment is a clear indicator of this situation (Plough and Krimsky 1987).

Arena Theory as a Tool to Investigate Risk Conflicts

Arena theory is not a new theory. It has been proposed by several scholars (Lowi 1964; Kitschelt 1980; Hilgartner and Bosk 1988) and has been endorsed by others for providing a particularly rewarding framework for the analysis of risk and environmental policies (Tierney 1989; Rucht 1990). So far, however, the theoretical foundations of arena theory have been scattered over the literature, and its application to risk and environment has been no more than cursory. It is my conviction that arena theory provides an excellent conceptual and sequential framework for conducting sociological research for explaining risk conflicts. In an idealized format, such a research project could be organized in the following way:

- Selection of an arena (or a stage within an arena);
- Identification of major actors and their *stated* objectives (through interviews, value trees, etc.);
- Identification of the formal and informal arena rules (through document study, interviews, etc.);
- Search for clues about the availability of resources to each actor (financial situation, legal authority, social status, cultural affiliations, and access to scientists or science institutions);
- Analysis of the role, position, and strength of the rule enforcing agencies (legal power, image, trust, etc.);
- Analysis of the communications patterns between the actors, issue multipliers, spectators, and the general public;
- Design of a model capable of explaining actors' behavior and conflict outcomes as a function of resource availability and mobilization potential; and
- Transfer of model to other risk arenas or political arenas in general.

The social arena theory can be used as a structural tool to conduct exploratory studies or as a modeling tool to interpret and structure empirical data. One of the many challenges of using this theory is quantification of the resource reservoir and of the mobilization potential. Money and legal power can be measured at least on an ordinal scale, whereas value commitment, social influence, and evidence are difficult to quantify. It may also prove difficult to measure the dependent variable: influence on policies. Competing theories, however, have nothing better to offer. They either are fixated on easily measurable variables or use anecdotal evidence for their claims. I believe that arena theory has the potential to become a theoretical concept that can be operationalized for empirical research, but it will need further conceptual and instrumental specification.

In terms of a normative theory for risk policies, the arena concept can provide a framework for organizing discourses on risk or structuring conflict resolution procedures. Furthermore, it provides an analysis of constraints and problems any risk policy maker is likely to face in the respective arena. If actors in an arena can win only by mobilizing resources, they will not engage in an organized discourse unless they are convinced that this route will help them to add resources to their reservoir. Although resource mobilization is not a strict zero-sum game, actors are aware that not every participant can win in a discourse. For this reason, they will cautiously evaluate their opportunities and risks and then decide whether to participate or stay outside. Actors with lots of available resources are particularly reluctant to get involved in a discourse in which their equal footing with all other parties would erode their position of strength. Arena theory helps policy makers gauge the responses they can expect and the problems they are likely to face.

CONCLUSIONS

Arena theory is capable of explaining social group responses to risk issues and of interpreting institutional and political actions directed toward risk reduction and risk management. What are the advantages and problems with this approach compared with other competing approaches?

First, arena theory explains the obvious observation that risk conflicts may not be about risks at all but about symbolic issues associated with risk debates. Many analyses of risk debates focus on the perception of risks of the various actors without acknowledging the social, political, or cultural context in which the risk debate takes place (Otway and von Winterfeldt 1982). The arena metaphor focuses on both the structural rules of the arena and the perceptions of the actors.

Second, arena theory tries to encompass all those social factors that researchers have identified as influential for the social experience of risk. Among them are the symbolic and moral content of issues, the possibility of using risk as a surrogate for other issues, the influence of the media and social networks, the importance of interests, values, and cultural affiliations, the structure and style of the political regulatory system, and the dynamics of social interactions among the major participants. The breadth of influential factors notwithstanding, the theory suggests a clear focus and structure. Its emphasis is on social resources and their impacts on policies. This focus makes the theory valuable for designing research projects and for selecting relevant phenomena for analysis.

Third, arena theory makes no inference about the actors' intentions or motivations. It focuses on their ability to mobilize resources. Conflicts in an arena are certainly grounded in differences in goals, values, and interests. Whether social research can measure them objectively or reveal them beyond speculation about true motives is still an open question. There is no need to provide a final answer to this question, however, if the focus is only on the means by which actors can influence the process. If these means include the overt statement of goals (which may often be the case, especially for value commitments), then they become part of the general strategy and thus an incentive for generating resources. Making resources the focus of research avoids the structural imperialism of Marxist approaches ("we know the real interests of the actors") and the relativism of the social constructivist, who would insist that only empathy with each group can help us reveal their real motives.

Fourth, by avoiding the question of motivation, arena theory does not imply a rational actor approach (in choosing ends or means), nor does it assume that groups want to maximize their interest, nor does it prestructure a group profile, as does the cultural theory of risk. Whatever the goals of the actors are, they can only accomplish them by mobilizing resources. Availability of resources provides the bargaining power to influence the outcome of the policy process.

Fifth, arena theory avoids the relativism or solipsism of the social construction theories and at the same time the structural determinism of neo-Marxist theories and many applications of critical theory. It provides an intersubjective anchor for determining success in a political arena. The fundamental axiom is that resource availability determines the degree of influence for shaping policies. If this axiom is correct, social arena theory provides an elegant and powerful instrument for the analysis of social issues in general and risks in particular.

No theoretical framework is without limitations, however, The social arena concept leaves the impression of politics as a game in which players want to win and spectators want to be entertained. Although some political debates support this impression, others certainly do not. Many debates are characterized by a good faith effort of all actors to improve a situation or to resolve a conflict. The emphasis on social resources may obscure the fact that not all political actions are strategic and that people often mean what they say. In addition, the division between actors and spectators seems to support a concept of democracy in which elites fight for power and influence and the masses are used as instruments for these elites to gain relative advantages.

I do not share this impression. I strongly believe that the arena concept can account for honest and altruistic actors and an aware and attentive public. As in modern theater, the audience may participate in the play if they so wish. The exclusion of motivations from arena theory is not premised on the assumption that people lie all the time, but by the observation that motivations do not count as a mobilization resource unless they are strategically linked with one of the five generic social resources. Nonetheless, the arena metaphor does lend itself to a cynical interpretation of the political process. As with most metaphors, there are limits beyond which the analogies become counterproductive.

Another problem with arena theory is its empirical operationalization. Since resources include economic, social, political, cultural, and scientific aspects, almost any social behavior can be interpreted as a resource mobilization effort, and any policy outcome can be interpreted as a product of these prior mobilization efforts. If this is true, the theory may still be good as an explanatory framework or a guide for data selection, but it cannot be tested empirically. Thus we do not speak about the theory as true or testable, but rather as functional. Although this is a serious problem, I believe that attempts to quantify the resources and link them to policy outcomes will show that arena theory provides nontrivial relationships between resource mobilization and policies. If the five resources can be operationalized so that they do not include all behaviors that groups demonstrate, the theory can be tested and potentially falsified.

As indicated earlier, social arena theory may produce only weak predictions of arena outcomes because the structural rules of arenas change and synergistic effects of interactions are difficult to anticipate. The theory may advance our knowledge, however, about present arenas and the actors within each arena. This knowledge can also help to restructure arenas or to assist the actors in the arena to overcome stalemates and to reach a viable compromise.

Finally, arena theory is limited to the social processing of risk issues in political debates. It does not include individual perceptions or the motivations of individuals or groups to join a specific arena. Furthermore, it is based on a pluralistic and democratic policy style that is prevalent in the United States and many European countries, but is certainly not a universal style throughout the world. Arena theory does not pretend to be an integrative approach to include all relevant risk experience. It is rather a specialized framework for studying group responses to risk and to explain the dynamics of social conflicts within a special political system.

_____

CHAPTER 8

Social Drama and Risk Evaluation

Ingar Palmlund

Theater forms a central part of life in my country, Sweden, in a way that I have not encountered in the United States. In Stockholm, with its 1 million inhabitants, there are over 120 theaters and theater groups. The importance of theater in Swedish culture is profound. It is, therefore, not surprising that a theater review of Henrik Ibsen's *A Doll's House* was my first publication.

Academic studies in Romance languages, economics, statistics, law, and political science brought me into the Swedish civil service. There I was trained in "computerese" and began my professional life as a systems analyst and manager. At the same time, in another segment of my life, I was raising my two children and learning about love and grief.

During the 1970s, as a civil servant, I dealt much with risks to human health and the environment. For several years, I was Executive Director of the Swedish Council of Environmental Information and later Deputy Director General of the Swedish Agency for Administrative Development. In those posts, I had many international assignments regarding environmental management. I also led three governmental committees investigating governmental policies for improving occupational health and safety. One of them specifically dealt with information about risks in the workplace. These experiences as policy maker and administrator eventually caused me to return to the academic world to explore what really happens when societies evaluate risks to health and the environment.

My theory of drama in societal risk evaluation draws upon the works of many social philosophers. Reading Aristotle, Victor Turner, Murray Edelman, and Kenneth Burke deepened my understanding of drama and symbolic action in social and political life; they provided me with a vocabulary and a conceptual framework. From Bertrand Russell, Ludwig Wittgenstein, Karl Popper, and Thomas Kuhn I learned that scientific statements are nets cast to catch what we call reality and that the catch may differ depending on how the net is cast; I also learned that the essence of scientific work is doubt, not confirmation. By reading Michel Foucault and Pierre Bourdieu I saw that social interaction and dominance may define reality more than we admit. But I have also humbly learned from authors whom we honor by using only one name: Shakespeare, Racine, Molière, Chekhov, Strindberg, Ibsen, Brecht, Ionesco, and Beckett. Mary Douglas and Aaron Wildavsky's book *Risk and Culture* (1982b) showed me a direction. A book by Robin Erica Wagner-Pacifici, *The Moro Morality Play: Terrorism as Social Drama* (1986), and wise friends in Sweden and at Clark University in New England gave me courage to braid rational thinking and emotional understanding in the social dramatism over risk.

The understanding that social drama may be a pattern in societies' risk evaluation emerged out of my empirical research in the United States and Sweden—a comparative study of politics in the two countries over risks associated with a certain type of pharmaceuticals. Although the flow of scientific information and policy discussions between the two nations was extensive, there were obvious differences, both in the public awareness of risk and in the nature and timing of the political responses. The natural question then arose: Why the difference?

In my search for measuring rods to compare the two countries' politics in this risk issue, I found theories in the risk analysis field singularly lacking in explanatory power. The commonplace explanations of differences in U.S. and Swedish policy-making style did not sufficiently address the fundamental distinctions between the two societies. The notion of using theater as the common denominator and measuring rod came to me out of the foreign policy field. If nations of the world are viewed as theaters, in which nuclear arms can be positioned or politicians can act, why should they not be regarded as theaters in other respects as well?

INTRODUCTION: RISK AS SOCIAL INTERACTION

Anyone interested in process in the natural world would be greatly rewarded by a study of theatre conditions. His discoveries would be far more applicable to general society than the study of bees and ants. (Brook 1988, 111)

When society deals with risks, whether of aggression, natural hazards, or a controversial technology, it is engaged in a political process. The politics concern allocation both of tangible benefits and costs and of symbolic assets and liabilities. Often at stake are human life and health and the quality of life. Also at stake seem to be tangible economic values in the form of property, markets, and business opportunities. Ultimately at stake is control of reality and trust in the elites elected to handle difficult decisions regarding the commonweal.

I have some discomfort with the tradition that is evolving in risk studies: that risks to human health and the environment can be defined by quantitative estimates and priced as commodities. There is also an emphasis on risk as a management issue, with risk communication as the preferred tool to manage opinions so that they do not get in the way of the dominant modes of technological development.

I believe that a different vision of risk is needed, one that emphasizes the role of social interaction, emotions, and power in public life. Risk must also be understood as essential uncertainty. The social interaction over risk has strong roots in existential anxiety and in the needs we have to exert control over the unknown and uncontrolled. In this interaction it is possible to discern patterns that are continually created and recreated through emotional and intellectual experience.

Societal evaluation of risk must be seen as a contest, where the participants offer competing views of reality. They compete to define what should be viewed as the benefits and the risks of prevailing production practices. If truth rests in the eye of the beholder, there are, by definition, many claims for truth in a pluralist society. The contest is a social process, colored by emotions, created by the action of several participants, some of whom have conflicting interests in the outcome. It contains blaming games and games of celebration. All the participants position themselves in response to concerns that matter to them, emotionally or economically, in order to convince an audience. I plan to show that these contesting players are essentially acting out a social process before an audience. I call this process "social dramaturgy." It is useful to view it as such in order to understand what actually takes place when societies evaluate technological risk.

I shall draw on a body of theory from philosophy, literary criticism, semiotics, sociology, and anthropology in order to develop categories that may be useful in the analytical studies of decisions on technological risk. The separation between actors and audience, a classification of the roles in the process, and genres of performance are the major analytical categories I propose. I call this a theory of social drama.

TOWARD A THEORY OF SOCIAL DRAMA AND RISK

Let us view the "real" social world as a spectacle offered to an observer, in the form of a performance with risk controversies enacted center stage. Such objectification leads the observer to a scrutiny of social interactions as symbolic exchanges (Bourdieu 1990, 52). It also forces us to understand decisions about the acceptability of risk as socially chosen agreements with some ingredients from science but mostly as reflections of the prevailing patterns of social power and dominance. In order to study risk evaluation in this way we need a vocabulary, a set of categories for sorting relevant phenomena, and a conceptual framework that can be used for analytical purposes. In this theoretical exploration, I shall be drawing an analogy between classical drama and the political response to risk events. This analogy offers a set of concepts—audience, roles and agents, the shape of the dramatic process, the characteristics of the plot, and the choice of genre—that help us examine these events.

The major concepts in the world of drama—performance, theater, stage, setting, roles, actors, scenario, script, crisis, catharsis, audience—have become part of the language commonly used in analysis and discussion of political events and processes. The use of social drama as metaphor and as paradigm is particularly fertile in an age when the mass media instantly bring political initiatives and confrontations directly into our living rooms. On a daily basis, the audience is offered close-up views of the main protagonists on a social stage. The protagonists, in turn, plan their activities with an eye to enlisting the media to give space and volume to their performances. Appearances in front of television cameras and the releasing of messages via the press have become inescapable ingredients in political maneuvering. Participation and recognition in the public dialogue across the media legitimate the protagonists as participants in the political games presented to the public and heighten the significance of their policies and actions.

Social controversies over technological risk have their roots in fear of death and in fear of losing control over reality. Concealed beneath discourses about hazards and possible loss of health, life, and economic prosperity are flows of emotions and a groping for the power to define—and thereby control—reality. The discussants repeatedly deal with death and disease to present competing visions of the future. Morbidity and mortality figures are not only offered in the abstract bodycounts of risk estimates, but are in many situations also reflected by a real loss of health, life, and property. Those who bear risk in these controversies are victims, sacrificed in the name of technological progress. And, as in ancient rituals, the sacrifice has a particularly strong emotional appeal when the victims are children or young women of childbearing age. Social controversies, where victims can be identified, resonate with an underlying, ancient theme: human sacrifice in order to ensure the good life for social elites. Thus, not only do these controversies manifest the constituent element of tragedy (loss, grief, and moral responsibility); in their content they can also be traced to the dramatic elements of sacrificial ritual.

In addition to fear of death, social controversies about risk have other characteristics in common with classical drama, and tragedy in particular. In form, the tragedy has a limited number of actors, who take leading parts in a dialogue, and a chorus, which comments on and interprets the action. The action is serious. Language is important. A tragedy has incidents arousing pity and fear, which may induce a catharsis in the audience. The action involves agents who have distinctive qualities both of character and thought.

The classical theory of drama as a form of universal representation of historical events was formulated by Aristotle. Since then, humanist and literary theorists have built a considerable body of knowledge regarding the social uses and importance of theater and drama. Contemporary social scientists (including Joseph Gusfield, Murray Edelman, Victor Turner, Clifford Geertz, Erving Goffman and Robin Erica Wagner-Pacifici) have added to the development of a theory concerning the function of drama in society. In studies of social controversies over technological risk, Helga Nowotny (1979) is one of the few writers who has used a social drama paradigm to interpret her findings.

The Audience

Social decisions about risk are always taken with an eye to one or more audiences. Without an audience, no decision on acceptable risk would be taken. There are specific audiences, constituencies, or target groups, for whom the "stage actors" perform as their agents. There is also the large, heterogeneous audience referred to as the general public.

In the social dramas over risk, some agents call for action on the stage; others make efforts to keep the audience quiescent. Many of the decisions taken aim at pleasing and appeasing audiences. Legislative and regulatory records are full of evidence that decisions to intervene in the free market and define levels of acceptable risk result from political pressures. Political leaders and administrators in governmental bureaucracies speak and act as reflections of a series of situations or confrontations.

In conflicts about risk, one audience consists of the groups that are threatened and the people who speak and act politically on their behalf. Fear and compassion for victims can be discerned as two major driving forces in legislative and regulatory decisions on risk. If it becomes known that there are victims—especially suffering children and women of childbearing age—the risk issue carries a deep emotional appeal with roots in survival instincts.

Another audience is the group that produces and uses the technology: the producers of the controversial technology and the professional groups that base their living on the existence, dissemination, and further development of the technology. The definition, by professional groups, of consumer and client needs that should be met by applying technology—the more advanced the better—is a strong driving force promoting the existing and future use of a particular technology (Illich et al. 1977). Much social interaction deals with the celebration of a technology or a set of products in a competition, where a critique of the underlying assumptions, the *doxa*, about the need for the technology or the products would be an act of self-destruction (Bourdieu 1984, 244–256, 466–475). Within a certain setting, as a *modus vivendi*, open conflicts regarding the definition of situations are avoided (Goffman 1959, 10). The fate of many so-called whistle-blowers is a good illustration of the social punishments meted out to those who dare speak out about the limitations of the dominant view.

A third audience is the citizenry at large, mostly complacent or indifferent to what is being advanced by elites in government and the private sector. Maintaining that complacency and quiescence is the reason for much political maneuvering (Edelman 1976, 22–41). In the end, it is not what those in power do that is important, but what they can get away with. If an important constituency or the citizenry at large is aroused, those in power may be thrown out and markets may be lost.

As soon as we introduce the notion of an audience for decisions we have a separation: activity from passivity; actors from spectators; a stage with a fairly limited number of actors elevated above a diffuse multitude of people with a multitude of characteristics; the bright light on the stage in contrast to the darkness where the audience watches; the performance by the visible few before the quiescence of the concealed. The action on the stage has to do with the attention of the audience. As theater director Peter Brook states: "The only thing that all forms of theatre have in common is the need for an audience. This is more than a truism: in the theatre the audience completes the steps of creation" (Brook 1988, 142).

In politics, as well, the audience completes the performance. A statement that is not directed to an audience or received by an audience, whether friendly or hostile, is devoid of social function. When society deals with risk, the statements before the audience have a double aim: to demonstrate a rift in the social fabric and to mend that rift so that a sense of equilibrium can be restored. The rift itself appears when a particular group feels threatened by a hazard. A group that feels unprotected and excluded from the processes where the hazard is defined or controlled expresses distrust and calls for redressive measures. By acting out, the group expresses its outrage and distrust in the social elites. Different groups in the audience see the rift in different lights, from different sides. What appears as an expression of distrust or manipulation to some is a manifestation of autonomy and group identity to others. Statements about risk serve the social function of creating separation and distance, bonding and unity. Their meaning on the surface deals with defining and comparing risk, with communicating and persuading. On another level their meaning concerns changing or preserving the prevailing social order.

The Roles and the Agents

Metaphors from the world of theater are often used to describe political events, but they may be more than metaphors. The moment an actor chooses to appear in a certain way, on a certain stage, with a specific type of message directed to a specific audience, a conscious choice of paradigm has been made.

Actors are agents, persons acting to promote certain interests. *Person* is a concept derived from the Latin word *persona*, which means face mask. All social interaction is performed by persons, singly or in groups, just as all contributions to scientific work or technical construction are produced by persons, singly or in groups. Conventional sociology and anthropology view human beings and organizations as agents who by their behavior reveal underlying interests and causal relationships. Persons are viewed not as individual, unique human beings but as *personae*, as human beings with face masks that may be changed depending on the context (Goffman 1959; Bourdieu 1990, 52). As human beings we are social creatures whose personalities, worldviews, and behavior are molded by the standards of the groups to which we belong (Frank 1974, 5–6). Social construction and search for consensus and approval have a great influence on human perceptions. The behavior of individuals is related to the institutions to which they are linked. Concepts are formed and learning takes place in social settings. Social concerns influence our selective perception of risk (Douglas 1985, 38–39).

Viewing social processes as shaped out by roles and agents—rather than by particular individuals or particular organizations—facilitates an analysis of structural and causal relationships in social controversies. Moreover, it allows emotions and attitudes to be addressed as "facts," worthy of the same importance as the results of analytical scientific endeavors. The behavior of the individual in the societal evaluation of risk can, in general terms, be regarded as a coded behavior, a role. That role is to some extent defined by the relationship to the risk(s) in question, but more by the institutional pattern in which the individual belongs. Both the agents and the audience know, both before and during the performance, that the role has certain demands that the player must meet in order to be allowed to perform the role and to stay on the stage.

The combination of functional roles in a specific social controversy characterizes the situation and the succession of events. The individual qualities of the agents may only shift the emphasis in the drama, change the tempo of the action, and engage the emotions of the audience in differing ways. The roles are characterized by a rational search for satisfaction of the interests that define them. The individual agents on different stages may express that interest in different ways, but the basic rationale for their actions remains the same, defined by their roles.

In social controversies over technological risk, one important distinction is between the *risk bearer* and the *risk generator*. Wars, disasters of nuclear energy, and hazards due to the handling and consumption of toxic and potentially toxic chemicals are good illustrations of how the two principal functional roles in a risk conflict—risk bearing and risk generating—are often separate and adversarial in nature, seldom congruent. The majority of those who bear risk related to many major threats to life, health, and environment in the modern world are not directly engaged in generating these risks. The soldiers and civilians who die in the high-tech wars have little say about why and how the war is conducted. The people living in the neighborhood of hazardous industrial plants have little say in how the hazardous materials and processes should be managed. Representing the risk bearer in the action is the *risk bearer's advocate*, who enters the public stage as a protagonist desiring the Good (truth, justice, prevention of harm), not necessarily on his or her own behalf but for another individual or for the community at large.

The opposing interests of the risk bearer and the risk generator are the counterweights in the balancing act that the dramatic tension generates in conflicts over technological risk. The agents for these juxtaposed interests act as stakeholders in a conspicuous struggle (the *agon*) in each risk controversy.

Apart from the two generic roles of risk bearer and risk generator, other generic roles, mediators in the conflict, can be discerned. They intervene in the conflict by gathering, creating, and providing information, both descriptive and normative, about the nature of the risk. One of these roles is taken by the *risk researcher*, who attempts to gather evidence on why, how, and under what circumstances a phenomenon may be assigned the value of "risk"; on who is exposed to the risk; and on when the risk may be regarded as acceptable. The *risk arbiter*, engaged in arbitration of the conflict, seeks to determine the distribution of risk, that is, the extent to which risk should be accepted, or how it should be limited or prevented; risk arbiters also judge how those exposed to risk should be compensated for running risk and experiencing harm. The *risk informers* in the mass media are engaged in placing the issues on the public agenda and scrutinizing the action. Their function is analogous to that of the chorus in classical dramas—portioning out praise and blame.

The risk bearer's advocate is the incarnated thematic force in a social drama over risk, desiring the Good—truth, justice, and the prevention of harm. The risk generators are his opponents or antagonists who present obstacles to the fulfillment of the goal. The risk arbiters have as their role to attribute the Good to protagonists or antagonists and thereby resolve the conflict. And the risk researchers and risk informers act as helpers to reinforce the action by one or other of the agents in the dramatic process.

These roles neatly correspond with the universal functions identified in semiotic analysis of dramatic situations (Elam 1980, 126–134). The six generic roles in a social drama over risk can be summarized in a matrix (Table 8.1). In each issue raised in societal risk evaluation the specific agents can be sorted into the fields of the matrix, thus revealing the structure of the various interests. A division that seems relevant for understanding the positions and acts of the agents is whether they appear as agents for private or public interests. Risk bearing—the suffering of harm and loss—is always in the private realm. All other roles may be performed either in the private or in the public realm, and sometimes in both, depending on the type of society and the type of issue that is investigated. It is easy to attach conventional dramatic labels to these generic roles defined by their position in social conflicts over risk. To illustrate, Table 8.1 portrays the controversy

Table 8.1
Generic Roles in the Societal Evaluation of Risk: An Example from the Conflict over the Cancer Risks of Hormone-Treated Meats in the United States

Generic Roles	Dramatic Labels	Private Actors	Public Actors
Risk Bearers	• Victim	• Consumers • Workers	
Risk Bearers' Advocate	• Protagonist • Hero	• Consumer organizations • Health organizations • Labor unions	• Members of Congress acting to prevent use of hormone-treated feeds
Risk Generators	• Antagonist • Villain	• Pharmaceutical industry • Cattle industry • Veterinarians • Agricultural extension advisors	• Agricultural extension advisors
Risk Researchers	• Helper	• Scientists in private sector research • Scientists funded from private-sector sources	• Scientists in government agencies and laboratories • Scientists funded from public sources
Risk Arbiters	• *Deus ex machina*	• Law firms • Mediators	• US Congress • USDA • USFDA • Courts
Risk Informers	• Chorus • Messengers	• Producers and journalists in news media, journals, books, films, etc.	• USFDA

in the United States over cancer risks associated with hormone growth promotants used in beef production.

A role does not necessarily have to be performed by one agent or a single organization. Even in theatrical drama, masks are shifted. A player can act in more than one role, just as one role can be performed by more than one player. An actor may be among both risk generators and risk bearers, having to choose which role to play. A manager of a pharmaceutical company, for instance, may discover in himself the adverse effects of a drug promoted by his company; a scientist/risk researcher may step out of the role of helper and into the role of protagonist. In the role of, say, risk arbiter, many actors may succeed each other within the same social drama. There may even be conflicts between the roles a single player performs. An agent's appearance in more than one role adds to ambiguity—but it also adds to his or her influence and control over events.

Acts and agents are heavily influenced by the scene and the setting where the action takes place. In principle, the nature of the acts and agents in a social drama is consistent with the nature of the scene (Burke 1945, 3, 11–20, 77–83). The social structures—laws and institutions—that provide the setting for new dramas are the remainders of previous dramatic action. So the national theaters in which controversies over technological risk are acted out condition the roles as well as the performances. Laws and public institutions created to safeguard the public interest in a specific technological risk issue merely reflect how earlier agents, who represented the general common sense, expected the risk to be handled in the future.

The Dramatic Process

A drama is a representation in universal form of a process of conflict. Awareness of the dramatic form directs participants' and spectators' attention not to individual persons or incidents but to the anatomy of the constituent conflicts as they develop over time. Drama is also a powerful paradigm for social action. One salient example is the national election process, where the action in front of the electoral audience often seems of greater importance than the underlying ideologies. Another example is the judicial process, in most countries set up as a dramatic process before an audience. Characterized by very carefully defined roles and even scripts for the participants, it is a process for the production of meaning, but also a process in which the meaning is open to interpretation.

Risk is a code word that alerts society that a change in the social order is being requested. Persons and groups have different attitudes to change in the prevailing order. Within the social order risk issues are used to provide leverage in action to change or to defend the existing pattern. Every reference to risk contains a tacit reference to safety. And our need for safety and security is related to our need for control. Conflicts over risk are processes played out over time, where anxiety is contrasted with security, and where perceptions of chaos and risk are intermingled with perceptions of order and certainty. It is not always obvious that the actors are players, agents presenting themselves to the public as representatives of different interests, and that their acts in a sense are conditioned by the structure of the conflict.

Conflicts over technological risk have their characteristic life cycles, which have been analyzed by some commentators. Anthony Downs suggests a characteristic pattern in the evolution of risk controversies: pre-problem stage, alarmed discovery, risk assessment reflective, decline of public interest, and post-problem stage (Downs 1972). Edward Lawless traces how risk controversies rise and fall in intensity (Lawless 1977). Robert Kates, Christoph Hohenemser, Jeanne Kasperson, and others present a synthetic sequence of human activities for coping with hazards (Kates, Hohenemser, and Kasperson 1985). In examining the social dynamics of technical controversy, Alan Mazur (1981) also identifies peaks of intensity. These descriptions are highly formalistic and fail to take account of the symbolic dimensions of risk controversies.

The anthropologist Victor Turner has developed the Aristotelian concept

Figure 8.1
Phases in the Social Interaction over Risk

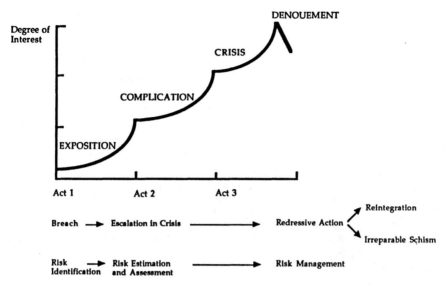

of drama in a way that is pertinent to the study of how society copes with conflicts over technological risk. Turner defines social drama as a unit of aharmonic or disharmonic process, arising in situations of social conflict. In social drama, Turner identifies four diachronic phases of public action: *breach*; *crisis*; *redressive action*; and *reintegration* or *irreparable schism* (Turner 1974, 37–42). These phases roughly coincide with the conventionally defined phases *risk identification*, *risk assessment*, and *risk management* (NRC 1983). They also coincide with the phases *exposition, complication, crisis*, and *dénouement* which can be discerned in the construction of dramas (see Figure 8.1).

The dramatic action in the societal evaluation of technological risk has the structure of a "well-made" play as it is defined in the drama literature (Styan 1965). A *breach* of regular, norm-governed social relations between persons or groups of persons within the same system of social relations is a manifestation of distrust among elites. It is a breaking of connections, a disjunction, a rift in the social fabric, a cohesion undone by fear of death and loss and by pity for victims. In dramatic terms, there is an exposition of the conflict so that the audience is engaged by actions on the stage.

Two types of dramatic breach can be discerned in the controversies over technological risk. A breach may be triggered by a sudden hazard or accident that is perceived as a violation or as a sign that violation may occur. Many of these accidents are known by the name of the place where the accident occurred: Seveso, Three Mile Island, Love Canal, Bhopal, and Chernobyl.

A breach may also appear when scientific findings reveal threats to socially important interests. The controversies over the use of the drug Thalidomide in the 1960s and diethylstilbestrol (DES) in the 1970s illustrate the anxiety over the potential harm to the fertility and newborns of the politically influential, affluent middle class.

A third type of breach that is less abrupt can also be observed. Carefully compiled scientific evidence may be used by social elites to raise issues on the political agenda. These initiatives are starting points for processes with a surface similarity to the social dramas over risk. They are, however, formed with a great deal more intentional strategic planning and projection than dramas driven by fear and pity. No victims can be shown. No strongly emotional appeals are associated with the breach. No injured group steps forward with demands or even threats to the establishment. Examples of this kind of breach include political actions in response to ozone depletion and global warming.

In the breach, the code word *risk* functions as a signal of a deviation from an expected pattern. Even if the word denotes only a factual, normal uncertainty, in the public mind it is easily translated into threats to life and well-being. Often, in the social contests (the *agon*) over the evaluation of risk, the protagonist intends to create these connotations, and the antagonists resist the claims. If the protagonist succeeds in gaining legitimacy to act out this issue on the political stage, the action is associated with intentions to safeguard a public interest.

In a social drama over risk, the breach is the precipitating event in a mounting *crisis*. Unless the breach can be sealed off quickly within a limited area of social interaction, there is a tendency for it to intensify and expand. In dramatic terms, the conflict grows in complexity and intensity, heightening the audience's interest in the action on stage.

During a mounting crisis, attempts to assert control are common. It is not unusual that the professional and scientific communities claim ownership: the problem is a common technical problem; the evidence of risk has not been brought forth by generally accepted methods; there are several well-known technical solutions to the problem. When these efforts are not successful, the *crisis escalates*, whereupon the risk attracts wider public attention, and demands for public participation grow. Often the crisis conforms to the existing patterns of social conflict.

The peak of the crisis is always one of those turning points or moments of danger and suspense when a true state of affairs is revealed, and when it is least easy to don masks or to pretend that nothing is wrong. In crisis, attitudes are peeled away to lay bare the underlying values and interests. The crisis appears as a menacing presence in the center of public life itself, challenging the representatives of order, who may wish to ignore it or wish it away, to confront it. The crisis forces latent anxiety and conflicts of interest into visibility and recognition. It causes the participants to sharpen their own positions and to articulate their values with greater clarity.

The third phase in the societal response to risk is *redressive action*. To manage the crisis, redressive mechanisms are brought into operation by representatives of those most affected by a system adjustment. The mechanisms they use vary in type and complexity with such factors as the depth and shared social significance of the breach, the social inclusiveness of the crisis, and the nature and autonomy of the social group or groups affected by the breach. The redressive mechanisms may range from personal advice and informal mediation or arbitration to formal juridical and legislative machinery set in motion in a public ritual. Legislation, regulation, and other redressive measures carry the message that the crisis should be over.

In a social controversy about technological risk there will be symbolic action—perhaps in the end of greater political importance than the redistribution of tangible benefits—in order to reassure the ostensible beneficiaries of the response (consumers, workers, or community at risk). Symbolic action is inevitable if social conflicts loaded with anxiety over death and dying are to be brought to closure.

The fourth and final phase is one of either the *reintegration* of the disturbed social group, or the public recognition and legitimation of an *irreparable schism*. This phase marks many public processes concerning the evaluation of risk. In some cases, the organizations that have been created in response to a risk survive beyond the specific issue that caused the crisis. They may become part of the institutional structure of society. In other cases, existing institutions adjust themselves by incorporating the objectives of the disturbed social groups. And in other cases, again, the conflicts may remain open and unresolved. As in Beckett's *Waiting for Godot*, the end could also be the beginning of a continued enactment of the theme that already has been enacted before the audience; there is no catharsis, no dénouement, no perceivable end; there is just a waiting for acknowledgment and absolution.

The Plot

Order and equilibrium appear as central issues in social dramaturgy. The significance of a breach is that it upsets the prevailing order. It is a manifestation of acute distrust and thus a disturbance in social life. Social dramas seem to be driven by one strong wish: to return from a state of disorder and disequilibrium to order and equilibrium (Wagner-Pacifici 1986, 231–232).

The plot in social dramas over technological risk reflects two opposing impulses in modern, industrialized society: the celebration of technological progress as against the protection of the health, safety, and property rights of individuals. The conflicts from these opposing impulses are made visible by a precipitating event—real or socially constructed—that fuels the underlying dissatisfaction and frames it as anxiety over a certain technological risk. What determines whether a specific technological risk is adopted for social controversy? There are several candidate criteria:

1. The risk should be tied to effects that appear familiar and close to people.
2. The effects should stir up emotions of fright and fear.
3. The risk should concern a large or important enough group of people for politically appointed politicians and senior administrators to worry about their support.
4. Raising the issue of risk in national politics should not obviously threaten fundamental national interests of major importance.
5. The issue should ideally be such that the mass media grasp it and assist politicians in placing it and keeping it on the agenda in national politics so as to satisfy the public's need of spectacular drama. (Palmlund 1989, 613)

The Choice of Dramatic Genre

Building on the theatrical analogy, we might expect that there are different modes of social dramaturgy over risk; social drama exhibits genre, just as theatrical drama may be expressed in different genres, such as tragedy, comedy, romance, satire, or melodrama. Wagner-Pacifici argues that generic choices of mode in the theater of politics condition the amount and quality of public participation, as do the character richness and psychological complexity. She makes a distinction between two ends of a generic continuum: tragedy and melodrama. Tragedy allows for and encourages the audience to identify with the tragic victims and their decisions, dilemmas, weaknesses, and fates. Melodrama excludes the audience both from such identification and from engaged participation beyond that of the prescribed booing of the villain and applauding of the hero (Wagner-Pacifici 1986, 1–21, 40–43, 272–294).

Do the participants in a social controversy consciously choose which type of drama they want to enact on the public stage? The participants in a risk drama differ in their understanding of the type of drama in which they participate. There may be expectations among risk bearers and their representatives that they act in a tragedy, expecting a conflict resolution that permits an integration of the experience of harm and injury as an increased moral awareness in the social consciousness. And there may be cynical interpretations by other participants in the action that the controversy merely is one more round in a game that is much broader than the particular conflict, a game that will continue long after the particular conflict is ostensibly settled.

Dürrenmatt provides the analyst with a key to interpreting the genre in the controversies over technological risks to human health and environment: "Tragedy presupposes guilt, despair, moderation, lucidity, vision, a sense of responsibility." But in the modern world we may only be capable of a form of Punch-and-Judy show. It is always "We couldn't help it" and "We didn't really want that to happen." And, indeed, things happen without anyone in particular being responsible for them. "Everything is dragged along and everyone gets caught somewhere in the sweep of events. We are all collectively guilty, collectively bogged down in the sins of our fathers and our forefathers.... That is our misfortune, but not our guilt: guilt can exist only as a personal achievement, as a religious deed. Comedy alone is suitable for us" (Dürrenmatt 1964, 33–34).

One important criterion for the choice of mode in tragic dramas may be embedded in the relationship between the agents on the stage and the audience. The tragic drama allowing for catharsis permits the public real political participation in public decision making. The mode of drama that does not appeal to the audience for emotional involvement leaves the public as a passive, watching audience, permitted to act politically only in moments when formal elections are necessary for the legitimation of political agents. The only difference between social tragedy and social melodrama would then be a difference in the control exercised by social elites.

Perhaps it is an exaggeration to claim that societies choose the genre of their social dramas with consciousness of the dramatic qualities inherent in the choices. However, there are important implications in the point made by Wagner-Pacifici that there is a significant difference in the dénouement of a social tragedy with an open acknowledgment and participation in catharsis, and the dénouement of a social melodrama without such a cathartic effect in the closure. To the extent that societies choose a genre of drama, they choose between, on the one hand, open reconciliation, acknowledgment, and transcendence of the constituent conflict and, on the other hand, repression of the conflict. The choice reveals something about the sense of morality in society.

CONCLUSION

There is an elusive reality with which we humans cope. An understanding of that reality emerges out of successive attempts to discover the truth about it. It is simplistic to assume that we can describe or represent that reality if we eliminate the human emotional experience of fear, grief, pity, compassion, and love. In studies of risk perception, risk evaluation, and risk management, we should therefore accept the relevance of emotive statements as well as positivist assertions. Since human action always produces a future and a present continuing from a past, we have to deal with the three basic dimensions in social analysis—time, space, and action—if we want to explain how society deals with risk. We have to explore the provisional character of our understanding of reality, in scientific work as well as in our personal construction of beliefs.

The theory of theater and drama provides categories for analysis of social conflicts over technology neglected by the mainstream risk assessment literature. It provides a critical perspective on the discourse and the symbolic action in societal risk evaluation and also on the field of risk analysis.

It raises questions, finally, about culture in modern society. Even though our trappings and technological arrangements for production and reproduction have changed through the ages, biologically *Homo sapiens* has not changed much. We are, in fact, in our social adjustment to risk, reproducing patterns of social interaction that have been carried down through generations. Our interest in social controversy over technological risk may well be a reproduction in modern social settings of earlier generations' anxiety, pity, and excitement surrounding the sacrifice of individuals to further the strength of the group.

PART III

The Role of Science in Risk Assessment

CHAPTER 9 _____

Public Wisdom, Expert Fallibility: Toward a Contextual Theory of Risk

Harry Otway

I began risk studies about twenty-five years ago as an engineer with some background in social psychology. Since that time I have made a steady transition to the point where I now work only on the social science side, having only faded memories of my life as an engineer. My initial involvement in the risk field was stimulated by wanting to understand public opposition to technologies, especially nuclear power, which had been judged by many experts and policy makers to be acceptable. Although no longer involved with energy systems, my main interest is still in problems arising from the integration of technical and social systems, for example, major chemical hazards and information systems in large organizations.

The people who have most stimulated my thinking on risk matters are, in alphabetical order, Martin Fishbein, Jerry Ravetz, and Brian Wynne. Fishbein's work (e.g., Fishbein and Ajzen 1975) was instrumental in bringing order to the previously confused field of attitude theory. His attitude model provided me with a framework for understanding what has become known as "risk perception," and we collaborated for several years in applying it to study public beliefs and attitudes toward technologies. Ravetz's and Wynne's writings on the social, philosophical, and political dimensions of risk (e.g., Ravetz 1971; Wynne 1982b) are unusual for their richness and depth and their ability to provide an unexpected new insight at every rereading. I have enjoyed collaborating with both of them as well.

The acknowledgment of my intellectual debts would not be complete without mentioning that many papers that I found to be particularly disagreeable have also provided an important and continuing source of intellectual stimulation and motivation. In this respect I am grateful to several of my colleagues for their unintentional encouragement.

GENESIS AND TRANSITION: THE INFLUENCE OF EARLY PARADIGMS

Duncan (1978, 19) postulated "a steady evolution in which problems are initially defined as scientific and technical, later as economic, and still later ... as intrinsically social and political." In pursuing my original quest to understand what was then commonly known in technical circles as "the public acceptance problem," I went through precisely this sequence. As a consequence, I have used a succession of incompatible frameworks over the years.

I began by trying to quantify technical risks, thinking that if they were "put into perspective" through comparison with familiar risks we could better judge their social acceptability (Otway and Erdman 1969). I am ashamed now of my naïveté, although I have the excuse that this was more than twenty years ago, while some people are still doing it today.

This was followed by a short-lived attempt to quantify and compare risks and benefits. This was stopped short by the realization that trying to quantify "fragile values" drains them of much of their meaning (Ashby 1978) and that the implicit assumptions that underlie the various methods of quantification act to perpetuate existing social and economic relationships. For example, a central problem in applying cost-benefit analysis to activities that involve potential loss of life is that of placing a monetary value on life saving. All of the methods proposed for doing this (e.g., willingness to pay, insurance, or court awards) are in some way based on the wealth or income of the victim and thus implicitly encourage saving the lives of the wealthy and imposing risks on the poor.

My involvement with cost-benefit analysis concluded with a methodological critique of Chauncy Starr's (1969) seminal paper. Starr offered a good philosophical discussion of risk regulation, but went on to propose a set of numerical risk-benefit relationships based on analysis of national-level statistics. These relationships purported to reveal society's past preferences with respect to risk taking and were suggested as guidelines for judging the acceptability of present and future activities. The results that received the most attention were that the public appeared to be willing to accept voluntary risks roughly 1,000 times greater than involuntary risks, and that the acceptability of risk appeared to be proportional to the third power of the associated (perceived or real) benefits.

Our critique (Otway and Cohen 1975) has been frequently misunderstood (Shrader-Frechette 1985). This was partly due to careless reading, but also because we demonstrated the limitations of the method and data base by presenting very different results, which we obtained using the same approach with different, but equally reasonable, assumptions. Some people missed our philosophical objections to the method and assumed that we were proposing an alternative set of numerical risk-benefit relationships.

To set the record straight, not only did we find that the Starr numerical results did not reflect accurately the data upon which they were based but, more important, that it would be impossible to get any meaningful relationships at all using this method, partly because the data do not reflect the qualitative dimensions of risk that are so important in the acceptance of technology, such as the credibility of the institutions involved. This caused me to look into surveys as a potentially more promising way to elicit public preferences.

In searching through the psychology literature I was struck by the similarity between *attitudes* toward risk and what was beginning to be called "risk perception." After much thought it seemed that the relevant issue was not risk per se, but attitudes toward the technology associated with the risk. Obviously, it is the *technology* as a whole that is ultimately accepted, not its risks in abstract isolation. Hence I embarked on a series of empirical studies with Fishbein and other colleagues, looking at public and expert attitudes toward different energy sources in terms of their underlying belief and value structures (Otway and Fishbein 1977; Otway, Maurer, and Thomas 1978; Thomas, Swaton, et al. 1980).

Fishbein's attitude model offered an established and tested theoretical framework ideally suited to accommodate the "stale innovation" (a lovely phrase coined by the Italian novelist and essayist Primo Levi) of risk perception, especially since "the word *perception* is used ... to refer to various kinds of attitudes and judgments" (Slovic, Chapter 5, note 1).

An important feature of the Fishbein model is that attitudes are measured in terms of their underlying beliefs and values. Further, attitude measurements from the model can be correlated with an independent, global measure of the same attitudes, thereby ensuring that the set of beliefs and values that people were asked to rate were indeed *salient* (relevant) to the particular attitude in question and that the set was complete. A serious limitation of much of the scaling done under the risk perception label is that it is difficult to know if the beliefs given people to rate really mattered to them and that they were complete. People will usually respond to the questions asked on a survey even if they do not seem particularly relevant.

Although attitude theory was used in some risk studies, primarily in Europe, it never really caught on, and the psychometric scaling approach of Slovic and his colleagues (e.g., Fischhoff, Slovic, et al. 1978) has become a dominant and influential research tradition, which is "now at a stage where we can begin to piece together theories and frameworks" (Slovic, Chapter 5).

Wynne (1989a) has criticized the psychometric approach for its sociological weaknesses and its failure to account for the context specificity of risk problems. Kerry Thomas and I have expressed reservations both about its technical limitations and the legitimacy of using risk perception results in policy processes (Otway and Thomas 1982). My own opinion is that if risk perception studies are going to be done, the attitude framework is aesthetically and methodologically more appealing than most others.

Risk perception studies continue to produce interesting findings, although by now they are mostly adding detail to the important general results that were already emerging when Paul Slovic hosted the Eugene workshop in 1980. However, the results of application to specific policy problems are both very specific indeed and highly perishable, and there still remains the delicate problem of whether or how one can legitimately use the results of specific risk perception studies in policy making. Perhaps the most important practical application of risk perception research is the use of its general findings in tutorials for those who still believe in "objective risk" and, more recently, to inform the promising work in risk communication.

The approaches used by different researchers, when viewed from a certain emotional and temporal distance, are more similar than dissimilar and have provided general insights that are largely consistent. In fact, the general findings, such as the multidimensionality of risk perception, are the important thing and, in principle, it would not even have been necessary to do empirical studies to get them—they could have been deduced anyway from long-established theoretical considerations. This makes arguments about the methods used to arrive at them seem a bit superfluous.

My current perspective is characterized by two key beliefs. The first is simply that ordinary people (i.e., the lay public) are pretty good at acting in accordance with their own beliefs and values to attain their own goals. Or, as Fiorino (1989, 294) succinctly put it, "The lay public are not fools." People do not necessarily behave in a highly efficient way to satisfy their goals but, in the long run, they do manage to muddle through quite well, demonstrating what the psychohistorian Robert Jay Lifton has called "inchoate wisdom."

The idea that people largely behave rationally is not uncommon in many social science disciplines, such as social psychology, sociology, and anthropology. Anyone whose interest is descriptive rather than normative should be comfortable with it. However, despite faith in the fundamental rationality of people, I realize that the public is not always right; the tyranny of the majority is no better than the tyranny of the elite.

My second key belief concerns the fallibility of experts. (Although I have not thought it out, these two beliefs may often go together.) One reason is that experts are often blinded by the received wisdom of their discipline and fail to realize that the present state of knowledge is not the ultimate one; if they do recognize their fallibility, they may trust that future developments will provide a "fix." They tend to be overconfident and reluctant to change their views, even when confronted with conflicting opinions from other, equally qualified experts.

It is sometimes even difficult to know who the experts are. In the short term, the policy establishment and expert peer groups often have trouble distinguishing between "breakthrough" perspectives and novel ideas that are just plain wrong. Both may look equally wrong when first proposed. Members of the peer community, who have helped to establish the conventional wisdom of the discipline, may be especially inclined to defend it against challenge. Thus expert selection and recognition are likely to be biased on the side of conservatism.

The use of experts in regulatory settings brings in some special features (Otway and Ravetz 1984). Some regulatory agencies deal with a specific technology (such as nuclear energy), while others, such as environmental agencies, deal with the side effects of many different industries. Agencies in the former category often share a pool of consultants with industry and may work with the same consultants over long periods of time, giving rise to the phenomenon known as "captive consultants."

Another human failing of experts is that success in one field can lead them to assume (sometimes without knowing it) that their opinions are equally valid in other areas. As an example (see Otway and Misenta 1980), a number of prominent nuclear energy experts demonstrated a rather striking ignorance of the human factors literature in their proposals for improving operator performance following the Three Mile Island accident.

Quite apart from the problem of motivational biases, the use of expertise in public arenas often has a peculiarly antidemocratic flavor because problems are defined in such a way as to make them the province of experts, thereby excluding nontechnical aspects that are important to people (Otway 1987). People are concerned about much more than the level of risk to which they will be exposed. They also care about qualitative aspects, such as who is exposed, who gets the benefits, what social institutions are favored by the particular technology, how the risk will be physiologically manifested, what the catastrophic accident potential is, which effects are delayed, and so on.

If a public debate is structured to consider only the technical system and its observable (sometimes equated with insurable) risks, then many of these other, but important, concerns may be ruled out of bounds. Anyone who insists on discussing them will certainly be considered disruptive and is likely to be labeled "irrational" as well. It follows, therefore, that whoever has the power to define the limits of the system in public discourse also implicitly decides who is being rational. You can quite rationally oppose a technical system that engineers have certified as "safe" if it turns out that their definition of "the system" did not include the things you care about the most.

SOME IMPLICATIONS OF MY PERSPECTIVE

The two beliefs just discussed have many implications for risk analysis and management. I will discuss several of them below, including objective and subjective notions of risk, the measurement of risk, the acceptability of risk, risk perception, cognitive limitations, and human and organizational aspects.

Objective Versus Subjective Notions of Risk

Policy decisions about hazardous technologies have the paradoxical quality that they are likely to be most urgent just where scientific knowledge is the most uncertain. The origins of the problems addressed by risk analysis guarantee their relative insolubility because they are often outside of current experience. They have been discovered either as unexpected and unwanted side effects of an existing technology or as theoretically projected side effects of a new and untested technology. In these situations, the "objective" risks are in principle both unknown and unknowable.

Facts do not exist independently of people; their articulation requires a human observer. In contrast to what is popularly thought of as a dry, passionless search for abstract truths, there is an intrinsic human element in knowledge. The attempt to be as objective as possible by using formal methods cannot obscure the fact that, for most risks that really matter, even the objective component of the risk still contains a strong subjective element. There is nothing wrong with this; it must be so. It only becomes a problem when self-deception prevents conscious awareness of it.

Those at risk also have subjective knowledge about how the risk-producing activity will affect their lives and their community. This knowledge, although less formal and more intuitive, represents a different kind of expertise. The impacts of most concern to those affected are often not included at all in the technical definition of risk.

What is commonly thought of as objective risk has a large subjective component, which may be based on one's experience of being at risk. These two notions of risk complement each other, and both need to be considered in policy. As an extreme example, if a bridge is not safely designed and solidly built, all the citizen subjective knowledge in the world will not keep it up. Yet, even if well-designed and beautiful, it could still be a failure as a sociotechnical system if it causes unacceptable changes in the social life of the community.

Krimsky and Plough summed it up nicely, recognizing that "a cultural approach that seriously considers popular behavior ... distinguishes two forms of rationality applied to risk: technical and experiential. Both make contributions to the problem of constructing and analyzing a risk event, but neither is sufficient" (Krimsky and Plough 1988, 304).

The Measurement of Risk

The only risks that can be "measured" are the relatively uninteresting ones for which there are statistical or epidemiological data. The kinds of risks that gave rise to risk analysis in the first place are those associated with what Alvin Weinberg (1972) called "trans-scientific" problems, those for which the methods of science can, in theory, provide answers but which, in practice, because of financial and sample-size constraints, cannot be answered.

Subsequently, several researchers (Funtowicz and Ravetz 1990a; and this volume, Chapter 11) have begun to discuss and analyze an even more intractable kind of problem: "post-normal science" issues where ignorance is the main feature and no amount of resources can provide "scientific" answers, for example, global environmental change.

Formal risk analysis of technical systems is a very useful design aid, helping to reveal weak points in a design or to facilitate the comparison of alternatives. However, the final estimates of risk to the public are notoriously unreliable, adding uncertainties in exposure calculations and dose-response relationships to the already considerable uncertainties in the analysis of the technical system itself.

For example, Mandl and Lathrop (1983) compared ten studies of the risk to people living near liquified natural gas terminals. These studies, made in the Federal Republic of Germany, the Netherlands, the United Kingdom, and the United States, found risks to vary over a factor of 100 million, although the technical facilities were similar. The differences were due mostly to the assumptions made by the analysts and the methods they chose to use in making their quantitative assessments.

In a large benchmark exercise in Europe (Amendola 1986), teams from ten countries independently estimated the failure probability of the auxiliary feedwater system of the same French nuclear power plant. Each team carried out its own analysis, using its own problem structures, fault and event trees, models, and data. The estimated mean failure probabilities ranged over a factor of forty-five. In a second phase of the study, the teams met to discuss their analyses and, once again working separately, had the opportunity to revise them, but without a requirement to converge. After a discussion of results and an exchange of ideas, the estimates still differed by a factor of thirty-six.

It should be noted that these were not estimates of risk to the public, but only estimates of the probability of failure in one subsystem of a very large and complex facility. The relative lack of change after learning of the other experts' approaches and results illustrates how confident experts tend to be and how difficult it can be to get them to change their views even when they find themselves at odds with other experts. This is a familiar phenomenon to those who have followed expert debates in public arenas.

In practice, there are no "true" measures of the industrial risks that concern us the most. The risk numbers we see floating about are based on expert judgment, as expressed through models, theoretical predictions, extrapolations, and so on. The most valuable product of risk analysis is not the risk estimates generated, but what is learned about the system from the analytic process. We must beware of any suggestion that we know what the "true" (or objective) risks are because of the size of the effort made to make and refine the estimates.

The Acceptability of Risk

It would be nice to think that no one still believes in the normative idea of quantitative criteria by which the social acceptability of risks and, by implication, of technologies can be decreed. Among others, Detlof von Winterfeldt and I wrote about this quite some time ago (Otway and von Winterfeldt 1982). It would be theoretically possible to establish some quantitative criterion as a minimum condition for regulatory acceptability, necessary for the risk producer to meet, but not sufficient of itself to ensure public and political acceptability.

Even this kind of criterion is deceptive, sharing one of the technical problems of "acceptable risk," that is, that it is virtually impossible to show convincingly, on the basis of calculations, whether it has been met or not. Obviously, a safety goal is of little value if the stakeholders are unable to satisfy themselves that it has been met. The probable consequence of this would be to switch debate from risk levels to risk analysis techniques—but without reducing its political content. Acceptability is finally decided by political negotiations among stakeholders, informed by expert advice.

Risk Perception

As alluded to earlier, I have some trouble with the concept of risk perception. My first difficulty is with the name itself—a concern that is not as trivial as it may seem at first glance. To begin with, the term *risk perception* is technically inaccurate because we cannot really perceive risks. Its use represented a departure from the traditional use of "perception" to refer to the processing of *sensory* information to apply to the processing of *conceptual* information (Slovic 1972). This is significant because some sensory perceptions can be measured, and we are familiar with the quantification of perceptual defects of this kind (e.g., in vision and hearing).

The concept of risk perception was used first in fields other than technological risk, for example, the risk of apprehension following criminal behavior (Claster 1967) or in the perception of the risk of gambles (Slovic 1967). Again, these were situations where the accuracy of people's judgments could be examined by comparing them to statistical arrest figures or to the mathematically correct expected value of a proposed gamble.

A brief review of the early literature on technological risk suggests that the term entered discussions in this field in the early 1970s. The notion of risk perception presented a happy and convenient intersection for some well-established, but quite different, concerns of technologists and cognitive psychologists. However, it was an area of application in which there were no real answers with which perceptions could be compared; there were only shades of opinion, some arrived at more formally and/or better informed than others.

Many technologists (whether in industry, government, or academe) were genuinely puzzled by active public opposition to technologies that they thought to be not only safe, but also providers of essential benefits. We can paraphrase their thinking with a three-part oversimplification: (1) obviously the public was perceiving something differently than they were; (2) something had to be changed to remedy the situation; and (3) the technologies in question were "safe" and did not require any fundamental changes.

Coincidentally, cognitive psychologists had a long-standing interest in discovering and documenting human limitations in handling probabilistic information. Called cognitive limitations or biases, these shortcomings were seen as impediments to making good decisions. Psychologists spoke of "decision technologies" to help decision makers overcome their limitations and of the need for public education to improve people's abilities to think probabilistically.

The technologists' concerns provided a concrete area of application for the psychologists' research interests and some (in the event, limited) new funding as well. Both groups seemed to accept implicitly that people's perceptions were faulty and that correcting them would be a perfectly reasonable and harmless thing to do. Because of its origins, the concept of risk perception retains a somewhat negative connotation and is unfortunately used sometimes to support the idea that nontechnical views are merely mistaken and irrational misperceptions.

The second point is that the risk perception paradigm acts to reinforce the technical definition of risk to the exclusion of the many nonrisk attributes that underlie public perceptions of the technologies or activities that create the risk. Risk is not accepted in the abstract; it is only part of a package of attributes that people must accept when they accept, for example, a technology that causes a risk. Risks are not sited; technologies or industries are. Perhaps the only time that nothing but risk is being "perceived" is when respondents are filling out a risk perception questionnaire.

It is completely normal and rational for people to consider more than just risk when judging a technology. Perceptions of a technology are also influenced by qualitative dimensions of its risks (e.g., *how* you die, if you have consented to the risk exposure, if its effects are delayed), by perceptions if its benefits, the social and political outcomes associated with its use, the legitimacy accorded its institutions, confidence in the plant operator, and so on.

This is not a new idea, and it should not need to be repeated, but many people who must surely know better still continue to refer to "risk perception" and "acceptance" when what we really mean is the perception and acceptance of the totality of whatever activity causes the risk. A person who considered only the statistical probability of death to the exclusion of all other information would be truly irrational.

In theory, there cannot even be a complete list of the salient attributes that underlie perceptions of technologies because people characterize a technology by whatever they have "learned" to associate with it. For this reason, the attitudes of different groups (e.g., experts and laypeople) toward the same technology may well be based on different underlying sets of determinants (beliefs). It follows, then, that attitudes toward different technologies are also based on different sets of attributes.

There has been much discussion about the "cognitive dimensions" that underlie risk perception, but people do not really have cognitive dimensions in their heads as innate structures. They are simply artifacts we use to simplify representation and discussion of data. These are examples of what philosophers of science (e.g., Hospers 1967) call "indirect objects" or "theoretical constructs," which "exist" only as long as the theories in which they have meaning are accepted.

The factors that underlie perceptions, as well as their relative importance, depend on the characteristics of the technology, its history, whom you ask, the particular moment in time when you ask them, what psychometric method you used, who designed the instrument, how the interviewing was done, how the data were analyzed and interpreted, and so on. The debates about cognitive dimensions have been useful in illustrating that risk perception is a complex, multidimensional concept, but one without fixed and universal dimensions.

Cognitive Limitations

I do not doubt the results of research on cognitive limitations (although I would like to understand better the effects of settings and subjects), but I do sometimes wonder how important they are in practice. After all, if we have these limitations, and nevertheless have managed to survive successfully as a species (things could be worse), perhaps they are not so important in practical terms. The finding that laypeople do not handle probabilistic concepts very well is not very disturbing either. Political and military leaders, and their like, have caused a great deal of mischief with their ability to handle probabilistic concepts and to think the unthinkable. Perhaps it's an overrated virtue.

Saying that people cannot think probabilistically is often technocratic code for saying that opposition to a technology is irrational because opponents are intellectually incapable of understanding how low its risks are. Proposals that people be "educated" in probability concepts are similarly suspect and could equally well be countered by public demands that technologists be better trained in the humanities and in the principles of democratic process, not to mention some specialized instruction on the limitations of science and expertise.

Human and Organizational Aspects

In recent years the tidy calculus of risk analysis has been upset by the realization that the human element in technical systems does not always behave in predictable ways and may be the most important cause of accidents. Its importance was underlined, for example, by the mistakes of the reactor operating crew at Three Mile Island and by the failure of maintenance procedures at Bhopal.

Although it is convenient for management to blame such accidents on low-level employees, it is a bit like blaming the victim for the crime. Most of these incidents are ultimately failures of the organization, being the logical outcome of policies regarding employee selection, training, and supervision, or, too often, of operators being confronted with grossly inadequate hardware and software interfaces with the technology. Management, occupied by higher-level imperatives, creates a situation where an accident is "waiting to happen." Relatively little attention has been given to organizational influences on risk and to the problems of implementation and evaluation of regulations (Baram 1985).

Regulation is primarily the use of state power to influence the behavior of organizations. In other words, organizations are the object of regulations. Thus, understanding what motivates organizational behavior is important because the regulations that shape risks are formulated in organizational settings and are implemented by organizations (Hall and Quinn 1983).

There are always differences between the formal, "paper" organization and the informal, real-world behavior of people in it. There are official procedures, communication channels, and lines of authority, but there are also allegiances to memberships in wider professional communities, different perceptions and expectations of individuals and subgroups, and unwritten procedures used when formal rules are inadequate.

This can be especially significant in the regulation of hazardous technologies, because the genuine uncertainties about what the risks really are and how best to manage them are exacerbated by differences in professional training, disciplinary orientations, and intellectual styles. This leaves room for maneuvering among the parties involved, allowing informal and unarticulated organizational and personal goals to play a subtle role.

Organizational realities mean that decision makers operate within rather narrow limits: "horizontally" in terms of their authority, and "vertically" in terms of financial and staff resources. For example, an agency may have authority in a safety area that does not allow it to consider the mental health aspects of its decisions. Limited resources might force an agency to choose among a number of safety problems that do fall within its charter. Similarly, the comparisons of risk that are often featured in hyperrational discussions of risk acceptance and management are irrelevant to an agency that has responsibility for only one type of risk. A decision to act on a risk problem may depend less on the magnitude of the risk than on the organizational possibility of acting and whether taking action is in the agency's own best interests.

Risk management studies require the analyst to know the goals of the "decision makers" so that options can be developed to satisfy them. There is a general problem of goal elicitation: it is not that decision makers do not know their objectives, but rather that they often cannot be made explicit for organizational or personal reasons. For example, one goal of an organization is to ensure its continued existence; thus it will not happily take a decision that will benefit a competing agency at its own expense, especially if the underlying scientific basis for the decision is soft. Likewise, individual managers and politicians have career goals that may be favored by one option and hurt by another. Risk studies may even be undertaken to legitimize the implementation of decisions already taken in private, an objective that cannot be freely communicated.

The behavior of organizations, both regulatory and regulated, is another nonanalytical factor that complicates the simple notion of acceptable risk, and one that deserves more attention than it has been given so far. The *Challenger* and Chernobyl accidents, affecting the parade of technical programs of the world's two largest superpowers, revealed surprising organizational and management deficiencies which significantly overshadowed their technical dimensions.

CONCLUSION: POLICY IMPLICATIONS

If there is a core issue at the heart of the "risk" debate, it is one of power or, more precisely, of knowledge merging with power (Ravetz 1990). Whoever has the power to select the technologies that will be developed and deployed is also implicitly shaping the future of the society in which we will all live. Recent catastrophic accidents have graphically demonstrated the fallibility of experts and further undermined confidence in political and administrative systems that have uncritically used expert advice while too often turning a deaf ear to public concerns.

Much of the opposition to industrial developments can be interpreted as public demands for more democratic control of technology. By their opposition, the electorate is implicitly redefining the mandate given to officials so as to exclude many decisions about potentially hazardous (or in other ways threatening) technologies. Perhaps the best example of the trend toward more social control of technology is recent legislation in the United States and Europe that requires administrators and experts to take the initiative in providing information to the public and to workers about the risks to which they are exposed.

Entering into communication with someone creates the expectation of a social relationship; it is this expectation that allows information to become communication. Entering into communication with the public about the risks to which they are exposed will inevitably lead them to assume that they will play a more significant role in shaping decisions about the source of these risks (Otway and Wynne 1989). However, and perhaps exactly for this reason, risk communication requirements are often interpreted merely as a matter of providing credible information that the public will believe and passively accept.

The idea of advertising is to make information credible through attractive packaging and presentation, but credible information is not necessarily authentic or true. There is a difference between providing information and communicating. Authentic communication involves sustained relationships in which mutual trust and respect are nurtured.

Risk communication requirements are a political response to popular demands. It therefore seems unlikely that the public will be content with cold, technical facts from a loudspeaker if what they really want is reassuring human contact with those who understand and can manage a potential threat, or perhaps to be consulted before decisions have been taken and options closed. The main product of risk communication is not information, but the quality of the social relationships it supports. Risk communication is not an end in itself; it is an enabling agent to facilitate the continual evolution of relationships.

In their seminal study of regulation, Graham, Green, and Roberts (1988) conclude by contrasting two polar views of the role of science and scientists in regulation. One view is that the key to resolving policy conflicts is to work toward short-term scientific consensus bolstered by long-term research to reduce uncertainties as a way of reducing policy disagreements. Science and scientists are seen as "tools" in the process of conflict resolution. The opposite view is that regulation is a fundamentally political activity and that science and scientists are "merely ammunition" in a larger debate about values, interests, and power. Resolution of conflicts in the latter view would require institutional innovation to strengthen democratic processes and to enhance public participation.

The authors go on to propose a middle course, with which I agree, which they call "neoseparationist." This view recognizes that it is impossible to separate science and policy in regulatory processes. In this perspective, science and scientists (and, of course, risk experts) have a "modest yet important" role to play in informing regulatory decisions. Scientific knowledge and judgment can provide essential guidance about regulatory choices, but they cannot answer the ultimate regulatory questions which, rightly, also have an inherent political dimension.

Acknowledging the limited role science can play in conflict resolution allows policy issues to be addressed directly, reduces unrealistic public expectations of scientists and, in the end, strengthens both science and democracy. This is an essential step toward a new paradigm that conceives authentic communication between experts and citizens as an integral part of the social relations of technology and the sharing of power and responsibility.

CHAPTER 10 ⎯⎯⎯⎯⎯⎯⎯⎯⎯⎯⎯⎯⎯⎯⎯

Heuristics, Biases, and the Not-So-General Publics: Expertise and Error in the Assessment of Risks

William R. Freudenburg

I approach the study of risk from the perspective of a sociologist—a student of society—who happens to be particularly interested in societal interrelationships with technology and the physical environment. I began my professional career with studies of large-scale developments in rural areas, particularly the so-called energy boomtowns of the western United States and Canada. My earliest research focused primarily on coal and oil-shale development in an arid region, well above sea level; when I moved to Washington State University in the late 1970s, I decided to counterbalance the earlier work with a study of nuclear power development in a rainy area, close to sea level, in Washington State. While the earlier work had led to findings of significant social impacts (see, for example, Freudenburg 1976, 1981, 1982, 1984, 1986a; Freudenburg, Bacigalupi, and Landoll-Young 1982), I had *not* previously encountered anything like majority opposition to the energy developments, and thus I was ill-prepared for the high level of public opposition inspired by the nuclear power plants. The obvious question was whether there might indeed be something "special" about nuclear energy developments; this possibility was explored in a book I edited with Gene Rosa (Freudenburg and Rosa 1984) and a series of other publications (Freudenburg 1985, 1987; Freudenburg and Baxter 1984, 1985; Rosa and Freudenburg, forthcoming).

When I became the first Congressional Fellow of the American Sociological Association to serve in the U.S. House of Representatives, in 1983–84, it was my expertise on nuclear issues that was of interest to the Subcommittee on Energy Conservation and Power. As often happens on congressional staffs, however, I soon found that I was expected to focus not on my areas of past research, but on the committee's areas of current need (see the report in Freudenburg 1986b).

More specifically, the need had to do with probabilistic risk assessments, or PRAs. The Subcommittee on Energy Conservation and Power was one of several having responsibility for overseeing the activities of the Nuclear Regulatory Commission (NRC). Several of the committee members (and staffers) had concerns that the NRC's growing enthusiasm for PRAs may have had more to do with the desire to sell the benefits of nuclear power than with managing its risks appropriately. Virtually everyone at the committee, however, already had too much to do; as the newest staffer, I was thus given the task of taking a closer look at the use of PRAs. While I had already been devoting attention to issues of risk for quite some time, if only in that risk is inherently an important concept for someone who is interested in the societal management of technology and the environment, it was this committee assignment that first led to my systematic involvement in issues of risk and their management.

Given my training and experience as a sociologist, I was immediately struck by the one-sidedness of the nuclear risk debate. At least among the persons employed full-time in the business of nuclear PRAs—virtually all of whom worked either for the nuclear industry or its regulators in the federal government, as opposed to the local and environmental groups found so often on the other side (cf. Dietz and Rycroft 1987)—the tendency was to assume that the agency dealt with "real" risks, while the public focused on "perceived" ones. In reality, of course, the so-called real risks were also perceived, albeit through a more complex set of calculations, and by persons whose livelihood just happened to depend directly on the continued health of the nuclear industry. Most of my superiors on the committee had the training and proclivities of lawyers, and they quickly became deeply suspicious about such an obvious potential for a conflict of interest. My own inclinations were more charitable, as I believed that most of the risk professionals genuinely did try to overlook their ties to the nuclear industry when they were performing their calculations, and my firsthand contact with technical-level people in the nuclear establishment generally reinforced my respect for their scientific professionalism. Still, I came to share some of my superiors' concerns that at least a minority of the policy-level personnel might have a personal interest in trying to construct something like a mythology of purportedly "real" risks (cf. Nichols and Wildavsky 1987), and I saw genuine reasons for concern in the apparently *un*intentional blind spots of even the well-meaning technical personnel. The errors and omissions struck me as being particularly serious in two areas that were familiar to me from my own training: those involving statistical assessment of probabilistic factors, and those involving behaviors of human beings and their institutions. These are the two areas that will be summarized in the pages that follow.

While I have discussed a number of problems in my previous work (see, for example, Freudenburg 1988, 1989, 1992; Freudenburg and Pastor, in press), much of my work on risk has dealt instead with the risk-related perceptions held by members of the broader public (see also Freudenburg 1987, 1990; Freudenburg and Gramling, in press; Freudenburg and Jones 1991). The current chapter marks my broadest effort to date to discuss some of the heuristics and biases that tend to be found *among members of the technical community*. This work is not as fully developed as are many of the other approaches in this book, such as the psychometric paradigm (see Chapter 5 by Slovic in this volume), and the area is still rapidly developing. Some examples of other key contributions include Clarke's (1990) study of the *Exxon*

Valdez oil spill and its aftermath; the work of Kroll-Smith and Couch (1990) (and earlier authors, notably Levine 1982, and Erikson 1976) on anthropogenic disasters; the work of Vaughan (1989, 1990) on the explosion of the *Challenger*; and the work of Paté-Cornell (1990; Paté-Cornell and Bea 1992) on risks of offshore oil platforms. Important but broader overviews are provided by Perrow (1984), Shrader-Frechette (1991), Wynne (1982b), and Otway (see his overview piece, Chapter 9 in this volume); still broader is the work of Shapiro (1987, 1990) on the problematic challenges involved in the "impersonal control of trust" (see also Barber 1983; Freudenburg 1990).

The discussion that follows is divided into two parts. The first discusses four sets of human and organizational factors that tend to exert a far stronger influence on probabilistic estimates than is commonly recognized. The second part discusses three sets of statistical weaknesses that are particularly worrisome in the case of estimates that are often the center of intense policy debates—high consequence events that are represented as having extremely low probabilities of occurrence. The discussion of problems is followed by a set of suggestions about potential next steps and a conclusion.

HUMAN ERROR IN ESTIMATION TECHNIQUES

Due in part to the publication of a paper on the topic by Kasperson and his associates (1988), and in part to the practical significance of the topic, "the social amplification of risk" has begun to receive increasing attention in the risk analysis community. Two particularly significant aspects of social amplification have received relatively little attention to date, however. The first is that human and social processes can lead to the *attenuation* of risk estimates as well as to their amplification; the second is that the problems can exist among experts as well as among the general public. Recent years have seen an increasing awareness that many of the techniques used in probabilistic risk assessments, particularly in earlier assessments, are prone to systematic errors, but while evidence of the problem continues to grow, the caveats are often overlooked or forgotten once an "overall risk" estimate is produced. Four sets of problems are particularly noteworthy.

Overconfidence in the Ability to Foresee All Possible Failure Modes

A number of estimates appear to have suffered from a misplaced belief that all relevant failure modes had been adequately foreseen. For example, the accident at Three Mile Island began when a valve failed to close, although the instrument panel showed that it had closed properly; the plant operators' reactions served to make matters worse (Flynn 1984). The worst oil spill in U.S. history occurred on a calm, clear night when the *Exxon Valdez*, the largest and most expensive oil tanker owned by the third-largest corporation in the United States equipped with state-of-the-art navigational equipment, crossed over a "buffer" lane, another lane reserved for incoming tanker traffic, and an additional stretch of open water before running aground on a well-known hazard that is marked clearly on navigational charts. Less than two months later, a train hauling sixty-nine carloads of potash derailed in San Bernardino, demolishing a row of houses and most of the railroad cars. The cause of the accident was a series of errors that led to speeds of 90 miles per hour on a steep grade where the train's speed limit should have been only 30 miles per hour (Mydans 1989). In 1984, by contrast, a train's speed was within acceptable limits, but an accident occurred when a series of upstream beaver dams gave way after heavy rains and washed out a gap in the railroad bed that was 53 feet long and 23 feet deep (Burkhardt 1984).

In another case reported by an Associated Press wire story, "Man Stomps Snake; Home in Flames," a home was destroyed by an incident probably unforeseen by even the most creative of insurance actuaries:

If you don't like to mess with snakes, here's a good reason why.
It happened to Al Fitzwater of Fort Wayne, Indiana. He'd been working on his car, and got inside to start it, when he disturbed a three-foot snake that had been napping under the seat.
Fitzwater says the snake bit him on the ankle. Worse was yet to come. As Fitzwater stomped the snake, he hit the gas. The car, the snake and the driver then slammed into the house—which spilled a can of gas on the bumper while flames shot out of the open carburetor, setting the car and the house on fire. (July 29, 1988)

From the frightening to the funny, these and many other such incidents illustrate the principle that even a lifetime studying natural laws does not give anyone the ability to *repeal* such laws—and that may include Murphy's Law. This principle is often a source of frustration to risk assessors, sometimes because members of the affected public will insist on the impossible condition that technologies not be allowed to go forward until literally all potential accidents have been foreseen and planned for—and sometimes because overly zealous entrepreneurs and policy makers make the equally implausible claim that we *have*, in fact, foreseen all such problems (Dubé-Rioux and Russo 1988; see also the discussion in Perrow 1986). The problem, as many risk assessors are already well aware, is that the often-irreducible inability to foresee all possible instances of Murphy's Law creates a potential for any estimate to be insufficiently conservative (see also Fischhoff 1977; Primack 1975; Holdren 1976). As will be noted below, this problem is particularly noteworthy for relatively complex systems and for estimates of extremely low probabilities. For such systems, in fact, the problem is so pervasive that it has even earned a name: the "disqualification heuristic" (Clarke 1990), or the temptation to conclude that certain highly unpalatable outcomes simply "couldn't" occur. Unfortunately, an assumption to that effect is not likely to provide much protection—and it may even provide disincentive for an organization to devote adequate attention to being prepared for such undesirable events.

Insufficient Sensitivity to Problems of Small "Sample" Sizes

Risk assessors are often placed in a situation of needing to produce estimates on the basis of incomplete or inadequate data. Under the circumstances, analysts are often forced to make do with whatever data happen to be available. In general, such isolated bits of data provide an important basis for calculations and extrapolations, and often even low-quality data may be better than no data at all. As scientists are all too well aware, however, the results of the first few trials, first few interviews, initial case studies, and so forth, often will wind up differing significantly from the results of a more thorough research program. This is the principle behind the well-known emphasis on replicability in scientific research, and it is often a cause of problems for risk assessments that are forced to rely on whatever data may be available. Even if an experiment is of high quality, the results from that experiment may provide little more than a sample of size $N = 1$ from the universe of all possible experiments; even if the initial results are replicated in a second experiment, a "sample size" of two is not normally one in which a great deal of confidence would be placed.

This problem is exacerbated by the fact that "samples" may be not only small but biased. This is particularly likely to be a problem in "big science" (Clark and Majone 1985; cf. Henrion and Fischhoff 1986). The high cost of purchasing equipment, developing procedures, and so forth, may mean that only one or two laboratories in the nation or world will be capable of conducting a given experiment—meaning by implication that there will be little chance for unforeseen or underestimated sources of problems to be challenged or corrected by other researchers. Particularly if it is important to anticipate all the ways in which something might go wrong, many heads are probably far better than one, if only because of the possibility that a given laboratory will be subject to "blind spots" or to unknown or unforeseen sources of bias.

Failure to Foresee System Interactions and Interdependencies

In general, one would assume or hope that, if errors are known to the persons designing and engineering the system, the errors will be corrected. In many cases, however, the most troubling problems may be precisely the ones that were not foreseen. Virtually by definition, these "unforeseen" errors are unlikely to be taken into consideration in the calculation of risk probabilities (cf. Perrow 1984).

In relatively clear-cut cases, it is tempting to refer to "designer error"— as when a designer misreads a specification, misplaces a decimal point, or makes a mistake in a calculation, and the error fails to be corrected before the system falls apart. In dealing with technological systems of increasing complexity, however, such examples of clear-cut errors may come to be less important than the more subtle "errors" created by the difficulty of fore-seeing system complexity.

The importance of this problem in the context of risk estimates is that risk assessment methodologies tend to be and perhaps need to be analytical. The normal approach to the calculation of risk probabilities, in other words, is to break down the tasks in terms of the constituent components of a system—looking at each pump, pipe, valve, axle, relay, switch, drive-shaft, and so on—and calculating the probability of failure for each. Some of the most vexing of technological risks, unfortunately, are related instead to systemic or conjoint problems (the simultaneous occurrence of two or more problems that might not have been individually significant) and to factors that only exert an influence after a system has been operational for a significant period of time. Perrow (1984), in fact, has characterized the problems of complex interdependencies as being so pervasive, and so predictable, as to warrant the designation of "normal accidents." Perrow draws special attention to cases where systems are so "tightly coupled" that little time is available for operators to respond to unforeseen combinations of events.

Part of the problem of dealing with many real-world risks is that the effort to delimit an analysis—for example, by examining a single shipment of radioactive materials—is likely to divert attention from errors that may exert a broader set of effects, such as an error in manufacturing or designing a given cask that would then affect all of the shipments in a cask or set of casks (Audin 1987). A second part of the problem is that most of us have only limited ability to appreciate the complexities that exist outside our own areas of disciplinary expertise, while the real world is rarely sufficiently courteous or orderly to hand us·problems that stop within the boundaries of our own disciplines. As Otway notes elsewhere in this volume, a "human failing of experts is that success in one field can lead them to assume (sometimes without knowing it) that their opinions are equally valid in other areas"—a problem that may be especially severe when persons who have expertise about *hardware* start making assumptions about *humans*. A third aspect of the problem is that the components of technological systems are often interrelated in ways that are not foreseen by any one person. For example, "the rupture of a liquid natural gas storage tank in Cleveland in 1944 resulted in 128 deaths, largely because no one had realized the need for a dike to contain spillage. The DC–10 failed in several of the early flights because none of its designers realized that decompression of the cargo compartment would destroy vital parts of the plane's control system running through it" (Slovic, Fischhoff, and Lichtenstein 1984). A fourth and perhaps even more significant part of the problem is what I have called elsewhere the "diffraction of responsibility" (Freudenburg 1989, 1992). The complexity of an *organization* can compound the difficulty of managing a complex *technology*; the larger and more complex the organization, in fact, the greater may be the likelihood that we will encounter the familiar complaint that an important detail simply slipped through the cracks. In such situations, even the persons who sense the potential significance of a problem may fail to take the initiative to correct it, often under the assumption that "that's somebody else's department."

In the case of many technological risks, the interrelationships and interdependencies of greatest significance may be associated with systems that involve both humans and hardware. For example, while many accidents are blamed on human error, the true causes may be more complex. The accident at Three Mile Island provides an illustration; while the accident is commonly blamed on "human error," usually meaning "worker/operator error," closer examination reveals a different picture. A key cause of the accident was the failure of a valve to close, although the indicator light in the control room indicated (erroneously) that it had closed. Within minutes, the operators were subjected to an incredible sensory overload of alarms, warning bells, and flashing lights—the President's Commission on the Accident at Three Mile Island (1979, 11) referred to it as "a cascade of alarms that numbered 100." The operators did what virtually any human being would have done: they turned off as many of the distractions as possible, while trying to figure out what was "really" causing the problem. In many cases, once an alarm had been shut off, there was no record of just which of the switches had been tied to which problems. Perhaps the main rationale for blaming the accident on "operator error" is that there were two instruments in the control room that could have told the operators the source of the problem—assuming it is reasonable to expect even a genius to have been able to identify the two relevant stimuli in such a cacophony of confusion. One of the instruments, however, was on the opposite side of the control panel, not visible without getting up and physically walking around the panel; the other was obscured by a tag attached to a neighboring handle that indicated that it was in need of repair (for further details/discussions, see Rubinstein 1979; Marshall 1979; Flynn 1984; President's Commission on Three Mile Island 1979; Rogovin and Frampton 1980). Even though some of the best minds in the American nuclear industry came to the control room over the next several hours in the effort to get the situation under control, moreover, the situation was "dangerously out of control for at least 48 hours," according to a report on the accident in *Science* (Marshall 1979).

While this brief discussion is clearly an oversimplification, it does lead one to wonder whether the risk assessment community would be justified in blaming the Three Mile Island accident on the operators who were unable to get the system under control in the first few seconds, when even the best experts in the country were unable to get the system back under control in a matter of many hours. At a minimum, the Three Mile Island example should illustrate the need for human behavior to be taken into account more systematically in the design and development of technologies. Before a given pump is installed in a nuclear power plant, it is generally expected to have gone through sufficient testing to provide reasonably reliable statistical data on such considerations as the mean time between failures of a given type. Perhaps the risk assessment community needs to begin now to devote more attention to the behavior of "human components" in order to identify with increased accuracy the types of "human failures" that are likely to occur, under what kinds of circumstances, and with what degree of frequency—not just in the laboratory, moreover, but under the often-perverse realities of real-world operation. In addition, however, the experiences of Three Mile Island point out the need for much greater attention to the ways in which *organizations* tend to work, and to the ways in which we combine humans with hardware. Ironically, the early evidence suggests that typical engineering responses often make matters worse. The blurry vision of the Hubble Space Telescope apparently stayed that way despite at least two tests on earth that pointed to problems, with technicians disregarding the tests because an earlier procedure had already "certified" the telescope as being accurate (Waldrop 1990). More generally, the common response—designing a system that requires even less in the way of human attention except in times of crises—amounts to the worst possible way to make use of human strengths while avoiding human frailties (Rochlin, La Porte and Roberts 1987; Rochlin 1987).

"Calibration Errors" and Cognitive Dissonance

While members of the risk assessment community often refer to the difficulties experienced by members of the general public in calculating probabilities, it is less well understood that calibration errors—mistakes in estimating probabilities—also present serious problems for persons with scientific training. The most serious problems occur in the absence of reasonably definitive data, but the general tendency in risk assessment is for even reasonably definitive data to be in unreasonably short supply.

As one way of illustrating the difficulty of calculating confidence intervals, even for scientifically trained persons, I recently conducted a small, informal experiment. In a series of four presentations to technically oriented audiences with a combined attendance of approximately 700 persons, I asked those in attendance to produce a simple estimate of a 90 percent confidence interval—a pair of estimates sufficiently far apart to guarantee a 90 percent probability that "the true number" would be contained between them. The topic is one with which most persons have at least a reasonable level of commonsense familiarity: the risks of driving.

As might be expected, not all hours of the week are equally "risky" in terms of the likelihood of fatal accidents per mile driven. Common sense even provides a reasonable inkling of which are the safest and least safe hours: The riskiest time is around 3 A.M. on "Saturday night" (i.e., Sunday morning), when a relatively high proportion of the drivers on the road are tired and returning from parties or other forms of social relaxation, often including the consumption of alcohol. The safest hour of the week is roughly nine hours later, around Sunday noon, by which time partygoers have returned to their homes, and a high proportion of the drivers on the road are taking family outings or returning home from places of worship, presumably being on their best behavior. Each audience was asked to estimate the ratio between the safest and the riskiest hours of the week. Are persons 10 percent more likely to die, per mile driven, at 3 A.M.? Ten times as likely? Ten thousand times as likely? Readers are urged to pause for a moment here to decide what their own estimate would be.

Next, persons in attendance were asked to come up with a 90 percent confidence interval—a pair of estimates sufficiently far apart that each person in attendance had a 90 percent level of confidence that "the true number" would be found somewhere between these extremes. Given that, for most people, the bottom end of this confidence interval is "practically no difference," attention was focused on the upper bound. (Readers are urged to select their own upper 90 percent confidence bound at this point; pick a number sufficiently high so there is a 90 percent probability that the empirical ratio between the safest and riskiest hours of the week will be lower than the upper bound you select. Given this chapter's emphasis on the problems of overconfidence, you may want to follow the advice that was given to each of the four audiences, namely, to compensate for the usual tendencies toward overconfidence by choosing a larger number than you might otherwise pick.)

If in fact the confidence intervals so selected had averaged out to be true 90 percent confidence intervals, roughly 630 of the persons in attendance— 90 percent of the 700 or so persons in the four audiences—should have picked upper bounds high enough to have included the "correct" number. In fact, only 34 of the estimates were even close. According to the best estimate available (Schwing and Kamerud 1987), deaths are over 100 times as likely, per mile driven, during the 3 A.M. hour than at noon on Sunday. Only 34 of the 700 estimates—roughly 5 percent of the total—called for deaths per mile to be at least 100 times as likely. Despite the emphasis on the importance of trying to compensate for the usual tendencies toward overconfidence, in other words, virtually none of the estimates were sufficiently high to include the figure developed on the basis of empirical experience. Even under the relatively generous criterion of accepting as a "hit" any estimate that the ratio was at least 100:1, what was supposed to be a "90 percent confidence interval" actually wound up, in the aggregate, deserving only about a 5 percent level of confidence.

While the vast majority of the persons in these audiences held advanced degrees, usually in engineering or the sciences, and virtually all of them presumably had at least some experience with the risks of driving, it could be argued that the estimates would have been closer to the mark in cases where persons were making estimates of probabilities *within* their own areas of specialty. Unfortunately, the real world often refuses to stay within the disciplinary boundaries that are set up for intellectual convenience, meaning that risk assessors are often forced to tread outside their own specialty areas. Perhaps even more tellingly, however, available evidence suggests that even disciplinary expertise might not be sufficient to guarantee a high "hit rate."

Instead, the general tendency appears to have been for scientists to express an excessive confidence in their own estimates, even in fields as well-developed as physics and when dealing with a quantity as fundamental and as carefully measured as the speed of light. A compilation of the twenty-seven published surveys of the speed of light between 1875 and 1958 that included formal estimates of uncertainty found that the measurements differed from the official 1984 value by magnitudes that would be expected to occur less than 0.0005 of the time, by chance alone, when using the original estimators' *own* calculations of the uncertainties in their estimates (Henrion and Fischhoff 1986). The straightforward conclusion is that "the respective investigators' uncertainties ... must [have been] significantly underestimated." Although the absolute magnitude of the errors declined significantly over time, there was no significant improvement in the accuracy with which the remaining uncertainty was estimated. The 1984 estimate of the speed of light (which has since been used to calibrate the length of a meter, rather than vice versa) falls entirely outside the range of standard error (1.48 × "probable error") for all of the estimates of the true speeds of light that were reported between 1930 and 1970 (Henrion and Fischhoff 1986, Figure 2).

Other examples can be reported for scientists who range from engineers to physicians. One study asked a group of internationally known geotechnical engineers for their 50 percent confidence bands on the height of an embankment that would cause a clay foundation to fail; when an actual embankment was built, not one of the experts' bands was broad enough to enclose the true failure height (Hynes and Vanmarcke 1977). Another study followed a group of patients who were diagnosed on the basis of an examination of coughs to have pneumonia; of the group listed by physicians as having an 85 percent chance of having pneumonia, less than 20 percent actually did (see Christenson-Szalanski and Bushyhead 1982; De Smit, Fryback, and Thornbury 1979; Lichtenstein, Fischhoff, and Phillips 1982). Other studies of the ability to assess probabilities accurately—the problem of calibration—have found that calibration is unaffected by differences in intelligence or expertise (Lichtenstein and Fischhoff 1977), but may be increased by importance of the task (Sieber 1974). Overall, one would expect that only about 2 percent of the estimates having a confidence level of 98 percent would prove to be surprises, but nonspecialist assessors may have a "surprise index" on the order of 20 percent to 40 percent (see, for example,

Fischhoff, Slovic, and Lichtenstein 1977; Lichtenstein, Fischhoff, and Phillips 1982).

In general, scientists may be subject to an understandable problem of doing a good job of "predicting" more of something that is already familiar, while missing the likelihood of sudden discontinuities. For example, Henshel (1982) notes that while demographers have often done a reasonably good job of "predicting" populations during times of relative stability, they have generally failed to anticipate "surprises" such as the baby boom of the 1940s and 1950s or the birth dearth of the 1960s and 1970s.

Other studies suggest a more troubling implication: It may be that the underestimation of risks is particularly likely when people are reflecting on the risks of the activities in which they normally engage. Weinstein reports a pervasive "it can't happen to me" (or "it probably won't happen to me") attitude when people are estimating the risks of a wide range of everyday behaviors, from automobile accidents to radon contamination (Weinstein 1984, 1987, 1988; Weinstein, Klotz, and Sandman 1988). This apparently reflects in part the assumption that, if a person has not experienced a given problem in the past, he/she may be exempt from experiencing it in the future. In another study, Newcomb (1986, 915) has referred to "a macho or omnipotent response . . . to nuclear power plant accidents" among persons who work in such facilities, perhaps reflecting a tendency on the part of at least some workers "to deny and minimize" rather than to perceive risks accurately (Newcomb 1986, 916). While this point has not been proven, the underestimation of risks does appear to be widespread in "risky" occupations, including fishing (Tunstall 1962), coal mining (Fitzpatrick 1980; Lucas 1969), offshore oil drilling (Heimer 1988), police work (Skolnick 1969), high steel iron work (Haas 1972, 1977), paratrooper training (Weiss 1967), and even recreational parachute jumping (Epstein and Fenz 1967) and professional gambling (Downes et al. 1987). While it is possible to hypothesize that experience will breed accuracy, in short, the limited evidence available to date suggests just the opposite; in fact, familiarity appears to generate at least complacency and a numbness to danger, if not exactly contempt. The "cognitive dissonance" perspective (Festinger 1957) would suggest a stronger conclusion: It may be that persons in "risky" occupations will *tend* to ignore, minimize, or otherwise underestimate the risks to which they are exposed, thus reducing the "dissonance" that might be created by focusing on the risks that are inherent in their occupational choice.

STATISTICAL VULNERABILITY OF LOW-PROBABILITY ESTIMATES

The problems of inaccurate estimation become particularly troubling in the case of low-probability estimates, which appear to be especially prone to error. Partly in the interest of minimizing the creation of additional gloom, and partly because a somewhat fuller discussion is already available elsewhere (Freudenburg 1988), I will attempt to be relatively brief in summarizing these additional problems, three sets of which are especially noteworthy.

Nontestability

Particularly for some of the more bizarre or unthinkable sets of threats to a technological system, ranging from terrorist attacks on casks for transporting nuclear waste to catastrophic, multivehicle crashes involving fires and explosion with caustic materials, we may never be able to know what the "worst" possible threat would be. In most senses, this is quite a good thing; most of us would rather not find out the hard way that there is something even worse than whatever we decide to be the "worst credible" set of circumstances. Unless challenges to the system of at least such a magnitude actually occur, moreover, such considerations will have little practical effect. Still, while it is to be hoped that there will be no "opportunities" for such tests to take place, hope is not the same as knowledge; until or unless the systems are actually tested by "unlikely" or "impossible" events, we are actually placing faith in untested assumptions.

When we consider new or previously untried technological systems, there is a potential for a special case of nontestability. As Weinberg (1972) pointed out in his classic essay on "trans-scientific" questions, some technologies are likely to be so complex and expensive to develop that there really is no way of "testing" them before they are built; the cost of a test would be comparable to the cost of building the system itself—potentially running into billions of dollars—and in the case of a technology having relatively unique requirements, such as an underground nuclear waste repository, there may be so few potentially acceptable sites that it would be politically unacceptable to devote one of those sites to a testing program that might later make that same site unsuitable for a repository itself. Quite literally, there may be no way to test our full set of assumptions about something so complex as a nuclear waste disposal site and associated transportation system without actually building and operating the system. The decision to build may or may not be justified in the absence of the testing that would normally be desired, depending on values and other considerations; in any case, however, such a decision needs to be made only with the full recognition that the assumptions have not had the opportunity to be tested before being applied in what will amount to an initial but real-world test.

Nonfalsifiability

In at least one respect, those of us with training in probability theory may be subject to a potential bias that is rarely found among the general public.

Nearly all of us have had the frustration of attempting to explain to the lay public, or even to our own students, that events with one-in-a-million probabilities are not impossible; a low estimated probability is not necessarily called into question if an unlikely event does in fact occur. Of all the events that are expected to occur only once every thousand years or so, we explain, some can be expected to occur each year, and a tiny proportion may even occur more than once per year. Yet our very understanding of these principles may sometimes cause our hypotheses about extremely low probabilities to become effectively nonfalsifiable.

The familiar statistical problem of Type I and Type II error—of rejecting hypotheses that are ultimately found to be true, on the one hand, or failing to reject those that are actually false, on the other—can take on a new complexity in cases of incidents that are expected to occur once in a million reactor years, for example, but that actually occur twice in a single year (Marshall 1983). If empirical operating experience is limited, we have no scientific basis for "proving" whether the estimated probabilities are too low or too high. If we stick with our original estimates, we avoid discarding our estimates on the basis of what may prove to be isolated experiences, but in doing so, we make a de facto decision to trust estimates that may be incorrect. While many areas of risk assessment provide us with enough experience to permit the identification of such errors, events that are truly rare—or technologies that are still new or untried—may provide too little information to permit such corrections.

The Statistical Power of the Hidden Flaw

Perhaps the most serious problem, however, is also the most straightforward. Low-probability estimates are especially vulnerable to the inaccuracies created when our calculations fail to take account of unforeseen events. Contrary to what some might see as a "commonsense" expectation, the failure to recognize a problem in one portion of a probabilistic analysis is often not offset by an exaggerated conservatism in another portion of the analysis; instead, the lower the calculated probability, the higher the susceptibility to any given instance of Murphy's Law.

Consider a technology estimated to have a one-in-a-million chance of failing. For simplicity's sake, assume that risk assessors had succeeded in identifying all potential risk factors but two—one of which made the technology safer than the official estimate, and the other of which made it less safe. To keep the example simple, imagine that the technology would still operate at the one-in-a-million level of risk in 80 percent of operational circumstances, but that 10 percent of the time, the real risk would be one in a thousand, and 10 percent of the time the risk would be one in a billion. Then the true risk of the technology would be $(.1 \times 10^{-9}) + (.8 \times 10^{-6}) + (.1 \times 10^{-3})$—that is, 10 percent times 10^{-9} (one in a billion), plus 80

242	The Role of Science in Risk Assessment

percent times one in a million, plus 10 percent times one in a thousand, respectively—for an overall probability of .0001008001, or slightly more than one in ten thousand. Rather than being offset by the presence of the unexpected safety factor, the unexpected problem dominates the ultimate risk probability. Indeed, even if the risk assessment were to have been so conservative in other respects that the "real" risks were to be no higher than one in a *trillion* except for the 10 percent of the operating experience where the one-in-a-thousand estimate would hold, the overall probability would still be higher than one in ten thousand.

ALTERNATIVE APPROACHES

To return to issues of professional and personal development, one of the lessons I have learned is that it can be simultaneously challenging and rewarding to work with colleagues who ask tough questions about my own assumptions and inclinations, rather than simply allowing me to ask questions about theirs. The present chapter offers an example that is both clear and timely. Rather than being content merely to allow me to discuss the origins and outlines of my thinking on issues of expert error—these already being tasks that involve no small challenges, particularly in attempting to move beyond the relative safety of intellectual considerations and on to the kinds of personal and autobiographical factors that we scientists are more inclined to forget than to analyze—editors Krimsky and Golding have challenged me to do more. They have asked me at least to suggest the initial outlines of an approach that might help to facilitate the testing of my still vaguely formed expectations in future research. What follows will reflect my well-intentioned if not entirely satisfactory efforts to respond.

To simplify in a way that I hope is useful, three sets of factors appear to be involved, and only the first of them has the kind of ready testability that I prefer; at least to date, I have been unable to devise satisfactory approaches for the latter two, but perhaps readers will be able to suggest approaches that have not occurred to me to date. The first or testable factor involves selective processes of recruitment, promotion, and retention; the second involves what I call the attenuation of vigilance; and the third involves the expectation that the leaders of some of societies' most important institutions, like most of their fellow humans, may have some vulnerability to the temptation to act in self-serving ways—ways that sometimes include defensive responses to criticism.

Selective Recruitment, Promotion, and Retention

As would be the case for virtually all sectors of society, the institutions that manage science and technology are likely to exert a selectivity in recruiting, retaining, or rewarding workers; several kinds of selectivity could be expected to encourage relatively low levels of sensitivity to many kinds of technological risks. All other things being equal, for example, young persons with relatively high levels of faith in science and technology should have a higher-than-average probability of being attracted to studies in science and technology, then of completing their degrees in the same fields, and then of successfully pursuing employment in the institutions that manage technological risks.

Within those institutions, particularly given that it is often necessary to make decisions or take actions on the basis of less-than-perfect information (see Chapter 11 by Funtowicz and Ravetz), several factors would be expected to lead to the differential promotion, reward, and retention of persons having relatively fewer doubts about their own abilities to foresee and control events—or at least of persons who are able to convince *others* to have fewer doubts about their own abilities. Performance should not be irrelevant, however; organizational selectivity should work against the promotion or retention of persons making memorable errors, as well as of persons who desire the "academic luxury" of waiting until all data are in before making any decision. All other factors being equal, success would be expected to come to those who could combine a high level of loyalty to the organization and its goals, plus overcome a track record of having the kinds of obstacles and hazards that might have stymied others.

It would be a relatively simple matter to perform at least indirect tests of this first set of expectations, doing so by assessing the levels of faith in science and technology (and in the likelihood that risks will be successfully controlled) among various groups of scientists and engineers. If this chapter's expectations are correct, for example, we would expect higher levels of faith among college students who choose to major in scientific and technical fields than in, say, the humanities, and we would expect further that, within groups of college freshmen picking majors in a technological field, there might be change effects as well as differential retention effects: Students whose faith in science and technology would go up during the course of study, for example, might be more likely to graduate in the same field, while those who report declining faith might be more likely to transfer into other disciplines, and among students with relatively stable scores, we would expect a relatively high level of faith to be predictive of graduating and of seeking and obtaining jobs in technical fields. Within a given field, moreover, we might expect to find systematic differences both across employing institutions and across levels of experience, with the scientists employed in the private sector, for example, being likely to express more faith in market mechanisms and seeking lower levels of regulation than would scientists who were trained in the same field but worked instead in regulatory agencies or academic settings (a set of expectations already beginning to be borne out by empirical research—see Dietz and Rycroft 1987; Rycroft, Regens, and Dietz 1987; Lynn 1986). We would also expect to see differential effects of organizational loyalty, with scientists who had been advanced to positions of organizational responsibility tending to show higher levels of commitment to organizational goals—perhaps even accompanied by lower levels of commitment to public health and safety, per se, than found among younger scientists in the same organizations still holding roles "as" scientists (with this expectation, again, already having been supported in at least one empirical study of public health professionals—see Sewell 1971; see also Nichols and Wildavsky 1987; Lawless 1985, 1991).

The Atrophy of Vigilance

A second expectation is that, whatever might be the *initial* level of attention to safety and quality control, that level will tend to decline over time. This hypothesis runs counter to the more common expectation for "learning effects," or for organizations to become *more* effective over time at performing their tasks, presumably including the tasks of risk management. The expectation here may not be so counterintuitive as it appears, however; instead, it may be that the key factor has to do with the frequency of experience and the interpretation of near-misses. As noted quite effectively by Clarke (1990), organizations are always organized to do certain tasks well, and while they may not succeed even in performing these central or core tasks, the more common problem is that they will focus on the performance of the core tasks while devoting less attention to the performance of others. All other factors being equal, I would suggest, organizations should be expected to improve (to "learn") in dealing with the challenges and risks they encounter routinely, while often failing to learn (or even "forgetting") how to deal with challenges that are rarely encountered or less central to their mission. Indeed, it is even possible to argue that the very essence of efficiency is to avoid having one's energy and attention diverted by problems that are "unimportant."

The atrophy of vigilance itself is represented by the "sawtooth" function in Figure 10.1. The key factor here is the distance, in time, between the "teeth." My basic expectation is that if time passes without the occurrence of accidents, not only do *individuals* begin to get lazy or complacent, but *organizations* cut back quite systematically and consciously on their own vigilance capabilities. If only a few days pass between accidents, the board of directors or the management of an organization would normally be expected to ask whether the incidents might be evidence of a broader pattern, or even of a problem that needs to be fixed. On the other hand, given that all organizations seem to encounter the need to tighten their belts on a regular basis, one would normally expect such belt-tightening to fall disproportionately on those activities the organization considers to be less central to its mission, if only to protect its core functions—and risk man-

Figure 10.1
The Atrophy of Vigilance

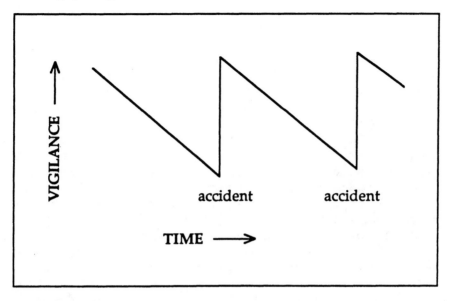

agement activities tend to be classic examples of so-called noncore functions (Clarke 1990; Freudenburg 1989).

According to this logic, even if risk management activities initially receive a high level of organizational attention, the most predictable thing in the world is that if accidents are extremely rare, the attentiveness will decrease over time. In the aftermath of the *Exxon Valdez* oil spill, for example, the petroleum industry announced plans for an ambitious system of well-equipped centers around the United States to respond to any future spills, all to be managed by the Petroleum Industry Response Organization, or PIRO. Roughly a year later, in a move that critics called a weakening of the planned response capacity (and perhaps in response to unkind jokes about "PIRO-maniacs"), the industry announced plans for a different new organization, the Marine Spill Response Corporation, or MSRC (immediately dubbed by critics as "mess-wreck"). At the time this chapter was being completed, the salience of response capacity had been reinforced by the enactment of the Federal Ocean Pollution Act, but if another six to eight years go by without a new oil spill in Prince William Sound, for example, it would seem only to make sense for the industry to ask whether there is really a need to "continue spending" or even to spend millions of dollars each year in cleanup exercises, for example. Even if we assume that the corporations' top leaders will be well intentioned (and that their task managers will be reasonably adept at protecting their budgets with the usual defenses—it would be bad for public relations; you can never be too safe;

etc.), the safest possible prediction is that such arguments will prove to be less persuasive than arguments from the organizations' "productive" divisions. Even if the risk management divisions survive the early budget-cutting exercises, moreover, another two or three years without a big spill would make it even more likely that the budgets would be cut in the next round of belt-tightening, particularly if the organizations' leaders genuinely believe their own public relations claims that "safety improvements" will by then essentially have eliminated the likelihood of such disastrous accidents—which, after all, by then would not have occurred even once in almost a decade. After another two or three years, the spill-preparedness exercises might be cut back further, with similar cutbacks being likely in other areas not having an obvious link to the organizations' core production goals. For organizations that decide their budget allocations on an annual or even a quarterly basis, in short, it can be difficult to maintain the level of vigilance that would be desirable for dealing with the kinds of accidents that, in practice, only occur once every ten or fifteen years.

The very nature of this argument makes it clear that it would be difficult to identify an appropriate universe of incidents that, for example, occur only once every ten or twenty years, let alone come up with a reasonable technique for sampling from within that universe, all while technology would presumably be continuing to change and evolve. One potential response, albeit one that is only partially satisfactory, would be to focus on so-called near-misses. As noted in a recent and very careful article by Bier and Mosleh (1990), near-misses provide decidedly mixed messages for risk management, perhaps in part because they have the potential to provide two kinds of directly contradictory information. On the one hand, so long as a disaster is averted, a near-miss (or more accurately, a near-hit) can be read as showing that the existing disaster management plans are capable of providing an appropriate margin of safety—perhaps even providing a higher level of performance than is asked of them in the organization's official planning documents. On the other hand, the near-misses also tend to show that the so-called prior probabilities—the events leading toward, if in this case not entirely *to*, disastrous outcomes—are *more* common than heretofore appreciated. To think again of the accident at Three Mile Island, for example, the interpretation evidently endorsed by nuclear power critics, as well as by a significant fraction of the broader populace, was that the accident demonstrated the fundamental *danger* of nuclear power; but the equally defensible interpretation that, not surprisingly, was put forward by supporters of the nuclear power industry, was that the accident demonstrated the fundamental *safety* of the technology, given that only tiny levels of radiation appear to have escaped from the facility during the accident.

One potentially testable expectation growing out of this chapter's logic would be that, in industries where near-misses are taken very seriously—meaning, operationally, that workers might be encouraged and even rewarded for reporting such incidents to authorities, who then would analyze the reports seriously as well, as appears to be the case for commercial aviation in the United States (Tamuz 1990)—we should see relatively little evidence of the atrophy of vigilance. In contrast, for industries where near-misses are taken largely as evidence that the system is working properly, we should see a much more serious problem of decreasing vigilance (and increasing probability of accidents) over time. Bier's analysis, incidentally, led her to the conclusion that, while the two messages from near-misses are intrinsically at odds with one another, the overall message is that near-misses tend to suggest the real risks of technology to be higher than previously anticipated. Bier's conclusion is thus consistent with the reasoning here, as are the media reports that so often follow major accidents, detailing evidence of apparent sloppiness in the industry or facility in question. Such media reports appear to show that the industry and its managers had been ignoring warning signs that are at least retrospectively obvious. In fairness, however, while it is a simple enough matter to list such reports as having come out in the aftermath of accidents such as the *Exxon Valdez* (Bartimus et al. 1989; McCoy 1989), or a few months later, in the aftermath of a smaller spill off Staten Island (Wolff 1990), I would not claim that such reports provide solid support for the perspective identified here; what I would most like to find, but have so far been unable to devise a way of obtaining, would be "fair" data on the extent to which such warning signs are found in a wide range of facilities and industries, coupled with long-term follow-up data on the number and severity of accidents experienced in those same industries over the next decade or more. If readers can assist me in sharpening this conceptualization or obtaining appropriate data, I would be most appreciative.

Responses to Criticisms

As suggested by the foregoing discussion of near-misses, my third expectation would be to find greater levels of success in organizations that attempt to learn from criticism than in those that attempt to belittle or discredit it. Yet this expectation, too, is likely to be difficult to measure quantitatively, given that most organizational actors will find it to be at least in their short-term interests to avoid being blamed for mistakes. As discussed more fully in a paper with Susan Pastor (Freudenburg and Pastor, in press), the basic argument is that deference from the public makes an agency's job easier (and a corporation's products more profitable); that criticism detracts from such deference; and thus that if it appears possible to "get away with" doing so, either a governmental or a private organization may find its best interests to be served by trying to undermine the legitimacy of its critics rather than by responding to them.

Notably, some of the most obvious approaches for trying to discredit critics would be to raise precisely the sorts of complaints about ignorance or irrationality (or, more charitably, about the need to "educate the public") that have in fact been raised repeatedly about the public concerns over technological risks. In fact, one of the considerations that points to the need to develop new approaches and conceptualizations is the fact that, while there is considerable evidence that faulty reasoning is not limited to experts, but is found among members of the general public as well, studies have repeatedly and consistently found that the supposed linkages between ignorance and opposition are either trivial or nonexistent. In short, if we are searching for the causes behind the growing public opposition to certain forms of technology, and if we begin with the assumption that public ignorance or irrationality is at fault, then, to borrow a common expression, we would appear to be barking up the wrong fault tree.

Again here, however, one of my reasons for hesitancy is that to raise this possibility is also to raise hackles. Persons who have not thought carefully about the issue are likely to have a visceral reaction—arguing, for example, that they know the differences between their own defensiveness and someone else's intellectual shortcomings. There is no real way to deal with such defensive reactions except to point out the problems that begin to arise when attention turns from the assertion of such convictions to the measurement of the underlying concepts. It is all too easy to conclude that defensiveness, like ignorance, is a malady that mainly afflicts other people, while we (and those who agree with us) are of course in the position of being hard-working professionals who, if we have failings, simply need to do a better job of educating our critics. The closest thing to an obvious solution to this problem might be to rely on the views of objective observers, although such a solution might prove to be more difficult to implement in practice than to describe in principle. Even if it were possible to identify a panel and a process that would be scrupulously fair, moreover, the persons and organizations judged to be guilty of defensiveness would normally be expected to defend themselves, presumably doing so by attacking the legitimacy of judges (as being either ignorant or deliberately biased, for example). Whatever the difficulties of assessing the extent to which official reactions to criticism might reflect defensiveness instead of a willingness to learn from criticism, however, the logic sketched out here would appear to suggest that such an effort would be worthwhile; here again, my hope is that perhaps readers will be able to assist in identifying approaches to operationalization that go beyond the ones that have come to mind to date.

CONCLUSION

The point of this line of research, of course, is not to create a sense of gloom, nor to dwell on errors or cases of unscientific behavior by scientists, regrettable though each of them may be. Instead, the purpose is to examine whether or not it is prudent to assume that the current or "official" estimates of risks can safely be taken as reasonable approximations of the "real" risks. On the basis of the accumulated evidence, the answer to that question appears to be negative, particularly in cases involving extremely low estimated probabilities. Instead, perhaps the most reasonable conclusion that can be drawn from the existing professional literature is that, *even in cases involving no conscious effort to produce biased estimates*, a combination of social and statistical factors will tend to lead to the *attenuation of risk estimates*, and through the misplaced complacency that is engendered by the conclusion that such low-probability incidents are "not credible," to a resultant *amplification of risks themselves*.

I would like to close this chapter by noting that I have written these observations, and all of my related work, as a loyal member of the risk assessment community. While of course I wish to minimize the likelihood of unprofessional behaviors by scientists, I also believe, on the basis of first-hand observations, that the vast majority of scientists are indeed careful, honest, and scrupulous, often to a fault. The problem, in short, is not that the scientists involved in risk assessment are bad or biased people; in general, they clearly are not.

Unfortunately, the problems identified in this body of work are in some ways more serious, and more difficult to counteract, than if deliberate or even conscious sources of bias were in fact involved. Instead, the problem is that a variety of factors that are far more subtle—unseen, unfelt, and yet unfortunate in their consequences—exert an influence that could scarcely be more disturbing even if they were based on deliberate malice. Systematically and repeatedly, the factors operating on risk assessors that have been identified in this report serve both to *attenuate* the estimates of risks and to *amplify* the risks themselves. Given that the field of risk assessment is committed to doing the best job possible of assessing risks accurately and fairly, I conclude that such a systematic set of biasing factors is one that we cannot afford to ignore.

CHAPTER 11 ⸻⸻⸻⸻⸻⸻⸻

Three Types of Risk Assessment and the Emergence of Post-Normal Science

Silvio O. Funtowicz and Jerome R. Ravetz

Before our paths crossed in 1981, our work had been proceeding, all unknown, along complementary lines. In Buenos Aires, Silvio had studied and taught mathematics and philosophy of science in the more formal, logical style, although his experience of teaching research methodology had already warned him of the limitations of the received views about both fields. Jerry had gone through science and philosophy at Swarthmore and a Ph.D. in mathematics at Cambridge before he got to Leeds to research and teach history and philosophy of science. There he eventually found himself needing to articulate a philosophy of science based on his experience of research, be it in mathematics, history, or critical analysis of leading pseudo-sciences like nuclear strategy. This effort culminated in *Scientific Knowledge and Its Social Problems* (Ravetz 1971), after which his efforts seemed most fruitfully applied outside academe. At the Council for Science and Society in London he headed a study group for which he drafted *The Acceptability of Risks* (Ravetz 1977). In this the integration of political and methodological issues was discussed for the first time. This work got him onto the Genetic Manipulation Advisory Group in London, and a visit to Princeton in 1977 gave him a ringside seat at the regulatory games as played at home and abroad.

When Silvio arrived in England in 1981, he intended to continue his studies for the Sociedad Argentina de Analisis Filosofico on Imre Lakatos' dialectical philosophy of mathematics. Jerry's earlier friendship with Lakatos had given him insight into that approach, and his interest in Eastern philosophy heightened his awareness of complementarity. Thus in our meeting it was, as it were, dialectics meeting complementarity. Together we realized that as the leading contradictions of our civilization have passed from simple class struggle and nuclear warfare to the destruction of the natural environment by our industrial system, the sciences of ecology and risk assessment have become central. Since these fields are both essentially affected by high uncertainties and high decision stakes, the political manipulation of uncertainty is now the focus of any relevant epistemology.

With these policy considerations in mind, we began our program of reforming quantitative thinking, which has hitherto been the paradigm case of absolute and unconditioned truth. Building on our common philosophical interests, we undertook the bold task of exhibiting the qualitative aspects of quantitative statements. We highlighted the complementarities of their "hard" and "soft" aspects, identifying their different sorts of inherent uncertainty, with the background of their dialectical interplay of knowledge and ignorance. Rather than doing conceptual analysis for its own sake, we designed a notational system whereby practice could be improved and mathematical nonsense identified and weeded out.

Its name, NUSAP, is an acronym standing for the five places of a complete quantitative statement. The first three, numerical, unit, and spread, are familiar from standard scientific practice. The last two, assessment and pedigree, describe the more qualitative judgments on the quantity. Spread is on the bridge between the two aspects; it expresses technical uncertainty, as in "random error" in experiments. Assessment conveys unreliability, as in "systematic error," while pedigree exhibits the deepest sort of uncertainty, which we call "border with ignorance." The five categories make up a notational system, which enables the maximum clarity, flexibility, and nuance in the expression of quantitative information. The system, together with its philosophical background, is fully described in our recent book, *Uncertainty and Quality in Science for Policy* (Funtowicz and Ravetz 1990b).

This endeavor of ours formed the background to the diagram of the threefold methodologies (described below), which was first introduced at the NATO ASI Summer School on Risk Analysis at Les Arc, France, in 1983 (Funtowicz and Ravetz 1985). This clarified an awareness which many workers in this field had been developing without being able to articulate: that the science involved in risk assessments is somehow radically different from that of classical lab practice. Also, it thereby provided a way through the confusions which then prevailed after the collapse of technocratic scientism in risk analysis. Several positions needed to be analyzed critically: philosophically naive *subjective probabilism*, elevating experts' guesses to the status of scientific facts; *radical social reductionism*, implying that "pollution is in the nose of the beholder;" California style *touchy-feelies*, solving all problems with good vibes; and finally the well-meaning *populism* which assumes that the knowledge and the feelings of real people are always good and true.

For us, risk analysis has functioned mainly as a leading example for our study of the way scientific methodology operates in its societal context, and particularly how mathematics functions as a means for dogmatism and elitism, little changed in principle since the time of the Pharoahs. Our work on NUSAP can therefore be seen as a first step in the genuine democratization of mathematics, and through it of science itself. Since then our work has moved in two directions. On the practical side, we are applying NUSAP in several directions, including radiological protection, ecological economics, and hazard analysis (e.g., the propagation of quality of data through fault trees). On the theoretical side, we are developing a new political epistemology for science, in which we articulate an ecological method for science. There, quality, complementarity, and plurality are the essential themes. We call this "post-normal science."

INTRODUCTION: THE PROBLEM

Our work has been motivated by the realization that the new problems facing our industrial civilization, although requiring scientific inputs for their resolution, involve a problem-solving activity that is different in character from the kind that we have previously taken for granted. Taking the example with which our own work began, we found that the analysis of risks involves uncertainties of many sorts, not all of which can be effectively controlled in practice. Attempts to solve such problems by bringing in more mathematical tools, as with Bayesian statistics or fuzzy sets, were all doomed to failure, because they missed the basic point of the presence of ineradicable uncertainties in a value-laden context.

The science of the textbooks, which effectively defines the world of practice for those becoming scientists or experts, has no place for either uncertainty or values. Every problem is a well-defined puzzle, which has a unique solution within its own terms. Although straightforward "applied science" can supply many useful results as inputs to policy making on risks and the environment, it is a delusion to believe that this approach is sufficient. Similarly, the approach of professional practice and consultancy, as exemplified in senior engineers and expert advisors, is frequently inadequate to these new tasks. Although such practitioners are aware of the complex and value-laden character of their problems, they, too, are trained to presuppose a stable and manageable context. In coping with these new problems, they can find that their tools and techniques are stretched beyond the point where they can be effective or meaningful.

We came to see that a full analysis of scientific problem solving in the modern world requires awareness of both the factual and the value dimensions of problems, and of the complexities in both. Our diagram has as its axes *systems uncertainties* and *decision stakes*. Its usefulness is as a heuristic tool rather than as a metric tool, so it is understood that there is no quantification along the axes. Accepting qualitative distinctions, we say that puzzle-solving science deals with problems low in both dimensions, and professional consultancy is involved when either is significant. Our innovation was to appreciate the possibility that in some important cases, either or both dimensions are extreme, so that the traditional methods are inadequate. We then mapped the three sorts of problem-solving strategies on a simple diagram, providing a graphic form that displays and also explains the distinctions (see Figure 11.1). For the "wild" area that lies beyond professional practice, we now assign the name *post-normal science*.

The problem situations that involve post-normal science are ones where, typically, facts are uncertain, values in dispute, stakes high, and decisions

Figure 11.1
Three Types of Problem-Solving Strategies

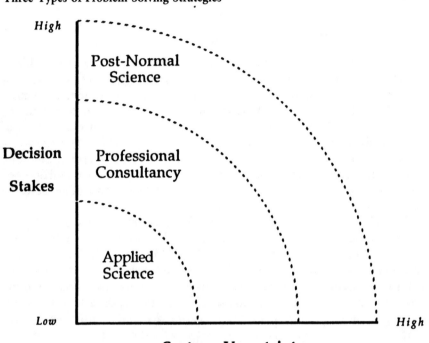

Systems Uncertainty

Source: Redrawn from Funtowicz and Ravetz (1985).

urgent. Because applied science and professional consultancy are inadequate, something extra must be added onto their practice which bridges the gap between scientific expertise and a concerned public. This is post-normal science, comprising a dialogue among all the stakeholders in a problem, regardless of their formal qualifications or affiliations. For the quality assessment of the scientific materials in such circumstances cannot be left to the experts themselves; in the face of such uncertainties, they too are amateurs. Hence there must be an *extended peer community*, and they will use *extended facts*, which include even anecdotal evidence and statistics gathered by a community. Thus the extension of the traditional elements of scientific practice, facts, and participants creates the elements of a new sort of practice. This is the essential novelty in post-normal science. In this way we envisage a democratization of science, not in the sense of turning over the research labs to untrained persons, but rather bringing this relevant part of science into the public debate along with all the other issues affecting our society.

Some people are uncomfortable with the idea that this new sort of practice is *science*. But science has continuously evolved in the past, and it will evolve further in responding to the changing needs of humanity. We are showing that the traditional problem-solving strategies of science, the philosophical reflections on them, and the institutional, social, and educational contexts need to be enriched to solve the problems that our science-based industrial civilization has created. To experience discomfort at the discovery of the uncertainties inherent in *science* is a mark of nostalgia for a secure and simple world that will never return.

APPLIED SCIENCE AND PROFESSIONAL CONSULTANCY

From the time of the Scientific Revolution onwards, the progress of science seemed to consist of the conquest of ignorance and uncertainty in one field after another, with no apparent limits. In the present century, theorists and philosophers have rediscovered uncertainty in mathematics and physics; but this has not prevented the continued achievements of pure and applied science to the present. Uncertainties in knowledge have reasserted themselves in practical fields with the development of technologies that are so novel and complex that the traditional skills of industrial safety assurance are inadequate. In such enterprises (notably civil nuclear power), it was science rather than engineering that experienced a crisis, for it was scientists rather than engineers who took credit for the achievements and created the public expectations of a brave new technological world.

When the new problems arose, scientists were not well prepared for them, because previous generations had led a sheltered existence inside universities and academies. In such circumstances, those with a scientific training, whose research was directed by an employer (private or state) rather than by an informal peer community, could be envisaged as doing the same sort of thing as their more fortunate academic colleagues, though with rather less freedom. In historical experience, such applied science provided (along with teaching) the bulk of the career opportunities for science graduates. It was a hybrid activity, very similar to core science on the cognitive side, while on the institutional side lacking many of the advantages and amenities of academic science. Problems were chosen by superiors with a view to applicability, solutions evaluated similarly, and intellectual property belonged to the employer. Historically this applied science was quite distinct from engineering, having different tasks and a different social organization.

During World War II all this changed, as the world's most famous scientists congregated in the military research laboratories of the United States and Great Britain, solving problems of military engineering with their scientific approach. (In addition to the obvious case of the atomic bomb, there was the solution of the "queuing" problem by Norbert Wiener and John von Neuman, and the ingenious code breaking by Alan Turing and his colleagues in mathematics and logic.) In the early postwar period, these scientists and their students were involved in the conception and development of the most advanced technologies (such as electronics, nuclear power, and space), and therefore these great engineering projects were generally conceived in the image of science. Science itself was being transformed, becoming "big" or industrialized, with gigantic research projects, so that the distinction between science and engineering was further blurred.

The basic distinction between scientific validity and engineering feasibility was overlooked, particularly in the euphoria of the 1950s. Hence the characteristic problems of the development and regulation of these new technologies, which could have been familiar to any engineer, were for a long time completely unnoticed. And the lack of scientific conclusiveness to the calculations of risks, which every engineer knew and managed through engineering judgment and good practice, came as an unwelcome surprise to the scientists who tried to apply the laboratory style to these new and difficult problems.

The conflict between the dominant self-image of science and the demands of a new form of practice was first exposed in the case of the politically sensitive problems of industrial risk assessment, particularly in relation to civil nuclear power. This was the occasion for Alvin Weinberg's pioneering essay on the new problems of uncertainty in science, in which he coined the term *trans-science* (Weinberg 1972). The presenting problem was of the possible carcinogenic effects of radiation at 1 percent of the natural background level; to test for this would require 8 billion mice! Weinberg recognized this as a case of a problem that could be framed scientifically and yet be unfeasible to solve, and so he called it trans-science. He did not then appreciate the importance of decision stakes, nor the need for extended peer communities and facts, but his insight of new problems, like science but lying beyond it, was fundamental.

The lesson of Weinberg's trans-science was slow in being learned, and most experts in risk assessment remained confident that their quantitative estimates were meaningful and valid. Only a few years separated the naive confidence of the Rasmussen report on reactor safety (NRC 1975) from the patent bewilderment of the experts during the weekend of the Three Mile Island accident. During the repeated crises of the 1970s and 1980s over industrial and environmental risks, fields of technology that had previously legitimated themselves as sciences suddenly revealed their fallibility. The old conception of science as the guarantor of the Good and the True had passed into history.

The fields of professional consultancy had long been familiar with the problems of risks and responsibilities. Whereas the scientist's task is completed when he has solved a problem that in principle can function as a contribution to a body of knowledge, the professional's task involves the welfare of a client, and the science that is deployed for that is subsidiary to that goal. One way of appreciating the difference between the two vocations is in their degree of recognition of skills and judgments. Among professional consultants these are known to be paramount; indeed, the fee structure reflects the knowledge of how to do a job (and being certified as such) more than its simple performance. Integral to a genuine profession is prolonged apprenticeship, which may involve years of initiatory rituals of hard study or overwork. This is most notorious in the case of physicians, the oldest of the professions. Senior architects and engineers are also professionals in this sense, along with those in any policy-related field who offer independent advice to clients. The real utility of the extended education and lengthy apprenticeships is the training in professional craftsmanship, which involves skills at the intellectual and behavioral levels. All this is in striking contrast to traditional science, where a single piece of supervised research, registered in a Ph.D. degree, has been deemed an adequate warrant for a lifetime career in independent research.

Further, the professional consultant can never escape from the tension between the scientific facts as established in the course of training and the elements of a decision in everyday practice. For this practice involves the management of uncertainty of many sorts. The tasks as presented will (particularly in the challenging cases) correspond imperfectly to the idealized categories of formal education. On occasion, the professionals may have to cope with situations for which their training provides little or no direct guidance. Faced with such contingencies, someone inside a scientific tradition would tend to protect himself by qualifying his conclusions with many caveats and always demanding more time for further research. The professionals know that they cannot afford such luxuries. Responsibility for the consequences of decisions and actions, rather than the guarantee of the validity of conclusions, is their metier. (For a detailed description of professional practice, see Schön 1983.)

Directly relevant to our present study is the difference between applied science and professional consultancy in the case of a decision that formally depends on the results of research, but where the stakes are high. In the traditional approach of science, even of applied science, such a consideration was deemed irrelevant. Scientists were to find the facts to the best of their ability, and that was the end of the matter. But in a real conflict of interests, any stakeholder can find ways of strengthening his position by criticizing the methodology of the other side's work. Because of the open texture of scientific argument (as distinct from logic or mathematics), such arguments can be prolonged indefinitely. In such a situation, the role of the professional consultant takes on another dimension. In this forensic context, the client's concern is less for the (contested) *facts* than for his own threatened interests.

The professional's responsibility for the well-being of his client can come into conflict with his own long-term interests and those of his profession. It is not only in such situations that the professional encounters ethical problems. However imperfectly ethics may have been incorporated into the training and institutional practice of professionals, there has never been any

Table 11.1
Traditional Forms of Problem-Solving Strategies

Type	Goals	Direction	Social Organization	Training
Core science	basic knowledge	peer community	university/academy	Ph.D.
Applied science	functional knowledge	managers	mission-oriented institution	Ph.D.
Routine engineering	working devices & systems	managers & clients	corporation	B.Sc. & experience
Professional practice & consultancy	practical problem-solving & advice	clients & professional peers	small-scale company	Postgraduate training & experience

doubt of its existence. This is in striking contrast to the research scientists, who until very recently were not even aware of having clients to whom they had ethical or societal responsibilities. In the present period, however, even the professionals' degree of awareness of these issues may be insufficient for the effective use of scientific inputs in the decision process. This is why an enriched conception of problem-solving practice is necessary for the effective application of science to the new environmental problems; and that is the background to *post-normal science.*

Before proceeding to a discussion of this new form of problem-solving practice, we will illustrate a variety of traditional forms (Table 11.1). Although these traditional forms of scientific problem solving are involved in coping with risk and environmental problems, by themselves they are not sufficient. Just as industrial risk assessment exposed the inadequacy of the *applied science* approach, so the newer risk problems, either global environment on the one hand, or toxics on the other, show the need for a form of practice that both includes and goes beyond applied science and professional consultancy. These two existing forms of practice fit neatly into a threefold classification scheme, whereby we can easily show why new forms are necessary.

THREE TYPES OF PROBLEM-SOLVING STRATEGIES

The problems of risks, both technological and environmental, have structural features that illustrate the inadequacy of traditional forms of problem solving. In these practices, decisions must be made involving the distribution of costs and benefits to different interests on the basis of future contingencies that are unknown and unknowable. In some cases numerical probabilities can be estimated and monetary costs guessed at, but these offer only limited assistance to decisions. We may state the situation in a paradoxical form: Whereas formerly we had the contrast between *hard* science and *soft* values, now we must take hard decisions between discrete alternatives, with only soft scientific inputs to them. Under these circumstances of radical uncertainty, a new type of problem-solving strategy is emerging; we call it postnormal science, where the traditional description, "the art of the soluble," is no longer appropriate. In this work, it is issues rather than problems that are being engaged, however much special scientific researches may be conducted and professional consultancy utilized.

We can compare the different sorts of problem-solving strategies that are now employed, through a biaxial diagram which exhibits them in terms of the two attributes of *systems uncertainties* and *decision stakes*, ranging from low to high, as in Figure 11.1. For systems uncertainties, the three intervals along the horizontal axis correspond nicely with the distinctions we have already made among the different sorts of uncertainty, namely, technical, methodological, and epistemological.

An integrated approach to the problems of uncertainty, quality, and values has been provided by the NUSAP system (see, for an introduction, Funtowicz and Ravetz 1987). In its terms different sorts of uncertainty can be expressed and used for an evaluation of quality of scientific information. NUSAP enables us to make the distinction between the sources and the sorts of uncertainty. Classification by sources is normally done by experts in a field when they try to comprehend the uncertainties affecting their particular practice. But for a general understanding, we have to distinguish among the technical, methodological, and epistemological levels of uncertainty; these correspond to *inexactness, unreliability*, and *border with ignorance*, respectively (for a longer discussion, see Funtowicz and Ravetz 1990b).

Uncertainty is managed at the technical level when standard routines are adequate; these will usually be derived from statistics (which themselves are essentially symbolic manipulations) as supplemented by techniques and conventions developed for particular fields. The methodological level is involved when more complex aspects of the information, as values or reliability, are relevant. At that level, personal judgments depending on higher-level skills are required, and the practice in question is a professional consultancy, a "learned art" like medicine or engineering. Finally, the epistemological level is involved when irremediable uncertainty is at the core of the problem, as when modelers recognize *completeness uncertainties*, which can vitiate the whole exercise, or when *ignorance-of-ignorance* (or *ignorance-squared*) is relevant to any possible solution of the problem. In NUSAP these levels of uncertainty are conveyed by the categories of spread, assessment, and pedigree, respectively.

It is easy to see how the different types of practice correspond to these different sorts of uncertainty. The vertical axis of the diagram relates practice to the world of policy; and the zones on the two-dimensional figure provide a full specification for any issue. For decision stakes, we understand in general the costs, benefits, and commitments of any kind for the various parties to an issue. There are three divisions, corresponding naturally to the three types of practice that we have discussed. In the case of applied science, the costs and benefits are minimal; only in exceptional cases does a policy decision depend on a single research result. For professional consultancy, they range from moderate to severe; the medical doctor normally cares for the health or life of a single patient, though he may also protect a wider community, as with epidemiological problems; for the engineer there is the welfare of a client, and in connection with safety, that of a wider community. In post-normal science, when global environmental issues are involved, the stakes can become the survival of civilization as we know it or even of life on the planet. Although these distinctions are real, there is no pretence of quantifying either of the factors. The intervals, and the zones they define, provide a rough gauge that forms a part of a heuristic tool for distinguishing the three types of problem-solving strategies.

Figure 11.1 illustrates that applied science is performed when both factors are low. Under these conditions, *puzzle solving* in the Kuhnian sense is adequate (Kuhn 1962). This would apply to the great mass of research that yields information on the behavior of materials or processes, either under controlled laboratory conditions or in nature. This is not the same as routine testing or monitoring, where there is hardly any novelty at all and the work can be done by a technician or an automatic machine; but in *puzzle-solving research* the element of possible surprise is small. In routine engineering practice the uncertainties are greater, for every local environment will have its novel features, and so this form of problem solving lies on the border of applied science. It is when either factor is significant that a more sophisticated sort of practice is involved. In the case of a surgeon, the uncertainties might be very well controlled, but the stakes (in the survival of the patient) are sufficiently high that what we call *professional responsibility, skill,* and *judgment* are involved.

One very useful feature of the diagram is the way it displays the fact that even when uncertainties are low, if decision stakes are high then puzzle solving alone will not be effective in a decision process. No scientific argument can be logically conclusive; even the received views in the philosophy of science acknowledge this. Scientific arguments evolve in a continuous dialogue that is incapable of reduction to logic; what it is that makes scientists "rationally" change their opinions is a matter of ongoing debate among philosophers and sociologists (Chalmers 1990). Applying this lesson to policy debates, we can appreciate that when a party finds its interests threatened, it can always find a methodological issue with which to challenge unwelcome results. This is particularly easy in the case of research on risks or the environment. Thus the forum for decision becomes enlarged from that of the technical experts, to include more of those with a strong stake in the outcome.

All these tendencies to debate appear still more strongly in the case of post-normal science. Although there is still an essential place for professional consultancy and even for applied science, the extremes of decision stakes or of systems uncertainties render them inadequate for the whole work. Research work and the deployment of skills have a central role to play, but this must be done in the epistemological framework in which the narrowly defined problems are integrated into larger issues. In this way they are provided with direction, quality assurance, and also the means of reaching a consensual solution to policy problems in spite of their inherent uncertainties.

Examples of issues with combined high decision stakes and high systems uncertainties are familiar from the current crop of global environmental problems. Indeed, any of the problems of major technological hazards or large-scale pollution belong here. The paradigm case for post-normal science could be the design of a repository for long-lived nuclear wastes, to be secure for the next 10,000 years. The strength of our diagrammatic scheme can be illustrated by consideration of cases located close to either of the axes. For a problem with low systems uncertainties, we have examples among the major disasters that have afflicted our modern industrial societies in recent years. In many cases, subsequent inquiries have established that the disaster had been "waiting to happen" through a combination of physical predisposing causes and management practices that had been well known in advance (e.g., Bhopal, the *Challenger, The Herald of Free Enterprise*, or the *Exxon Valdez*). Yet for the managements concerned, the costs of policies that would have prevented such disasters were unacceptably high; and so the high decision stakes dominated over the low systems uncertainties in safety policy.

The symmetries of the diagram lead us to ask about the cases with high uncertainty and low decision stakes. In policy-related fields, this is a recipe for low interest all around; if you won't get certainty and it doesn't matter anyway, why bother? However, this area on the diagram provides us with a link with earlier forms of scientific practice, when speculation was driven by curiosity and fields flourished in spite of a lack of assurance of either certainty or profit. Before science became the basis of a regular career (within the past century), most research was conducted in this spirit. For examples of such fields nowadays, we must look to areas where amateurs (in all senses) have an important part to play. One such field is cosmology. There the data are so sparse, theories so weakly testable, and public interest so lively, that the field is as much natural philosophy as science; and experts must share the platform with amateurs, popularizers, philosophers, and even theologians. Indeed, when leading scientists in the field write popular books in which they speculate on the theological implications of their theories, the distinctions become happily blurred, just as in the preprofessional past. This example may help to remind us how, in spite of the permanence of the greater achievements of science, the characteristic forms of scientific practice do depend on the societal context of the work. Post-normal science is the successor to earlier forms, appropriate to the needs of the present.

By the use of the diagram in Figure 11.1, we can better understand the different aspects of complex projects in which all three sorts of practice may be involved. For this we may take the example of a dam, originally discussed in connection with an analogous classification of problems as scientific, technical, and practical (Ravetz 1971). First, in the construction of a dam much basic, accepted scientific knowledge is deployed. Particular research projects of an "applied science" character will determine the relevant features of the local environment for the dam and the details of its construction. But the making of the dam is in the first place a design exercise, where the shape and structure are not determined by the scientific inputs. If nothing else, there will be a design compromise among the various possible functions of the completed dam, which may include water retention, hydroelectric power, flood control, irrigation, and leisure, together with their associated costs. Achieving the optimum balance among these, given both the uncertainties in scientific inputs and the value conflicts among interests, is a task for a professional. But the matter does not stop there. Some people may find their homes, farms, and religious monuments inundated by the artificial lake; can they possibly be adequately recompensed? There may be a possibility of long-term deterioration of the hydrological cycle in the district, and perhaps even local earthquakes. Dams, once seen as completely benign instruments of human control over raw nature, have suddenly come to be seen as a sort of predatory centralism, practiced by vast impersonal bureaucracies against local communities and the natural environment. When such issues are in play, we are definitely beyond professional consultancy and in the realm of post-normal science.

We can also use the diagram to illustrate how a problem can evolve so that it is tamed and brought some way in toward manageability. When, for example, a risk or pollution problem is first announced, it will almost always be in a condition of considerable uncertainty. Since it had not been appreciated previously, there is unlikely to be substantial evidence about it. Hence the information will tend to be anecdotal on the experimental side and speculative on the theoretical side. But the strength of the decision stakes will ensure that all interests, aided by the independent media, will offer their opinions with apparently complete certainty. The first phase of the discussion will therefore resemble ordinary political debate, but of a particularly confused kind. For each side will attempt to define the problem in the terms most favorable to its interest. Typically, proponents present it as applied science, while opponents stress its uncertainties and ethical objections. It is a new phenomenon for such debates to be effective; hitherto commercial viability or state security was the overriding consideration for industrial development, subject to a natural concern for health and safety. Indeed, in recent decades scientists and engineers have experienced bewilderment and dismay in confrontation with those who try to block progress on the basis of such intangible and nonscientific arguments. One of the last debates of the old sort was that over recombinant DNA research in the 1970s, when the evolving problem was kept firmly in the control of the scientists (Ravetz 1990); in its sequel, on genetic engineering, the critics have scored some signal successes, as in Germany, and are now generally accepted as legitimate participants in the debate (Fincham and Ravetz 1991).

If such issues remained in the realm of pure power politics, the outlook for our policies for science, technology, and the environment would be grim. But there is a pattern in the evolution of these issues that suggests that science may yet have an important role in such debates. For as the debate develops from its initial phase, positions are clarified and new research is stimulated. Although the definition of problems is (as we have seen) never free of politics, an open dialogue ensures that such considerations are neither one-sided nor covert. In the developing discussion on the technical aspects, no advocates need admit they were wrong; it is sufficient for there to be a tacit shifting in the terms of the dialogue. And as new research eventually introduces new facts, the issue becomes more amenable to the approach of professional consultancy. A good example of this evolution is the changing attitude toward lead in gasoline, where, in spite of the absence of conclusive environmental or epidemiological information, a consensus was eventually reached that the hazards were not acceptable.

Thus the simple diagram of the three strategies for problem solving enables us to see where traditional scientific practice is not effective, and why new dimensions need to be added to the problem-solving process. By its means we can make a dynamic analysis of the evolution of an issue involving science and policy. Post-normal science is thereby given its place as the natural and appropriate enrichment of the traditional problem-solving strategies.

QUALITY ASSURANCE AND POST-NORMAL SCIENCE

It is important to appreciate that post-normal science functions as complementary to applied science and professional consultancy. It is not a challenge to the traditional practice of science, nor does it contest the claims to reliable knowledge or exclusive expertise that are made on behalf of science in its legitimate contexts. Recent critical philosophies of science, concentrating on scientific knowledge alienated from its social context, have led to a view that "anything goes" in science. It is as if any charlatan or crank should have equal standing with qualified scientists or professionals (see notably Feyerabend 1975). Our critical analysis proceeds on another basis, that of quality assurance. The technical expertise of qualified scientists and professionals in accepted spheres of work is not being contested; what can be questioned is the quality of that work, especially in respect to its environmental, societal, and ethical aspects. Previously the ruling assumption was that these were somehow "external" to the work of science itself, and that such problems as arose could be managed by some appropriate societal mechanism. Now the task is to see what sorts of changes relevant to the quality of work in the practice of science and in its institutions will be entailed by these extended problems. We have introduced these new aspects through the three strategies of problem solving. Now we will develop their implications through an analysis of quality assurance in science.

Assessments of quality, and their use in quality assurance, have recently been appreciated as essential to successful practice in industrial production; this has been the lesson of the Japanese experience. We also know that many major disasters have been caused by defects or low quality at the interface between mechanical and information systems and the humans who operate and control them. Probabilistic analyses can indicate the relative likelihoods of different sorts of accidents, but real disasters tend to arise through sequences of events that no one had thought to put into the model. Now it is generally recognized that the quality of information, as a component of real systems of communication, command, and control, is critical.

Any policy decision on environmental and technological risks is made in the context of uncertainty, dependent on inputs of variable, or even unknown, quality. There is a growing concern among experts, politicians, and the public about the uncertainties affecting data for major environmental issues, such as global warming. There seems to be no systematic solution to this problem; instead, uncertainty is manipulated politically, to accelerate or defer major initiatives, depending on the outlook of the advocate. By contrast, the problem of assuring the quality of information has been almost universally ignored. One reason for this neglect may be in the confusion between uncertainty and quality, and the naive belief that there is a straightforward relationship between them, high quality being equivalent to low uncertainty.

Whereas uncertainty is an attribute of knowledge, quality is a pragmatic relation. It can be defined as "the totality of characteristics of a product that bear on its ability to satisfy an established use" (see British Standards Institution 1979). Uncertainty and quality are two distinct attributes; information of lesser certainty may yet be of good quality for its intended function. An extreme case of this is provided by deforestation in the Himalayas; although the estimates of the per capita fuelwood consumption vary through a factor of almost a hundred, all serious studies agree that their numerical predictions imply that the problem exists and that its solution is urgent (Thompson and Warburton 1985). An example of high certainty and very poor quality is provided by a prediction of a rise in the average temperature of the earth of 0 to 10°C over the next forty years due to the greenhouse effect. On a commonsense basis, we may say that the true value is almost certain to lie within that range; but the climatic consequences in this range vary from the trivial to the nearly catastrophic. The prediction is nearly true by definition; its quality decreases accordingly because the statement approaches being analytical rather than synthetic. In other words, it tells us very little about the real world.

Thus there are inherent limitations to the reduction of uncertainty in this kind of research. There is no point in risk assessment trying to emulate experimental physics in its control of uncertainty. Each field of practice has a characteristic grade of information appropriate to its needs (rather like hotels or restaurants in grading schemes); within that grade, information may vary in quality (as with hotels), depending on how well its uncertainties are managed and hence how well the information fits its function as an input to a decision process.

In ordinary scientific practice, considerations of values are largely implicit; even if they are operative in the choice of problems, once the research is under way they are put in the background. However, they are always present as part of the framework of the research; the myth of "value-free" science can be sustained only by ignoring the routinely used statistical methods. In any genuine statistical exercise, the design must take account of the error-costs of the possible alternatives; thus no single test can optimize both selectivity and sensitivity (avoiding the errors of false positives and false negatives). The choice, as expressed in numerical confidence levels, reflects the background of values, realized as costs and benefits, which condition every experimental program.

When ordinary scientific practice does not provide conclusive solutions for its problems, the values become explicit in the assignment of rules of inference. The growing use of scientific expertise in the courts frequently reveals a mismatch between the traditional value-implicit rules of scientific inference and those appropriate in tribunals. Thus in the law courts, various special principles for controlling error-costs are invoked, including *balance of probabilities* and *burden of proof*. Thus in the latter case, the error-costs of convicting an innocent person are deemed to be higher than those of acquitting the guilty, at least in the Anglo-Saxon tradition. Tribunals of inquiry provide an illuminating case of bridging the two approaches and their respective conceptions of value and error-cost. In the Black enquiry on excess child leukemia cases in the neighborhood of the Sellafield nuclear re-processing plant, the Scottish concept of a "not proven" verdict was explic-itly applied to the possible cause of the excess leukemias (Macgill 1987).

In problems of risk and the environment, the value considerations in scientific practice may be quite explicit. A classic example is the statistical design of a program for testing defective items in a large shipment. If it is of apples, then a bad one spoils only its barrel; but if it is of landmines, a premature explosion can take the whole neighborhood with it. The relative costs of false positives and false negatives are very different in the two cases. This example also serves to illustrate the factor of *dread*, an important dimension of public perception of novel risks like nuclear power and the release of genetically engineered organisms into the environment.

If we keep the issues of quality in mind, we are in a position to understand how post-normal science is different from its predecessors. In his classic work *The Structure of Scientific Revolutions*, Thomas S. Kuhn (1962) defined *normal* science as "puzzle solving" within an unquestioned "paradigm," an exemplar for practice. This definition is adopted by a subject-specialty community that consists of all those with the appropriate educational qualifications who also accept (generally unself-consciously) common standards of quality for problems and solutions. "Progress" takes place by means of such routine puzzle solving, as the ruling paradigm becomes ever more articulated; indeed, in "matured" fields, this is the defining property of normal science. Only when this approach fails to an embarrassing degree to resolve anomalies of practice does the community lose its unanimity and undergo crisis. This leads to a "scientific revolution" and, eventually, to the enthronement of a new paradigm—not so much building on the old one as replacing it and rendering all its associated puzzle solving irrelevant and obsolete.

Kuhn did not merely describe the practice of "matured" science; as a historian, he was also very concerned to see how sciences achieved this state, evolving out of the "immature," embryonic early stages through which all sciences passed. His account of the achievement of the state of "maturity" has a most important ambiguity, which bears directly on the social aspects of post-normal science. For the transition he imagines a sort of *social contract* among the practitioners of an immature field, in which they agree to a closure of the endless debate about foundational questions. Indeed, it was his experience of the contrast between argumentative behavioral scientists and acquiescent physical scientists that gave him the clue to the essentially social character of scientific maturity. He already knew that the foundational questions of physics are no more settled than those of psychology; why, then, do physicists normally ignore them? There seem to be two sorts of reasons: one is that puzzle solving *works* in a way that the community accepts as successful and progressive. The other is that dissidents are thenceforth ignored, or dismissed as nuisances. If we look at the unquestionably successful fields of academic scientific research, then the difference between these reasons is inessential; only cranks and occasional rebels disagree with the consensus. But when we consider fields that are not so favored, the ambiguity in Kuhn's picture becomes crucial. For we may then ask, how is the uniformity enforced? Kuhn himself indicated that there is something of a dogmatic, totalitarian element in normal science, as when he compared education in natural science to that in orthodox theology. This interpretation has been useful both to those academics who would like to achieve maturity by fiat, forcing all members of a department to follow the line, and also to rebellious students who recognize no inherent virtue in the subject's ruling paradigm or its intellectual puzzles.

Kuhn did not deal explicitly with questions of quality in science, for his problem lay within the scope of the classic philosophy of science, concerned with claims to knowledge and progress. But his social model of scientific practice lends itself naturally to an analysis of quality assurance. Using his framework for the new problems facing science, we may say that in normal science quality assurance is effected by the closed community of practitioners on a well-defined set of problems in whose solution they have exclusive esoteric expertise. In pre-normal science, quality assurance is a matter of continuous controversy, and this is taken as a sign of its immaturity. From the vantage point of post-normal science, we can appreciate the fertile ambiguity of Kuhn's formulation. For we are now familiar with the cases where a body of scientific or technological puzzle solving is radically flawed or nearly vacuous when viewed from the outside, while the community of practitioners have by some means maintained a consensus that all is well or will be soon. It is difficult for a layperson to argue effectively that this or that field of academic science is not as mature as its proponents claim. But when the responsible experts are unable to produce a class of environmental models that predict reliably, or an experimental practice that protects sentient beings, or an epidemiology that identifies environmentally caused illnesses without protracted political and legal struggles, then by default we are in the realm of post-normal science, and we need an extension of the peer community for the exercise of quality assurance.

The phenomenon of reality breaking into a social or intellectual system has recently been most obvious in connection with the societies of Eastern Europe, when the hollowness and ineptitude of the regimes' normal practice suddenly became a topic for public discussion and active dissent. Our technological systems have generally not suffered from such pathologies to the same degree within their defined spheres of operation and in their centers of origin; but the ongoing problems of both space and nuclear technologies remind us that competence should not be taken for granted anywhere. We have previously described this as the "Ch-Ch syndrome," after *Challenger* and Chernobyl (Ravetz, Macgill, and Funtowicz 1986). We could interpret the global environmental issues as an extension of this syndrome, in which our scientific puzzle solving has, all unknown to practitioners and general public alike, been seriously defective in important aspects of its quality.

Normal science still occupies a central position in the study of risk, in two ways. As part of the solution, there is always a need for scientific information that is as sound as it can be, much of it produced by well-tried techniques on limited problems. Indeed, as public interest in a problem leads to resources being invested in it, the relevant sciences gain in strength, and (as we discussed above) the problem is brought back in toward the professional consultancy domain. In this way, the characteristic uncertainties are brought back from the epistemological state, toward the methodological and perhaps even the technical. But normal science can also be part of the problem, in ways that are unfamiliar and disturbing to the individuals involved. The great risk problems have to a large extent been created by the practice of normal, puzzle-solving science and technology. Scientists and engineers who always thought that their work was purely beneficial to humanity, either directly or indirectly, now discover new problems thrown up by their past successes. Worse, their training and their inherited approach do not equip them for the solution of the problems directly associated with their work. Thus nuclear physicists are not skilled in oncology or epidemiology; nor are molecular biologists familiar with microbial ecology. Even more, specialists in human reproduction engineering are not systematically educated in ethics. Hence when such people in matured sciences try to cope with the problems created by their work, whether they are made manifest as hazards, pollution, or ethical dilemmas, they are no longer working within their disciplinary paradigm. They find that their normal-science practice has created problems of a post-normal sort, and in the face of these, their skills are only partly effective; in important aspects of the problem, they are as amateurs.

Traditionally trained scientists who venture into the fields of post-normal science thus find themselves in unfamiliar territory. The relevant disciplines (such as toxicology, epidemiology, ecology, and risk analysis) are weaker, technically and socially. They deal with more complex systems, are less well developed theoretically, and historically have tended to lack prestige and resources. Furthermore, their relations with the public are very different. It is not a case of popularizing esoteric results to an appreciative lay audience. Rather, the post-normal sciences address the worries of people, as residents, parents, and human beings, perhaps even the families of those involved in creating the problem in the first place. The criteria of quality are broader than (say) theoretical interest or industrial applicability; they include considerations of health and well-being, of the environment and of humanity. The forums in which issues are debated are not restricted to the closed communities of subject-specialists, but will involve the media and various sorts of tribunals. In these, the scientist is not protected by his academic qualifications and may be subjected to criticisms and interrogations that he may justifiably consider to be unscientific and unfair. In spite of these personal and professional hazards, the narrowly defined puzzle-solving disciplinary community can no longer maintain a monopoly on the quality assurance of their work; and so normal science must in these fields be superseded. There is a need for a new, more pluralistic strategy of inquiry, where the power embodied in quality assurance is more equitably shared among those with a legitimate concern for the consequences of scientific and professional work.

SOCIAL ASPECTS OF POST-NORMAL SCIENCE

Although knowledge has its objective aspect, especially when embodied in books or taught impersonally in schools, it is a social product and as such is involved in the distribution of power in society. This applies to science as much as to literature or art; and a political epistemology is now necessary for the understanding of the new proper uses of scientific knowledge.

In what we might now call *pre-normal* science, before the professionalization that took place through the nineteenth century, nearly all the practitioners were amateurs. They could and did debate vigorously all aspects of the work, from data to methodology, but there was no in-group of established practitioners in conflict with an out-group of critics. In normal science, any outsiders were effectively excluded from dialogue. Only in a Kuhnian "pre-revolutionary" situation, when the ruling paradigm (cognitive and social) could not deliver the goods in steady puzzle-solving progress, would outsiders get the chance to be heard. In post-normal science there is still a distinction between insiders and outsiders, based (on the side of knowledge) on certified expertise and (on the social side) on occupation. But since the insiders are manifestly incapable of providing effective conclusive answers to many of the problems they confront, the outsiders are capable of forcing their way into a dialogue. When the debate is conducted before a lay public, the outsiders (including community activists, lawyers, legislators, and journalists) may on occasion even set the agenda.

In the United States, where community activism is a recognized part of the political process, there is even a term for the work of the extended peer communities: *popular epidemiology* (Brown 1987). This displays an important aspect of post-normal science, namely, the struggles for legitimacy by nontraditional researchers. In the terms of our diagram, the decision stakes involve not merely the results of the research for the relevant health policies, but also the monopoly of accredited expertise hitherto enjoyed by various groups of academics, professionals, and officials. Of course, such battles for status are of long standing in health care; what is new here is that nonestablished practitioners are challenging the established groups on their own ground. They perform all the necessary operations of quality assurance on their research except for the crucial one of leaving it to the official experts. Here, as in the case of "accidents waiting to happen," these societal decision stakes can dominate the problem to the point where debate continues even when the system uncertainties are completely controlled.

As extended peer communities become more coherent and effective, the political process becomes enhanced with new structures whereby dialogue can be maintained and perhaps controlled. Thus mathematical decision analysis, historically a tool for a hypothetical decision maker with perfect knowledge and power, now embraces processes with a multiplicity of stakeholders and even of disagreeing experts (see von Winterfeldt, Chapter 14). But from the point of view of NUSAP and of post-normal science, it is questionable whether the gross quantitative uncertainties in the risk and environmental variables, to say nothing of those of the stakeholders' values, can be carried through a formal computation without yielding a totally indeterminate result.

An appreciative study of local knowledge in solving scientific and technological problems is only now getting under way. Some authors have recognized this as the key to genuinely sustainable development. Arnold Pacey illustrates how a highly successful technology is the outcome of a "dialogue" between what is an apparently more advanced innovative culture and the apparently traditionalist receiving culture. Thus, in African agriculture, the previous dominance of colonially introduced temperate zone concepts is being replaced by the integration of tree and field crops (incomprehensible to Western experts), together with irrigation and minimal engineering (Pacey 1990, 203).

In Europe, a recent study by Brian Wynne of the University of Lancaster on the sheep farmers of Cumbria after Chernobyl has provided a classic case of the contrast between farmers with a craft knowledge of their animals, their habitat, and the requirements of their businesses, and the "official" side of the problem. This included well-intentioned Ministry scientific experts whose knowledge of local conditions was derived from a different sort of experience, and official advisors and spokesmen whose apparent main concern was to utter reassuring noises so long as they could. A farmer's reaction to a typical piece of Ministry advice on husbandry was, "When you hear things like that, it just makes your hair stand on end" (Wynne 1989c).

It is not merely in Third World countries that "appropriate technology" can solve problems better than the official sort. Even in the midst of our high-technology culture, the official experts can be deficient on several fronts: problem identification, traditional knowledge, evaluative understanding, and intuitive and particularized knowledge (Krimsky 1984). All such extensions of *facts* have tended to be neglected in the formal training of the professionals who are accredited for solving practical problems. When introduced into a debate, they remind the professionals of uncertainties and complexities for which they have no preparation. They also raise the decision stakes by challenging professional authority through the proposed extension (perhaps to quite humble or unlettered persons) of the peer group performing quality assurance on the technical materials. Hence any theory of scientific knowledge in this broader context must be a political epistemology.

Because of these human aspects of the issues giving rise to post-normal science, there must be an extension of all the elements of the scientific enterprise. To begin with, there must be present an expertise whose roots and affiliations lie outside that of those involved in creating or officially regulating the issue. These new participants, enriching the traditional peer communities and creating what might be called *extended peer communities*, are necessary for the transmission of skills and for quality assurance of results. For in the case of the new sort of science, who are the *peers*? In Kuhn's normal science, they are colleagues on the job, engaged in that "strenuous and devoted attempt to force nature into the conceptual boxes supplied by professional education" (Kuhn 1962, 5). Such peers are still here, as scientists and experts; and they exercise quality control within the technical paradigm of their expertise. But the problems of the new sort of science are not ones of purely *knowing that* within stable paradigms; they include *knowing how*, along with broad and complex issues of environment, society, and ethics. Hence it is necessary and appropriate for quality assurance in these cases to be enriched at the very least by the contribution of other scientists and experts, technically competent but representing interests outside the social paradigm of the official expertise.

It is important to realize that this phenomenon is not merely the result of the external political pressures on science that occur when the general public is concerned about some issue. Rather, in the conditions of post-normal science, the essential function of quality assurance can no longer be performed by a restricted corps of insiders. When problems do not have neat solutions, when the phenomena themselves are ambiguous, when all mathematical techniques are open to methodological criticism, then the debates on quality are not enhanced by the exclusion of all but the academic or official experts. Knowledge of local conditions may not merely shape the policy problems; it can also determine which data are strong and relevant. Such knowledge cannot be the exclusive property of experts whose training and employment incline them to abstract, generalized conceptions. Those whose lives and livelihood depend on the solution of the problems will have a keen awareness of how general principles are realized in their backyards. It may be argued that they lack theoretical knowledge and are biased by self-interest, but it can be argued equally well that the experts lack practical knowledge and have their own forms of bias (see Freudenburg, Chapter 10).

Along with the enrichment of the traditional scientific peer communities we have a parallel enrichment of the cognitive basis of post-normal science; we speak of *extended facts*. This is the material that is effectively introduced into a scientific debate on policy issues. It is now widely appreciated that the beliefs and feelings of local people, whatever their source and validity, must be recognized and respected lest they become totally alienated and mistrustful. But extended facts go beyond that purely subjective base. There will also be anecdotes circulated verbally, as well as edited collections of such materials prepared for public use by citizens' groups and the media. These will not usually be in traditional scientific form, but they may be essential for establishing a prima facie case for the existence of a problem, and therefore the urgency of systematic research. When such testimonies are introduced into scientific debate and subject to some degree of peer review before reporting or acceptance, they approach the status of scientific facts. Of similar strength are the experiences of persons with a deep knowledge of a particular environment and its problems, like the hill farmers of Cumbria reported by Wynne. We should not forget material discovered by investigative journalism. Finally, the category of extended facts can also be applied to information that is quite orthodox in its production, but that for political or bureaucratic reasons is officially secret in some way or other; such facts can then function covertly, forming a background to loaded public questions. This last sort of "fact" may seem very strange to those whose idea of science is derived from the textbook and the academic research laboratory. But for those who are familiar with science in the policy context, such extended facts may be quite crucial in the accomplishment of the quality assurance of results on which health and safety depend.

As post-normal science depends so critically on data that are frequently inadequate in quantity and quality, the pitfalls in its production and interpretation are particularly severe. Scientists who are engaged in an academic exercise, or those working for a bureaucracy with a vested interest in the issue, will not normally be inclined to check for all the possible hidden traps that could vitiate their results. It is entirely natural and appropriate for those with a personal interest in the issue, and a personal knowledge of the phenomena, to engage in a dialogue on quality assurance. As yet this has happened only sporadically, and in a context of conflict and polarization of interests. The task is to create the conceptual structures, along with the political institutions, whereby a creative dialogue may be developed. For this, post-normal science is a foundational element.

We might finally ask, what sort of scientific practice would we call it, if unproblematic routine monitoring and research into risk and environmental problems were to be carried out by citizens (who had obtained the necessary competence) rather than by official experts? That is, the legitimacy of their practice would derive not from their official accreditation but from their standing with their own community. This is not yet the case; as we mentioned in connection with popular epistemology, the established official and professional bodies do not welcome such a broadening of the scientific franchise. Such a situation could be seen as a new sort of applied science, with an accepted extension of the peer community beyond its traditional boundaries; there, we might say that post-normal science would have sublimated itself. There are historical precedents: in nineteenth-century America, inventors were free agents (provided they could survive the inequalities of wealth and power); and in medicine, the status division between "orthodox" and "alternative" was not very sharp. The present local struggles over risks and the environment, usually manifesting as NIMBY issues, are reflections of conflicts over power and authority in knowledge that go back continuously through the ages. The successes in the developments of post-normal science are therefore part of a long process in the democratization of society.

CONCLUSION: THE DEMOCRATIZATION OF EXPERTISE

We have now reached the point where the narrow conceptions of science and knowledge are no longer appropriate for our needs. Unless we find a way of enriching our science to include practice, we will fail to create methods for coping with the challenges of technological and environmental risks, in all their complexity, variability, and uncertainty. Fortunately, in the changing social distribution of knowledge and skills, the conditions are ripe for broadening the conception of science. For now the liberal arts, as rhetoric, are no longer restricted to a tiny privileged elite in society, and the manual arts have lost the stigma of belonging to the oppressed majority. The improvement of manners and morals, from the Enlightenment through industrialized society, has been real. In modern societies there are now large constituencies of ordinary people who can read, write, vote, and debate. The democratization of political life, to include ordinary people and women, is now a commonplace; its hazards are accepted as a small price to pay. Now it becomes possible to achieve a parallel democratization of knowledge, not merely in mass education but in enhanced participation in decision making for common problems.

The democratization of science in this respect is therefore not a matter of benevolence by the established groups, but (as in the sphere of politics) the creation of a system that, in spite of its inefficiencies, is the most effective means for avoiding the disasters that in our environmental affairs, as much as in society, result from the prolonged stifling of criticism. Let us be quite clear on this: we are not calling for the democratization of science out of some generalized wish for the greatest possible extension of democracy in society. The epistemological analysis of post-normal science, rooted in the practical tasks of quality assurance, shows that such an extension of peer communities, with the corresponding extension of facts, is necessary for the effectiveness of this new sort of science in meeting the great challenges of our age.

NOTE

We are grateful to the editors for their suggestions for the improvement of the earlier draft, in particular Table 11.1 on the traditional forms of problem-solving practice.

CHAPTER 12

Risk and Social Learning: Reification to Engagement

Brian Wynne

I came across the risk field by accident, largely thanks to my longer-standing interest in the democratization of science and technology. This interest sparked an early critique of the technocratic pretensions of technology assessment (Wynne 1975). Having completed 95 percent of my doctoral thesis in physics/materials science (with, as my supervisor encouragingly put it, the other 95 percent still to do), I began belatedly to awaken to the social dimensions of science. I immediately saw the need for a systematic intellectual framework to find my bearings in a completely new and dauntingly open-textured field. My postdoctoral move to study the history, sociology, and philosophy of scientific knowledge, at the Science Studies Unit in Edinburgh, was a crucial formative influence in developing a deeper understanding of the nature of scientific rationality (Edge and Barnes 1982).

In addition to the treatment of the authority of science in politics by authors such as Ezrahi (1974, 1990), anthropological perspectives on knowledge were especially relevant to the way I subsequently approached the risk area (Horton and Finnegan 1973; Douglas 1966, 1975; Hollis and Lukes 1982). These offered accounts of the subtle ways in which natural knowledge is constructed as a central element in the rationalization of social arrangements as if they were objectively and unavoidably given in nature (Barnes and Shapin 1979). The similar way in which scientific discourses represent risk is a central reason why I have never felt intellectually or politically comfortable with the field and its dominant paradigms.

As a scientist I had always admired the philosophical sensibilities of Niels Bohr. I later found that one of his mentors, the existentialist theologian and writer Soren Kierkegaard, had something important to say about risk perceptions and social relations. Communication between social actors is intrinsically limited by the primary process of self-confirmation by which individuals or communities try to maintain (and develop) their identities. We reconstruct the meanings offered to us by others into forms that correspond with our fundamental identities. In the process, the original meanings are transformed, or perhaps we should say violated. Kierkegaard (1985) wrote with great power about the tragedy, not just that we are confined to distorting each others' meanings, but more that we are confined to pretending that it is otherwise.

My profound skepticism toward techniques that purport to quantify public risk perceptions, such as "willingness to pay" surveys (Wynne 1987, 1989a), was probably prepared by another strand of anthropological work, which addressed the politics of expropriated meaning in an identical way. F. G. Bailey's "A Peasant View of the Bad Life" (1968) was a classic demolition of the modernist myth that the Third World "primitive" lives in a constitutional state of ignorant bliss, unable to face up to the risks, opportunities, and bracing drafts of market relations, instrumental rationality, and the rest of the Western "package." Bailey noted that Third World peasants were fully aware of the unstated social uncertainties and social control—including extra dependency on unfamiliar outsiders—that were inadvertently embedded in "objective" technical advice from outside experts. The peasants often resisted passively if not explicitly on the reasonable grounds that they were effectively being asked to hand over social control to aliens. This was falsely defined by those same aliens—Western scientific experts—as incompetence or unreasonable resistance based supposedly on a naive expectation of certainty and of complete protection from risk.

From these perspectives, I have argued (Wynne 1982a) that the prevailing treatment of public risk perceptions creates an ideological smokescreen that avoids the underlying issue, namely, the social relations of technology. Thus my own contributions to the risk literature—whether primarily focused on expert risk analyses (Wynne 1989b), public risk perceptions (Wynne 1980, 1989a), or risk communication (Wynne 1989c)—have all been concerned with the broader issue of how authority is generated and maintained, and how we should best interpret conflicts that are ostensibly about risks. Much of my work has been centered outside the risk field as such, concerned with the role of scientific knowledge in public policy—for example, in energy modeling (Wynne 1984b; Keepin and Wynne 1984) and decision making about technology (Wynne 1982b). Even when I have focused on risk, my ultimate interest has been to develop more constructive concepts of technology, science, and social learning. This requires more reflexive frameworks than currently recognized.

A corollary of this approach to knowledge and risk conflicts is that I dissociate myself from the bipolar notion that the wisdom of the people is pitted against the brittle knowledge of the experts. I prefer to conceive of all knowledges (i.e., distinct bodies of knowledge deemed "expert" or otherwise) as *conditional*. The main challenge to risk assessment and technology assessment is to unearth and debate the conditions of legitimate authority for different risk knowledges in a social learning process.

The reflexivity introduced from the sociology of scientific knowledge emphasizes that validity depends upon whether the world—natural and social—can be restructured or manipulated to accord with and thus "validate" the tacit models embedded in the technology or knowledge claim. It is the unawareness of the open-ended, underdetermined (social and physical) properties of technologies that allows unconscious concealment of this social/natural manipulation. Obsession with uncertainty rather than *indeterminacy* in scientific knowledge and technologies has consolidated this problem. The directly associated preemption of negotiation and learning is the central failing in existing discourses of risk.

In addition to anthropology, and the mainstream history and sociology of scientific knowledge inspired by Polanyi (1958) and Kuhn (1962), Nelkin's case studies of public controversies and scientific expertise (Nelkin 1971, 1979) were original and timely. These studies contradict the conventional wisdom that conflicts about environmental impacts and technological risks can be resolved "naturally" by allowing the technical experts to debate their scientific positions fully. Nelkin and her co-workers show that intensified expert interaction, far from producing the supposed natural scientific consensus which could then be handed down to the political arena, simply deepens the technical conflicts and uncertainties. Different social values and interests seem to be embedded within the competing technical knowledges, structuring them in ways that reflect covert social interests, although they appear natural and objectively given. The notion of "interests" as constituents of scientific knowledge now has an extensive theoretical and empirical literature (Barnes 1977; Edge and Barnes 1982; Woolgar 1981).

TRUST AND THE SOCIAL LOGIC OF RISK DEFINITION

My first venture into case studies of major conflicts involving technical expertise was encouraged by Nelkin, but eventually went beyond the "politics of expertise" paradigm. As a participant observer of the 1977 Windscale Public Inquiry into a planned oxide fuels reprocessing facility at the Sellafield-Windscale nuclear complex, I explored the political implications of discourses on rationality (Wynne 1982b). In particular, I examined the way that the dominant rationality silently and systematically deleted my questions about institutional commitment, behavior, and trustworthiness, as if they had nothing to do with the risk. This same rationality constructed the decision issue as one of objective discovery rather than social commitment, and hence also constructed the opponents and their concerns as factually wrong or irrational.

Although the nuclear experts and the judge who chaired the inquiry automatically reduced the issue to technical risk questions about the plant per se, my analysis revealed that opponents approached the issue with a completely different frame of reference. The opponents believed that the social institutions that managed nuclear power were committed to its indefinite expansion, were unresponsive to criticism or alternative technological social trajectories, and were therefore untrustworthy as impartial arbiters. Hence, logically, not just as a matter of "perception," the risk problem was for them multiplied in proportion with the envisaged "natural" future expansion of nuclear facilities.

This was the origin of the general observation (Wynne 1980) that the heart of risk perceptions and risk conflicts was not the issue of technical risk magnitudes, but rather trust in institutions. Although this was an original insight for the risk field, trust had long been of interest to sociologists and others as a tacit but essential dimension of social life and institutional viability (Garfinkel 1963).

A crucial, often overlooked part of my analysis of the Windscale Inquiry was that although the official expert framing of the risk issue was taken to be the natural rational perspective, it was just as much derived from prior social-institutional assumptions as the public framing of the issue. Not surprisingly, however, this expert framework accepted existing decision-making institutions as trustworthy, natural, impartial, and open-minded about the future. Thus, future development and expansion, feared as part of the present risk by opponents, was absent from the expert framing of the risk problem. Nevertheless, this framing was also socially constructed.

Each of these "natural" but incompatible framings was symmetrically socially embedded, but with contradictory substantive precommitments. There was no a priori reason for considering one to be more rational than the other. "Rationality" required consensus on these founding social commitments before it could begin to be constructed. Unless these tacit dimensions of institutional belief and commitment were recognized and articulated, objections on institutional grounds would continue to be treated by established institutions as simply "antiscientific," with further polarization and degeneration of public debate. Social learning can be defined as this kind of progressive, reflexive unearthing and negotiation of the precommitments shaping knowledge frameworks. It is reflexive in the sense that it critically examines and enlarges the self-knowledge of the social actors involved (Wynne 1989b).

While these deeper, unexpressed conflicts between different social worldviews could not be resolved by empirical evidence alone, there was nevertheless relevant empirical evidence. For example, patterns of past and present behavior of relevant decision-making institutions could be drawn upon to structure this level of argument. This kind of evidence is of course unfamiliar to scientists and has to be gathered by ethnographic, sociological, or anthropological work. As explained later, my own work has attempted to take this *critically engaged* stance. It tries to articulate what are usually unarticulated belief systems about social relations and institutions. It focuses on the social identities underlying explicit risk definitions, which people are continually struggling to develop and defend. It is in this domain that the important theoretical and normative concept of social learning in relation to risk needs to be rooted. Failure to recognize the social foundations of risk framing by expert institutions only provokes a greater sense of denigration and skepticism of authority on the part of the public. Thus public debate and social learning are undermined.

Analysis of the Windscale Inquiry also indicated that the prevailing nuclear decision-making institutions were deeply insecure. They were particularly anxious about their own social legitimation on precisely those grounds (i.e., institutional demeanor) which were the foundation of public anxiety and opposition. The chair of the inquiry vigorously prosecuted an extreme, reductionist rationality that automatically precluded uncomfortable questions about institutional performance and trustworthiness. The inquiry thus offered a public discourse on risk assessment and technological decision making that was profoundly comforting for the nuclear establishment.

This historical-institutional interpretation of the Windscale nuclear risk conflict demonstrated the central importance of trust and credibility, which was my first major contribution to the risk field (Wynne 1980). By then I had recently read the work of Harry Otway and his group in the International Institute of Applied Systems Analysis-International Atomic Energy Agency (IIASA-IAEA) joint project on public attitudes to risk. From a very different starting point this work coincided strongly with my own developing ideas about the basis of what were called, misleadingly, "public perceptions of risks." I saw that Otway's methodologically more structured research on perceptions also contradicted the dominant conventional wisdom that risk definitions, as framed by technical experts, were more real than those defined by laypeople (Otway and Pahner 1976). Prior to questions of measurement and quantification, there were more basic issues about what dimensions of social experience should be given recognition and meaning, and which ones were being denied altogether.

Policy and professional languages of risk preempted such questions and imposed particular answers in the name of objective risk. Like Otway, I thought it profoundly unscientific to elicit attitudes toward a socially constructed abstraction like quantified mortality risk without first being interested in how this artifact related to people's own constructs. There was nothing especially natural or automatically privileged about this particular meaning—pregnant as it was with political implications—as compared to other possible framings. More sense could be made of public responses to "risks" by treating them as responses to the more grounded experience of technologies as both hardware and historically rooted social-organizational relationships. It is important to note that there is nothing in this interpretive perspective that denies the importance and value of science; it allows the opportunity to place scientific knowledge on a more legitimate, properly conditional, and ultimately more effective footing.

Acceptable Risk as Institutional Neurosis

Otway and von Winterfeldt's (1982) critique of the "acceptable risk" paradigm is among the classic contributions to the field. My own approach only offers an interpretation of why that paradigm should have been so popular, despite so much contrary evidence. Consistent with the earlier approach to the ritual role of rationality in the Windscale Inquiry, I found psychoanalytic work to be highly suggestive. Daly's (1970) paper, "The Specters of Technicism," analyzes clinical experience of the many people who allow condensed images of technology to hold absolute power over them. They have simplified the threatening complexities of the impenetrable forces that they experience as controlling their lives into condensed symbols, centralizing those diffuse forces onto all-powerful unicentric agencies—technological specters. Daly also observed that these conditions were no longer individual, but collective—mass neuroses transmitted in mainstream culture and experience.

This condition could be interpreted as the lay public's being frightened to confront the complexities of modern life. On the other hand, it reflects the ways technology and science have actually been symbolized in legitimation processes: as magic black boxes whose esoteric inner workings need not interest people.

The more important point in the present context is that an argument can be made for precisely equivalent simplifications of threatening social complexities by expert institutions. Faced with the confusing variety of contexts, subcultures, and responses thrown up in public reactions to technological and scientific programs, expert institutions have responded in a way parallel to Daly's mass neuroses. They have artificially simplified the recalcitrant and threatening complexity of social life into condensed, but context-free, quantified scales of "acceptable risk," as if the imposed singular meaning of risk—estimated quantified mortality rates—were the only meaningful element of experience. In particular, this discourse obliterates any questions about the role(s) of expert institutions in shaping people's lives, risks, and experiences.

Daly described how people created technological specters using symbols of their own biological systems, investing them with unconditional powers to decide, and thereby cutting a comfortingly clean swathe through otherwise overpowering ambiguities. They would obsessively refer to a simple biological measure such as their pulse rate as an "objective" authority for decision making, in place of facing the challenge of disentangling the complexities they experienced.

The acceptable risk paradigm is akin to an institutionalized version of consulting pulse rates, on the part of experts confused and threatened by the prospect of respecting and interacting with diverse publics (Wynne 1987). It could be seen as a self-delusory discourse that allowed such institutions to avoid the ambiguities and social risks of *negotiating* the conditions of acceptability, case by case. Failure to acknowledge lay social experiences of expert institutions has left those same bodies unaware of themselves and their social role in engendering public reactions and risk perceptions. The acceptable risk paradigm has therefore been a central pillar of a systematic expert self-delusion. It has projected institutional insecurities about authority under possible conditions of mutual recognition and authentic interaction into false constructs of the public as naive (expecting zero risk) and irrational (unresponsive to scientific persuasion). Yet "zero risk" demands should perhaps be interpreted as expressions of "zero trust."

EXPERT RATIONALITIES: SOCIAL AND TECHNICAL CONDITIONS

Some Central Tenets

At this point it is worth restating in more consolidated form some of the central tenets of my perspective on risk. I will then define and illustrate some key terms via empirical examples before going on to discuss criticisms and issues for further development.

1. Scientific definitions of risk require a prior framing, which is not normally subject to explicit formulation and examination. This framing involves setting an assumed context of actors, behaviors, and processes, in which a particular kind of risk is thought to arise.

2. In addition to introducing a particular social meaning of risk (such as probable fatalities per unit of time), scientific risk discourses depend upon such foundational social models in order to begin to analyze risks. They abstract the risk analysis from such risk situations, or contexts, and rarely carefully examine the dependency of the analysis on the implicit model of the risk situation, nor question the validity of the framing model. Hence expert risk knowledge is only artificially divorced from social and organizational dimensions and is *conditional* upon the validity of those unstated situational precommitments. This is what is meant by expert knowledge being *conditional* knowledge.

3. The social-situational factors, such as the competence and trustworthiness of organizations or individuals, are an essential part of the risk process, hence the risks. Expert risk analyses usually misrepresent the intrinsically open-ended, *indeterminate* nature of these dimensions, treating them as if they were deterministic, and assuming that technical imprecision can be overcome by statistical rules and techniques of uncertainty analysis. Alternatively, they adopt naively idealistic models that assume that social and organizational behavior follows dependable laws.

4. These conditional models and precommitments are rarely explicated and analyzed, yet they are embedded within, and shape, the expert risk assessment. The experts may be least qualified to identify and judge the validity of the embedded situational models or assumptions and may ignore the knowledge of others who have more experience of the risk situations. In the relatively open-ended social situations of risk-generating activities, the tacit social model may in effect become prescriptive. It implicitly requires

the reshaping of social behavior in its own image to validate the expert risk knowledge.

5. The inadvertent imposition of these basic risk meanings and models upon people by experts and related institutions creates an objective social threat to those people and thus intensifies whatever risk they perceive. This is a rational response, brought about by lack of critical reflexive awareness on the part of the expert institutions and their dominant risk discourses.

6. This, often legitimate, social anxiety tends repeatedly to be misinterpreted by experts as ignorance, irrationality, or naive expectations of zero risk, thus morally denigrating the relevant public. This in turn exacerbates the public's sense of being threatened by institutions that do not respect its identity, rationality, and legitimate standing in the issue in question, hence further expanding the sense of risk, in a negative cycle of polarization.

7. Social learning would involve breaking into this cycle of polarization by first appreciating the *conditionality* of "objective" risk analytic knowledge; and second, by understanding the social-institutional basis of all risk definitions, expert and lay. It would then involve institutional self-learning of this conditionality, of the precommitments tacitly shaping its own knowledge, recognition of the legitimacy of other social actors' precommitments and framing processes, and collective negotiation of authoritative risk meanings, definitions, and assessments, from situation to situation. It would thus enlarge the dimensions of "risk" recognized in social debate and decision making, from elaborated technocratic definitions and attributes alone, to include relevant institutional track records, social demeanor, intentions, and institutional structures in the whole area of social practice in question.

8. Studies of public risk perceptions, often built around the aim of identifying an objective level of acceptable risk, unconsciously presuppose what is meant by risk. They then measure public attitudes toward that imposed meaning, without first questioning whether the people involved share that meaning. Technical experts thus assume that the "natural" meaning of risk is a physical measure such as probability of mortality. They do not recognize that the indigenous meanings that people give to risk may include many other objective dimensions, such as whether valued social relationships and identities are threatened, or dependency on what may be inscrutable and distant social actors or institutions. Thus one of the favorite pastimes of the risk field, measuring attitudes to "risk," may be a misbegotten and misleading exercise; instead of attempting to understand people's indigenous meanings of risk and negotiating with these from a position of respect, they distort and denigrate those indigenous meanings from the outset. They do this by insisting on a singular basic universal meaning, measuring "attitudes" toward it, and then expropriating these indigenous meanings in the form of those measurements, to use them as surrogates of public concern in inaccessible and nonnegotiated expert decision-making processes. This very process, in its institutionalized way of denigrating, distorting, and expro-

priating people's indigenous meanings and identities, itself imposes an objective risk on those people it supposedly represents (Wynne 1983, 1987, 1989a). Elaborating technical methods in this way avoids constructive, critical development of new institutional structures, which could allow continued social access to negotiation over the practical meaning of risk. Since the very term *risk* is laden with political and moral implications, it should be open to continued negotiation and redefinition, as an essential part of democratic life. A social learning process would deepen and expand the definitions of risk, without eliminating conflict, ambiguity, or indeterminacy.

Contested "Natural" Meanings

The sociology of scientific knowledge offered an analysis of a major scientific policy controversy of the 1960s and early 1970s that was effectively a precursor and model treatment of the risk issue. In that debate the concept of intelligence was central (Ezrahi 1974). The analogy with risk lies in how its public meaning was constructed.

A group of scientists led by the U.S. psychometrician Arthur Jensen and a leading physicist, William Shockley, advanced the view that intelligence was genetically inherited, and that mean differences of intelligence between blacks and whites were inherited. These views were espoused at a time of massive government support for compensatory education programs to discriminate positively in favor of black people, on the assumption that such extra educational support would have a sustained effect on black educational abilities and social advancement. The Jensen-Shockley work was, therefore, an explicit scientific attack on this liberal policy, arguing that compensatory programs of this kind were based on a scientific falsehood, and thus were futile.

Against the "right-wing science" of inheritance, various scientists asserted that intelligence was indeed improved by social and educational environment and not determined by genetic inheritance. *Nurture*, not *nature*, was the dominant factor. Scientific claim and counterclaim flew back and forth amid escalating controversy and ad hominem attack. Significantly, however, what both sides inadvertently achieved in the entrenchment of these opposed stances was to reify the concept of *intelligence* at the center of the debate, as if it matched a real objective entity existing "out there" in nature. Each side treated intelligence as objectively measurable, then argued violently about whether the evidence was based on nature or nurture.

The "nurture school" claimed that the concept of intelligence used by the "nature school" was biased toward white cultural experiences. Some scientists midway between the two extremes argued that intelligence was determined by both nature and nurture, and the central question was, by how much of each? None of these important qualifications to the debate, however, introduced the larger question of whether IQ measures imposed a distorted and reduced meaning to intelligence as a concept with moral and political force in social debate. The construction of the social debate in scientific terms only gave the reduced concept of intelligence a (false) natural status, limiting public discourse to the sterile argument over whether "it" was racially inherited or environmentally determined.

Any wider social debate and broader responsibility for what richer meaning society might want to give to this powerful concept was effectively hijacked by this all-around scientific reduction of the concept to an appendage of psychometric techniques. Interestingly, and perhaps cause for optimism, a return to the issue at the 1991 annual meeting of the American Association for the Advancement of Science saw more explicit appreciation among scientists that there was a lot more to intelligence beyond whatever IQ tests could measure, even culturally adapted IQ tests (Sternberg 1991).

A fundamentally identical syndrome blights treatments of risk and risk perceptions today. Instead of encouraging wider social debate about the diverse meanings of risks, heated argument and endless analysis focuses on whether a given quantitative risk estimate is correct, what quantity is acceptable, and what factors affect people's acceptance (or tolerance). Risk is assumed to have an intrinsic, objective natural meaning that everyone should share, rather than a meaning that has been created and imposed by particular dominant social institutions with their own interests and anxieties, and that systematically conceals certain issues and questions from public attention.

There is an important role for quantification, measurement, and modeling of risks, a role that needs to be defended. Neglecting the institutional dimensions, however, as scientific treatments usually do, often exacerbates public anxieties over the treatment of risky activities. This sets off a further round of intensification in scientific frameworks, which only makes matters worse in an escalating negation of collective learning. Thus, a key challenge to risk research is its development of a better definition of "context." I have attempted to do this, by focusing on the institutional dimensions of risk. A central part of this perspective, consistent with my analysis of the Windscale risk controversy, is that what we call *context* is often better described as the social and technical *constitution* of risk. I explain the significance of this with reference to expert risk assessments as institutionalized in regulatory settings.

Risk Analysis: From Formal Model to Real World

As noted earlier, however much scientific risk analysis tries to separate itself from social or institutional dimensions of a risk system, it cannot avoid making intellectual commitments to a social model. Even the "hardest" of risk-analytic sciences, like nuclear reactor pressure vessel safety analysis, has to make assumptions about the quality of social organizations in order to produce figures for the expected frequency of failure of components and subsystems. Even when these are based on empirical data from reactor operation, assumptions are still made that the organizational quality of the new situation will be at least as good as those from which the data have been extracted. Even when there is apparent consensus about these assumptions, it is important to recognize that they are necessary but not sufficient *conditions of validity* of the risk analysis. As experience has shown, we should not take their fulfillment for granted, and implicit, legitimate differences of view about this dimension underlie many risk conflicts.

Many typical risk/regulation problems are less well structured than the reactor pressure vessel problem. For example, one illuminating case involved the extensive public controversy over the herbicide 2,4,5-T in the United Kingdom (Wynne 1989b). The scientific Pesticides Advisory Committee effectively assumed that the real world of pesticides production and use was identical to the controlled world of the laboratory toxicologist. By reference to that research literature, the committee repeatedly dismissed labor union claims of health damage as imaginary. Eventually, the committee qualified its dismissals with the caveat that *"pure 2,4,5-T offers no hazards to users, nor to the general public... provided that the product is used as directed"* (Wynne 1989b, 36; emphasis added).

Yet this apparently trivial qualification, so painfully extracted, was precisely the issue. The scientists' reference to the laboratory toxicology literature tacitly demanded the belief that the world of pesticide manufacture and use was an idealized social world. Among other things, it was assumed that the manufacturing process conditions for pesticides never varied sufficiently to produce dioxin and other toxic contaminants, and drums of herbicide always arrived at the point of use with full instructions intact and intelligible. In spite of the inconvenience, farmers and other users would comply with the stated conditions, such as correct solvents, proper spray nozzles, pressure valves, and other equipment, appropriate weather conditions, and full protective gear. As a model of the *real* social world and thus of the typical risk system, this was utterly naive and incredible, however good the laboratory science. One farm worker's researcher described the scientists as "living in cloud-cuckoo land behind the laboratory bench" (Wynne 1989b, 37).

Thus, the scientific risk analysis did not avoid, and could not have avoided, making social assumptions in order to create the necessary scientific knowledge. It was *conditional* knowledge in that its validity depended, *inter alia*, upon the conditions in this embedded social model being fulfilled in actual practice. The scientists did not recognize this conditionality until they had long since forfeited credibility. What is more, the validity was conditional not merely because of uncertainty, but due to *indeterminacy*: Could the real risk system be policed and reorganized to correspond with the scientists' implicit ideal model? In terms of the risk issue in question, it is artificial to call the social conditions of herbicide production and use *contextual*, as if exogenous or parallel to the "real" situation. They were *constitutive* of the risks and of the real knowledge of them. Each party, both scientists and workers, tacitly defined different actual risk systems. They built upon different models of the social practices controlling the contaminants and exposures.

Although the scientists repeatedly patronized them as imagining things, the farm and forestry workers had real empirical experience. Indeed, they had expertise that was directly relevant to an *objective* risk analysis, but this knowledge was rejected, and in the process their social identity was denigrated and threatened. When one appreciates the institutionally defended resistance of the scientists to the possibility that their *objective* knowledge might be conditional, and their arrogant and provocative denigration of the workers, it is easy to sympathize with a populist interpretation of the "wisdom of the people against the fallible experts."

It is important, however, to see *both* kinds of knowledge as conditional, with their different constitutive social assumptions buried. The key is to recognize that this will always be true, and to explicate the buried conditional assumptions or commitments, so that debate and negotiation can address these dimensions properly. Too often the social world is portrayed as deficient because it does not match the assumptions of the technologists or risk analysts. Negotiation about these social models would be more constructive, and would constitute a more reflexive learning process.

This interpretation of the herbicides risk controversy draws support from work in the sociology of science (Latour 1983, 1986; Callon and Latour 1981; Krohn and Weyer 1989). The case illustrates how science confirms its truth by reorganizing the world beyond the laboratory to fit the implicit models in the scientific program in question. In risk discourses the essential indeterminacy of these processes is reconstructed in terms only of uncertainty, which obstructs enlargement of the social debate into negotiation of the social relations of technology.

In the 2,4,5-T case and several others I have analyzed, there is no reflexive recognition of the social models that are essential constituents of the expert risk analysis. For the expert risk assessment to be correct, the social world would have to be controlled as in a laboratory. The social identities of publics are threatened when experts tell them how stupid and irrational they are, while simultaneously conducting "objective" risk assessments that ignore public knowledge and impose naive assumptions about behavior in the social world.

It is easy to attribute the failings of risk discourse, with the exclusion of public knowledge and concerns, to congenital expert arrogance or even conspiracy. I prefer to analyze them as the results of the institutional structures of decision making within which scientific experts naturally operate. Unfortunately, the effects of this institutional lack of awareness and learning are polarization and understandable public mistrust of expert institutions.

CRITICISMS AND RESPONSES

Three sorts of criticism have been made of the perspective I have developed: that it is methodologically weak; populist and even antiscientific; and too complicated to offer practically useful proposals for policy makers.

Methodology and Engagement

My interpretive approach to definitions of risk attempts to articulate the most authentic and plausible arguments and identities of the relevant social groups. In the case of the Windscale Inquiry, my analysis was based on listening extensively to diverse arguments, intensive debate and participation, and comprehensive documentary immersion. My analysis of sheep farmers' responses to the Chernobyl accident (Wynne 1989c) involved in-depth, structured, but flexible interviews and numerous informal conversations with farmers, scientists, and others. In the case of 2,4,5-T, my analysis involved a fairly straightforward paraphrasing of statements made by people directly involved.

In this and other work, my goal has been to articulate what has been unarticulated but discernable, and to see if these portrayals resonate with the social groups in question. By discernable, however, I do not pretend to observe a fully and independently existing reality, in a quasi-Newtonian sense. My attempts to articulate the reality of a group's position in the very process help to *shape* that reality. This reflects the theoretical understanding that our values and social identities are not entirely complete or intrinsic to us. They are radically indeterminate and ready to be further developed in the relations and interactions that we engage in with others. This directly contradicts the vision underlying conventional approaches. These unreflectively draw upon and confirm the rational, instrumental, individual paradigm, in which social interactions are seen only as a means to achieve prior individual ends, and are not *intrinsically* of any worth. Identities are thought of, wrongly in my view, as independent and complete, not subject to the constructive forces of interaction. From my relational-interpretive stance, which proposes that our social identities are chronically incomplete, it is illusory to pretend to observe free-standing beliefs or to measure objective attitudes. My methodology thus recognizes the inevitability of engagement, and attempts only to be sensitive, explicit, and self-critical. Observation at this level also helps the observed groups, be they scientists or publics, come to a more developed state of being, by articulating what is not fully articulated. This is more than simply unveiling *hidden* agendas and meanings. This dialectic between observation and engagement thus ensnares me as analyst and creates a less tidy, but more exciting and authentic analytical existence.

This so-called compromise with conventional canons of objectivity is grounded in the paradigms of critical theory, relational moral philosophy, and interpretive sociology (Habermas 1975, 1984–87; Strauss 1969; MacIntyre 1981; Bernstein 1983). These different currents coincide on the essential point that individuals are not discrete beings with completely separate and fully finished values and beliefs. The form and quality of our social interactions shape our identities, beliefs, and values, in an endless attempt to complete the incompletable. As a direct corollary, the models of nature and the technological artifacts and systems we establish do not merely shape our values and identities, they are necessarily reflections of them. They may be played back to us as if completely objective, but our values are completed and further articulated in the forms of knowledge we thus "naturalize." There is therefore a latent level of necessary debate that is suppressed and distorted by our culture of scientism.

This position is one step more intellectually radical than Otway's justifiable critique of attitude measurement on risk (Otway, Chapter 9). It also cautions against objectification of values and beliefs, and related assumptions that these can be measured or at least definitively described (Sperber 1982 Wynne, Forthcoming).

This idiosyncratic perspective on methodological issues may appear casual and eclectic, but it only tries to render explicit what is concealed in more apparently objective methodologies. All observation of the social world (1) is based upon often unrecognized, and invariably unstated, precommitments, which lie outside the control of even the most rigorous methodological discipline; and (2) helps to constitute the object observed.

Making Sides: Critical Engagement

There is an unavoidable element of intuition and empathy in this interpretive stance that does not have the luxury of sheltering behind any ritual of objectivity. This does not mean, however, that it fails to adopt a critical distance from its objects, or that evidence cannot be systematically deployed to criticize its conclusions. Although some readings of my work have claimed that it takes sides with the people against the lampooned scientists, this is not the case. The framework has analyzed the conditional nature of scientific knowledge and the naive, tacit sociology that often underpins that knowledge. It has also identified the similarly socially based logic of public risk definitions. This offers no judgment as to which side is right; indeed, it suggests that the question is often meaningless because the issue is open—whose risk definition is correct depends *inter alia* upon how relevant social organizations will behave.

I argue that all sides tend to obstruct broader social learning by not recognizing this dimension of indeterminacy in risk definition and assessment (Wynne 1991b). Whether social institutions are *likely* to, or do typically, behave in accordance with one or the other side's embedded assumptions, or whether the social assumptions are *acceptable* (for example, policing farmers to avoid misuse of animal growth hormones) is something that can be debated with relevant evidence, but only if this dimension is first recognized.

In my analysis of sheep farmers' responses to scientific advice about the Chernobyl fallout (Wynne 1989c), I identified not an information gap, nor even a gap in trust or credibility, but a cultural dislocation between two different styles of knowledge; each reflected different kinds of social relations within which knowledge existed. Identifying the basis of farmers' seemingly truculent attitudes is bound to suggest some sympathy toward them, as is identifying elements of their local expertise that were ignored by the scientists and authorities. This is far from claiming, however, that the farmers had *better* knowledge than the scientists. Each group could say that it had better knowledge than the other, but only on specific, partial (and not necessarily overlapping) ground. The point is that each had *conditional knowledge*, which was parochial to the conditions of its tried and tested use. The Chernobyl emergency presented a situation that would have benefited from an awareness of both bodies of knowledge and experience, negotiated into a practically integrated form. This could have taken the form of intercultural negotiation and learning about the rationality and legitimacy of the other parties' worldviews, and of the normative epistemological commitments shaping one's own.

This perspective is therefore independent of the "truth" of any side in a risk debate, but it is avowedly and inevitably engaged in the articulation and development of parties' stances and identities. Better for this to be recognized, so that it can be systematically and critically evaluated. As for the antiscience criticism, this is based on a false idea that scientific knowledge is unconditional. Defining the proper conditions of authority for scientific knowledge would defend science against the disillusionment brought about by its unconditional expression in typical institutional settings.

Policy Implications

There is no formula of prescriptions for the risk manager that follows from this institutional perspective on the constitution of risk. Yet several pieces of work within it have had significant and, I hope, constructive policy impacts.

For example, my work on the controversy over growth hormones was appreciated in the European Community. Policy makers realized that the validity of their risk assessments rested shakily on the assumption that laboratory-style controls and conditions could be implemented on a large scale. Whether this was an ad hoc response or reflects the understanding of the underlying principle remains to be seen.

In the field of toxic wastes, my perspective has had an impact on the debate over regulation in the European single market after 1992. The original expectation was that a single free market in wastes would exist throughout all twelve member states, based on a single set of waste and hazard definitions, uniform standards, and a comprehensive system of documentation recording all waste movements from cradle to grave. The fact that each country had different definitions and standards was expected to be overcome simply by *technical* negotiation of hazard criteria into a single European Community (EC) system. An implicit faith was that technical criteria were context-free and that their adaptation had no implications for the institutional context in which they existed. Our analysis demonstrated that this was not true (Laurence and Wynne 1989).

The imprecise toxicity criteria of the U.K. system reflected its *general* institutional culture of discretionary local regulatory decision making. To have had precise, unambiguous quantitative criteria as in the Netherlands would undermine the *social* basis of trust and negotiation among relevant actors in the U.K. culture. We therefore argued that harmonizing technical hazard criteria in the EEC, far from being a purely technical issue, implied institutional harmonization to some significant degree—a completely different order of problem. Such harmonization of technical definitions was a prerequisite of a single market for the free but controlled movement of wastes throughout the EEC. Thus, an inescapable logic of our analysis was the need to restrict waste movements as far as possible to within a single homogeneous system of regulatory definitions and arrangements (as exists in Bavaria and Denmark), with a legal restriction on export of toxic wastes from the catchment. In practice, this argument has hit home, since despite an overwhelmingly strong commitment to the single market, a competing principle of waste treatment "self-sufficiency" by each member state has now been created.

In these two cases, significantly, there was some institutional flexibility, since institutional arrangements had not stabilized into set patterns. In other policy arenas this may not be true, and this approach has been criticized as too complicated or radical for practical use. For example, in the radioactive waste field the response to public hostility has been a reduction in risk design criteria from a national 1 in 10 million to 1 in 100 million, as if this might enhance acceptability. I have instead argued that people's concerns are institutional and include, for example, the fear that decision makers are under the control of the industry and are committed to endless future expansion of radwaste generating activities; the fear that once the proponents have an opening they will push open the door as much as they can; and a belief that the controlling authorities are not independent of the promoters and are not accountable to local democratic institutions. All of these concerns can be addressed by institutional responses rather than by converting them into spurious technical safety demands. Policy makers are unfamiliar with these kinds of options, however, and usually do not have the powers to implement them. More significantly, they do not have the inclination to consider them because they have become institutionalized themselves into set terms of reference and boundary conditions.

One of the principal "natural" boundary conditions is that existing institutional structures and routines are not disturbed and rendered uncertain. There is no good reason, however, for researchers to accept the assertion that generating constructive insights for policy means accepting these timid terms of reference. Indeed, there is every reason not to accept this kind of intimidation, so long as one strives to make the resultant tension between research and policy creative and constructive. My approach could be summed up by defining its aim as the enlargement of policy consciousness, rather than the provision of policy tools.

Intellectual Relations

I have already outlined the correspondences between my approach to scientific risk analysis and that of others. The indeterminacy that this perspective highlights was earlier called structural uncertainty in conjunction with Thompson, Warburton, and Hatley (1986). Ravetz's (1986) work on ignorance has also been important, though my work lays more stress on the *indeterminate* element of risk systems and the legitimate roles of publics as unrecognized participants in negotiating the terms of the social-natural experiments that new risk activities (technologies) bring before us. The intrinsic underdetermination of scientific knowledge and its "closure" (that is, its acceptance as natural) by *social* processes is not fully recognized by Ravetz's approach.

The nearest paradigm to my own in many senses is the cultural theory of risk pioneered by Douglas (Douglas 1985; Thompson 1983; Rayner 1984). Both share the fundamental tenet that *all* rationalities of risk definition are shaped within more holistic complexes of social experience and the defense or nurture of familiar social identities. All rationalities therefore embody moral and social prescriptions. In contrast to Douglas et al., my own perspective focuses on middle-range institutional questions—a level that may vary according to the overt issue arena. Cultural theory also appears to adopt a more structurally determinate model of social identities with which I am uncomfortable. For example, in my fieldwork with Cumbrian sheep farmers, I found ambivalence in their beliefs on the source of the radioactivity, depending on whether, at a particular time, they considered their identity as part of family and neighborhood networks that depended for jobs upon Sellafield, or whether they viewed their identity as part of the wider farming community. This may well be explicable as a structurally determined cultural process of belief and risk definition, but the units of cultural structure would apparently need to be more refined and flexible than cultural theory presently allows.

CONCLUSIONS: NEW DIRECTIONS AND UNRESOLVED ISSUES

The approach I have developed highlights the systematic (though usually inadvertent) suppression of the constituting institutional dimensions of what are called risk issues. This analytical stance does not at all involve the claim that risks can be reduced to social factors alone, to the exclusion of physical dimensions. Its novelty lies in the claim that whether their authors realize it or not, technical risk definitions do require framing commitments to models of the social realities in which risks are generated, defined, and experienced.

This social framing has two components. First, because of different assumptions about relevant social behavior, there is a legitimate variance in the estimates of the magnitude of the "physical" risk. Second, there is a negotiable framing of what is to be meant by *risk* for social decision-making purposes, including but not restricted to quantitative estimates of physical harm.

Social Learning

All too often these prior framing questions are preempted by institutional structures and decision-making cultures that take existing tacit commitments for granted as answers. This socially constructed nature is obscured, resulting in an impoverishment of social debate and learning. The concept of learning here deserves attention. It is not learning about some complex reality of risks believed to exist *sui generis*. It is learning in the sense of recognizing the conditional nature of one's own knowledge, and the implicit assumptions and commitments that constitute it. Thus the social learning that eventually took place patchily in the 2,4,5-T case was that risk assessment drawn from toxicology is committed by default to an ideally controlled social world in the image of the laboratory. Other questions and domains of knowledge are inappropriately excluded. Tied to this realization of the limitations and conditions of one's own knowledge is appreciation of the legitimacy of other sources of knowledge, organized in other forms, and carried by other social actors. At the same time these other actors may learn that science can provide reliable and robust knowledge, within conditions that need to be identified and debated, and that it may be responsive to extrascientific criticism.

The proper concept of learning is therefore reflexive in that it enlightens institutional self-knowledge and mutual knowledge between different social actors. It creates a basis for negotiation of mutually authoritative knowledges across paradigms rather than merely intensifying the brittle circles of (attempted) self-reassurance within existing paradigms. In so doing it recognizes the real indeterminacy of such social interactions, and the crucial point that quality and value—positive or negative—are created and reside within the interactions themselves. Thus social interactions are not merely means to ends defined in people's supposedly preexistent, discrete, and completed values and identities. They are constitutive of value and identity in their own right.

The critique of decision analytic approaches, including the multi-attribute elaborations on public perceptions of risk, is based on this relational model of human nature and value (Wynne 1989a). Learning institutions would not exclude their own structure, power, and social relations from the discourse about risk.

Such institutions are what Thompson (1991) has aptly called clumsy institutions. They trade narrow, and in the end self-defeating, efficiency for greater resilience and much richer learning capability by embracing multiple rationalities. This is a social parallel with Schön and Argyris' (1978) reflexive model of organizational learning, in which a central element is the developing identity of the organization itself, through deeper appreciation of its relations with others. Developing and establishing this social learning concept as a framework for technology negotiation will be a key challenge to the theoretical capabilities and policy sensitivities of the risk field. Its closer interaction with the social analysis of technologies (Bijker, Pinch, and Hughes 1987; Bijker and Law 1991) and the new field of constructive technology assessment (Schot 1991) would be a valuable learning experience.

The social learning concept is ambivalent because it is so easily misunderstood to imply that an external trajectory exists by which to define and measure it (as is the case, for example, with conventional concepts of learning in education). It is the connected dimensions, of self-exploration combined with developing relations with others and their forms of knowledge and experience, which constitute the crucial *reflexive* and *interactive* learning. This has no preordained or guaranteed direction; indeed, it needs recognition of the *indeterminacy* of values, identities, and knowledges in order to be possible. Use of the term *social learning* to describe the reflexivity I describe here is itself risky in that it is easily reduced to the more authoritarian version.[1]

Extended Peer Groups and Relegitimated Science

Defenders of decision analytic uses of psychometric risk perception analysis argue that these frameworks should not be taken at face value. In good hands they are simply a vehicle—a kind of enabling ritual—for facilitating the very same negotiation processes that I have advocated. This is a fair comment, up to a point. The same could be said of scientific risk analyses—that they should not be taken at face value, but seen as a common discourse for all parties to enter the debate about the social and institutional dimensions, and the richer meanings of the risk issue. However, this looks a dubious proposition. My analysis of cases stretching from Windscale to pesticides via biotechnology and back to Windscale is that scientific rationality as an institutionalized form of knowledge and relationships systematically obstructs such reflexive learning and negotiation. In this mode science is inadvertently delegitimating itself with publics, actively aiding and abetting any antiscientific extremist who may be on the loose (Wynne 1987, 1991b).

The cases also show that the extrascientific knowledge lay communities possess is relevant to science. These nonscientific peers are becoming more and more significant as the research process and the generation of scientific knowledge extend beyond the laboratory and merge with knowledge application. Technologies are inadvertent social experiments, or, as Krohn has put it, society is the laboratory (Krohn and Weyer 1989). In this situation relevant publics are no longer merely "impacted," they are knowledge generators. For example, the Cumbrian sheep farmers told the environmental scientists that feeding sheep with bentonite to flush radiocesium would not work because the sheep were being held in artificial conditions. The farmers were proven correct, after first being ignored.

Thus the sciences, and especially sciences like risk assessment, need to reconceive themselves as being controlled intellectually by extended peer groups (Funtowicz and Ravetz 1990a), which may include relevant actors with no scientific pretensions. This self-reconception would require institutional and political reorganization to give standing and influence to such extended networks. This is tantamount to recognition that scientific knowledge is essentially indeterminate, and that valid "closure" requires the involvement of the appropriate social networks, which need to stretch beyond scientific communities alone. In this way the proper *conditions* of validity of the relevant knowledges would be explored. In exchange for yielding power, scientists would gain greater legitimacy and social effectiveness.

Such reinstitutionalization of science would correspond with social learning as already outlined. Different forms of knowledge would find a field for the negotiation of mutually authoritative knowledges and policies. In this new institutional and cultural mode science could indeed act as the facilitator and not the obstructor of constructive learning.

Many large-scale modern technologies, notably but not only nuclear, demand intense and disciplined collective commitment that requires the eradication of doubt, and hence the denial of uncertainties, conditions, and qualifications. This is a Catch–22 situation for nuclear power because these necessary properties are precisely those that encourage arrogance and manifest self-delusion, hence understandable public opposition and fear. It remains an open question whether a demythologized, relegitimated science— full as it would be of explicit conditions and uncertainties, and socially more open-textured—could allow such monolithic technologies to be protected by the constitutive myth systems of which current risk discourses are a part (Wynne 1982b). As the risk paradigm is developed in future, these are the questions that need to be addressed.

Public Sciences, Credibility, and Postmodern Beliefs

My approach emphasizes the indeterminacy of knowledges. Stretching beyond Otway's paradigm of belief systems and public experiences of technology-as-power, and in parallel with the modernism-postmodernism debate in social theory (Giddens 1991), it places social identity at the heart of the problem in analyzing responses to risks and risk information. This first surfaced in the notion of risk perception decision methodologies as social identity-stripping by imposing the assumption that people give meaning and respond only to the physical risk aspects of technological interventions. The use of methodologies such as "willingness to pay" surveys of risk valuation, however, shows that some people do enter into such discourses without overt protest, even if they do not identify with any of the processing of their responses. This is testimony to the multiple social identities we are all busy trying to manage in the bewildering diversity of the postmodern world.

Beck (1986) has given a thorough sociological analysis of the deep structure of risk apprehension that pervades modern culture. We are told ad infinitum that our age is awash with choice in all things. Yet endless horizons of choice (supposing it were true) also entail endless horizons of responsibility and existential doubt and uncertainty. This is accentuated by the fundamental insecurities involved in trying to manage multiple social identities from one context of relationships to another. How can institutions be trusted, hence risky activities be accepted, in this context of fragmentation and pervasive background anxiety, when the very discourses and institutions supposed to manage risks for us are involved in putting our social identities at risk?

A key shift required by the perspective described here is that definitions of risk, and knowledge, and responses to information and uncertainty are based ultimately on the attempted maintenance of familiar social identities. This is fundamentally more complex and comprehensive than the dominant idea that (objectively existent) risks are perceived and valued according to a person's preexistent and discrete "values" or "interests." Physical risks thus have to be recognized as embedded within and shaped by social relations and the continual tacit negotiation of our social identities. As Beck and others have argued, this will become an increasingly explicit and prominent part of public risk issues.

The modernist paradigm of singular unconditional rationality, of which dominant risk discourses are a pillar, entails a concept of social identities as unproblematic and completed. This modernist perspective has incorporated the observation that social trust and credibility underpin physical risk perceptions and responses. But it has done this by reifying trust or trustworthiness as just another attitudinal dimension or attribute, from within the same model of (unproblematic) social identities and values.

I would suggest that trust and credibility also need instrumental programs of manipulation (Otway and Wynne 1989). This in turn has allowed trust and credibility to become the object of deconstruction, to identify the ambivalence that pervades them. People may have to act *as if* they trust a social actor—a person, organization, or institutional complex—because they are, or see themselves to be, socially *dependent* on that other actor. They may well then construct beliefs that rationalize this dependency, resulting in "credibility" and "trust" that are only skin deep and conceal a deeper level of ambivalence. Thus alternative attitudes and beliefs may be held by the same person, as functions of alternative social identities reflecting a complex existence within different social networks. A key challenge to risk research and theory development will be to engage seriously with these more complex perspectives on trust and credibility. Such basic ambivalence underlying "trust" may have to be recognized as an essential condition of postmodernism and not a symptom of intellectual or moral weakness, supposedly to be overcome by the further advance of scientific rationality in its modernist version.

The postmodernist perspective in social theory has made important crucial inroads into the relentless social disorientation brought about by institutionalized monopolistic versions of rationality and human nature. However, in its stronger forms (Lyotard 1984) it so relativizes values and fragments identities as, in effect, to allow whatever succeeds in imposing itself as a new order to create its own conditions of legitimation. The reflexive framework on risk offered here could be a necessary middle way, consistent with the broader perspective of reflexive modernization (Beck 1986).

While the modernist paradigm of singular rationality may have exhausted itself, the hesitant many who have seen through it may not be enticed by the postmodern celebration of incoherence. Rational instrumental individualism has shown itself to be an inadequate framework for collective reason in technological and risk decision making. The critical challenges for the future of the risk field will be to provide an adequate account of the (not fully determinate) social nature of technologies and to relate these to a much richer, less determinate concept of human beings, our aspirations and identities. The institutional correlates of these cultural and intellectual transformations will also have to be charted.

Latour (1991) has suggested the alternative term *amodern* to encompass his dissolution of the social and the natural (Latour 1986) as a conceptual underpinning to the new project of identifying our human selves with the protection of nature. But this dissolution per se does not address the need to open up from natural discourses of science and risk, to address the tensions and indeterminacies involved in human possibilities (Grove-White 1991). It is just conceivable that risk as a field could do this; but a condition would be its radical, and regular, reconstruction.

NOTES

I am especially grateful to Robin Grove-White for many conversations that have helped me to shape the thoughts reflected in this paper.

1. F. Birrer, personal communication, 1991.

PART IV

Policy and Decision Frameworks

CHAPTER 13 _____

A Conceptual Framework for Managing Low-Probability Events

Howard Kunreuther

My initial interest in risk and uncertainty began in September 1964 when I undertook a study at the Institute for Defense Analysis with Douglas Dacy on the economic problems facing Alaska following the Good Friday earthquake of March 1964. We were both surprised to find that behavior did not conform to the patterns prescribed by economic theory. Food prices and rents went down in the short run even though there were shortages in perishable goods and a limited supply of housing. Most residents and businesses did not have earthquake insurance and hence turned to the federal government for relief and were rewarded with low-interest loans and forgiveness grants. It was not unusual to hear many victims remark that financially they were better off after the earthquake than prior to the event due to liberal disaster relief.

Our conclusions from the study were influenced by other studies on behavior following natural disasters (White 1953; Kates 1962; Fritz and Mathewson 1957) and discussions with geographers such as Robert Kates and Gilbert White as well as sociologists like Charles Fritz. It is thus not surprising that in summarizing the findings of our study we noted that sociological and psychological factors play an important role in influencing economic behavior and must be explicitly considered in order to develop meaningful and workable policy formulations (Dacy and Kunreuther 1969).

A look at disaster relief activity following the Alaska earthquake revealed that the generous aid given the Alaskans rapidly became the norm due to an unparalleled series of hurricanes, tornadoes, and floods that affected all parts of the country during the next eighteen months. If people did not protect themselves prior to a disaster by undertaking mitigation measures and purchasing insurance, then they would turn to the federal government for assistance, and Congress would respond.

Government relief reached a peak in the summer of 1972, when Tropical Storm Agnes caused approximately $2 billion in damage to the northeastern section of the United States. Few homeowners and businesses had flood insurance even though it was highly subsidized by the federal government and was available in some of the stricken areas. As a result, the Small Business Administration provided $5,000 forgiveness grants and 1 percent loans to uninsured victims. The total SBA-approved loan amount was $1.2 billion, with over $550 million in the form of forgiveness grants (Kunreuther 1973).

The lack of interest by homeowners in purchasing flood insurance led a group of us to study the factors influencing individuals' actions to protect themselves against low-probability/high-consequence events. Through field surveys (Kunreuther, Ginsberg, et al. 1978) and controlled laboratory experiments (Slovic, Fischhoff, et al. 1977), we contrasted two alternative models of choice: the expected utility model, which forms the cornerstone of economic analysis; and a sequential model of choice, which incorporates principles of bounded rationality (Simon 1955). Our conclusions from this study suggest that individuals have a difficult time dealing with the concept of probability and tend to rely on salient data (e.g., past experience) and easily accessible sources (e.g., friends and neighbors), rather than utilizing statistical data and making tradeoffs between benefits and costs. These findings suggest that consumers may be the source of market failure when it comes to adopting protective measures prior to a disaster. To avoid liberal relief by the government following a catastrophic event, there may be a need for regulatory mechanisms regarding the adoption of cost-effective loss prevention measures or the institutionalization of insurance requirements as a condition for a mortgage.

The need for regulatory measures and the involvement of the public sector became even clearer when my own interests moved from natural to technological disasters. While at the International Institute for Applied Systems Analysis (IIASA), I became involved with a large project on the siting of liquified natural gas (LNG) facilities in four countries. An international team undertook detailed interviews with key interested parties to contrast the processes involved in making siting decisions in four different countries (Kunreuther and Linnerooth 1982). Although our studies were descriptive in nature, they raised a number of issues related to the role of compensation, insurance, and regulation in facilitating the siting process.

Since returning from IIASA to the University of Pennsylvania, I have pursued research related to both natural and technological hazards. A group of us from different disciplines in the social sciences formed the Center for Risk and Decision Processes at the Wharton School in 1984. Its mission is to understand better the decision-making processes regarding low-probability/high-consequence events and thereby to encourage the design of more effective policies. As director of the center, I have been involved in a variety of projects related to the siting of the high-level radioactive waste repository in Nevada; determining the role of mitigation measures and insurance in dealing with earthquake problems; and gaining a better appreciation of how companies cope with catastrophic disasters such as the chemical explosion at the Union Carbide plant in Bhopal, India.

During the past three years a group of center researchers has been involved in a National Science Foundation sponsored project on "The Role of Insurance, Compensation, Regulation and Protective Behavior in Dealing with Risk and Misfortune." We approach these issues from three perspectives: normative, descriptive, and prescriptive. The normative research develops a set of standards, such as efficiency and equity, for evaluating choices under risk, uncertainty, and ambiguity. The descriptive work focuses on how consumers, businesses, insurers, and government agencies actually make decisions about what type of protective activities are appropriate for coping with low-probability/high-consequence events. The prescriptive phase of the project develops risk management strategies to improve group and individual decision processes and choices.

In reflecting on my approach to problems involving health and safety risks, the work of psychologists such as Baruch Fischhoff, Daniel Kahneman, Paul Slovic, and Amos Tversky has greatly influenced my thinking. In particular, I have greatly enjoyed my collaboration with Paul Slovic over many years.

Three leaders in their fields have played a key role in much of my research over the past twenty-five years. Kenneth Arrow encouraged me from the outset to question the assumptions upon which the theory of the economics of uncertainty is based, contending that we need to do a better job of modeling the ignorance of the economic agent. Herbert Simon's pioneering efforts in understanding human behavior and his theory of bounded rationality provided a foundation on which to develop alternative models of choice. Finally, Gilbert White has served as a mentor from the start of my forays into natural disasters through my more recent work on the siting of hazardous facilities. His wisdom with respect to decision processes of individuals and groups, coupled with his recognition of the importance of institutional arrangements, suggested a framework for developing prescriptive analyses. He has been a friend and source of guidance over the years.

Much of my research on risk has addressed the linkage between descriptive and normative analysis for low-probability/high-consequence (LP-HC) events through prescriptive recommendations. By low probability I am referring to events that are perceived by the public and/or the experts as having a relatively small chance of occurring.

Normative models have been developed by economists and management scientists as guides for good decision making. In the case of individual behavior, the expected utility model is the cornerstone for guiding choices between alternatives under risk. It is based on a set of axioms that imply that a rational individual should choose the alternative that maximizes his or her expected utility. Decision analysis, which utilizes expected utility analysis, is a normative approach for incorporating probabilities and outcomes so that one can make the right choices under conditions of risk. In practice, many individuals violate the axioms on which these approaches are based, either because they take into account other factors (e.g., responsibility, justification) that are not incorporated in the expected utility model, or because they have difficulty processing information on uncertainty and consequences.

When one turns to LP-HC events, one faces additional problems. Low-probability events, by definition, do *not* enable individuals to learn easily from the past. At a *descriptive* level, empirical studies reveal that experts often disagree with each other on the potential risks from natural and technological hazards. People often use rules of thumb that either enable them to disregard the possibility of a disastrous event (e.g., "It cannot happen to me") or cause them to exhibit disproportionate concern about other potential hazards (e.g., "I want zero risk"). These heuristics imply that much of the public fails to make calculations that mirror the computations suggested by normative models of choice. This may be a principal reason why residents in hazard-prone areas do not invest in loss-reduction measures or purchase insurance even though their own subjective risk and cost data suggest that they should avail themselves of this protection.

Sound *prescriptive* analysis should be guided by normative models but modified by the lessons of descriptive behavior. Thus, in developing strategies for dealing with LP-HC events, it is important to gain an understanding of individuals' decision processes within the context of existing institutional arrangements. For example, if one is interested in developing strategies for dealing with natural hazards, it is important to know what programs are currently in effect and how they influence behavior. If the public knows or feels that the government will bail them out of a disaster with forgiveness grants, then it is quite rational for them *not* to purchase insurance. On the other hand, if people *do* reflect on the likely consequence of a severe flood or major earthquake, and still choose not to purchase insurance, then their decision is likely to be based on nonnormative decision rules.

Prescriptive strategies involve the use of a combination of different policy tools for managing risks, ranging from information provision and market-based incentive systems to compensation, insurance, and regulation. In evaluating a particular strategy, one needs to consider its impact on resource allocation across all interested parties (the efficiency question), and the differential impact on each of the different interested parties (the equity question).

The tension between efficiency and equity considerations raises an important set of policy questions. Certain programs, which may appear to benefit society when looking across all the stakeholders, may place an undue hardship on a particular group and, therefore, may be unacceptable politically. For example, suppose a large number of disaster victims were forced to go bankrupt following a catastrophic earthquake because they were uninsured. This policy might be justified on efficiency grounds by serving as a signal to homeowners and business that they should seriously consider protecting themselves with insurance and adopting loss-reduction measures in the future. Our society, however, may not tolerate this callous response to misfortune.

A potential strategy for dealing with this problem would be to determine whether certain protective measures should be required prior to a disaster (e.g., purchasing earthquake insurance as a condition for a mortgage), or after the event (e.g., forcing individuals who get a government loan to buy insurance at the same time). When is it appropriate to rely on positive incentives (e.g., subsidies) or negative sanctions (e.g., fines) to induce certain actions? What are some of the implementation problems with different strategies? These and other questions raised in the phase of prescriptive analysis can only be evaluated if one has a descriptive understanding of the problem and normative guidelines by which to judge proposed solutions.

The next section of this chapter turns to a normative analysis of individual decision making by exploring the expected utility model of choice, the standard approach utilized by economists and policy analysts to guide prescriptive analysis. The following two sections deal with the limitations of this theory as a descriptive model of choice and the development of a prescriptive framework for managing risk based on our understanding of human behavior and current types of institutional arrangements. The concluding section outlines future research directions.

NORMATIVE ANALYSIS: EXPECTED UTILITY THEORY

My particular perspective on risk has its origin in expected utility theory. The demand for insurance illustrates the use of this theory as it applies to consumer behavior. Suppose a person with a utility function U has wealth W and faces a p chance of an economic loss L or can buy full-coverage insurance for a price I. Without insurance, the expected utility is

$$p \ U \ (W-L) \ + \ (1-p) \ U \ (W)8 \qquad (1)$$

With insurance coverage, expected utility is $U(W-I)$. The price I^* at which $U(W-I^*) = p \ U(W-L) + (1-p) \ U(W)$ is the certainty equivalent of the risk. Whenever the price of insurance $I<I^*$, an individual should prefer full insurance to remaining unprotected.

A similar analysis can be applied to an insurer who has a utility function V and is considering selling insurance coverage with the objective of maximizing expected utility. Suppose the firm has assets A and is determining what price I to charge for insurance against the loss that the consumer faces. If the firm offers an insurance policy to an individual with the above risk, then its expected utility is

$$p \ V(A+I-L) \ + \ (1-p) \ V(A+I) \qquad (2)$$

If it does not offer coverage, its expected utility is simply $V(A)$. The premium I^{**} at which $p \ V(A+I^{**}-L) + (1-p) \ V(A+I^{**}) = V(A)$ is the minimum premium that a firm would be willing to charge a consumer for full insurance coverage. Market failure occurs if $I^{**} > I^*$. In other words, the *maximum* price the consumer is willing to pay for coverage is less than the *minimum* price the insurer is willing to charge.

The above analysis can be expanded by introducing other features of a policy such as deductibles, coinsurance, and reinsurance. One can also consider the case of insuring many risks where there is a potential for a catastrophic loss. These variations will change both the indifference values of I* and I** and hence will determine under what circumstances markets exist and when they fail. Similarly, one could incorporate the response of the federal government to an uninsured victim by providing low-interest loans or grants. For example, if people knew that they would receive a grant of up to $5,000 if they suffered a disaster loss, then the value of L (assuming it was $5,000 or more) would be reduced by that amount in equation (1). If the loss were less than $5,000 then, of course, L would be zero.

In a similar fashion, one can utilize expected utility theory to analyze other types of problems such as the siting of hazardous facilities. Specifically, one can determine the *minimum* amount of benefits B* (perhaps in the form of reduced property taxes) that an individual would require to vote in favor of hosting a potentially hazardous facility in her community, where there is a probability p of some accident with consequences denoted by L. Those providing these benefits (e.g., the developer, the government) would specify the maximum amount B** they could offer each person. If B*<B** then an individual presumably would favor the facility; otherwise the person would oppose the siting of the facility in her backyard. Such an analysis does *not* consider the negative social aspects of compensation, such as the person viewing it as a bribe. For these individuals, a tradeoff between receiving benefits and increased risk will be viewed as inappropriate, which would lead them to vote against the facility.

DESCRIPTIVE ASPECTS OF INDIVIDUAL BEHAVIOR

Economics is a theory of market behavior. Until recently it paid little attention to individual decision making, since it assumed that people utilize normative models of choice, such as expected utility theory, to choose between alternative courses of action. By contrast, cognitive psychology has been concerned with the many factors influencing individual judgment and choice. Recently, there has been considerable research on the factors influencing risk perception (Slovic 1987), judgmental biases (Kahneman, Slovic, and Tversky 1982), and the alternative decision rules for making choices under uncertainty for low-probability events (Weinstein, ed. 1987). Studies by psychologists have shown that the expected utility model is an inadequate description of individual choices under uncertainty (e.g., Schoemaker 1982; Machina 1987). Some of these studies are summarized below, and a more complete set of references related to LP-HC events can be found in Camerer and Kunreuther (1989a).

Biases in Probability Judgments

Many people utilize heuristics for estimating probability, and these rules yield systematic errors in judgment.[1] The *availability bias* reflects the tendency for many people to estimate the probability of an event by the ease with which they can retrieve information about it from memory. People perceive the likelihood of deaths from sensational, highly reported disasters, such as fires and homicides, to be higher than those of less sensational events, such as individual deaths from diabetes and breast cancer. These two diseases together actually take twice as many lives as the two more dramatic events (Combs and Slovic 1979).

Motorists often exhibit an *optimism bias* by taking the attitude that an accident "can't happen to me." This may explain why Svenson (1981) found in a survey that almost 90 percent of drivers felt that they were better than the median driver. Individuals also *ignore low-probability events* by assuming that they are below a threshold worth worrying about. This may explain the reluctance by residents of flood-prone areas to buy flood insurance even when 90 percent of the cost was subsidized by the federal government (Kunreuther, Ginsberg, et al. 1978). With respect to seat belts, individuals may be reluctant to buckle up because they perceive the chance of a fatality on any one trip to be extraordinarily low (Slovic, Fischhoff, and Lichtenstein 1978).

Importance of Other Attributes

Some of the violations of expected utility theory (EU) are due to attributes other than outcomes. Ambiguity or vagueness about probabilities is an attribute that is ignored in EU but that appears to affect choices people make (Ellsberg 1961). In the earlier example on insurance, suppose that the probability of loss p is not known exactly, but instead has a distribution $f(p)$ with expected value p^*. Under EU, the expected probability p is all that matters.

Yet empirical evidence suggests that ambiguity does matter. In a series of experiments related to insurance, sophisticated subjects (including professional actuaries and underwriters) indicated a strong aversion to ambiguity for low-probability events, such as product defects, earthquakes, and leakage from an underground storage tank. When the actuaries were asked to assume the role of an insurer, they showed greater aversion to ambiguity than in their role as a manufacturing firm or consumer seeking coverage (Hogarth and Kunreuther 1989). One reason that the private market has been thin or has failed to provide coverage against such risks as environmental pollution, flood disasters, and nuclear power plant accidents is that $I^{**} >> I^*$ for many potential firms who would be interested in purchasing insurance.

Laypersons' judgments of riskiness are based on dimensions other than probability and losses. Risks that are uncontrollable, unknowable, or have catastrophic potential are feared by the public even when they are unlikely (Fischhoff, Watson, and Hope 1984; Slovic 1987). In other words, laypersons often dread risks over which they have little control, or about which there is limited knowledge and statistical data, or where many people could be adversely affected in a catastrophic event. Experts are generally less concerned with these attributes. By incorporating such attributes as fear and catastrophic potential as part of a multi-attribute utility model, one may be able to explain why the public perceives hazardous waste storage facilities, nuclear power plants, or chemical operations as much riskier than do the experts.

One reason why individuals may be reluctant to think about particular risks is because they feel that there is little they can or want to do to mitigate the consequences. Few people are testing their homes for radon, perhaps, because they may not want to know whether they and their children have been exposed to the risk over a long period of time. They may also be unwilling to incur the personal expense associated with eliminating radon from their home, particularly if actions such as opening windows mean higher heating bills in the winter (Smith et al. 1988).

Purchasing insurance may relieve dread in some cases and may be attractive for that reason. For example, flight coverage is frequently purchased at the airport, but life insurance is a much better buy. For other risks, insurance may remind people of their vulnerability to forces beyond their control. This may partially explain the limited demand for earthquake coverage in California, and for flood insurance in high-hazard areas of the country.

Decision Processes

The expected utility model is based on a set of axioms of rational behavior that individuals are assumed to follow. In practice, people often use heuristics where they make tradeoffs between dimensions of alternatives such as probability and utility (Tversky, Sattath, and Slovic 1988). The weights placed on these dimensions will vary depending on the type of problem, how it is framed, and past experience with the hazard.

In studying individual decision processes for low-probability/high-consequence events, it is useful to distinguish between events where individuals focus on the small chances of their occurrence and other hazards where they attend to the severe impacts of a disaster. For the first class of risks, individuals often treat the hazard as if "it cannot happen to me." In other words, if the probability of an event falls below a critical level, they do not take any protective action. The failure of individuals to purchase insurance or adopt mitigation measures against possible disaster losses illustrates this behavior.

For other risks, for which experts have estimated the probability of occurrence to be extremely low, such as a nuclear power plant accident or leakage from a high-level radioactive waste repository, much of the public focuses on the severe consequences of an accident rather than emphasizing the chances of its occurrence. This is one reason why we observe the not-in-my-backyard (NIMBY) syndrome for siting those hazardous facilities which the experts perceive to be safe but where the public focuses on the impact of a radioactive leak, an explosion, or some other potential disaster without concern for how likely such events will be.

The weights on the relevant dimensions can also change over time, particularly if an accident or disaster has occurred in the interim. For example, the Nuclear Regulatory Commission (NRC) utilized a probability threshold in making its safety-design procedures, not concerning themselves with events that were below a critical level (Fischhoff 1983). The public did not concern itself with this procedure until after TMI. The emphasis since that time has been on worst-case scenarios, which is one reason why the development of nuclear power in the United States has come to a standstill.

To summarize, low-probability/high-consequence events are particularly troublesome at a *descriptive level* for several reasons.

Ambiguity. Experts often disagree about the chances and potential consequences associated with specific events, and there are limited scientific data to reconcile these differences. Ambiguities associated with the chances of an event and/or its consequences influence both consumer and firm decision processes.

Risk Perception. Even when experts agree, individuals often exhibit perceptions that differ systematically from those of the experts. For example, some events are perceived by individuals as sufficiently low that they are not worth worrying about even though the experts rank the hazard as dangerous (e.g., radon in the home), while others are considered by the public to be much more likely than the experts estimate them to be (e.g., hazardous waste; Allen 1987a).

Labile Preferences. Individuals do not have clear, stable preferences with respect to these risks, often being unduly influenced by a recent event that may have little to do with the long-term probability. For example, individuals often have an interest in protection following a recent disaster such as a flood or earthquake, rather than taking steps to mitigate both the physical and economic losses prior to the event.

PRESCRIPTIVE ANALYSIS FOR MANAGING LOW-PROBABILITY RISKS

Each of the descriptive features listed above has implications for *prescriptive analysis*:

Ambiguity. If there is considerable ambiguity related to a particular risk, then private insurance markets may dry up. Consider the problem of predicting environmental pollution damage from a hazardous waste storage facility. The large uncertainty associated with the relationship between a person's exposure to a particular chemical should the facility leak, and the possibility that he or she may contract cancer in the future, makes it difficult for insurers to estimate the *probability* of damage. In addition, new toxic torts, new environmental legislation,' and recent court decisions have increased the uncertainty associated with the *magnitude of the losses* should a suit be filed. Given these characteristics of the risk, it is not surprising that practically all insurance companies are reluctant to provide environmental impairment liability coverage today.

Risk Perception. If individuals perceive risks differently than the experts, private market mechanisms may not be appropriate ways for dealing with these risks. The failure of individuals to adopt voluntary protective measures, such as wearing seat belts, raises the question as to what decision processes these individuals are following in making this decision. At a prescriptive level, what programs are most appropriate for dealing with this problem? For example, when should regulations such as seat belt laws be utilized as a way of increasing seat belt usage?

At the other end of the spectrum, it is now well known that communities are strongly opposed to having hazardous technological facilities sited in their backyards, even though they recognize the potential benefits to society and that the scientific estimation of the risks of such facilities is very low. At a prescriptive level, one can ask what role can market-like solutions such as compensation for risk play in facilitating the siting process? The answer depends on the circumstances under which the public is willing to make tradeoffs between risk and money.

Labile Preferences. If individuals are greatly influenced by recent events and disregard long-term probabilities, then one has the worst of both possible worlds. Failure to mitigate structures and purchase insurance in areas subject to natural disasters makes individuals extremely vulnerable to the forces of nature. Following a disaster there will be enormous pressure by the victims for liberal relief in the form of low-interest loans and grants to help them recover.

To the extent that the government responds with aid, all taxpayers are helping to finance the losses of a few. The problem is exacerbated if the private insurance industry is reluctant to provide coverage to homes and businesses facing the hazard due to the catastrophic loss potential, as was the case twenty-five years ago with flood insurance and is presently the case with earthquake coverage (Litan 1991). From a prescriptive vantage point, we need to determine whether certain types of regulations (e.g., specific building codes) are appropriate and whether the government should be

Figure 13.1
Conceptual Framework for Developing Policy Programs

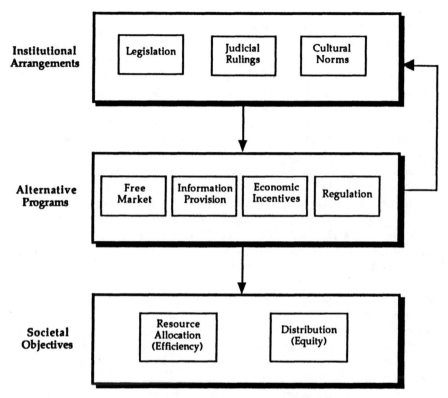

involved in providing some type of reinsurance protection for catastrophic losses.

Figure 13.1 depicts a conceptual framework for the development of alternative policy programs. The current institutional arrangements associated with a particular problem affect the relative benefits and costs of alternate programs, which range from a free-market approach at one extreme to regulatory mechanisms at the other. The performance of these programs may then change the institutional arrangements in place.

The changing climate with respect to seat belt usage illustrates the interaction between institutional arrangements and alternative programs. Even though it has been recognized that seat belts save lives, there were no seat belt laws in the United States until the early 1980s. The prevailing cultural norm was that individuals should have the freedom to decide whether or not to protect themselves against injury or possible fatality from accidents. Automatic restraints were available in some cars, but individuals had to purchase them as an accessory at an additional price—an example of the free market in action. Educational programs and information provision by groups such as the Insurance Institute for Highway Safety, however, failed to stimulate additional seat belt usage (Robertson 1987).

More recently there has been a shift in the attitude toward voluntary seat belt usage, as indicated by the promulgation of new laws and regulations. In 1984, the Department of Transportation ruled that unless states comprising two-thirds of the nation's population passed seat belt laws by 1989, automatic restraints would be required in all new cars beginning in 1990. This ruling led to the passage of seat belt laws in a number of states (Williams and Lund 1988). In terms of Figure 13.1, the failure of the free market and information-provision programs to increase seat belt use led to new legislation and laws. These new institutional arrangements used fines as the principal means of increasing seat belt use.

The use of alternative policy tools is intimately connected to the ideological question as to how much government should interfere with individual choice. Public policies that force people to buy insurance or wear a seat belt infringe on individual rights. On the other hand, regulations may be more desirable than current programs such as federal disaster relief or subsidized medical care after a car accident. In this sense, some degree of paternalism by requiring certain actions *ex ante* may be viewed as desirable to protect individuals against themselves and spare others from bearing these costs *ex post* (Schelling 1984).

In evaluating the effectiveness of policy tools, societal objectives need to be considered. These include the impact of the policy tool on overall resource allocation or social welfare (i.e., efficiency considerations) and the effect of the policy tool on the distribution of resources across different stakeholders (i.e., equity considerations).

The approach outlined below is based on the premise that it is most desirable to let individuals make their own choices through the use of a private market. Government action may be required in dealing with LP-HC events, however, for several reasons: imperfect information processing by individuals; the need for more equitable distribution of resources across different parties; and negative externalities. By externalities we mean situations in which the actions of one individual or entity affect the welfare of others. The use of public funds to cover the costs of an uninsured disaster victim is an example of a negative externality associated with the failure of a person to purchase insurance prior to disaster.

To explore these issues further we consider two societal problems that involve low-probability risks and where the behavior of individuals has enormous implications at a societal level: (1) protection against natural disasters, and (2) siting hazardous facilities. In both examples, I will examine first private market solutions and then other approaches. The prescriptive solution for a particular problem may involve a mix of different mechanisms.

For example, in promoting auto safety, certain regulations may be desirable (e.g., speed limits), while private auto insurance markets may encourage the purchase of automatic restraints by offering discounted insurance to car owners who have these devices installed.

Protection Against Natural Disasters

If individuals do not protect themselves against the consequences of natural disasters through the purchase of insurance and/or adoption of loss prevention measures, then the financial consequences from a major disaster are likely to be severe to the potential victim. To the extent that the federal government provides liberal disaster relief in the form of low-interest loans and forgiveness grants, the general taxpayer will be partially responsible for financing the costs of recovery. Hence there are private and social costs associated with individuals not adopting protective measures prior to a disaster.

The *free market* offers one line of attack. Empirical evidence on both the demand and supply side, however, indicates that this approach will not work well in practice. Consumers have little interest in voluntarily purchasing flood or earthquake insurance, in part, because they are not fully aware of the costs of insurance and also because they do not believe that the disaster will happen to them (Kunreuther, Ginsberg, et al. 1978). Insurers have been concerned with the catastrophic consequences to them of a large-scale flood or earthquake. In the case of floods, no private insurance company has offered coverage since the severe floods of 1927 and 1928 (Manes 1938). Hence Congress passed the National Flood Insurance Program of 1968, which offered federally subsidized flood insurance on a nationwide basis with coverage marketed by the private sector.

One way to correct for market failure on the consumer side is the *provision of information* about hazards and available protective measures. The *availability bias* suggests that media publicity, vivid films, or visual displays such as plotting flood heights on photographs of familiar buildings may help create concern for the hazard (Kates 1962). To date, there is no evidence that these approaches have increased the demand for protection.

If individuals only attend to a hazard when they perceive the probability to be above a given threshold, then changing the time dimension may make them more sensitive to the consequences and lead them to adopt protective actions. For example, rather than indicating that the annual probability of a hundred-year flood is .01, a homeowner could be told that if she lived in her house for the next twenty-five years, the chances of at least one severe flood would be .22. Experimental evidence with respect to presenting data on the chances of a fatality from an automobile supports this conjecture. Motorists are more likely to consider using seat belts when the evidence is presented in terms of a lifetime of driving rather than on a single trip (Slovic, Fischhoff, and Lichtenstein 1978).

Insurance agents could also provide homeowners with better data on the costs and terms of a policy. If insurers view coverage in terms of an investment, they should educate their clients that the best return is no return at all. Otherwise those who purchase policies against low-probability events are likely to cancel coverage after a few years of not suffering any losses. Evidence from the flood insurance program reveals that this is likely to occur (Lave and Lave 1991).

A more direct approach is to provide some form of *economic incentives* to encourage individuals to protect themselves against potential losses from a disaster. In the case of flood insurance, the subsidized rates still did not encourage many consumers to purchase coverage. One interpretation of this behavior is that individuals knew that they would receive liberal disaster relief in the wake of a catastrophic disaster. Our field surveys in flood- and earthquake-prone areas revealed that few uninsured homeowners anticipated federal relief following a disaster even if their anticipated losses were greater than $10,000 (Kunreuther, Kleindorfer, et al. 1987).

As an incentive for homeowners to adopt loss prevention measures, insurance rates could be reduced to reflect the lower risk. One example that appears to be moving in this direction is the National Flood Insurance program. A proposed community rating system has been developed, whereby insurance premiums for all structures are reduced should specific building codes be imposed as part of a communitywide mitigation program.

From an efficiency standpoint, the federal government could indicate that *no* disaster assistance would be provided to uninsured victims of natural disasters. Alternatively, any uninsured victim who received federal relief would be required to purchase coverage in the future. There is no guarantee that those homeowners required to purchase insurance would maintain their policies for more than a few years, thus leaving them open to future catastrophic losses. From a political standpoint, distributional considerations often dictate legislative actions, so that if many victims of a large-scale disaster were uninsured, special relief measures would be forthcoming.

If information provision and incentives are relatively unsuccessful, one can turn to some form of *regulation* to force homeowners to adopt protection. In the case of insurance, banks and financial institutions could require flood and earthquake coverage, much as they require homeowner's insurance as a condition for a mortgage. Today, all homeowners in designated flood-prone areas with federally insured mortgages are required to purchase flood insurance, but this condition does not generally apply to other mortgages with commercial banks. Specific building codes and land-use regulations could also be imposed on communities.

Siting Hazardous Facilities

The siting of facilities that are perceived by the public to pose risks to health and safety has become an especially conflict-ridden issue in recent years. These facilities include solid and hazardous waste treatment plants, landfills, power plants, sewage-treatment facilities, and other locally unwanted land uses (LULUs). Opposition to these facilities has been so effective that not a single new hazardous waste disposal facility has been sited in the United States since 1980.

Society faces a dilemma in resolving this conflict. On the one hand, people demand the goods and services the production of which yields waste. There appears to be widespread agreement that there is a need for properly designed and managed disposal facilities since, in the aggregate, their presence would yield benefits in excess of their risks and costs. On the other hand, opposition by citizens is vehement when they learn that their community is being considered for a trash disposal or hazardous waste facility. This results in the NIMBY phenomenon (Popper 1983), which is now part of our American culture. In other words, society may need the facility, but no community wants to be the site.

The *free-market* approach to this problem can be simply stated. Those who advocate siting the facility should provide sufficient compensation to those who incur costs from it. If the anticipated benefits exceed the required compensation costs, then the facility should be sited. Otherwise it is not needed.

This approach to the problem has not worked in practice for two principal reasons. People prefer clinging to the status quo even when it may be costly for them to do so. Samuelson and Zeckhauser (1988) provide an illustrative example of a small town in West Germany that was given an offer by the government to pay for its own relocation due to a strip mining project in the area. Despite many options for redesigning the town, the citizenry opted to maintain its serpentine layout, which had evolved without any rhyme or reason over the centuries.

A second reason for the inability of free-market approaches to find suitable sites for hazardous facilities is the unwillingness of individuals to trade additional money for increased risk. The findings of a telephone survey of Nevada residents faced with the prospect of hosting a high-level radioactive waste facility at Yucca Mountain (approximately 100 miles from Las Vegas) illustrate this point. Each respondent was asked a pair of "willingness-to-accept" (WTA) questions that varied the dollar rebates to be given to residents over a twenty-year period should the repository be located at Yucca Mountain. Residents had to decide whether they would vote for or against the repository if they were given a credit or rebate on their federal income taxes of either $1,000, $3,000, or $5,000 for each of the next twenty years.[2] If the person voted for the repository, the question was asked again, but the credit or rebate was half the original amount; if the person voted against the repository, then the question was asked again and the credit or rebate was double the original amount.

The response to the questions suggests that there was little enthusiasm for compensation even though there were assurances that the facility would meet government safety standards. Approximately 25 percent of the sample was willing to accept the credit or rebate for hosting the facility in their backyard. Even more surprising to us was residents' insensitivity to the amount of compensation. There was no statistical difference in the percentage of Nevadans favoring the facility regardless of whether the initial annual dollar rebate was $1,000, $3,000, or $5,000 (Kunreuther, Easterling, et al. 1990).

These findings suggest that other prescriptive approaches may be more effective in siting new facilities. With respect to *information provision*, there is a need to highlight the default option to all those affected by the siting process. The status quo bias creates a false sense of security or well-being with the current situation that often leads to inertia. For example, a presentation of comparative figures on the expenditures associated with shipping waste to a distant location versus the lower disposal costs associated with a new facility in the region is an important input into any siting debate.

In a similar fashion, one can present information on the risks associated with the current methods of disposal in relation to a new facility. To the extent that the health and safety risks associated with modern disposal facilities are lower than the current processes being utilized, an argument on risk grounds alone should provide convincing evidence to adopt the new technology.

With respect to *economic incentives*, there are limitations as to the role that compensation can play in facilitating the siting of facilities. Creative benefit-sharing packages can be developed so that community residents feel that they are better off with the facility than under the status quo. These benefits may be more appropriate in the form of in-kind compensation such as better health facilities or improved educational facilities. The advantage of presenting community residents with a package that addresses health and safety needs is that it enables one to demonstrate that the addition of a hazardous waste facility may actually reduce overall risks to the citizenry.

The host community should also be fully compensated for any negative impacts that might occur as a result of the facility. Residents often fear that their property values will fall once a facility is slated for their community and hence that they will be hurt economically should they sell their house in the future. Champion International addressed this problem directly before siting a paper sludge landfill in Hamilton, Ohio. They implemented a program to protect owners of property within two miles of the facility from any loss in resale value due to the location of their landfill. The property was priced by two independent appraisers, one chosen by the owner and the other by Champion. Comparable homes in nearby areas that had similar characteristics to Hamilton are used as a barometer for real estate value changes in the absence of the landfill (Ewing 1990).

Assuming that there is a perceived need for the facility, some type of competitive bidding procedures between candidate sites might prove useful. One procedure that addresses both equity and efficiency concerns is a lottery-auction mechanism (Kunreuther, Kleindorfer, et al. 1987; Kunreuther and Portney 1991). In the first stage, each of the potential host communities indicates how much it would demand in compensation to host the facility. Let us call the maximum amount that any community demanded t^*. Assuming that t^* is considered an acceptable amount by all interested parties, a lottery is used to determine a candidate site. At the end of this stage, the winner of the lottery is designated as the default host site, and t^* would be earmarked for their use if the facility is sited there.

The second stage involves an auction whereby each of the candidate communities (including the lottery winner) has an opportunity to specify the maximum amount it would require to serve as a host community. All of the communities are aware that they may be required to pay a portion of the final compensation package if they are not chosen as the host site. The developer and other users of the facility may also be required to contribute money to this pool. If no community bids less than t^*, then the lottery winner is declared the actual site and would receive t^*.

In siting a potentially hazardous facility, economic incentives are not likely to be effective if there is concern expressed by community residents about the risks from the facility to current residents and future generations. Recent siting experience supports this hypothesis. In the evaluation of a monitored retrievable storage facility in Tennessee, a local task force needed assurance that the facility was safe before even considering its operation, desirability, and benefit-sharing package (Peelle and Ellis 1987). Former Governor Richard H. Bryan of Nevada, in discussing the importance of impeccable scientific studies of the repository as part of the siting process, affirmed the essential role of safety when he stated that "no amount of compensation or federal 'incentives' can ever substitute for safety and technical suitability in the site selection effort" (Bryan 1987).

Guarantees that regulations and stringent safety standards will be met are critical ingredients to a successful siting process. Several steps can be taken for achieving this objective. Appropriate monitoring and control procedures can be established that are agreeable to both the developer and the host community to ensure that community-approved safety standards are maintained. Plans and restrictions for the use of the facility (such as those eligible to ship waste) can be specified. Finally, and perhaps most important, the community could have the power to shut down the facility temporarily or permanently if the preestablished regulations and standards are not adhered to by the operator.

There is another dimension to the siting process that goes beyond the policy tools outlined above. There is a need for a participatory process that involves all the stakeholders and identifies the nature of the problem and potential solutions. Trust between the various parties can be established by identifying past difficulties and mistakes in siting, and by allowing for independent assessment of project risks, costs, and benefits. By seeking acceptable sites with a voluntary process, there is some chance that a host community can be found.

A set of guidelines emerged from a National Workshop on Facility Siting in 1990 that constitutes a general approach for allowing the different interested parties in a siting dispute to arrive at a mutually acceptable set of terms for the siting and operation of a facility (Consensus 1991). The guidelines represent a set of operational principles and mechanisms that local and regional governments might incorporate into their own approaches. Each siting case requires specialized treatment due to the nature of the affected participants, the project itself, and the political culture.

CONCLUSIONS AND FUTURE RESEARCH DIRECTIONS

The research to date on LP-HC events suggests that a problem-focused approach is necessary to develop a meaningful set of prescriptive recommendations for meeting specific goals and objectives. Each problem has a unique set of institutional arrangements and dynamics between the relevant stakeholders that needs to be clearly specified. The strategies chosen for inducing people to buckle up their seat belts depend on the relationship among the automobile manufacturers, insurance companies, regulatory agencies, the relevant legislative bodies, and the public. Siting a hazardous waste facility involves an entirely different set of interested parties.

For each problem, the policy objectives need to be clearly stated and will depend on the relative power of the concerned stakeholders. What are the tradeoffs between efficiency and equity? What policies are best suited to cope with economic and political concerns? These questions depend on who is affected by the particular hazard in question and their ability to cope with the situation. For example, in developing strategies for reducing the costs of natural disasters, there are questions as to what policies should be developed to meet the long-run goals of society while still satisfying the immediate concerns of the victims, many of whom have limited financial resources to cope with their loss. The increasing societal concern with environmental issues requires us to examine the benefits and costs from different technologies with both short- and long-run goals in mind. The mix of policy tools such as insurance, regulations, and incentives will partially depend on what these objectives are and how the different parties react to the potential hazard.

We also need to understand how individuals and groups process information with respect to LP-HC events. Recent research in this area suggests that most people do not collect enough information or process the data they have to maximize their expected utility. They rely on simplified models of choice, which vary according to the problem context. If individuals show little concern with some hazards that are potentially costly, not only to themselves but to the general taxpayer, then this needs to be taken into account when developing policies. If, on the other hand, many people are worried about hazards that experts agree pose little danger to them or future generations, then very different strategies will have to be considered for dealing with these issues.

Some of the questions that future research on LP-HC events might address are listed below:

1. What are the characteristics of specific hazards that influence decision processes of individuals? Can one link a typology of different hazards to the behavior of individuals under uncertainty? The different typologies that have been presented (e.g., Hohenemser, Kates, and Slovic 1983; von Winterfeldt and Edwards 1984; Slovic 1987) may provide a convenient starting point for relating the characteristics of hazards to how individuals deal with them.
2. What different decision processes are utilized by individuals in dealing with different LP-HC events? For some risks, individuals focus on the magnitude of the consequences of the event, while for others they focus on the low probability. Can one determine when individuals are likely to use one strategy rather than another? Attributes such as justification, accountability to others, and responsibility may play a key role in decision processes. By understanding the relative importance of these attributes we may be able to design more meaningful public policies.
3. What is the effectiveness of different prescriptive strategies utilizing efficiency and equity criteria as guidelines? How does one implement specific policies, recognizing the importance of current institutional arrangements, and how difficult is it to change the status quo?

Laboratory experiments and field surveys provide insight into decision processes. The computerized process technology used by Payne, Bettman, and Johnson (1990) may help us understand the variables influencing individual decisions and the tradeoffs between effort and accuracy. Experiments on markets and groups' choices are useful in determining how different programs will work when aggregated across individuals. It is unclear how policy tools such as incentive systems (e.g., fines and subsidies) and regulations affect individual behavior in a market context when there is uncertainty and information asymmetry.

Finally, published data on the success of various policy tools should be examined more carefully. There are many states with seat belt laws, and their relative performance can be compared using variables such as the level of fines and types of enforcement mechanisms. There are successes and failures in siting potentially hazardous facilities, and these experiences should be contrasted. It would be useful to know how variables such as trust, public participation, and the nature of the siting process (e.g., voluntary, legislated) play a role in the final outcome.

NOTES

The research described in this chapter reflects interactions and joint efforts with many colleagues, notably Colin Camerer, Jack Hershey, Paul Kleindorfer, Paul Schoemaker, Paul Slovic, and Gilbert White. Thanks to Dominic Golding and Sheldon Krimsky for their helpful comments and suggestions on earlier drafts of this chapter. Partial support was provided by the Wharton Center for Risk and Decision Processes and NSF Grant #SES–8809299.

1. Many of these biases have been documented elsewhere (e.g., Kahneman, Slovic, and Tversky 1982) and will only be briefly summarized here. Additional examples related to natural hazards can be found in Slovic, Kunreuther, and White (1974).

2. Respondents were randomly assigned to one of the three initial dollar figures of $1,000, $3,000 or $5,000.

CHAPTER 14

Expert Knowledge and Public Values in Risk Management: The Role of Decision Analysis

Detlof von Winterfeldt

Decision analysis is a systematic procedure to assist decision makers in making wise choices in the presence of uncertainty and multiple objectives. The methodology of decision analysis consists of decomposing a decision problem into its factual and value parts, analyzing the factual parts as probability problems, analyzing the value parts as utility problems, and reaggregating both by using explicitly stated and logical principles of probability and utility theory.

I came to decision analysis when it was in its infancy in the late sixties and early seventies. After four years at the University of Hamburg in Germany, I entered a Ph.D. program in mathematical psychology under the supervision of Clyde Coombs, Ward Edwards, and David Krantz at the University of Michigan. These three individuals influenced my thinking in very different ways. Clyde Coombs' interest was in describing how people make decisions and how they deviate from normative (utility and probability) theory. Ward Edwards searched for ways to make decision theory useful by applying Bayesian probability theory and multi-attribute utility theory to several real-world contexts. David Krantz's interest was in theories of measurement, including measurement of probability and utility. In addition to the impacts of my interactions with my three academic advisors, I was also strongly influenced by the work of Ron Howard, Duncan Luce, Howard Raiffa, Amos Tversky, and James Savage.

Following my dissertation at the University of Michigan in 1976, I spent three years at the International Institute of Applied Systems Analysis (IIASA), then headed by Howard Raiffa. This period had two major impacts on me: It confronted me with the messiness of real-world decision problems, and it introduced me to my colleague and friend Ralph Keeney. Trying my hand at the problems IIASA was chartered to tackle, I soon found that they did not neatly fit into the schematic of decision analysis. There never seems to be a single decision maker, decisions have to be invented rather than lying around for analysis, objectives are poorly understood, and there are as many ways to structure a decision problem as there are analysts. In short, I learned that the toughest task of decision analysis was the transformation of an initially vague and ill-understood problem into one that could be analyzed in a way that provides useful insights for thinking and decision making. Ralph Keeney, a master at that task, taught me some of his skills.

IIASA had strong environmental and energy programs, and, as a result, I focused on environmental management problems, often related to energy issues such as nuclear power safety, pollution from offshore oil platforms, and noise regulation. In my first applied study of offshore oil pollution in the North Sea, I encountered the problem of multiple stakeholders: Rather than dealing with a single decision maker, several groups—including environmentalists, regulatory agencies, and industry—interacted in complex ways. Decision analysis, with its single decision-maker focus, did not appear to be well suited to handle these problems. Game theory appeared better suited, but it seemed to provide somewhat artificial solutions to fairly contrived problems. I preferred an intermediate approach to decision analysis, now known as the *multiple-stakeholder approach*, in which I analyzed the same decision problem from the perspective of different stakeholders. The goal was not to find the best alternative (as in standard decision analysis), nor to find an equilibrium (as in game theory), but to clarify the values and opinions of the stakeholders, to pinpoint the sources of disagreement, and to develop compromise solutions.

I have pursued this work since leaving IIASA, including multiple-stakeholder analyses on problems as diverse as prioritization of research and development activities, air pollution control, offshore oil drilling and nuclear safety. In addition to value conflicts among stakeholders, I also often encountered conflicts and disagreements among experts. This recognition led to an extension of the multiple-stakeholder approach to include the involvement of multiple experts to provide diversity in judgments. This approach of using decision analysis to map out the views of multiple stakeholder values and multiple expert opinions is by now a mature methodology. However, some vexing problems remain: What role do experts versus the public have in this kind of methodology? How can values and facts be separated? What is the relationship between analysis and the political process of decision making? And finally, how does the implicit image of society controlled by special interests relate to the democratic image of society controlled by all individuals?

The purpose of this chapter is to describe the challenges of applying decision analysis to public policy problems in risk management, to summarize the multiple-stakeholder approach to decision analysis with its extension to multiple experts, and to reflect on some of the unsolved problems lying between the challenge and the methodology.

EXPERT KNOWLEDGE AND PUBLIC VALUES IN RISK MANAGEMENT

In the traditional approach to risk management, the expert was often the risk estimator, evaluator, and decision maker. A structural engineer could, for example, calculate the amount of concrete and steel it would take to build a bridge, provide reasonable estimates of the risks and margins of safety, and essentially make the technical decisions for the policy maker and the affected publics. This traditional approach worked well as long as there was opportunity for trial and error and a societal learning process with the risks implied by these decisions. To be sure, the experts' estimates of risks were not always correct and did not necessarily reflect public preferences for safety, but if the risks were fairly small and there was opportunity for learning, the experts' decisions were usually correctable. When the risk levels implied by experts proved incredulous to the public, they were eventually lowered. Trains and steamboats are examples (see Edwards and von Winterfeldt 1986).

For several modern technologies, this approach to resolving risk management issues does not work well anymore. First, the task of estimating risks has become much more difficult with many new technologies like nuclear power, bioengineering, and chemicals in food. Uncertainties in models and data, compounded with expert disagreements about model assumptions and interpretations of data, often lead to orders of magnitudes of differences among risk estimates. Second, the trial and error approach fails with many risks that either have such a large disaster potential that they should never happen or are so uncertain that no data accumulation will ever give final answers. Thus, the public has little or no feedback about how well the experts have estimated the risks or how appropriate an implied risk level is. Third, the experts are not necessarily in tune with the safety values and concerns of the public, and they consequently run the danger of superimposing their own values. The "acceptable risk" debate was essentially a controversy about expert versus public values.

The result has been an increasing mistrust by the public of experts and subsequent demands for more public control over experts and technological choice processes (Ruckelshaus 1987). In some instances, this has led to pushing a technology question to the top of the political agenda, as in the case of the supersonic transport (SST), nuclear power, and, currently, the issue of global warming. At the extreme, one could think of a process in which all technological risk questions would be put to a vote by those affected by the technology and its risks. But clearly, nobody would seriously suggest voting on whether a bridge design is safe enough or whether the costs and risks of a dam safety project outweigh its benefits. As desirable as it is to provide more public control over experts and technological choice processes, one has to recognize the limits of laypeople's knowledge and judgments in these extremely complex issues. On issues as technical as nuclear power, electromagnetic fields, global warming, and acid rain, to name only a few, the gulf between those who possess an in-depth knowledge of the problem and the rest of society is huge.

The dilemma is thus clear: The experts should not control society's technological choices, but the public and their political representatives are not sufficiently informed to assume complete control themselves.

THE ROLE OF DECISION ANALYSIS

Decision analysis can contribute to overcoming this dilemma in at least three ways:

1. By exploring the value side of the problem and by highlighting multiple conflicting values held by different stakeholder groups;
2. By analyzing the factual side of the problem through multiple elicitations of experts with differing views of the facts, data, and models; and
3. By studying the implications of conflicting stakeholder values and differing expert judgments on the evaluation of the available policy alternatives.

During the last ten years, decision analysts have developed methodologies that could assist in these tasks. The multiple-stakeholder approach to decision analysis (see, e.g., Edwards and von Winterfeldt 1987; von Winterfeldt 1987; Keeney and von Winterfeldt 1987) was designed to provide public value inputs into policy decision making. In this approach, stakeholders are identified, their values and concerns are elicited, and their evaluation strategies are quantified by a formal evaluation model. These models are then used to identify sources of agreement and disagreement in the evaluation strategies as well as in developing compromise solutions. Over the last decade, this approach has been applied to problems as diverse as offshore oil drilling, water resources planning, earthquake-proofing of houses, nuclear waste transportation, and pollution control planning.

In the last five years formal methods for eliciting expert judgments in risk problems have been expanded from early attempts to elicit probability judgments to a complete process for training experts, structuring decompositions of problems, and eliciting a variety of technical judgments from experts (see, e.g., Merkhofer 1987; Mosleh, Bier, and Apostolakis 1988; Keeney and von Winterfeldt 1989, 1991). While still an emerging methodology, formal expert elicitation is now increasingly applied to areas such as nuclear power safety, nuclear waste siting, and environmental assessments.

Decision analysis therefore now has two major capabilities, which in combination can address some of the analytic problems of using expert judgments in combination with public value judgments. In the following section, I will outline how the multiple-stakeholder methodology for obtaining public value inputs can be combined with formal methods for eliciting expert judgments to assist decision makers in controversial risk

Table 14.1
Steps in a Multiple-Stakeholder Decision Analysis

Problem Formulation	• Translate the risk problem into a decision problem • Identify stakeholders • Obtain broad stakeholder input and objectives
Development of Objectives and Attributes	• Constructing separate value trees with stakeholders • Building a combined value tree • Developing attributes
Estimation of Risks, Costs, Benefits and Other Impacts	• Identification and selection of experts • Training and assistance in decomposition • Modelling and data collection • Elicitation • Aggregation across experts
Elicitation of a multiattribute utility model from stakeholders	• Elicitation of value judgments • Testing and building a multiattribute utility model
Sensitivity analyses and option invention	• Putting the pieces together • Sensitivity analyses • Option invention

problems. Subsequently I will discuss issues regarding the foundation of this methodology, its uses, and its limitations.

THE MULTIPLE-STAKEHOLDER APPROACH TO DECISION ANALYSIS

Table 14.1 summarizes the steps of the multiple-stakeholder approach to decision analysis. It consists of an expansion—through the use of multiple experts—of the multiple-stakeholder approach described, for example, in von Winterfeldt (1987) and in Keeney and von Winterfeldt (1987). In this section, I will briefly elaborate on the steps outlined in Table 14.1.

Problem Formulation

The first step consists of translating a usually ill-defined risk problem (e.g., what can one do about chemical wastes?) into a decision problem with properly formulated alternatives (e.g., treatment alternatives or disposal sites). This is not always a trivial task. For example, when examining the offshore oil drilling problem, some stakeholders formulated the problem in terms of alternative drilling sites, some phrased it as a yes/no decision, and others simply refused to allow drilling in "their backyard" and wanted to examine alternative means of battling the drilling proposals (see von Winterfeldt 1987). In the case of nuclear risks, technical experts sometimes phrase the problem in terms of alternative safety standards, while other groups see the issues in terms of institutional controls. At this stage it is important to be open to alternative problem formulations and avoid settling in too early on the alternatives that are to be studied.

The next step in problem formulation is the identification of stakeholders. Stakeholders are groups—not necessarily organized—that share common values and preferences regarding the alternatives under consideration. For example, stakeholders related to offshore oil drilling are the fishermen, environmentalist groups, local city councils, business associations, and oil companies. It is usually not difficult to identify organized stakeholder groups in controversial problems. They will have taken sides before the analysis begins, and they often voice their opinions loudly. It is more difficult to recognize and involve stakeholder groups that are not represented by an organization. For example, in a water resources management problem in central Arizona, certain farmers were affected by some of the alternatives, yet no organization represented them (see Rozelle 1982). These farmers were stakeholders who should have been (and were) given a voice in the process.

After the identification of stakeholder groups, the decision analyst interviews one or several representatives of the groups to elicit their views of the problem to be analyzed as well as to obtain initial ideas of stakeholder objectives. Problem formulation presents us with a list of stakeholder groups, a description of their main objectives, and a description of the way they view the problem. Problem formulation concludes when a common formulation of the problem has been achieved that matches the stakeholders' views. If this common definition leaves out important aspects of some stakeholders, this should be made clear, and stakeholders should be asked whether they would like to participate in the analysis in spite of the fact that the problem as formulated may not completely coincide with their own view.

In some cases the stakeholders will refuse to do so. For example, when analyzing alternative energy policies for West Germany, a group representing the radical environmentalist movements refused to participate, since they disagreed with the problem formulation. This formulation pitted four energy scenarios against each other, while the environmentalists saw the choices as being between alternative processes for obtaining public control over energy policy issues (see, e.g., Keeney, Renn, and von Winterfeldt 1987).

The final step in problem formulation is the selection of a subset of stakeholders that should participate in the study. Often there are too many groups to involve all of them. For example, in the offshore oil study, we counted over 100 groups. The key point to keep in mind is that all relevant values should be represented by the participating stakeholders, but not necessarily all groups representing similar values. Thus, it is usually sufficient to involve one or two environmental groups, rather than all environmental groups, and one or two groups representing development interests, rather than all of them. In most cases, the spectrum of relevant values and concerns can be covered by involving five to ten groups.

Development of Objectives and Attributes

Constructing separate value trees with stakeholders. In a second round of interviews with stakeholder representatives, value trees are constructed (Keeney and Raiffa [1976] call them objectives hierarchies). The decision analyst should attempt to enlist the highest-ranking representatives of each stakeholder group, since such members are usually willing to participate and interested in exploring value questions. In the interview, the analyst asks questions such as, Why is a particular value (e.g., environmental protection) important to the group? How is the value defined? What is good about an alternative and what is bad? Means are pursued to identify underlying ends. For example, if pollution is stated as a concern, the analyst would pursue why this is so, presumably to discover that this concern reflects concerns with human health, visibility, and deterioration of flora and fauna. The interview usually lasts one to two hours.

The results of this interview are structured in a tree form with general concerns (e.g., "minimize environmental impacts") and increasingly more detailed objectives (e.g., "minimize human health impacts," "minimize the numbers of cancers," etc.). At each level of the value tree there should be a value-relevant objective (Keeney 1992) that is characterized by an object of preference (e.g., "human health impacts"), a direction of preference (e.g., "minimize"), and a context of preference (e.g., "from air pollution"). Lower-level objectives explain the meaning of upper-level objectives. Thus each stakeholder group is represented by a separate value tree.

The initial trees should be returned to the stakeholders for review and possible revisions. Examples of two stakeholder value trees for the problem of analyzing air pollution control strategies in the Los Angeles basin are shown in Figures 14.1 and 14.2.

Building a combined value tree. This task is carried out by the analyst. It consists of combining the separate stakeholder trees into a single tree. This should be done by maintaining the logic of individual trees and by attempting to include comprehensively all stakeholder values. Ideally, each stakeholder value tree should be identifiable as a subtree of the combined tree. The combined tree should be sent to all stakeholders for review and revisions. An example of a combined tree for the problem of air pollution control in Los Angeles is shown in Figure 14.3.

Developing attributes. A very important task is to define attributes that

Figure 14.1
Value Tree of a Member of the Lung Association of America

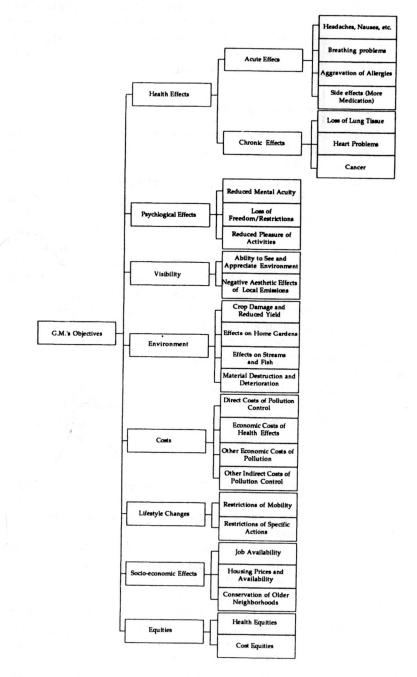

Figure 14.2
Value Tree of a Member of an Oil Company

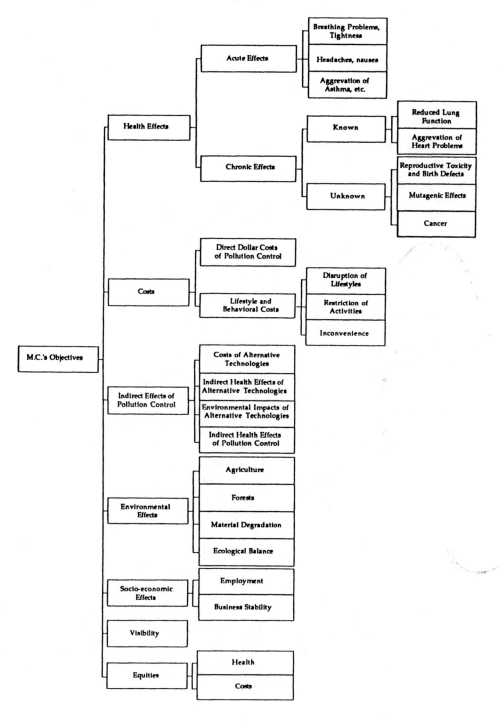

Figure 14.3
Combined Value Tree for L. A. Basin Air Pollution Control

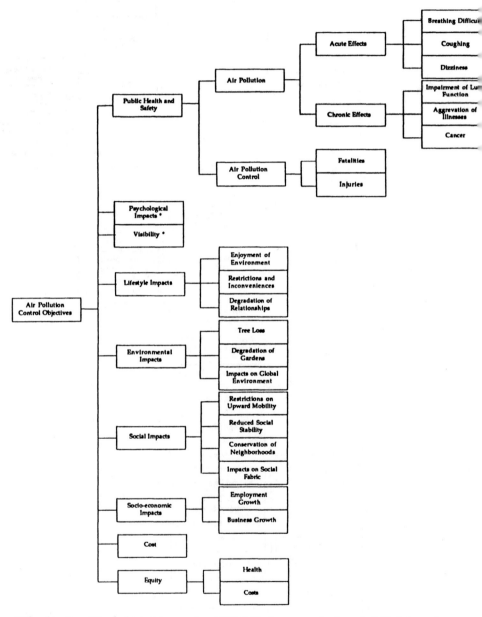

*The objectives "Psychological Impacts" and "Visibility" were not further subdivided. Instead they were operationalized at the highest level.

operationalize the meaning of the objectives in the combined value tree. Most commonly, these attributes are defined at the lowest and most specific level of the value tree. There are two types of attributes: natural and constructed. A natural attribute uses a common quantitative scale to express the degree to which an objective is achieved. For example, the attribute "number of lifetime cancers" may be an attribute for measuring the objective "minimize cancer risks to society." A constructed scale describes, often in words, several degrees of the level to which an objective may be achieved. Table 14.2 shows an example of a constructed scale for biological impacts of a project (Keeney and von Winterfeldt 1987).

The definition of attributes is important, because they provide the linkage between the factual and evaluative parts of the analysis. The stakeholder representatives will need the attribute definitions to express their tradeoffs in a meaningful way. The experts will need the attributes to understand what is being estimated and to develop models and estimation procedures that allow them to provide estimates on the aspects that are relevant to the stakeholders.

Having constructed attributes, the analyst should send them to both the stakeholders and the experts for review. The stakeholders should review them to determine whether the attributes truly capture their concerns. The experts should review them to determine whether they can provide estimates of the alternatives' performance on these attributes. The attributes should be revised to reflect comments by both groups.

Estimation of Risks, Costs, Benefits, and Other Impacts

Identification and selection of experts. In controversial risk problems experts are likely to take sides. For example, when examining the problem of health effects from electromagnetic fields (EMFs) created by power lines, some experts argue that there are no ill health effects, others state that the research regarding the health effects of EMF exposure is inconclusive, while still others claim that there is a real danger of cancer risks to children and others with long-term exposure. The multiple-stakeholder approach to decision analysis attempts to capture these different opinions by eliciting them from a number of experts with diverging views. Obviously, the selection of experts is a crucial step in this process. Experts should be selected on the basis of their knowledge about the subject matter(s) as well as on the basis of providing a variety of political views and preferences among the alternatives. Several criteria for selecting experts have been identified in Bonano et al. (1990). These include professional competence, peer recognition, command of the subject matter, and flexibility of thought. When assembling teams or panels of experts, several criteria concerned with diversity should be added: diversity of disciplines, political views, as well as opinions and attitudes toward the problem at hand.

Table 14.2
Example of a Constructed Attribute

Impact Level	Biological impacts on the affected area
0	No damage to species of plants or wildlife that are desirable, unique, biologically sensitive, or endangered, or to any habitats for such species.
1	Damage to individuals of desirable species or habitats for the species, but such species or habitats are common throughout the region.
2	Damage to individuals of biologically sensitive species or portions of their habitats, but this does not threaten their regional abundance.
3	Damage to, or destruction of, individuals of threatened and endangered (T&E) species or portions of their habitats that does not threaten their regional abundance; or sensitive species or resource areas are in the affected area, and damage to, or destruction of, individuals of these biologically sensitive species or portions of their habitats threatens their regional abundance.
4	Damage to, or destruction of, individuals of T&E species or portions of their habitats that does not threaten their regional abundance; and damage to, or destruction of, individuals of biologically sensitive species or portions of their habitats that threatens their regional abundance.
5	Damage, or destruction of, individuals of T&E species or portions of their habitats that threatens their regional abundance; and damage to, or destruction of, individuals of biologically sensitive species or portions of their habitats that threatens their regional abundance.

Training and assistance in decomposition. Experts are usually knowledgeable in their own discipline, but will have little or no background in decision analysis and probability elicitation. It is therefore useful to train the experts in the task of making probability judgments. Besides providing specific guidance about the tasks ahead, this training also should motivate experts to perform the task and make them feel comfortable in expressing

Figure 14.4
Decomposition of a Reactor Safety Problem

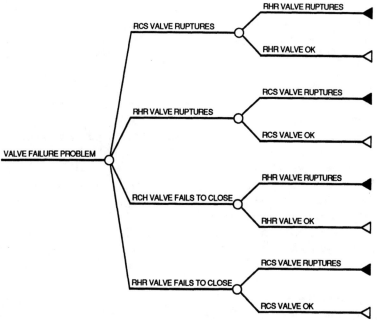

Note: There are two check valves in series, the RCS valve and the RHR valve. When both fail, there will be a catastrophic leakage of cooling water into the containment and beyond, initiating a loss of coolant accident. The decomposition breaks the failure modes down into several sequences of ruptures and failure to close on demand. The darkened triangles at the ends of the event tree indicate a catastrophic failure.

their views and opinions in terms of probabilities. Most important, the training is meant to make the experts aware of biases in their judgments and of ways to avoid these biases.

In addition to being trained in probability elicitation, experts should also be assisted in decomposing their judgmental task. Decomposition is aimed at simplifying the task by breaking it down into smaller subtasks, and then reaggregating the results of the subtasks. For example, when asked to provide probability judgments about a catastrophic failure of two check valves in a nuclear power plant cooling system, the experts found it easier to make judgments about certain component failures. This decomposition is represented in Figure 14.4 (see also Keeney and von Winterfeldt 1991).

Modeling and data collection. Eliciting expert judgments for decision analysis is no substitute for modeling, experimentation, and data analysis. Rather, it is meant to provide a snapshot of the state of knowledge based on modeling, experimentation, and data analysis. It is often useful to perform additional modeling, experimentation, and data analysis efforts after the task has been decomposed, but prior to the actual elicitation. For example, in an extensive nuclear safety analysis, experts had up to three months to carry out analysis and data collection activities prior to being elicited (Keeney and von Winterfeldt 1991).

Elicitation. The elicitation of expert judgments usually consists of a one-on-one interview between an analyst and the expert. First, the analyst attempts to clarify the elicitation variable or event, to establish boundaries, and to elicit probability distributions over the variable or events. Subsequently, the analyst elicits judgments by asking probability questions and documents both the answer and the reasoning of the expert. (Detailed approaches and techniques for this process can be found in Bonano et al. 1990 and in Keeney and von Winterfeldt 1991.)

An example of the elicitation for the previously mentioned check valve problem in nuclear power plants is shown in Figure 14.5. The three panels show the elicited component probability distributions over the several variables identified through the decomposition. Each panel in Figure 14.5 shows the five cumulative distributions that were elicited from the experts in this study. Figure 14.6 shows the reaggregated distributions for the five experts as well as an average distribution. Clearly, there is substantial disagreement among the experts on the frequency of a catastrophic check valve failure. The main source of this disagreement becomes obvious when inspecting Figure 14.5: While the experts agreed fairly well on the probability distributions over the unconditional rupture frequency (f_R) and even more so on the probability of a valve being stuck open (f_o), they strongly disagreed on the conditional probability of the RHR valve rupturing, given that the RCS valve ruptured ($f_{r|R}$). Expert A thought these events to be highly dependent, while expert D thought that there was a .99 chance that the events were independent and a .01 chance that there was some dependency, leading to a more conservative cumulative distribution.

Aggregation across experts. It is not unusual to find orders of magnitudes of disagreements in elicited probability distributions as exemplified in Figure 14.6. In case of such disagreements, the analyst has two basic choices: mechanical aggregation (e.g., averaging) or behavioral resolution (e.g., by a Delphi method or group interactions). Often a combination of both procedures is useful.

More important, the elicitation often shows where the experts agree and where they disagree. In the check valve problem, the main disagreement was in the assessment of the conditional probability of the second valve failing, given that the first valve failed. One expert (D) thought of those two events as nearly independent, while another (A) thought of them as highly dependent, pointing to a common-cause defect of the two valves. Clearly, in this case a simple averaging process would hide the true sources of the disagreements, and a behavioral resolution would be more desirable.

Figure 14.5
**Cumulative Probability Distributions over the Components of the Reactor Safety
Problem for Five Experts**

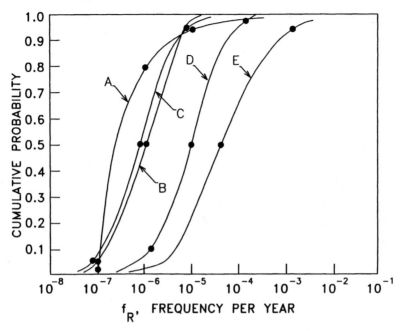

a. Cumulative probability distributions for five experts over the annual rupture frequency of
   the RCS.

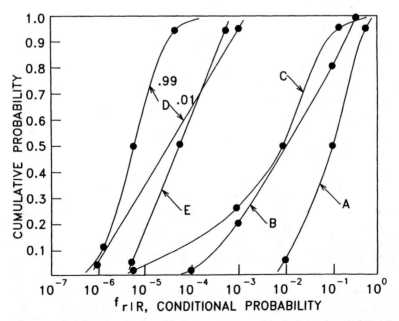

b. Cumulative probability distributions for five experts over the conditional probability that
   the RHR valve ruptures, given that the RCS valve ruptured.

Figure 14.5 (Continued)

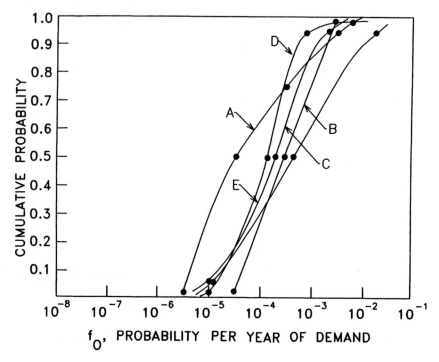

c. Cumulative probability distributions for five experts over the annual probability of the RHR or RCS valve failing to open upon demand.

In some cases, the disagreements may be so substantial that separate distributions have to be carried throughout the analysis to provide sensitivity results with respect to these differences.

Elicitation of a Multi-attribute Utility Model from Stakeholders

Elicitation of value judgments. The next step in the analysis is to elicit two types of judgments from stakeholder representatives. First are judgments of the relative desirability of different levels of an attribute. These judgments are translated into so-called single-attribute utility functions. Second are tradeoffs among changes in one attribute versus another. These judgments are translated into so-called attribute weights.

Single-attribute utility functions should reflect the decision maker's relative preferences for outcomes that vary only in one attribute. For example, in a job choice problem, the number of vacation days may be an important attribute. The relative desirability of numbers of vacation days can be represented by a—

Figure 14.6
**Cumulative Probability Distributions over the Aggregated Catastrophic Failure
Frequency in the Reactor Safety Problem for Five Experts**

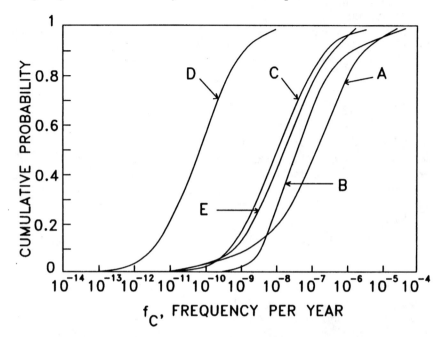

presumably decreasing—utility function over days. Several elicitation methods
for constructing single-attribute utility functions are described in Keeney and
Raiffa (1976) and in von Winterfeldt and Edwards (1986).

While single-attribute utility functions reflect relative comparisons within
an attribute, tradeoffs are meant to reflect comparisons of the desirability
of units across attributes. In a job choice problem, for example, a decision
maker may face a tradeoff between the number of vacation days and the
annual salary offered. In this case the decision maker may feel that within
the range of vacation days offered, a vacation day is roughly worth $500
in salary. This judgment, combined with the judgments about single-attribute utility functions, can be used to derive attribute weights. These weights
are elicited in interviews with stakeholder representatives using standard
techniques described in Keeney and Raiffa (1976) and von Winterfeldt and
Edwards (1986). They often determine the results of an analysis in important
ways. They also are most likely to differ among stakeholders. For example,
some stakeholders will emphasize the value of environmental impacts, while
others stress employment.

Testing and building a multi-attribute utility model. The most common
model to aggregate single-attribute utility functions is to take their weighted

average. In this model, an alternative is evaluated by first determining its single-attribute utilities, weighting these utilities by the attribute weights, and summing the products across attributes. Other aggregation methods may apply, depending on the independence assumptions that are acceptable in a specific case (e.g., Keeney and Raiffa 1976 and von Winterfeldt and Edwards 1986).

Sensitivity Analyses and Option Invention

Putting the pieces together. The evaluation of the alternatives in the multiple-stakeholder approach to decision analysis begins with an analysis of the judgments of one expert and one stakeholder. (If there are different experts for different attributes, the experts should be selected to represent a common point of view.) First, for each alternative and attribute, an expected utility is calculated, based on the expert's probability distribution and the stakeholder's single-attribute utility function. Next a multi-attribute utility model is used to calculate the overall utility across attributes.

This analysis is repeated for all stakeholders and experts, providing as many overall evaluations (rankings and numerical utilities) as there are combinations of experts and stakeholders.

Sensitivity analyses. These overall evaluations rarely agree on a single winning alternative. Sometimes the expert disagreements dominate the differences between the resulting evaluations, as, for example, in the case of air pollution control in the Los Angeles basin (Keeney 1992). Sometimes the stakeholder values drive the disagreements, as, for example, in the offshore oil study (von Winterfeldt 1987). In many cases both disagreements contribute to the differences in evaluations.

To determine the extent of these differences, numerous sensitivity analyses can be carried out. One type of sensitivity analysis is on expert judgments. Typically, one asks to what extent an expert judgment would have to be changed in order to change a particular rank ordering. Similarly, one can ask how much a tradeoff would have to be changed to change a rank ordering. This type of analysis provides information about the importance of the different judgments entering into the analysis and evaluation. Through the sensitivity analyses, the stakeholders can learn how their own and other stakeholders' judgments affect the resulting evaluations and how the experts influence both. Thus, the models become a vehicle for dialogue and communication.

Option invention. While this process is not likely to generate a consensus, in many cases it facilitates the invention of new compromise options. This was the case in the highly political analyses of alternative school desegregation plans for Los Angeles (Edwards 1981) and in the case of evaluating alternative sites for the first high-level radioactive nuclear waste repository (Keeney and von Winterfeldt 1988).

REFLECTIONS ON THE FOUNDATION, USES, AND LIMITATIONS OF THE METHODOLOGY

Methodological Issues

Decision analysis was originally developed as a theory for a single decision maker based on assessing both subjective probabilities and utilities from one individual. However, even in its first applications, it became clear that there is a necessary division between the "decision maker," who should primarily provide utility and value judgments, and the "expert," who should provide probability judgments. For example, in the classical oil drilling studies, geologists and other experts knowledgeable in oil exploration provided probability inputs, and the director or chairman of the board of an oil exploration and production company provided utility functions for money. The justification of maintaining a single decision-maker view was usually that the expert was simply the extension of the thoughts of the decision maker and that the decision maker essentially made the expert judgments his or her own in the analysis.

This justification became more difficult in public policy problems that involved both multiple stakeholders with conflicting values and multiple experts with conflicting opinions. Decision analysts had two possible answers to this problem: One, the multiple-stakeholder approach, was presented here; the other one was to expand decision analysis into the area of games and negotiations (see, e.g., Raiffa 1982). These approaches are not necessarily competing. In cases where the essence of the problem is joint decision making on an agreed-upon problem, the multiple-stakeholder approach is probably preferable. In cases where the stakeholders have different agendas, choose among different types of alternatives, and have different values, a game theoretic approach may be more useful.

Thus, a key assumption in the multiple-stakeholder approach is the existence of a jointly agreed-upon problem formulation. This means, at the minimum, that the stakeholders should be willing to agree on a set of alternatives. There is, however, no assumption that a best alternative can be found or created.

Another key assumption in the multiple-stakeholder/multiple-expert approach to decision making is that the *factual* and *value* parts of the problem can be separated. In practice, this is very difficult, and there will be many shades of gray among pure *factual* disagreements and *pure* value conflicts (see, e.g., von Winterfeldt and Edwards 1984). Clearly, values will influence opinions, and opinions will shape values. Moreover, values and opinions can shape the formulation of the problem and the definition of alternatives, and thus precondition the analysis results.

Having acknowledged the difficulty of separating out facts and values cleanly, decision analysts nevertheless feel that it is useful to carry that separation as far as possible in a given context. First, the separation emphasizes the different nature of the underlying disagreements about preferences among alternatives. Second, the separation allows a natural division of labor: experts—possibly assigned by the stakeholders—work on the factual part, and stakeholder representatives work on the value part.

A third assumption in the approach is that the factual and value parts can be addressed with probabilities and utilities, respectively. Regarding probabilities, there has been a long history of debates about this issue (for a recent summary, see Apostolakis 1988). Those promoting the use of probability to quantify expert judgments have argued that probabilities are more precise than qualitative expressions, that they are useful to represent existing knowledge, and that they plug into an extensive apparatus of probability calculus. On the utility side, the concept of tradeoffs is now generally accepted, at least in a qualitative sense. There does not seem to be a very large step from acknowledging the necessity and usefulness of making tradeoffs to the acceptance of making these tradeoffs explicitly and quantitatively.

There are many more technical assumptions in the multiple-stakeholder approach regarding, for example, the forms of the probability and utility decompositions, reaggregations, and the possible rules for combining expert and stakeholder judgments. There is a fair amount of flexibility in choosing a procedure for decomposition and aggregation that is appropriate for the specific problem at hand. The approach does not require or force any specific form of aggregation across experts and stakeholders (e.g., averaging across experts or stakeholders). In fact, the most useful insights from the procedure come from sensitivity analyses and comparisons of the most dramatic differences among experts and stakeholders.

Process Issues

The methodology itself is silent about the process of implementation, with the exception of prescribing a specific series of steps and providing some basic guidelines about how to interact with stakeholders and experts. However, in many cases the process is at least as important as the methodology itself.

The approach assumes a process involving multiple stakeholders who are essentially cooperative in striving for compromise solutions among a common set of alternatives. This image is not necessarily in line with a purely democratic process in which each individual has the same voting power. Thus, the point has been made, usually in informal discussions, that the methodology may have tendencies to give powerful, organized stakeholder groups a larger-than-deserved voice in the decision-making process.[1]

There are at least three comments in defense of the multiple-stakeholder approach. First, public policy, at least in the United States and many industrialized Western countries, is, in fact, shaped by interactions among multiple stakeholders. Second, the multiple-stakeholder approach not only brings organized groups into the process, but also ensures the involvement of groups that should have a stake but are not yet organized. Third, the main value of the approach is to inform decision making and debate, not to force decisions. Option invention and dialogue creation are as much products of the approach as (conditional) conclusions about what should be done. Ultimately, if some agency has to decide, it will do so either with or without a broad information base from multiple stakeholder values and multiple expert opinions.

Moreover, the multiple-stakeholder approach seems to enhance democratic tendencies, at least in one important way. One of the dangers in today's society has been the increasing reliance on experts who often become decision makers by default. In the multiple-stakeholder approach, experts are assigned a specific role appropriate to their knowledge and experience. Rather than asking experts for values and decision recommendations, they are asked to make judgments about the factual side of the problem only. Value judgments, often ignored in analysis, are actively solicited from stakeholders, not experts. Thus the process reduces expert control and provides public input where none or little exists in traditional procedures.

There are many additional process issues to which the multiple-stakeholder approach has not yet provided satisfactory solutions: When should the stakeholders meet, and what form should the meetings take? How should the stakeholders and experts interact? Should experts be encouraged to develop consensus opinions, and how could this be achieved? How can the role and influence of the analyst be limited? Many of the answers are likely to emerge from trial and error with the application of the approach over time.

Uses and Limitations

As stated earlier, one use of the approach is in situations in which an agency wants broad stakeholder and expert inputs in solving a particular problem. Such broad-based input is often mandated by regulations and oversight committees in government. Another use is to assist several different stakeholders who attempt to solve a common problem in a cooperative way. Examples of applications that generated useful insights or contributed constructively to decision making are the evaluation of school desegregation plans in Los Angeles (Edwards 1981), offshore oil drilling in southern California (von Winterfeldt 1987), air pollution control in the Los Angeles basin (Keeney 1992), water resource planning in central Arizona (Rozelle 1982), and energy planning in West Germany (Keeney, Renn, and von Winterfeldt 1987).

When there is no agency with ultimate decision-making power, or when an agency is not truly motivated to respect conflicting stakeholder values and expert opinions, or when stakeholders are essentially noncooperative, other political processes and other methodological approaches are preferable.

NOTE

1. R. Howard, personal communication, May 15, 1990.

CHAPTER 15

Inconsistent Values in Risk Management

Chris Whipple

Having a summer job as an undergraduate at the Atomic Energy Commission's Savannah River Plant as an instrumentation engineer, I was interested when technical issues regarding nuclear power plant safety began to receive public attention in the early 1970s. My graduate advisor, Milton Plesset, was a technical consultant on some nuclear safety issues and was later (several years after I graduated) named to the Advisory Committee on Reactor Safeguards. When I completed my Ph.D. at Caltech in 1974, I accepted a job with the new Electric Power Research Institute (EPRI), a nonprofit creation of the electric utility industry. Given the recent oil embargo, energy was topical.

EPRI's founding president, Chauncey Starr, offered me a choice between doing thermal-hydraulic analysis of power plant plumbing (something for which I was educated) or working for him on analysis of energy issues of the day. Chauncey argued (in hindsight, truthfully) that the latter would be more interesting and challenging. Chauncey's interest in risk analysis was well established, based on his early recognition of the potential contributions of quantitative risk analysis to engineering, and to his understanding, illustrated by his seminal 1969 *Science* article, that the social aspects of risk taking and risk analysis were both important and unexplored.

About half my time was spent on risk analysis issues, and the other half on analysis of energy supply and demand futures. This energy analysis complemented the risk work in that economics and social science analysis applied to energy forecasting were also useful in the risk area. Then, as now, the fact that one's viewpoint on energy futures (hard and soft paths) usually coincided with views on energy risks was apparent.

The community of researchers working on social aspects of technological risk was smaller then, but the most influential groups on my thinking are still prominent. They include Paul Slovic, Baruch Fischhoff, and Sarah Lichtenstein, Gilbert White's natural hazards center in Boulder, the Clark University group, including Bob Kates and Roger Kasperson, and the International Institute for Applied Systems Analysis (IIASA/International Atomic Energy Agency (IAEA) joint research project. An opportunity to teach a National Science Foundation (NSF)/American Association for the Advancement of Science (AAAS) Chautauqua short course on risk-benefit analysis gave me a push to learn more about risk and decision making; during the three years I taught the course I also met many people that I now see each year at the Society for Risk Analysis meeting. Finally, the Nuclear Regulatory Commission's safety goal exercise (described in this chapter) was a major event in the development and application of risk-based regulatory approaches; this activity gave me a chance to work once more with David Okrent.

My current interests are in radioactive waste issues, which I mostly see from the perspective of National Academy of Sciences committees reviewing Department of Energy (DOE) projects, and in risk assessment as practiced by and for the Environmental Protection Agency (EPA) under Superfund and the Resource Conservation and Recovery Act (RCRA). As with some of the early nuclear risk issues, radioactive waste repositories and hazardous waste sites are often characterized by experts as posing little risk, although they raise significant public concern.

A common approach in the social science literature dealing with risk is to segment conflict and controversy over risk into the realms of facts (or perceived risks) and values. This simplified approach has been criticized from many perspectives, for example, for its treatment of risk controversies from a solely individual perspective in which there is no role for social and cultural dynamics. These criticisms notwithstanding, in some contexts the facts/values model of risk attitudes is useful, in part because it is consistent with the dominant behavioral model in economics, expected utility theory. Its principal contribution to understanding conflicting views on risks and what should be done about them is that it does offer a simple disentanglement of attitudes about risk into two parts: how big the risk is, and whether such risks are acceptable. The subject here is with this second question, that of the values that underlie risk taking.

While there are obviously cases where social conflicts over risk are due to different values across different segments of the population or to different beliefs about the nature of risk, it is also likely that generally there is a social consensus that small risks are better than large ones, that inexpensive and easily implemented risk reductions are desirable, and that good risk management requires both democratic processes and competent technical input. But consensus on these points is not sufficient to establish consensus on risk management policy; conflicts over the social management of technological risk seem to arise continuously.

This chapter presents a slight variation on the "conflicting values" explanation for risk controversies. The thesis here is that many difficulties encountered in social risk management have their origins in a collectively held but internally inconsistent value structure. It may seem a question of semantics whether a social conflict over a risk is due to differences in values regarding risks among the affected parties or to different emphases in a set of social values that are widely shared but internally inconsistent. It is argued below that this distinction is important for what it suggests about our understanding of risk conflicts and conflict resolution.

As examples of internally inconsistent values in risk taking, one can consider (a) the desire to be free from involuntarily imposed risks of any magnitude versus the desire to achieve collective social benefits deriving from economic activities that generate small involuntary risks; (b) the desire to have the most informed experts involved in socially important risk decisions versus the view that socially important issues should be decided through a democratic process that does not involve delegation of decision-making power to specialists; and (c) the desire for liability policies that compensate those harmed by hazardous products versus concern regarding the detrimental effect of strict liability on the cost and availability of hazardous goods ranging from vaccines to ladders. These three examples were selected with the intention of identifying dichotomies where the emphasis of one objective necessarily leads to the neglect of another valued objective. It is the interplay of these values and the role of the technical risk assessor that are discussed here. In many ways, conceptual thinking about risks has grown and evolved as the insights from new disciplines have been added over the past twenty years. But for a field involving as many disciplines as does risk analysis, the integration of many distinct insights into a coherent framework remains an intriguing challenge.

An objective of the workshop for which this chapter was prepared was the examination of major frameworks for thinking about risk from disciplinary perspectives. Consequently, this chapter opens with a simplified view of how engineers, through training and tradition, have addressed risk. This description necessarily involves considerable generalization, and the usual caveats apply (i.e., all generalizations are false, including this one).

Much of the discussion that follows is aimed at deciding what questions are important. Many of the points below are speculative. The objective is similar to that of one of the major works influencing this paper, *Tragic Choices* (Calabresi and Bobbitt 1978, 195): "the business of this book is not to resolve tragic choices by means of discoveries of new methods, but to make it possible for us to get a clearer view of the state of affairs that troubles us." In thinking about the issues associated with risk and the social responses to them, the explanatory power of alternate frameworks can be supported by examples and arguments, but proof that one framework is "right" and another "wrong" is rarely possible. More often the critical question involves thinking about which framework is most appropriate in a particular context.

AN ENGINEERING PERSPECTIVE

Engineering risk management decisions range from apparently straightforward technical choices (e.g., how alternative designs compare in risk, cost, reliability) to complex social decisions involving groups and individuals with competing interests and conflicting values. As with other professions such as medicine, acceptable risk has traditionally been judged in engineering by whether good engineering practice has been followed, both in the application of appropriate design standards and in analysis resulting in engineering decisions where no standards apply precisely. For technical or "simple" cases, the tradition has been to try to reduce health and safety risks to some unquantified but small residual level, at which point the product or process is said to be safe.

While the engineering profession has long been concerned with risk as a matter of professional responsibility, a more general interest in social definitions of acceptability became evident only in the past several decades. This is largely because safe engineering practice was defined by engineers as a professional issue, not as a public issue. This perspective began to be challenged in the 1960s and 1970s, when the public nature of health and safety decisions became more apparent, and when public willingness to delegate decision-making authority over risk questions began to erode. Under the traditional engineering approach, engineers looked to their peers for determination of acceptable risk in engineering practice. Under the more recent approach, public participation in risk decisions, and particularly in the value judgments that determine the acceptability or nonacceptability of risk in a particular context, is recognized as essential.

A major motivation, if not the major motivation, for using quantitative risk assessments for risk management is that such an approach permits a conceptual separation between the technical factors that determine risk and the political factors that bear on risk management. The evolution of the use of quantitative risk assessment methods in engineering is still in progress, and some areas of application, for example, nuclear and aerospace engineering, have adopted its use more than other areas. A major consequence for engineers of this change is that acceptable risk, especially for newer technologies, is difficult to determine and defend. Yet the question of risk acceptability is inescapable in engineering as well as many other professions.

In engineering areas where quantitative risk assessment is in use, there is a broader recognition by engineers that seemingly narrow technical issues involve judgments of "How safe is safe enough?" (Starr 1969). The traditional engineering education provides little or no preparation for these questions. Usually, decisions regarding acceptable risk levels are made judgmentally, with risk comparisons serving as guidance. The engineering tradition for risk is generally based on achieving acceptable risk levels from an equity perspective (i.e., that no one is exposed to an excessively high risk) rather than on analysis of marginal cost-effectiveness.

Complex risk issues with significant social involvement are hard problems, not just for engineers. While it is evident that social concerns and processes do not easily translate to engineering criteria, the inability of the political and social science communities to provide operable guidance to engineers is a frustration (Whipple 1985). A common view among engineers is that "actual" risks should be dominant decision factors, despite the fact that often they are not. The notion of a "technical rationality" and a "cultural rationality" (Krimsky and Plough 1988) captures the effects of these alternative frameworks nicely.

Many engineers working on issues involving public risk and controversy, for example, nuclear power or handling and disposal of toxic chemicals, have become aware of the major points of the psychological literature on risk perception, especially the work of Slovic and colleagues. The work has great power to explain why controversy exists over what, to many engineers, seem to be trivial risks. However, this literature is often interpreted to mean that people systematically misperceive risks, an interpretation encouraged by words like "bias" and "misperception" in some risk perception papers, or through Sandman's explanation that risk = hazard + outrage (Sandman 1987, 21).

AN ANECDOTE

In 1981, a workshop was held by the Nuclear Regulatory Commission (NRC) to discuss quantitative safety goals for nuclear power plants. In addition to NRC staff and industry people with expertise in probabilistic risk assessment and regulation, attendees included critics of nuclear power, university faculty members, and others with interests in risk and regulation. The group's objective was to consider whether and how quantitative safety goals might be beneficially applied to the regulation of nuclear power.

One key aspect of the discussion was whether the safety goals should be constructed so that rare catastrophic accidents would be stringently weighted, that is, so that extreme events would be more tightly regulated than accident scenarios with equivalent expected consequences but with higher probabilities and lower consequences. In short, the issue was whether to make the goals reflect a risk-averse value structure. Behind this issue were two conflicting motivations: The risk perception literature of the time indicated that a significant factor in the public's view that nuclear power posed high risks was its potential for severe accidents; however, probabilistic risk assessment calculations did not identify the most severe accident scenarios as dominant contributors to expected losses. The Nuclear Regulatory Commission's Advisory Commission of Reactor Safeguards (ACRS) proposed a set of safety goals that explicitly included risk aversion. The basis for this proposal was that it was thought to represent, albeit crudely, a value structure more reflective of public values than did safety goals based on expected losses.

The expected value of a risk is calculated by multiplying consequences and probability, summing over all accident scenarios. The ACRS proposed method for weighting severe accidents was to raise consequences to some power greater than 1, and then to multiply by probability. In this way, accidents with large consequences received greater weight and priority than would be the case if expected values were used.

There was reasonably solid support for this approach at the workshop until Paul Slovic noted that one implication of the proposed weighting structure was that, for equivalent regulatory resources, the proposed goals would lead to higher expected losses than would goals without risk aversion. At this point, the group consensus quickly shifted to a risk-neutral approach. The common view was that including risk aversion sounded like a good idea before the implications of such a policy on overall risk were examined.

This was a surprising reversal. The NRC and ACRS staff, mostly engineers, had tried to develop goals reflective of public values. The group that reviewed the proposal and ultimately recommended that risk aversion be eliminated included a number of social scientists with a strong commitment to risk regulations incorporating public values, even if this meant using some measure of risk other than its expected value. In the nuclear power context, risk aversion was widely accepted as an important public value, so it was reasonable to expect that risk-averse safety goals would be proposed.

In current terminology, the group's recommendation was the result of a shift in the framing of the issue. When framed as a simple question of whether it was better or not to include risk aversion, the consensus was for risk aversion. When the question was reframed as "Are you for risk aversion if it means that, over the long run, more people may die?" the group's response was "no."

DISCUSSION—RECONCILING THE FRAMEWORKS

Because most participants in the NRC meeting wanted both to minimize expected consequences and to include risk aversion, this example seems to reflect a case of internally inconsistent values rather than one of competing paradigms. Preferences for risk aversion, initially, and for minimizing expected values, subsequently, were shared by engineers and social scientists and by both those with pro- and antinuclear power viewpoints. Moreover, the value conflict over the impossibility of simultaneously being risk averse and minimizing fatalities was apparently experienced by most of those present. This was not a case where values were in conflict across groups; in fact the consensus on values was remarkably solid, in spite of the internal inconsistency in views regarding technology. To illustrate the value consensus, at one point a prominent nuclear power critic remarked that he had no problems agreeing to the proposed goals, but that he did not think that the plants could meet them.

At the risk of overinterpreting this single case, it is interesting to speculate that many of the social phenomena involving risks can be viewed as due to alternative framings of decisions, but where basic social values are commonly shared although internally in conflict.

What does this have to do with the role of risk assessment in social risk management and with the issue of technological and cultural rationalities? Krimsky and Plough's conclusion regarding these two frameworks is:

Once it is accepted that two inconsistent decisions can be rational and consistent on independent criteria, it is possible to reach beyond the deviant model of risk communication.... If these forms of rationality are unalterably antagonistic, technical reason and popular response to risk may be truly incommensurable. Both forms of rationality must be capable of responding to a process of mutual learning and adjustment. If the technosphere begins to appreciate and respect the logic of local culture toward risk events and if local culture has access to a demystified science, points of intersection will be possible. (Krimsky and Plough 1988, 305, 306)

I read this conclusion to mean that Krimsky and Plough's two frameworks—technical and cultural—reflect conflicting perspectives between different segments of society. It may be a subtle difference between this view and one that holds that risk issues are difficult in part due to commonly held but conflicting values. Under this "conflicting values" view, technological and cultural perspectives are emphasized in varying proportions depending on specific contexts.

My view is that this distinction is important to our understanding of social processes involving risk, and that the distinction is important to progress in social risk management. The "alternative rationality" explanation points to conflicts between groups and prescribes "mutual learning and adjustment." The "inconsistent values" explanation, if mostly correct, suggests that a more cooperative social process could result if commonly held values are recognized and taken as the starting point for social dialogue.

CONTENT AND PROCESS

The nuclear safety goal example and associated discussion has treated the question of technical and cultural rationality as a question of content, that is, what values are emphasized and what decisions result. Of equal or greater importance are process questions involving how decisions are made and who participates in making them. From the viewpoint of process, the key issue in the reconciliation of technical and cultural perspectives is "How can risk decisions be made so that we can take advantage of what science can tell us without giving too much political power to experts?"

From this viewpoint, the "inconsistent values" explanation seems to offer significant explanatory power. The two rationalities can derive from the shared view that scientific knowledge is good and technocratic decision making is bad. This seems more plausible than a framework in which some people don't care much for science while others don't care much about democracy.

The incommensurability of the benefits of having good science versus the risks of shifting political power to scientists (or to those who hire scientists) suggests that there is little to be gained by trying to weigh these conflicting objectives and to arrive at the "right" amount of participation by technically trained people in risk decisions; there seems to be no right answer to the question of overall balance. A more constructive question is to consider how it is possible to improve on the current situation by getting both more science and less technocracy than current practices provide.

One important reason for the recent interest in risk communication has been this question of making science accessible for public decision making. The role of risk communication in public policy was a major topic of a recent National Academy of Sciences report (NRC 1989). While it is not possible to summarize here all the major points of that report, it is fair to say that it recommends that technically trained people work to inform (rather than to persuade) the public from a viewpoint that the public finds useful, that is, that the public should define the agenda.

A number of trends in risk assessment can be pointed to that seem aimed at making risk assessment more politically acceptable. One of these is the codification of risk assessment methods, especially for carcinogens, but also for some engineering applications, for example, nuclear power plants. The development and application of consistent analytical assumptions and techniques suggest that a relatively solid scientific consensus exists. In addition, in contrast to early risk assessments that reported results in terms of population risk, that is, expected losses, recent risk assessments have generally provided multiple measures of risk, with particular emphasis on measures of individual risk (such as risk to the maximally exposed individual). The shift has helped point out that risk assessment is not tied to cost-benefit or cost-effectiveness analysis; that risk assessment can provide information in various forms appropriate for various decision criteria. Finally, the recent emphasis on risk communication, and on training and credibility, suggests that the technical community is concerned with the limited acceptance its analyses receive.

These trends, taken together, reflect an effort by risk assessors to make risk assessment more acceptable to the political process. The approaches described above all involve the use of safeguards against technocracy—publishing and sticking to established protocols, better communication, and development of a service mind-set among scientists.

WHEN VALUES CONFLICT

Potentially helpful insights can be gained from the study of similar conflicts in other contexts stemming from collectively shared but internally inconsistent values. In *Tragic Choices* (Calabresi and Bobbitt 1978), the nature and social consequences of conflicting values are insightfully explored in the context of the social allocation of scarce essential resources.

The tragic nature of Calabresi and Bobbitt's subject arises in part from recognition that for social goods such as artificial kidneys, "scarcity is not the result of any absolute lack of a resource but rather of the decision by society that it is not prepared to forgo other goods and benefits in a number sufficient to remove the scarcity" (Calabresi and Bobbitt 1978, 22). This framework seems as applicable to decisions regarding production of social "bads" as it is to social goods. Any single risk could probably be reduced significantly if it were the only item of social concern. But because we value many things other than safety, risks are created and tolerated in spite of the moral contradiction in doing so.

One common strategy is to frame issues in a way that disguises the degree to which values are in conflict. We pay any sum to rescue an identified victim, for example, a child in a well. But far less is spent per life saved when the lifesavings are statistical and abstract, for example, for highway safety investments, perhaps because such budgeting decisions are made in settings where efficiency values are emphasized. Calabresi and Bobbitt argue that societies "must attempt to make allocations in ways that preserve the moral foundations of social collaboration. . . . Morally debasing outcomes are averted. But unless the values held in tension have changed, the illusion that denies their conflict gives way and the transformation will have only been a postponement" (Calabresi and Bobbitt, 1978, 18).

Another strategy is to use a mixture of approaches that represents a compromise between conflicting values: "The object of public policy must be, therefore, to define, with respect to each particular tragic choice, that combination of approaches which most limits tragedy and which deals with that irreducible minimum in the least offensive way" (Calabresi and Bobbitt 1978, 149).

In other words, explanations may be chosen that minimize social contradiction. Unfortunately, it appears that choosing framings that minimize contradictions only works for a while; contradictions inherent in social values eventually become apparent. We ban cyclamate and ethylene dibromide (EDB) in order to eliminate risk, but, later, questions of what to do about saccharine and methyl bromide raise the same issues.

A central characteristic of decisions made under conflicting values is that, over time, it becomes apparent that certain values have been slighted. When this happens, new approaches will emerge that redress the weakness of the prevailing system. Calabresi and Bobbitt (1978, 196–197) claim that the renewal and recycling of policies is in fact a strategy for dealing with problems of this sort:

The admission that cycle strategy occurs is an admission that society is attempting to preserve essential yet conflicting values. . . . Why do approaches to tragic allocations change? Such changes are not mindlessly made; they have, in fact, represented quite rational responses preceded by discussions as rational as discussions termed rational usually are. The criticisms of the pre-existing system have described in generally accurate detail its fundamental flaws and have invoked the basic values which that system degrades. But the defenders of the pre-existing system are just as rational. They usually are penetrating in their recognition of the flaws inherent in the proposed reform. And when the reform is accepted and has become the vested method, it is eventually seen to display the very shortcomings which its critics had predicted (and to degrade those values they had sought to protect). Are these mistakes? If they are not, why do we move restlessly from one system which proves inadequate to another?

The answer is, we have come to think, that a society may limit the destructive impact of tragic choices by choosing to mix approaches over time. Endangered values are reaffirmed. The ultimate cost to other values is not immediately borne. Change itself brings two dividends, although all too often of an illusory kind we have associated with subterfuges. First, a reconceptualization of the problem arouses hope that its final price will not be extracted; the certainties of the discarded method are replaced. Second, the society is acting, and action has some palliative benefit since it too implies that necessity can somehow be evaded if only we try harder, plan better than those we followed, avoid their mistakes, and so forth.

In the social management of risk, a number of conflicting values can be identified in addition to the conflict between good science and technocracy. A cycle such as described above can be observed in environmental regulation. In the early and mid–1970s, EPA regulations often were based on best available control technology (BACT). This approach was simple to understand and enforce, but it was seen as economically inefficient in that it did not permit industry to use cheaper than BACT methods where they could provide roughly equivalent environmental protection. In addition, this approach failed to provide incentives for improvement of control technologies. Over time, BACT was replaced by an approach based on cost-effectiveness (Portney et al. 1978). However, explicitly trading dollars for lives produced another value conflict, and regulation moved on to an equity or risk-level approach. Under this method, EPA developed risk-based approaches to protect individuals from excessively high risks due to air emissions of toxic materials. At present, Congress has revisited the Clean Air Act and appears to be moving toward MACT (maximally achievable control technology, like BACT, but new and improved), due to criticism of the slow pace of regulation under a risk-based approach. Each of the three approaches followed by EPA emphasizes some important value: under BACT, each firm is treated the same and regulations can, in theory at least, be easily established and enforced. Under cost-benefit–based regulation, economic efficiency is promoted, but at the cost of a population exposed to variable levels of risk. Risk-based standards (the approach used for carcinogenic air emissions since the vinyl chloride decision until the present) provide for consistent and small risks, but with economic and operational penalties.

A second value conflict concerns the issue of openness. Openness and honesty are valued, but some social decisions do not fare well under an open decision-making process (the old caution about not watching sausage being made is appropriate here). It appears that for engineering applications where decisions can be judged in hindsight after accidents have occurred (for example, the Pinto gas tank), a cost-effectiveness approach is unacceptable (Whipple 1988). One can hardly imagine that, at a hearing following an airplane crash, the administrator of the Federal Aviation Administration would say that additional safety equipment, capable of preventing the accident, was not required since it failed a cost-benefit analysis. Similarly, Milton Russell, former assistant administrator for policy evaluation at EPA, notes that a police chief is unlikely to refer to an "optimal number of child molesters," even though police department resources are devoted to many things other than prevention of child molestation (Russell 1986).

A final value conflict concerns the degree to which environmental regulation and enforcement are aimed at reducing risks to health versus providing sanctions and moral disapprobation against risk creators. It is often suggested that the reason that public concern over radon has not been high is because there is no one to blame. That this point is sometimes made by risk assessors as a derisive comment about the results of political risk management shows a lack of understanding that there is probably a long-term social benefit in establishing a social prejudice against risk creators (although this is certainly not a simple issue). But the key point of this argument is that social disagreements over risk are due more to inconsistent than to conflicting values, and that we are more likely to treat people who have similar values but different priorities with greater respect when we recognize the conflicting nature of our values.

CONCLUSION

If the ideas above about the role of inconsistent values in risk taking have explanatory power, then there are positive and negative implications. On the positive side, the continuing evolution in social approaches to risk management may reflect a sensible management strategy rather than a political inability to produce anything but a continuing set of inadequate policies. Conversely, this may imply that, at best, we can reach temporarily satisfactory compromises in risk management. Long-term policies that promote major social objectives may not be possible. This is not certain, however. With sufficient insight, it may be possible to achieve convergence and compromise rather than oscillation in policy.

In any case, a feasible objective may be to minimize the magnitude of the policy swings that accompany cycles in risk management. The lesson for those concerned with risk policies is that, to the extent that policy debates are conducted within a framework that recognizes that compromises are necessary because of inconsistent values, a more cooperative atmosphere for policy making may be fostered. The distinction between conflicting and inconsistent values is important to recognize for this reason alone.

Reflections

Sheldon Krimsky and Dominic Golding

The study of risk, once relegated to a narrow sector of the academic community and the insurance industry, has been nourished by the demands of public policy and has rapidly developed into a multidisciplinary field. On the technical side, toxicologists, epidemiologists, and others in the health sciences have concentrated on perfecting methods of hazard identification and risk estimation, including dose estimation, exposure assessment, and dose-response models. These methods have become canonized in the regulatory procedures of agencies such as the Environmental Protection Agency (EPA), the Food and Drug Administration (FDA), and the Occupational Safety and Health Administration (OSHA). Similarly, the engineering and physical sciences have labored to improve techniques such as fault and event tree analysis used in probabilistic risk assessments. These techniques have become the stock-in-trade of the chemical and nuclear industries, and regulatory agencies such as the Nuclear Regulatory Commission and Department of Energy. From these technical perspectives, risk is seen as an objective phenomenon that is amenable to measurement in terms of probabilities and severity of consequences. In the traditional models of risk assessment and risk management these estimates feed directly into the policy process: they provide a straightforward method for setting priorities and allocating resources. Public assessments of risk, and therefore implicitly the choice of priorities, have frequently been at odds with these expert views, however.

We believe that the principal contribution of the social sciences has been to broaden the debate about risks beyond the technical considerations of the engineers and the natural scientists, and to explain the divergence between public and expert views of risk. To be sure, there is a range of opinion within the social science community, from objectivist to subjectivist, from pragmatist to rationalist, and from monist to pluralist, as illustrated by Ortwin Renn in Chapter 3 (Figure 3.1). If you scratch any economist you are likely to find an underlying belief that risk is a one-dimensional concept for which there are universal measures. Such measures would allow us to set priorities and allocate resources *rationally*, if only we could improve the availability of information and levels of public knowledge. Like Howard Kunreuther (Chapter 13), however, most economists would also agree that there are many factors that cause public behavior to diverge from the normative model. Nonetheless, such economists are unlikely to go as far as some of the cultural theorists, who believe that risk is a wholly subjective and multidimensional phenomenon, lacking a common metric.

Social scientists have necessarily criticized the techniques of risk assessment (see Chapters 9 through 12), but this criticism has been constructive. They have pointed out that expert knowledge is not value-free but conditioned by the social context of research, and that experts suffer biases and limitations in their technical assessments. They have also broadened the debate to incorporate important concepts, such as the notions that risk is more than merely probability times the consequence of an event; that the public perception of an attitudes toward risks vary according to a wide range of variables (including voluntariness, catastrophic potential, dread, and so forth); and that public acceptance (or tolerance) of risk is largely a political problem that hinges on public involvement in the process of risk management. There are differences of opinion within the social science community on the nature of risk and the relative importance of different factors. Notwithstanding these differences, the principal unifying thrust of much of this research is the attempt to dispel the myth that the divergence between pubic and expert views of risks results from public ignorance and/ or irrationality. One measure of success in this regard is the degree to which these ideas germinating from social theory have influenced the formation and implementation of public policy.

MATURATION OF THEORY AND ITS IMPACT ON PUBLIC POLICY

Aside from psychologists, economists have had the most profound influence on risk policies and policy making. Expected utility theory, the central paradigm of normative economics, holds a favored status in many public policy arenas. Expected utility theory comprises a set of decision rules that define rational behavior. It is generally assumed that people would follow these rules if they had sufficient information and time to dwell on the consequences of alternative decision paths. In policy terms, expected utility theory provides a means of setting priorities among different categories of risk events. Through the use of techniques such as cost-benefit and risk-benefit analyses, the emphasis is on developing a common metric (e.g., dollars/lives saved) and optimizing an endpoint (e.g., maximizing the total number of lives saved by all risk management programs). Of all the social scientific approaches, economics is the most closely allied with the technical risk assessments of the engineers and the physical and health sciences. As illustrated in Chapter 3, all of these approaches follow a set of canonical procedures, and propose general principles that abstract from the concreteness of events.

The economic theory of risk is supported by those who seek a pure, rational approach to policy making and who believe that there is a single form of rationality. Among such proponents, Zeckhauser and Viscusi (1990, 559) argue, "Although in practice, the choices made by human beings under uncertainty frequently do not conform to the prescriptions of expected-utility theory, given time to reflect, most people would accept the theory's axioms." Many advocates of expected utility theory are likely to overformalize for the sake of elegance and in so doing lose the richness, specificity, and complexity of events. Nonetheless, there is a broad range of perspectives among economists, and many are more willing to accept, indeed they try to model, more subjective views of risk. For example, Howard Kunreuther (Chapter 13) incorporates empirical observations to explain divergence in behavior from the rigid normative model of expected utility theory and to derive prescriptive guidelines that conform more closely to social behavior.

Psychometric (or cognitive) theory is another leading risk paradigm, but unlike expected utility theory it departs from the view that risk may be reduced to a common metric. A significant body of empirical research on public attitudes grew out of the cognitive framework developed by the social scientists who sought to understand why the public's estimates of risk were at odds with those of experts. This theory has shown that risk decisions are made on the basis of multiple attributes that describe the risk event; these attributes are more complex than the simple estimates of expected mortality and the cost per life saved often used by economists.

The psychometric paradigm (Chapter 5) has had a significant influence in the debate over how to determine the acceptability of risk, which remains a concern today but was most hotly debated in the early 1980s. Those on the technical side of the field that adhere to the idea that risk is an objective phenomenon tend to believe that acceptable levels of risk can be determined by measuring risks of concern and comparing them with other similar, and not so similar, risks. Kasperson (1983a) calls this kind of comparison contextual analysis, and others have referred to it as comparative risk analysis. This approach assumes that if the measured risk of a new activity (e.g., the operation of a nuclear power plant) is lower than the risks of comparable activities (e.g., a coal-fired power plant) that are already *accepted*, then the new activity should be *acceptable*. Psychologists and other social scientists point out that this is like comparing apples and oranges—there are many other attributes beyond the probability and magnitude of harm that must be taken into account when determining acceptability. These include the degree of voluntariness, the nature of the harm (e.g., cancer versus bronchitis), catastrophic potential, the distribution of risks and benefits, and so on. Hence, determining acceptability requires broadening the analysis to examine public preferences and issues of equity. Other social and political scientists have broadened the debate still further, arguing that the acceptability of technologies such as nuclear power rests on issues unrelated to the risks per se, such as the nature of political control (e.g., centralized versus decentralized). They emphasize that debates about risk are often more about power, control, and access to resources than they are about risk. Indeed, many risks are not *accepted*, they are *imposed*, while others are merely *tolerated*.

Psychometric theory has been the driving force behind the burgeoning research area of risk communication, which has had enormous influence in the private and public sectors. Risk communication has become enshrined in laws such as SARA Title III Community-Right-to-Know, and agencies such as EPA, FDA, and DOE have spent considerable effort developing risk communication training manuals and materials for their staffs. Many of these agencies at the federal, regional, and state levels have full-time staff devoted to the development of these in-house and public risk communication programs. For some environmental problems, such as radon, risk communication is the principal risk management tool. The private sector has been similarly enthusiastic about risk communication. Many corporations and trade associations have developed high-profile risk communication programs that parallel government activities, although many critics are skeptical that these efforts are little more than revamped public relations exercises intended to mollify an increasingly antagonistic public. Some of these programs are in response to new legislation; others are responding to a new public mood (Baram and Partan 1990; Gow and Otway 1990).

Whatever the true nature of these programs, there can be no doubt that risk communication has been enthusiastically embraced by private and public sectors alike. It remains to be seen if these programs can deliver the goods. Given that there is often an almost evangelical zeal for and belief in risk communication as a universal panacea, there are sure to be future disappointments. It should be pointed out that while psychometric research was a principal driving force behind the development of risk communication, other disciplinary areas and theories have made significant contributions as these ideas have grown and been put into practice. These range from sociologists and cultural theorists who emphasize the need to consider the social and cultural contexts of risk communication (Nelkin 1985), to political scientists who have contributed their substantial knowledge of previous efforts in public participation (Portney 1991).

Cultural theory has been controversial and gained prominence in academic circles, but has had only limited influence in policy arenas. Cultural theory highlights the notion that controversies involving risk are often not about risk per se but about other factors like social roles (see Chapter 4).

In their book *Risk and Culture*, Douglas and Wildavsky (1982b) have advanced a structuralist-functionalist form of cultural theory that explains people's selection of risk on the basis of their institutional affiliation. On summarizing their thesis, Wartofsky (1986, 148) notes, "People think they are making choices about matters of risk, but what they are really doing is preserving a given set of social relations to maintain a certain social structure." Other variations of cultural theory are grounded on the view that risk is a collective construct but avoid the structuralist formulation of Douglas and Wildavsky. With the emphasis in cultural theory on the situational context of risk, objectivity and truth are treated as constructions derived from the scientific context, not as universal, not even as ideal types. The view that all truth is relational is dysfunctional to a scientific epistemology, which may explain the limited influence cultural theory has had in policy.

The social amplification framework (Chapter 6) is the most promising effort to date for integrating cognitive and sociological approaches to risk. It achieves this not by building a theory from basic concepts and axioms, but rather by setting up a framework that structures the interdependencies in a risk event, thereby establishing a foundation for empirical study. With an emphasis on signals and their amplification/attenuation, the social amplification framework has been able to integrate media analysis into a theory of risk. While the media's role in shaping risk selection is universally recognized, the particular function of the media has not yet been satisfactorily incorporated into a theoretical framework, which gives the social amplification framework an advantage over other theoretical approaches.

FUTURE DIRECTIONS OF RESEARCH

The field of risk studies in general, and theory in particular, is still in its early stages. No one can predict its direction, and much depends on the shape of events in the public sphere.

The growth of complex technologies, such as commercial airlines and nuclear energy, was the impetus behind the development of techniques such as probabilistic risk assessments to examine sources of system failure. Growing concerns about the impacts of individual lifestyle and the environment on health in general, and the incidence of cancer in particular, hastened the development of toxicological risk assessment. Events such as Times Beach and Love Canal further encouraged this development. Similarly, the tragedies at Bhopal, India, and Seveso, Italy, fostered the development of risk assessment models for chemical plants and greater attention to issues of emergency planning and risk communication. Theory building in risk will continue to respond to high profile events such as these that pose new challenges to social scientists. However, given the uncertain nature of such events in the future, it is not possible to say how the theory will evolve.

There are a few other indications of the directions that theory may be taking, however. At the risk of being proved wrong, we examine below what we believe are some likely areas of future research.

Social Factors and Risk Perception

Marxists and critical theorists have taken a prominent role in challenging the established theory and methods in natural hazards research, but they have been noticeable by their absence from the debates in the technological hazards arena. Technological hazards research has broadened its scope of analysis from cognitive to sociopolitical and cultural factors, but the effects of the traditional sociological variables of class, race, age, and gender remain largely unexplored.

There has been some research on the disproportionate concentration of noxious facilities in poor, politically weak communities, but otherwise there is surprisingly little research in what would appear to be fruitful areas, especially in regard to public policy. The dearth of research in this area is demonstrated by the unprecedented attention given to the United Church of Christ (1987) report *Toxic Wastes and Race in the United States*. This report received inordinate attention not so much for its findings (which were anticipated), but because it is one of the few pieces of research to document such socioeconomic biases in our risk management efforts. Since the release of this report and various other activities that followed in its wake, the EPA has placed a new emphasis on the issues of environmental equity.

With these kinds of stimuli, it is likely that research on these topics will increase in the future. Two particular areas in need of exploration are the impacts of racial and socioeconomic variables on the distribution of risks and the variation in public perceptions of and attitudes toward risk.

Within the psychometric field, increasing attention has been given to the contextual setting of technological risks. The notion of *trust in decision makers* has been identified as an important variable to explain public response to technologies. Another context-related factor is *stigmatization*: how do certain events and technology become stigmatized? What impact does stigmatization have on improving perceptions? These research trends indicate that psychometric theory has been widening its lens from the study of cognitive variables to a study of the interaction between cognition and the social variables (Slovic, Flynn, and Layman 1991).

"Rational" Risk Reduction

The divergence between public and expert views of risk was highlighted by the publication of *Unfinished Business* in 1987 (U.S. Environmental Protection Agency 1987). The report ranked thirty-one environmental problems based on expert evaluations of the risks they posed, and found that the rankings bore little relationship to EPA's programmatic priorities. The rankings were closely correlated, however, with apparent public perceptions of risks. Many within the agency find this mismatch discomforting and would prefer that agency priorities match the expert assessments more closely. In a follow-up report entitled *Reducing Risk: Setting Priorities and Strategies for Environmental Protection* (U.S. Environmental Protection Agency 1990), this is exactly what the EPA's Scientific Advisory Board recommended. Consequently, there is a considerable effort under way to encourage risk-based planning and budgeting. In other words, the risks that are considered by the experts to be the most severe would receive the highest levels of funding and the greatest attention. Such risk-based budgeting would dramatically reduce funding for programs such as Superfund, while increasing the funds available for controlling radon. While this may seem like a perfectly reasonable and *rational* way to set priorities, there are some major criticisms, most of which revolve around the issue of how broadly risk is defined and what is the appropriate role of expertise in public policy. If the experts believe the risks of a Superfund site are low, but the public believes they are high, should a publicly accountable agency such as EPA allocate a small or large part of its budget to solving the problem? Conversely, if the experts believe the risks of radon are high, should the EPA spend considerable sums of money trying to stimulate public concern? These and many other issues are going to be hotly debated as the pressure mounts for a more rational allocation of our scarce risk management resources, especially during times of fiscal austerity. Social scientists will have much to offer this debate.

The Role of Science

Science's role in risk assessment has been a recent subject for sociological study. The criteria for truth and objectivity advanced in science are not uniform. They may vary with the degree of uncertainty and the refractory quality inherent in the subject matter under investigation. Risk assessment has been applied to very different types of events, from industrial accidents to environmental carcinogenesis from chemically contaminated drinking water. Society's interest in uniform outcome measures persists, despite the fact that the methods used to discover the "truth" vary considerably. More research is needed to investigate the range of epistemic conditions in science that contribute to risk assessment. The comparison of two risk estimates cannot be legitimately made unless we also compare the methodologies and the value-ladenness of the predictive models. Funtowicz and Ravetz (Chapter 11) have begun to address these issues with their classification of different orders of science. More theoretical research will provide a more thorough accounting of how science contributes to our knowledge of risk.

Public discussion over risk rarely escapes controversy among scientists. There is need for theoretical explanation on how science addresses political controversy. What constitutes consensus among scientists? What role does scientific consensus play in allaying controversy within the popular culture? If expert knowledge about risk it conditional, is it conditional in the way that other areas of science are? When science is applied to the study of risk, are we relegated to an inferior form of science?

There is still much to learn about the relationship between science and public opinion. Do popular views about risk change in the wake of new scientific conclusions? What is the appropriate model to explain the relationship between science and popular opinion on risk? In particular, if scientific support grows for the thesis that humans consume more natural carcinogens than they do synthetic carcinogens in their food, will this change public attitudes about synthetic chemicals?

Theories of risk have yet to develop a satisfactory conception of "scientific objectivity." Cultural theorists and other sociologists of science have abandoned "objectivity" under the rubric of "social constructionism." Knowledge, it is claimed, is relative to the culture. With two beliefs in opposition, each legitimized by its functional role in its respective cultural context, the notion of universal objectivity loses its meaning.

On the other hand, proponents of technical risk assessment accept a view of objectivity uncritically. They neglect weaker from stronger epistemic systems in science. We are left with two unsatisfying positions. Either all knowledge, including scientific knowledge, is relativized, or we have an uncritical acceptance of scientific risk assessment that fails to distinguish levels of confidence.

Global Environmental Policy: Cross-Cultural Studies

Global environmental change in general, and global warming in particular, present relatively recent and unique challenges to the social science community in risk studies. The risks of global environmental change are quantitatively and qualitatively different from most of the risks with which the field has dealt in the past, in terms of geographical scale, temporal duration, political complexity, and our abilities to intervene. As Funtowicz and Ravetz (Chapter 11) point out, these problems are definitely in the novel realm of second-order science—they will require new techniques of analysis and new kinds of solutions. Several contributors to this volume have already turned their attention to these knotty problems. Ravetz and Funtowicz emphasize the importance of the quality of information, and suggest that we, as a society, are going to have to learn to make *hard* decisions based on relatively *soft* science. Kasperson and his colleagues are examining what social scientists with expertise in the risk field may contribute to the debate, and in particular what geographers have learned that may be of value.

Steve Rayner is turning his anthropologist's eye and his interest in institutions to examine the array of international efforts under way or necessary in the future to tackle the problems of global environmental change. These problems are inherently transnational, but the interpretation and public response to these risks may vary considerably according to the historical, sociopolitical, and cultural context of the different countries involved. This will present new opportunities for the extension of the cultural theory of risk.

These are only a sample of some of the ongoing efforts in this area. It is likely that research in this area will expand dramatically in the future. With this expansion we can expect risk researchers to pay greater attention to cross-national differences and political processes.

Bibliography

Agassi, J. 1984. "The Cheapening of Science." *Inquiry* 27:167–172.

Allen, F. W. 1987a. "The Situation: What the Public Believes, How the Experts See It." *EPA Journal* 13(9):9–12.

———. 1987b. "Towards a Holistic Appreciation of Risk: The Challenge for Communicators and Policymakers." *Science, Technology, and Human Values* 12(3–4): 138–143.

Amendola, A. 1986. "Uncertainties in Systems Reliability Modeling: Insights Gained Through European Benchmark Exercises." *Nuclear Engineering and Design* 93:215–225.

Apostolakis, G. 1988. Special Issue. *Reliability Engineering and Systems Safety* 23:293–298.

Appelbaum, R. P. 1977. "The Future Is Made, Not Predicted: Technocratic Planners vs. Public Interests." *Society* 5:49–53.

Arabie, P., and C. Maschmeyer. 1988. "Some Current Models for the Perception and Judgment of Risk." *Organizational Behavior and Human Decision Processes* 41:300–329.

Aristotle. 1909. *On the Art of Poetry*. A Revised Text with Critical Translation and Commentary by Ingram Bywater. Oxford: Clarendon Press.

Ashby, E. 1978. *Reconciling Man with the Environment*. London: Oxford University Press.

Associated Press. 1990. "Groups Challenge Value of Cancer Testing on Rats." *Register-Guard* (Eugene, OR), August 31, 6A.

Audin, L. 1987. *A Review of the Effects of Human Error on the Risks Involved in Spent Fuel Transportation*. Report Prepared for the Nebraska Energy Office. Lincoln: Nebraska Energy Office.

Bailey, F. G. 1968. "A Peasant View of the Bad Life." In T. Shanin, ed. *Peasants and Peasant Society*. Harmondsworth: Penguin.

Baram, M. S. 1980. "Cost-Benefit Analysis: An Inadequate Basis for Health, Safety, and Environmental Regulatory Decisionmaking." *Ecology Law Quarterly* 8:473–531.

————. 1985. "Implementation and Evaluation of Regulations." In H. Otway and
    M. Peltu, eds. *Regulating Industrial Risks: Science, Hazards and Public Pro-
    tection.* Boston: Butterworths, 37–75.

Baram, M. S., and D. G. Partan, eds. 1990. *Corporate Disclosure of Environmental
    Risks: U.S. and European Law.* Salem, NH: Butterworth Legal Pub.

Barber, B. 1983. *The Logic and Limits of Trust.* New Brunswick, NJ: Rutgers
    University Press.

Barnes, B. 1974. *Scientific Knowledge and Sociological Theory.* London: Routledge
    and Kegan Paul.

————. 1977. *Interests and the Growth of Knowledge.* London: Routledge and
    Kegan Paul.

Barnes, B., and S. Shapin, eds. 1979. *Natural Order.* London: Sage.

Bartimus, T., H. Spencer, D. Foster, and S. McCartney. 1989. "Greed, Neglect
    Primed Oil Spill." *St. Louis Post-Dispatch*, April 9, 1.

Bauman, E., and O. Renn. 1989. *Air Quality Standards and Regulatory Styles in
    West Germany and the United States.* CENTED Research Report No. 4
    Worcester, MA: Clark University.

Beck, U. 1986. *Die Risikogesellschaft. Auf dem Weg in eine andere Moderne.* Frank-
    furt am Main: Suhrkamp.

————. 1990. "Vom Überleben in der Risikogesellschaft." In M. Schüz, ed. *Risiko
    und Wagnis: Die Herausforderung der industriellen Welt.* Pfullingen: Gerling
    Akademie, Neske, 12–31.

Benthin, A. C., P. Slovic, and H. H. Severson. In press. "A Psychometric Study of
    Adolescent Risk Perception." *Journal of Adolescence.*

Bentler, P. M. 1980. "Multivariate Analysis with Latent Variables: Causal Mod-
    eling." *Annual Review of Psychology* 31:419–456.

Berkeley, G. 1710. *A Treatise Concerning the Principles of Human Understanding.*
    Dublin: Rhames and Popyat.

Bernal, J. D. 1939. *The Social Function of Science.* London: Routledge.

Bernstein, R. J. 1983. *Beyond Objectivism and Relativism.* Oxford: Blackwell.

Bier, V. M., and A. Mosleh. 1990. "The Analysis of Accident Precursors and Near
    Misses: Implications for Risk Assessment and Risk Management." *Reliability
    Engineering and System Safety* 27:91–101.

Bijker, W., and J. Law, eds. 1991. *Shaping Technology, Building Societies: Studies
    in Sociotechnical Change.* Cambridge, MA: MIT Press.

Bijker, W., T. Pinch, and T. Hughes, eds. 1987. *The Social Construction of Tech-
    nological Systems.* Cambridge, MA: MIT Press.

Bloor, D. 1976. *Knowledge and Social Imagery.* London: Routledge and Kegan
    Paul.

Blumer, H. 1931. "Science Without Concepts." *American Journal of Sociology*
    36:515–533.

Bohnenblust, H., and T. Schneider. 1984. "Risk Appraisal: Can It Be Improved by
    Formal Models?" Paper presented at the Annual Meeting of the Society for
    Risk Analysis, Knoxville, TN.

Bonano, E. J., S. C. Hora, R. L. Keeney, and D. von Winterfeldt. 1990. *Elicitation
    and Use of Expert Judgment in Performance Assessment for High-Level
    Radioactive Waste Repositories.* NUREG/CR–5411, SAND–1821. Albu-
    querque, NM: Sandia National Laboratories.

Bostrom, A. 1990. *A Mental Models Approach to Exploring Perceptions of Hazardous Processes.* Unpublished Ph.D. diss. School of Urban and Public Affairs, Carnegie Mellon University.

Bostrom, A., B. Fischhoff, and G. Morgan. Forthcoming. "Characterizing Mental Models of Hazardous Processes: A Methodology and an Application to Radon." *Journal of Social Issues.*

Bourdieu, P. 1984. *Distinction: A Social Critique of the Judgment of Taste.* Cambridge, MA: Harvard University Press.

———. 1986. *Kultursociologiska texter.* Stockholm: Salamander.

———. 1990. *The Logic of Practice.* Cambridge, UK: Polity Press.

Bradbury, J. A. 1989. "The Policy Implications of Differing Concepts of Risk." *Science, Technology, and Human Values* 14(4): 380–399.

Brehmer, B. 1987. "The Psychology of Risk." In W. T. Singleton and J. Howden, eds. *Risk and Decisions.* New York: Wiley, 25–39.

Brion, D. 1988. "An Essay on LULU, NIMBY, and the Problem of Distributive Justice." *Environmental Affairs* 15:437–503.

British Standards Institution. 1979. *The British Standard for Quality Assurance.* BS 4778. London: British Standards Institution.

Brody, B. A., ed. 1970. *Readings in the Philosophy of Science.* Englewood Cliffs, NJ: Prentice-Hall.

Brook, P. 1988. *The Empty Space.* London: Pelican Books.

Brown, H., and R. Goble. 1990. "The Role of Scientists in Risk Assessment." *Risk: Issues in Health and Safety* 6:283–311.

Brown, P. 1987. "Popular Epidemiology: Community Response to Toxic Waste-Induced Disease in Woburn, Massachusetts." *Science, Technology, and Human Values* 12:78–87.

Bryan, R. H. 1987. "The Politics and Promises of Nuclear Waste Disposal: The View from Nevada." *Environment* 29(8):14–17, 32–38.

Burke, K. 1945. *A Grammar of Motives.* Berkeley: University of California Press.

Burkhardt, R. 1984. "Rail Officials Testify on Crashes." *Journal of Commerce* (July 27):3.

Burns, W. 1990. "Introducing Structural Models and Influence Diagrams into Risk Perception Research: Their Value for Theory Construction and Decision Making." Unpublished doctoral dissertation, Department of Decision Sciences, University of Oregon.

Burns, W., R. E. Kasperson, J. X. Kasperson, O. Renn, S. Emani, and P. Slovic. 1990. *Social Amplification of Risk: An Empirical Study.* Carson City, NV: Yucca Mountain Socioeconomic Project, State of Nevada Nuclear Waste Project Office.

Burton, I., and R. W. Kates. 1964. "The Perception of Natural Hazards in Resource Management." *Natural Resources Journal* 3(3):412–441.

Burton, I., R. W. Kates, and G. F. White. 1968. "The Human Ecology of Extreme Events." *Natural Hazards Research Working Paper No. 1.* Toronto: Department of Geography, University of Toronto.

———. 1978. *The Environment as Hazard.* New York: Oxford University Press.

Buss, D. M., K. H. Craik, and K. Dake. 1986. "Contemporary Worldviews and Perception of the Technological System." In V. T. Covello, J. Menkes, and

J. Mumpower, eds. *Risk Evaluation and Management*. New York: Plenum Press, 93–130.

Butters, G., J. Califee, and P. Ippolito. 1981. "Reply to Steven Kelman." *Regulation* 5(2):41–42.

Calabresi, G., and P. Bobbitt. 1978. *Tragic Choices*. New York: W. W. Norton.

Callon, M., and B. Latour. 1981. "Unscrewing the Big Leviathan." In K. Knorr-Cetina and A. Cicourel, eds. *Advances in Social Theory and Methodology*. London: Routledge and Kegan Paul, 277–302.

Camerer, C. F. 1987. "Do Biases in Probability Judgment Matter in Markets? Experimental Evidence." *American Economic Review* 77:981–997.

Camerer, C. F., and H. Kunreuther. 1989a. "Decision Processes for Low Probability Events: Policy Implications." *Journal of Policy Analysis and Management* 8:565–592.

———. 1989b. "Experimental Markets for Insurance." *Journal of Risk and Uncertainty* 2:265–300.

Carroll, J. D., and J. J. Chang. 1970. "Analysis of Individual Differences in Multidimensional Scaling via an N-Way Generalization of 'Eckart-Young' Decomposition." *Psychometrika* 35:283–319.

Chalmers, A. 1990. *Science and Its Fabrications*. Milton Keynes: Open University Press.

Christenson-Szalanski, J.J.J., and J. B. Bushyhead, 1982. "Physicians' Use of Probabilistic Information in a Real Clinical Setting." *Journal of Experimental Psychology* 7:928–935.

Clark, W. C., and G. Majone. 1985. "The Critical Appraisal of Scientific Inquiries with Policy Implications." *Science, Technology, and Human Values* 10(3):6–19.

Clarke, L. 1988. "Explaining Choices Among Technological Risks." *Social Problems* 35(1):22–35.

———. 1989. *Acceptable Risk?: Making Choices in a Toxic Environment*. Berkeley: University of California Press.

———. 1990. "Organizational Foresight and the Exxon Oil Spill." Paper presented at the Annual Meeting of the Society for Study of Social Problems, Washington, DC, August.

Claster, D. S. 1967. "Comparison of Risk Perception Between Delinquents and Non-Delinquents." *Journal of Criminal Law, Criminology and Police Science* 58(1):80–86.

Coase, R. A. 1960. "The Problem of Social Cost." *Journal of Law and Economics* 3:1–44.

Cohen, B. L. 1983. *Before It's Too Late: A Scientist's Case for Nuclear Energy*. New York: Plenum Press.

———. 1985. "Criteria for Technology Acceptability." *Risk Analysis* 5(1):1–3.

Combs, B., and P. Slovic. 1979. "Newspaper Coverage of Causes of Death." *Journalism Quarterly* 56:837–843, 849.

Comfort, L. K., ed. 1988. *Managing Disaster: Strategies and Policy Perspectives*. Durham, NC: Duke University Press.

Consensus. 1991. "The Facility Siting 'Credo': Guidelines for Public Officials." *Consensus* 9 (January):5.

Coppock, R. 1985. "Interactions Between Scientists and Public Officials: A Comparison of the Use of Science in Regulatory Programs in the United States and West Germany." *Policy Sciences* 18:371–390.

Coser, L. A. 1956. *The Function of Social Conflict.* New York: Free Press.

Covello, V. T. 1983. "The Perception of Technological Risks: A Literature Review." *Technological Forecasting and Social Change* 23:285–297.

Covello, V. T., W. G. Flamm, J. V. Rodricks, and R. G. Tardiff, eds. 1983. *The Analysis of Actual Versus Perceived Risk.* New York: Plenum Press.

Covello, V. T., J. Menkes, and J. Mumpower. 1986. *Risk Evaluation and Management.* New York: Plenum Press.

Covello, V. T., and J. Mumpower. 1985. "Risk Analysis and Risk Management: An Historical Perspective." *Risk Analysis* 5(2):103–119.

Covello, V. T., J. L. Mumpower, P.J.M. Stallen, and V.R.R. Uppuluri, eds. 1985. *Environmental Impact Assessment, Technology Assessment, and Risk Analysis: Contributions from the Psychological and Decision Sciences.* Berlin: Springer-Verlag.

Covello, V. T., D von Winterfeldt, and P. Slovic. 1987. "Communicating Scientific Information About Health and Environmental Risks: Problems and Opportunities from a Social and Behavioral Perspective." In V. Covello, L. Lave, A. Moghissi, and V. Uppuluri, eds. *Uncertainty in Risk Assessment, Risk Management and Decisionmaking.* New York: Plenum Press.

Coy, P. 1989. "Radiation from VDTs, Power Lines Raises Fear." *Register-Guard* (Eugene, OR), December 3, 11C.

Crouch, E.A.C., and R. Wilson. 1982. *Risk Benefit Analysis.* Cambridge, MA: Ballinger.

Cummings, R. B. 1981. "Is Risk Assessment a Science?" *Risk Analysis* 1(1):1–3.

Dacy, D. C., and H. Kunreuther. 1969. *The Economics of Natural Disasters: Implications for Federal Policy.* New York: Free Press.

Daly, K. 1970. "The Specters of Technicism." *Psychiatry* 33:417–431.

Dawes, R. M. 1988. *Rational Choice in an Uncertain World.* San Diego: Harcourt Brace Jovanovich.

de Leeuw, J., and J. van Rijckevorsal. 1980. "HOMALS and PRINCALS: Some Generalizations of Principal Components Analysis." In E. Diday, L. Lebart, J. P. Pages, and R. Tomassone, eds. *Data Analysis and Informatics.* New York: North-Holland, 231–242.

Derby, S. L., and R. L. Keeney. 1981. "Risk Analysis: Understanding 'How Safe Is Safe Enough.' " *Risk Analysis* 1(3):217–224.

De Smet, A. A., D. G. Fryback, and J. R. Thornbury. 1979. "A Second Look at the Utility of Radiographics School Examination for Trauma." *American Journal of Radiology* 43:139–150.

Dietz, T., and R. W. Rycroft. 1987. *The Risk Professionals.* Occasional Report 14. New York: Russell Sage Foundation.

Dietz, T., R. Scott Frey, and E. Rosa. Forthcoming. "Risk, Technology, and Society." In R. E. Dunlap and W. Michelson, eds. *Handbook of Environmental Sociology.* Westport, CT: Greenwood Press.

Dietz, T., P. C. Stern, and R. W. Rycroft. 1989. "Definitions of Conflict and the Legitimation of Resources: The Case of Environmental Risk." *Sociological Forum* 4:47–69.

Dombrowski, W. R. 1987. "Critical Theory in Sociological Disaster Research." In

R. R. Dynes, B. de Marchi, and C. Pelanda, eds. *Sociology of Disasters:* Milan: Franco Angeli, 331–356.

Douglas, M. 1966. *Purity and Danger: Concepts of Pollution and Taboo.* London: Routledge and Kegan Paul.

———. 1970. *Natural Symbols.* London: Barrie and Rockliff.

———. 1972. "Environments at Risk." In Jonathan Benthall, ed. *Ecology: The Shaping Enquiry.* London: Longman.

———. 1975. *Implicit Meanings: Essays in Anthropology.* London: Routledge and Kegan Paul.

———. 1978. *Cultural Bias.* Royal Anthropological Institute Occasional Paper No. 35. London: Royal Anthropological Institute.

———. 1984. "A Backdoor Approach to Thinking About the Social Order." Address to the American Sociological Association, San Antonio.

———. 1985. *Risk Acceptability According to the Social Sciences.* New York: Russell Sage Foundation.

Douglas, M., and A. Wildavsky. 1982a. "How Can We Know the Risks We Face?: Why Risk Selection Is a Social Process." *Risk Analysis* 2(2):49–51.

———. 1982b. *Risk and Culture: An Essay on the Selection of Technological and Environmental Dangers.* Berkeley: University of California Press.

Downes, D. M., B. P. Davies, M. E. David, and P. Stone. 1987. *Gambling, Work and Leisure: A Study Across Three Areas.* London: Routledge and Kegan Paul.

Downs, A. 1972. "Up and Down with Ecology—The 'Issue-Attention Cycle.'" *Public Interest* 28:38–50.

Drabek, T.E. 1986. *Human System Responses to Disaster: An Inventory of Sociological Findings.* New York: Springer-Verlag.

DRMS (Decision, Risk, and Management Science Program). 1990. *Program Statement.* Draft. Washington, DC: National Science Foundation.

Dubé-Rioux, L., and J. E. Russo. 1988. "An Availability Bias in Professional Judgment." *Journal of Behavioral Decision Making* 1(4): 223–237.

Duncan, O. D. 1978. "Sociologists Should Reconsider Nuclear Energy." *Social Forces* 57(1):1–22.

Dunlap, R. E. 1989. "Public Opinion and Environmental Policy." In J. P. Lester, ed. *Environmental Politics and Policy: Theory and Evidence.* Durham, NC: Duke University Press, 87–134.

DuPont, R. L. 1981. "The Nuclear Power Phobia." *Business Week* (September 7):14–16.

Dürrenmatt, F. 1964. *Four Plays 1957–62.* London: Jonathan Cape.

Dynes, R. R., B. de Marchi, and C. Pelanda, eds. 1987. *Sociology of Disasters.* Milan: Franco Angeli.

Earle, T. C., and M. K. Lindell. 1984. "Public Perception of Industrial Risks: A Free-Response Approach." In R. A. Waller and V. T. Covello, eds. *Low-Probability High-Consequence Risk Analysis.* New York: Plenum Press, 531–550.

Easterling, D. 1989. "Individual Differences in the Perception of Risky Activities: Teenagers' Views of Personal Risks." Unpublished manuscript. Philadelphia: University of Pennsylvania, Wharton School, Department of Public Policy and Management.

Easton, D. 1965. *A Framework for Political Analysis*. Englewood Cliffs, NJ: Prentice-Hall.

Edelman, M. J. 1976. *The Symbolic Uses of Politics*. Urbana: University of Illinois Press.

———. 1977. *Political Language: Words that Succeed and Policies that Fail*. New York: Academic Press.

———. 1988. *Constructing the Political Spectacle*. Chicago: University of Chicago Press.

Edelstein, M. 1986. "Stigmatizing Effects of Toxic Pollution." Unpublished manuscript, Ramapo College, Department of Psychology.

———. 1988. *Contaminated Communities: The Social and Psychological Impacts of Residential Toxic Exposure*. Boulder, CO: Westview Press.

Edge, D. O., and B. Barnes, eds. 1982. *Science in Context: Readings in the Sociology of Science*. Milton Keynes: Open University Press.

Edwards, W. 1981. "Reflections on and Criticism of a Highly Political Multiattribute Utility Analysis." In L. Cobb and R. M. Thrall, eds. *Mathematical Frontiers of the Social and Policy Sciences*. Boulder, CO: Westview Press, 326–340.

Edwards, W., and D. von Winterfeldt. 1986. "Public Disputes About Risky Technologies: Stakeholders and Arenas." In V. T. Covello, J. Mumpower, and J. Menkes, eds. *Risk Evaluation and Management*. New York: Plenum Press, 69–92.

———. 1987. "Public Values in Risk Debates." *Risk Analysis* 7:141–158.

Elam, K. 1980. *The Semiotics of Theatre and Drama*. New York: Methuen.

Ellsberg, D. 1961. "Risk, Ambiguity, and the Savage Axioms." *Quarterly Journal of Economics* 75:643–669.

Emani, S., J. X. Kasperson, R. E. Kasperson, and O. Renn. 1990. "Characterizing Media Coverage of Hazards: Typical Profiles and Social Amplification of Risk." Unpublished paper presented at the Annual Meeting of the Society for Risk Analysis, New Orleans.

Engländer, T., K. Farago, P. Slovic, and B. Fischhoff. 1986. "A Comparative Analysis of Risk Perception in Hungary and the United States." *Social Behaviour: An International Journal of Applied Social Psychology* 1:55–66.

Epstein, S., and W. D. Fenz. 1967. "The Detection of Areas of Emotional Stress Through Variations in Perceptual Threshold and Physiological Arousal." *Journal of Experimental Research in Personality* 2(3):191–199.

Erikson, K. T. 1976. *Everything in Its Path: Destruction of Community in the Buffalo Creek Flood*. New York: Simon and Schuster.

Etzioni, A. 1961. *A Comparative Analysis of Complex Organizations*. New York: Free Press.

Evers, A., and H. Nowotny. 1987. *Über den Umgang mit Unsicherheit. Die Entdeckung der Gestaltbarkeit von Gesellschaft*. Frankfurt am Main: Suhrkamp.

Ewing, T. F. 1990. "Guarantees Near a Landfill." *New York Times* (National ed.), July 8, 27.

Ezrahi, Y. 1974. "The Authority of Science in Politics." In A. Thackray and E. Mendelsohn, eds. *Science and Values*. New York: Humanities Press.

———. 1990. *The Descent of Icarus*. Cambridge, MA: Harvard University Press.

Fairchild, H. P. 1955. *Dictionary of Sociology*. Ames, IA: Littlefield, Adams.

Festinger, L. 1957. *A Theory of Cognitive Dissonance*. Evanston, IL: Row, Peterson.

Feyerabend, P. K. 1975. *Against Method*. London: New Left Books.

Fincham, J.R.S., and J. R. Ravetz. 1991. *Risks and Benefits of Genetically Engineered Organisms*. Milton Keynes: Open University Press.

Fiorino, D. J. 1989. "Technical and Democratic Values in Risk Analysis." *Risk Analysis* 9(3):293–299.

Fischhoff, B. 1977. "Cost-Benefit Analysis and the Art of Motorcycle Maintenance." *Policy Sciences* 8:177–202.

———. 1983. "Acceptable Risk: The Case of Nuclear Power." *Journal of Policy Analysis and Management* 2(4):559–575.

———. 1985. "Managing Risk Perceptions." *Issues in Science and Technology* 2(1):83–96.

Fischhoff, B., B. Goitein, and Z. Shapiro. 1982. "The Experienced Utility of Expected Utility Approaches." In N. T. Feather, ed. *Expectations and Actions: Expectancy-Value Models in Psychology*. Hillsdale, NJ: Lawrence Erlbaum, 315–340.

Fischhoff, B., S. Lichtenstein, P. Slovic, S. L. Derby, and R. L. Keeney. 1981. *Acceptable Risk*. Cambridge, Eng.: Cambridge University Press.

Fischhoff, B., P. Slovic, and S. Lichtenstein. 1977. "Knowing with Certainty: The Appropriateness of Extreme Confidence." *Journal of Experimental Psychology* 3:552–564.

———. 1979. "Weighing the Risks." *Environment* 21(4):17–38.

Fischhoff, B., P. Slovic, S. Lichtenstein, S. Read, and B. Combs. 1978. "How Safe Is Safe Enough? A Psychometric Study of Attitudes Towards Technological Risks and Benefits." *Policy Sciences* 9:127–152.

Fischhoff, B., S. Watson, and C. Hope. 1984. "Defining Risk." *Policy Sciences* 17:123–139.

Fishbein, M., and I. Ajzen. 1975. *Belief, Attitude, Intention and Behavior: An Introduction to Theory and Research*. Reading, MA: Addison-Wesley.

Fitzpatrick, J. S. 1980. "Adapting to Danger: A Participant Observation Study of an Underground Mine." *Sociology of Work and Occupations* 7(2):131–180.

Flynn, C. B. 1984. "The Local Impacts of Three Mile Island." In William R. Freudenburg and Eugene A. Rosa, eds. *Public Reactions to Nuclear Power: Are There Critical Masses?* Boulder, CO: American Association for the Advancement of Science/Westview Press, 205–232.

Forester, J., ed. 1985. *Critical Theory and Public Life*. Cambridge, MA: MIT Press.

Fornell, C., ed. 1982. *A Second Generation of Multivariate Analysis: Methods*. New York: Praeger.

Foucault, M. 1979. *Discipline and Punish: The Birth of the Prison*. London: Allen Lane.

Frank, J. D. 1974. *Persuasion and Healing*. New York: Schocken Books.

Frank, P. 1957. *Philosophy of Science: The Link Between Science and Philosophy*. Englewood Cliffs, NJ: Prentice-Hall.

Freeman, A. M. 1986. "The Ethical Basis of the Economic View of the Environment." In D. VanDeVeer and C. Pierce, eds. *People, Penguins, and Plastic Trees: Basic Issues in Environmental Ethics*. Belmont, CA: Wadsworth, 218–226.

Freud, S. 1924. *Collected Papers*. London: Hogarth.

Freudenburg, W. R. 1976. "The Social Impact of Energy Boom Development on

Rural Communities: A Review of Literatures and Some Predictions." Presented at the Annual Meeting of the American Sociological Association, New York, August.

———. 1981. "Women and Men in an Energy Boomtown: Adjustment, Alienation, and Adaption." *Rural Sociology* 4(2):220–244.

———. 1982. "The Impacts of Rapid Growth on the Social and Personal Well-Being of Local Community Residents." In B. A. Weber and R. E. Howell, eds. *Coping with Rapid Growth in Rural Communities*. Boulder, CO: Westview Press, 137–170.

———. 1984. "Boomtown's Youth: The Differential Impacts of Rapid Community Growth upon Adolescents and Adults." *American Sociological Review* 49(5):697–705.

———. 1985. "Waste Not: The Special Impacts of Nuclear Waste Facilities." In J. G. McCray et al., eds. *Waste Isolation in the U.S. Vol. 3: Waste Policies and Programs*. Tucson: University of Arizona Press, 75–80.

———. 1986a. "The Density of Acquaintanceship: An Overlooked Variable in Community Research?" *American Journal of Sociology* 92(1):27–63.

———. 1986b. "Sociology in Legis-Land: An Ethnographic Report on Congressional Culture." *Sociological Quarterly* 27(3):313–326.

———. 1987. "Rationality and Irrationality in Estimating the Risks of Nuclear Waste Disposal." In R. G. Post, ed. *Waste Isolation in the U.S.: Technical Programs and Public Participation*. Tucson: University of Arizona Press, 109–115.

———. 1988. "Perceived Risk, Real Risk: Social Science and the Art of Probabilistic Risk Assessment." *Science* 242:44–49.

———. 1989. "The Organizational Attenuation of Risk Estimates." Paper presented at the Annual Meeting of the Society for Risk Analysis, San Francisco, October.

———. 1990. "Risk and Recreancy: Weber, the Division of Labor, and the Rationality of Risk Perceptions." Presented at the twelfth annual Department of Energy Conference on Low-Level Radioactive Waste, Chicago, August.

———. 1992. "Nothing Recedes Like Success? Risk Analysis and the Organizational Amplification of Risks." *Risk: Issues in Health and Safety* 3(1):1–35.

Freudenburg, W. R., L. M. Bacigalupi, and C. Landoll-Young. 1982. "Mental Health Consequences of Rapid Community Growth: A Report from the Longitudinal Study of Boomtown Mental Health Impacts." *Journal of Health and Human Resources Administration* 4(3):334–352.

Freudenburg, W. R., and R. K. Baxter. 1984. "Host Community Attitudes Toward Nuclear Power Plants: A Reassessment." *Social Science Quarterly* 65(4):1129–1136.

———. 1985. "Nuclear Reactions: Public Attitudes and Policies Toward Nuclear Power." *Policy Studies Review* 5(1):96–110.

Freudenburg, W. R., and R. Gramling. In press. "Community Impacts of Technological Change: Toward a Longitudinal Perspective." *Social Forces* 70(4).

Freudenburg, W. R., and T. R. Jones. 1991. "Attitudes and Stress in the Presence of Technological Risk: A Test of the Supreme Court Hypothesis." *Social Forces* 69(4):1143–1168.

Freudenburg, W. R. and S. K. Pastor. Forthcoming. "NIMBYs and LULUs: Stalking the Syndromes." *Journal of Social Issues*.

———. In press. "Public Responses to Technological Risks: Toward a Sociological Perspective." *Sociological Quarterly* 33(3).

Freudenburg, W. R., and E. A. Rosa, eds. 1984. *Public Reactions to Nuclear Power: Are There Critical Masses?* Boulder, CO: American Association for the Advancement of Science/Westview Press.

Friedman, S M., S. Dunwoody, and C. Rogers, eds. 1986. *Scientists and Journalists: Reporting Science as News*. New York: Free Press.

Fritz, C., and J. H. Mathewson. 1957. *Convergence Behavior*. Washington, DC: National Academy of Sciences–National Research Council.

Funtowicz, S. O., and J. R. Ravetz. 1985. "Three Types of Risk Assessment." In C. Whipple and V. T. Covello, eds. *Risk Analysis in the Private Sector*. New York: Plenum Press.

———. 1987. "The Arithmetic of Scientific Uncertainty." *Physics Bulletin* 38:412–414.

——— 1990a. *Global Environmental Issues and the Emergence of Second Order Science*. EUR 12803 EN. Ispra, Italy: Joint Research Centre of the Commission of the European Communities.

———. 1990b. *Uncertainty and Quality in Science for Policy*. Dordrecht: Kluwer.

Gale, R. P. 1986. "Social Movements and the State: The Environmental Movement, Counter-Movement and Governmental Agencies." *Sociological Perspectives* 29:202–240.

Galton, F. 1880. "Psychometric Experiments." *Brain* 2:149–162.

Gamson, W. A. 1990. *The Strategy of Social Protest*. 2nd ed. Belmont, CA: Wadsworth Pub. (originally Homewood, IL: Dorsey Press, 1975).

Gamson, W. A., and A. Modigliani. 1989. "Media Discourse and Public Opinion on Nuclear Power: A Constructionist Approach." *American Journal of Sociology* 95:1–37.

Garfinkel, H. 1963. "A Conception of and Experiments with 'Trust' as a Condition of Stable Concerted Actions." In O. J. Harvey, ed. *Motivation and Social Interaction*. New York: Ronald Press, 187–238.

Geertz, C. 1980. *Negara: The Theater State in Nineteenth Century Bali*. Princeton, NJ: Princeton University Press.

Gerlach, L. P. 1987. "Protest Movements and the Construction of Risk." In B. B. Johnson and V. T. Covello, eds. *The Social and Cultural Construction of Risk*. Dordrecht: Reidel, 103–145.

Gerlach, L. P., and S. Rayner. 1988. "Culture and the Common Management of Global Risks." *Practicing Anthropology* 10(3–4):15–18.

Gerrig, R. J., L. T. Maloney, and A. Tversky. 1985. "Dimensional Invariance in Psychological Spaces: Personality Traits and Emotional States." Unpublished manuscript, Department of Psychology, Stanford University.

Giddens, A. 1985. *The Constitution of Society*. London: Macmillan.

———. 1990. *The Consequences of Modernity*. London: Polity.

———. 1991. *Modernity and Self-Identity*. London: Polity.

Goffman, E. 1959. *The Presentation of Self in Everyday Life*. Garden City, NY: Doubleday.

———. 1963. *Stigma*. Englewood Cliffs, NJ: Prentice-Hall.

Golding, D. 1990. *The Differential Susceptibility of Workers to Occupational Hazards*. New York: Garland.

Goodenough, W. 1971. *Culture, Language, and Society*. Reading, MA: Addison-Wesley.

Goszczynska, M., T. Tyszka, and P. Slovic. 1991. "Risk Perception in Poland: A Comparison with Three Other Countries." *Journal of Behavioral Decision Making* 4(3):179–193.

Gould, L. C., G. T. Gardner, D. R. DeLuca, A. R. Tiemann, L. W. Doob, and J.A.J. Stolwijk. 1988. *Perceptions of Technological Risks and Benefits*. New York: Russell Sage Foundation.

Gow, H.B.F., and H. Otway. 1990. *Communicating with the Public About Major Accident Hazards*. London: Elsevier.

Graham, J. D., L. C. Green, and M. J. Roberts. 1988. *In Search of Safety: Chemicals and Cancer Risk*. Cambridge, MA: Harvard University Press.

Graham, J. D., and J. W. Vaupel. 1981. "Value of a Life: What Difference Does It Make?" *Risk Analysis* 1(1):89–95.

Griesmeyer, J. M., and D. Okrent. 1981. "Risk Management and Decision Rules for Light Water Reactors." *Risk Analysis* 1(2):121–136.

Grimshaw v. Ford Motor Co. No. 19776 (Superior Court, Orange County, California, February 6, 1978).

Gross, J. L., and S. Rayner. 1985. *Measuring Culture*. New York: Columbia University Press.

Grove-White, R. 1991. "Emerging Environmental Conflict." *Royal Society of Arts Journal* 139:437–447.

Gusfield, J. R. 1975. *Community: A Critical Response*. Oxford: Basil Blackwell.

Hass, J. 1972. "Binging: Educational Control Among High Steel Ironworkers." *American Behavioral Scientist* 16:27–34.

———. 1977. "Learning Real Feelings: A Study of High Steel Ironworkers' Reactions to Fear and Danger." *Sociology of Work and Occupations* 4(2):147–172.

Habermas, J. 1971. *Toward a Rational Society*. London: Heinemann.

———. 1975. *Legitimation Crisis*. Boston: Beacon Press.

———. 1984–87. *The Theory of Communicative Action*. 2 vols. Boston: Beacon Press.

Häfele, W., O. Renn, and H. Erdmann. 1990. "Risiko, Unsicherheit und Undeutlichkeit." In W. Häfele, ed. *Energiesysteme im Übergang—Unter den Bedingungen der Zukunft*. Landsberg/Lech: Poller, 373–423.

Hall, R., and R. Quinn. 1983. "Is There a Connection Between Organizational Theory and Public Policy?" In R. Hall and R. Quinn, eds. *Organisational Theory and Public Policy*. London: Sage Publications. 7–22.

Hance, B. J., C. Chess, and P. M. Sandman. 1988. *Improving Dialogue with Communities*. Trenton: New Jersey Department of Environmental Protection.

Hanson, N. R. 1963. *Patterns of Discovery*. Cambridge, Eng.: Cambridge University Press.

Harris, M. 1974. *Cows, Pigs, Wars, and Witches*. New York: Random House.

Hattis, D., and D. Kennedy. 1990. "Assessing Risks from Health Hazards: An Imperfect Science." In T. S. Glickman and M. Gough, eds. *Readings in Risk*. Washington, DC: Resources for the Future, 156–163.

Hauptmanns, U., M. Herttrich, and W. Werner. 1987. *Technische Risiken: Ermittlung und Beurteilung.* Berlin: Springer-Verlag.

Heimer, C. 1988. "Social Structure, Psychology and the Estimation of Risk." *Annual Review of Sociology* 14:491–519.

Henrion, M., and B. Fischhoff. 1986. "Assessing Uncertainties in Physical Constants." *American Journal of Physics* 54:791–798.

Henshel, R. L. 1982. "Sociology and Social Forecasting." *Annual Review of Sociology* 8:57–79.

Hesse, M. 1966. *Models and Analogies in Science.* Notre Dame, IN: University of Notre Dame Press.

Hilgartner, S., and C. L. Bosk. 1988. "The Rise and Fall of Social Problems: A Public Arenas Model." *American Journal of Sociology* 94:53–78.

Hogarth, R., and H. Kunreuther. 1989. "Risk, Ambiguity, and Insurance." *Journal of Risk and Uncertainty* 2:5–35.

Hohenemser, C., R. E. Kasperson, and R. W. Kates. 1982. "Causal Structure: A Framework for Policy Formulation." In C. Hohenemser and J. X. Kasperson, eds. *Risk in the Technological Society.* Boulder, CO: Westview Press.

Hohenemser, C. et al. 1983. *Methods for Analyzing and Comparing Technological Hazards: Definitions and Factor Structures.* CENTED Research Report No. 3. Worcester, MA: Center for Technology, Environment, and Development (CENTED), Clark University.

Hohenemser, C., R. W. Kates, and P. Slovic. 1983. "The Nature of Technological Hazard." *Science* 220:378–384.

———. 1985. "A Causal Taxonomy." In R. W. Kates, C. Hohenemser, and J. X. Kasperson, eds. *Perilous Progress: Managing the Hazards of Technology.* Boulder, CO: Westview Press, 67–89.

Holdren, J. P. 1976. "The Nuclear Controversy and the Limitations of Decision-Making by Experts." *Bulletin of the Atomic Scientists* 32(3):20–22.

Hollander, R. D., and N. H. Steneck. 1990. "Science- and Engineering-Related Ethics and Values Studies: Characteristics of an Emerging Field of Research." *Science, Technology, and Human Values* 15(1):84–104.

Hollis, M., and S. Lukes, eds. 1982. *Rationality and Relativism.* Oxford: Blackwell.

Hoos, I. 1980. "Risk Assessment in Social Perspective." In Council on Radiation Protection and Measurements, eds. *Perceptions of Risk.* Washington, DC: National Council on Radiation Protection, 57–85.

Horton, R., and R. Finnegan, eds. 1973. *Modes of Thought.* London: Faber and Faber.

Hospers, J. 1967. *An Introduction to Philosophical Analysis.* London: Routledge and Kegan Paul.

Hyman, E. L., and B. Stiftel. 1988. *Combining Facts and Values in Environmental Impact Assessment.* Boulder, CO: Westview Press.

Hynes, M. E., and E. H. Vanmarcke. 1977. "Reliability of Embankment Performance Predictions." In R. N. Dubey and N. C. Lind, eds. *Mechanics in Engineering.* Waterloo, Ont.: University of Waterloo Press, 367–384.

Illich, I., I. K. Zola, J. McKnight, J. Caplan, and H. Shaiken. 1977. *Disabling Professions.* London: Marion Boyars.

Jasanoff, S. 1982. "Science and the Limits of Administrative Rule-Making: Lessons from the OSHA Cancer Policy." *Osgood Hall Law Journal* 20:536–561.

————. 1986. *Risk Management and Political Culture.* New York: Russell Sage Foundation.

Jodha, N. S. 1987. "A Case Study of Degradation of Common Property Resources in India." In P. Blaikie and H. Brookfield, eds. *Land Degradation and Society.* London: Methuen, 196–207.

————. 1990. *Rural Common Property Resources: Contributions and Crisis.* New Delhi: Society for Promotion of Wastelands Development.

Johnson, B. B. 1987. "The Environmentalist Movement and Grid/Group Analysis: A Modest Critique." In B. B. Johnson and V. T. Covello, eds. *The Social and Cultural Construction of Risk.* Dordrecht: Reidel, 147–178.

Johnson, B. B., and V. T. Covello, eds. 1987. *The Social and Cultural Construction of Risk.* Dordrecht: Reidel.

Johnson, E. J., and A. Tversky. 1984. "Representations of Perceptions of Risk." *Journal of Experimental Psychology: General* 113:55–70.

Jones, E. E., et al. 1984. *Social Stigma: The Psychology of Marked Relationships.* New York: W. H. Freeman.

Jungermann, H. 1986. "Two Camps of Rationality." In H. L. Arkes and K. R. Hammond, eds. *Judgment and Decision Making: An Introductory Reader.* Cambridge, Eng.: Cambridge University Press, 627–641.

Jungermann, H., and P. Slovic. In press. "Die Psychologie der Kognition und Evaluation von Risiko." In G. Bechmann, ed. *Technik und Gesellschaft.* Opladen: Westdeutscher-Verlag.

Just, R. E., D. L. Heuth, and A. Schmitz. 1982. *Applied Welfare Economics and Public Policy.* Englewood Cliffs, NJ: Prentice-Hall.

Kahneman, D., P. Slovic, and A. Tversky, eds. 1982. *Judgment Under Uncertainty: Heuristics and Biases.* New York: Cambridge University Press.

Kahneman, D., and A. Tversky. 1974. "Judgment Under Uncertainty: Heuristics and Biases." *Science* 185:1124–1131.

————. 1979. "Prospect Theory: An Analysis of Decision Under Risk." *Econometrica* 47(2):263–291.

Kaprow, M. L. 1985. "Manufacturing Danger." *American Anthropologist* 87:357–364.

Kasperson, R. E. 1983a. "Acceptability of Human Risk." *Environmental Health Perspectives* 52:15–20.

————., ed. 1983b. *Equity Issues in Radioactive Waste Management.* Cambridge, MA: Oelgeschlager, Gunn and Hain.

————. 1986. "Hazardous Waste Facility Siting: Community, Firm, and Government Perspectives." In National Academy of Engineering. *Hazards: Technology and Fairness.* Washington, DC: National Academy Press.

————. 1990. "Social Realities in High-Level Radioactive Waste Management and Their Policy Implications." In *Proceedings, International High-Level Radioactive Waste Management Conference.* La Grange Park, IL: American Nuclear Society, Vol. 1, 512–518.

Kasperson, R. E., J. Emel, R. Goble, C. Hohenemser, J. X. Kasperson, and O. Renn. 1987. "Radioactive Wastes and the Social Amplification of Risk." In R. G. Post, ed. *Waste Management 87.* Tucson: Arizona Board of Regents.

Kasperson, R. E., and J. X. Kasperson. 1983. "Determining the Acceptability of Risk: Ethical and Policy Issues." In J. T. Rogers and D. V. Bates, eds. *As-*

sessment and Perception of Risk to Human Health. Ottawa: Royal Society of Canada, 135–155.

———. 1991. "Hidden Hazards." In D. C. Mayo and R. Hollander, eds. *Acceptable Evidence: Sciences and Values in Risk Management*. Oxford: Oxford University Press.

Kasperson, R. E., R. W. Kates, and C. Hohenemser. 1985. "Hazard Management." In R. W. Kates, C. Hohenemser, and Jeanne X. Kasperson, eds. *Perilous Progress: Managing the Hazards of Technology*. Boulder, CO: Westview Press, 43–66.

Kasperson, R. E., O. Renn, P. Slovic, H. S. Brown, J. Emel, R. Goble, J. X. Kasperson, and S. Ratick. 1988. "The Social Amplification of Risk: A Conceptual Framework." *Risk Analysis* 8(2):177–187.

Kasperson, R. E., O. Renn, P. Slovic, J. X. Kasperson, and S. Emani. 1989. "The Social Amplification of Risk: Media and Public Response." In R. G. Post, ed. *Waste Management '89*. Tucson: Arizona Board of Regents, 131–135.

Kasperson, R. E., S. Tuler, and J. Himmelberger. 1990. "Field Studies of the Social Amplification of Risk." Unpublished manuscript, Clark University, Center for Technology, Environment, and Development (CENTED).

Kates, R. W. 1962. *Hazard and Choice Perception in Flood Plain Management*. Research Paper No. 78. Chicago: Department of Geography, University of Chicago.

———. 1971. "Natural Hazard in Human Ecological Perspective: Hypothesis and Models." *Economic Geography* 47(3):438–451.

———. 1978. *Risk Assessment of Environmental Hazard*. Scientific Committee on Problems of the Environment, SCOPE 8. New York: Wiley.

Kates, R. W., C. Hohenemser, and J. X. Kasperson, eds. 1985. *Perilous Progress: Managing the Hazards of Technology*. Boulder, CO: Westview Press.

Kates, R. W., and J. X. Kasperson. 1983. "Comparative Risk Analysis of Technological Hazards (A Review)." *Proceedings, National Academy of Sciences* 80:7027–7038.

Keeney, R. L. 1992. *Value Focused Thinking: A Path to Creative Decisionmaking*. Cambridge, MA: Harvard University Press.

Keeney, R. L., and H. Raiffa. 1976. *Decisions with Multiple Objectives: Preferences and Value Tradeoffs*. New York: Wiley.

Keeney, R. L., O. Renn, and D. von Winterfeldt. 1987. "Structuring West Germany's Energy Objectives." *Energy Policy* 15 (August):353–362.

Keeney, R. L., and D. von Winterfeldt. 1987. *Operational Procedures to Evaluate Decisions with Multiple Objectives*. EPRI Research Report No. RP–2141–10. Palo Alto, CA: Electric Power Research Institute.

———. 1988. "The Analysis and Its Role for Selecting Nuclear Waste Repository Sites." In G. K. Rand, ed. *Operational Research '87*. Amsterdam: Elsevier, 687–701.

———. 1989. "On the Uses of Expert Judgment on Complex Technical Problems." *IEEE Transactions on Engineering Management* 36(2):83–86.

———. 1991. "Eliciting Probabilities from Experts in Complex Technical Problems." *IEEE Transactions on Engineering Management* 38(3):191–201.

Keepin, B., and B. Wynne. 1984. "Technical Analysis of IIASA Energy Scenarios." *Nature* 312:691–695.

Kelman, S. 1981a. "Cost-Benefit Analysis: An Ethical Critique." *Regulation* 5(1):33–40.

———. 1981b. *Regulating America, Regulating Sweden*. Cambridge, MA: MIT Press.

Kemp, R. 1980. "Planning, Legitimation, and the Development of Nuclear Energy: A Critical Theoretic Analysis of the Windscale Inquiry." *Urban and Regional Research* 4:350–371.

Keown, C. F. 1989. "Risk Perceptions of Hong Kongese vs. Americans." *Risk Analysis* 9(3):401–405.

Kierkegaard, S. 1985. *Philosophical Fragments*. Princeton, NJ: Princeton University Press.

Kitschelt, H. 1980. *Kernenergiepolitik. Arena eines gesellschaftlichen Konflikts*. Frankfurt: Campus.

———. 1986. "New Social Movements in West Germany and the United States." *Political Power and Social Theory* 5:286–324.

Klandermanns, B. 1984. "Mobilization and Participation: Social Psychological Expansion of Resource Mobilization Theory." *American Sociological Review* 49:583–600.

Kraus, N. N., T. Malmfors, and P. Slovic. 1992. "Intuitive Toxicology: Expert and Lay Judgments of Chemical Risks." Risk Analysis 12(2):215–232.

Kraus, N. N., and P. Slovic. 1988. "Taxonomic Analysis of Perceived Risk: Modeling Individual and Group Perceptions Within Homogeneous Hazard Domains." *Risk Analysis* 8(3):435–455.

Kreps, G. A. 1984. "Sociological Inquiry and Disaster Research." In Ralph H. Turner and James Short, eds. *Annual Review of Sociology* 10:309–330.

Kreps, G. A. 1987. "Classical Themes, Structural Sociology, and Disaster Research." In R. R. Dynes, B. de Marchi, and C. Pelanda, eds. *Sociology of Disasters*. Milan: Franco Angeli, 357–401.

———. 1989. *Social Structure and Disaster*. Durham, NC: Duke University Press.

Krewski, D., and P. L. Birkwood. 1987. "Risk Assessment and Risk Management." *Risk Abstracts* 4(2):53–61.

Krimsky, S. 1984. "Epistemic Considerations on the Value of Folk-Wisdom in Science and Technology." *Policy Studies Review* 3:246–262.

Krimsky, S., and A. Plough. 1988. *Environmental Hazards: Communicating Risks as a Social Process*. Dover, MA: Auburn House.

Krohn, W., and J. Weyer. 1989. "Die Gesellschaft als Labor: Die Erzeugung Sozialer Risiken durch Experimentele Forschung." *Soziale Welt* 3:349–373.

Kroll-Smith, J. S., and S. R. Couch. 1990. *The Real Disaster Is Above Ground: A Mine Fire and Social Conflict*. Lexington: University Press of Kentucky.

Kroonenberg, P. M. 1983. *Three-Mode Principal Component Analysis: Theory and Applications*. Leiden: DSWO Press.

Kuhn, T. 1962. *The Structure of Scientific Revolutions*. Chicago: University of Chicago Press.

Kunreuther, H. 1973. *Recovery from Natural Disasters: Insurance or Federal Aid?* Washington, DC: American Enterprise Institute for Public Policy Research.

Kunreuther, H., D. Easterling, W. Desvousges, and P. Slovic. 1990. "Public Attitude Toward Siting a High-Level Nuclear Waste Repository in Nevada." *Risk Analysis* 10(4):469–484.

Kunreuther, H., R. Ginsberg, L. Miller, P. Sagi, P. Slovic, B. Borkan, and N. Katz. 1978. *Disaster Insurance Protection: Public Policy Lessons.* New York: Wiley.

Kunreuther, H., P. Kleindorfer, P. Knez, and R. Yaksick. 1987. "A Compensation Mechanism for Siting Noxious Facilities: Theory and Experimental Design." *Journal of Environmental Economics and Management* 14:371–383.

Kunreuther, H. and J. Linnerooth. 1982. *Risk Analysis and Decision Processes: The Siting of Liquefied Energy Gas Facilities in Four Countries.* Berlin: Springer–Verlag.

Kunreuther, H., J. Linnerooth, and R. Starnes, eds. 1982. *Liquefied Energy Gas Facility Siting.* Laxenberg, Austria: International Institute for Applied Systems Analysis.

Kunreuther, H., and P. Portney. 1991. "Wheel of Fortune: A Lottery/Auction Mechanism for Siting of Noxious Facilities." *Journal of Energy Engineering* 117(3):125–132.

Lasswell, H. 1958. *Politics: Who Gets What, When, How.* New York: Meridian.

Latour, B. 1983. "Give Me a Laboratory and I Will Raise the World." In M. Mulkay and K. Knorr-Cetina, eds. *Science Observed.* London: Sage, 141–170.

———. 1986. *Science in Action.* London: Open University Press.

———. 1991. "The Impact of Science Studies on Political Philosophy." *Science, Technology and Human Values* 16(1):3–19.

Laurence, D., and B. Wynne. 1989. "Toxic Wastes in Europe: Towards a Single Market?" *Environment* 31(4):12–17, 34–35.

Lave, L. B. 1987. "Health and Safety Risk Analyses: Information for Better Decisions." *Science* 236:291–295.

Lave, L. B., and T. Lave. 1991. "Public Perception of the Risk of Floods: Implications for Communication." *Risk Analysis* 11(2):255–267.

Lave, L. B., and J. Menkes. 1985. "Managing Risk: A Joint U.S.–German Perspective." *Risk Analysis* 5(1):17–23.

Lawless, E. W. 1977. *Technology and Social Shock.* New Brunswick, NJ: Rutgers University Press.

Lawless, W. F. 1985. "Problems with Military Nuclear Waste." *Bulletin of the Atomic Scientists* 41(10):38–42.

———. 1991. "A Social Psychological Analysis of the Practice of Science: The Problem of Military Waste Management." In R. G. Post, ed. *Waste Management '91: Waste Processing, Transportation, Storage and Disposal, Technical Programs and Public Education* (vol. 2). Tucson: University of Arizona, 91–96.

Lee, T. R. 1981. "The Public Perception of Risk and the Question of Irrationality." In Royal Society of Great Britain, ed. *Risk Perception.* Vol. 376. London: Royal Society, 5–16.

Levine, A. G. 1982. *Love Canal: Science, Politics, and People.* Lexington, MA: Lexington.

Levins, R., and R. Lewontin. 1985. *The Dialectical Biologist.* Cambridge, MA: Harvard University Press.

Lichtenberg, J., and D. MacLean. 1988. "The Role of the Media in Risk Communication." In H. Jungermann, R. E. Kasperson, and P. M. Wiedemann, eds. *Risk Communication.* Jülich, Ger.: Research Center KFA, 33–48.

Lichtenstein, S., and B. Fischhoff. 1977. "Do Those Who Know More Also Know More About How Much They Know?" *Organizational Behavior and Human Performance* 20:159–183.

Lichtenstein, S., B. Fischhoff, and L. D. Phillips. 1982. "Calibration of Probabilities: The State of the Art to 1980." In D. Kahneman, P. Slovic, and A. Tversky, eds. *Judgment Under Uncertainty: Heuristics and Biases*. New York: Cambridge University Press, 306–333.

Lichtenstein, S., P. Slovic, B. Fischhoff, M. Layman, and B. Combs. 1978. "Judged Frequency of Lethal Events." *Journal of Experimental Psychology: Human Learning and Memory* 4:551–578.

Lind, N. C. 1987. "Is Risk Analysis an Emerging Profession?" *Risk Abstracts* 4(4):167–169.

Lipsky, M. 1968. "Protest as a Political Resource." *American Political Science Review* 62:1144–1158.

Litai, D., D. D. Lanning, and N. C. Rasmussen. 1983. "The Public Perception of Risk." In V. T. Covello, W. G. Flamm, J. V. Rodricks, and R. G. Tardiff, eds. *The Analysis of Actual Versus Perceived Risks*. New York: Plenum Press, 213–224.

Litan, R. 1991. *A National Earthquake Mitigation and Insurance Plan: Response to Manufacturers*. Boston: Earthquake Project.

Lopes, L. 1983. "Some Thoughts on the Psychological Concept of Risk." *Journal of Experimental Psychology: Human Perception and Performance* 9:137–144.

———. 1987. "The Rhetoric of Irrationality." Paper presented to the Colloquium on Mass Communication, November 19, Madison, WI.

Lowi, T. J. 1964. "Four Systems of Policy, Politics, and Choice." *Public Administration Review* 32:298–310.

———. 1975. "Ein neuer Bezugsrahmen für die Analyse von Machstrukturen." In W. D. Narr and C. Offe, eds. *Wohlfahrtsstaat und Massenloyalität*. Cologne and Berlin: Pahl-Rugenstein, 133–145.

Lowrance, W. 1976. *Of Acceptable Risk: Science and the Determination of Safety*. Los Altos, CA: William Kaufmann.

Lucas, R. A. 1969. *Men in Crisis: A Study of a Mine Disaster*. New York: Basic Books.

Luce, R. D., and E. U. Weber. 1986. "An Axiomatic Theory of Conjoint, Expected Risk." *Journal of Mathematical Psychology* 30:188–205.

Luhmann, N. 1982. *Soziologische Aufklärung*. Vol. 2. 2nd ed. Opladen: Westdeutscher Verlag.

———. 1986. *Ökologische Kommunikation*. Opladen: Westdeutscher Verlag.

———. 1990. "Technology, Environment, and Social Risk: A Systems Perspective." *Industrial Crisis Quarterly* 4:223–231.

Lundqvist, L. 1980. *The Hare and the Tortoise*. Ann Arbor: University of Michigan Press.

Lynn, F. M. 1986. "The Interplay of Science and Values in Assessing and Regulating Environmental Risks." *Science, Technology, and Human Values* 11(2):40–50.

———. 1987. "OSHA's Carcinogens Standard: Round One on Risk Assessment

Models and Assumptions." In B. B. Johnson and V. T. Covello, eds. *The Social and Cultural Construction of Risk.* Dordrecht: Reidel, 345–358.

Lyotard, J. 1984. *The Postmodern Condition.* Minneapolis: University of Minnesota Press.

McAdam, H., J. McCarthy, and M. N. Zald. 1988. "Social Movements." In N. Smelser, ed. *Handbook of Sociology.* Newbury Park, CA: Sage, 695–737.

McCarthy, J. D., and M. N. Zald. 1973. *The Trend of Social Movements in America: Professionalization and Resource Mobilization.* Morristown, NJ: General Learning Press.

———. 1977. "Resource Mobilization and Social Movements: A Political Theory." *American Journal of Sociology* 82:1212–1241.

McCoy, C. 1989. "Broken Promises: Alyeska Record Shows How Big Oil Neglected Alaskan Environment." *Wall Street Journal,* July 6.

Macgill, S. M. 1987. *The Politics of Anxiety.* London: Pion.

McGregor, D., and P. Slovic. 1989. "Perception of Risk in Automotive Systems." *Human Factors* 31(4):377–389.

Mach, E. 1926. *Erkenntnis und Irrtum.* 5th ed. Leipzig: Johann Ambrosius Barth.

Machina, M. 1987. "Choice Under Uncertainty: Problems Solved and Unsolved." *Economic Perspectives* 1(1):121–154.

Machlis, G. E., and E. A. Rosa. 1990. "Desired Risk: Broadening the Social Amplification of Risk Framework." *Risk Analysis* 10(1):161–168.

MacIntyre, A. 1981. *After Virtue: A Study in Moral Theory.* Notre Dame, IN: University of Notre Dame Press.

McKay, B. 1990. Petitioners Opening Brief: *State of Nevada v. J. D. Watkins, Secretary of the U.S. Department of Energy.* U.S. Court of Appeals for the Ninth Circuit (Docket Nos. 86–7308 and 90–70004).

MacLean, D. 1986. "Social Values and the Distribution of Risk." In D. MacLean, ed. *Values at Risk.* Totowa, NJ: Rowman and Allanheld, 75–93.

McLuhan, M. 1970. *From Kliché to Archetype.* New York: Viking Press.

Malinowski, B. 1948. *Magic, Science and Religion, and Other Essays.* Boston: Beacon Press.

Mandl, L., and J. Lathrop. 1983. "LEG Risk Assessments: Experts Disagree." In H. Kunreuther, ed. *Risk Analysis and Decision Processes: The Siting of Liquefied Energy Gas Facilities in Four Countries.* Berlin: Springer-Verlag.

Manes, A. 1938. *Insurance: Facts and Problems; Selected Lectures on Business Administration and Economics.* New York: Harper.

March, J., and H. Simon. 1958. *Organizations.* New York: Wiley.

Markowitz, J. 1991. "Kommunikation über Risiken: Eine Problemskizze." Unpublished manuscript, University of Bielefeld.

Marshall, E. 1979. "Public Attitudes to Technological Progress." *Science* 205:281–285.

———. 1983. "The Salem Case: A Failure of Nuclear Logic." *Science* 220:280–282.

Marx-Ferree, M., and F. Miller. 1985. "Mobilization and Meaning: Toward an Integration of Social Psychological and Resource Perspectives on Social Movements." *Sociological Inquiry* 55:39–51.

May, P. J. 1989. "Social Science Perspective: Risk as Disaster Preparedness." *International Journal of Mass Emergencies and Disaster* 7(3):281–303.

Mazur, A. 1981. *The Dynamics of Technical Controversy*. Washington, DC: Communications Press.

———. 1984. "Media Influences on Public Attitudes Toward Nuclear Power." In W. R. Freudenburg and E. A. Rosa, eds. *Public Reactions to Nuclear Power: Are There Critical Masses?* Boulder, CO: Westview Press, 97–114.

———. 1985. "Bias in Risk-Benefit Analysis." *Technology in Society* 7:25–30.

———. 1987. "Does Public Perception of Risk Explain the Social Response to Potential Hazard?" *Quarterly Journal of Ideology* 11:41–45.

Mechitov, A. I., and S. B. Rebrik. 1990. "Studies of Risk and Safety Perception in the USSR." In K. Borcherding, D. I. Larichev, and D. M. Messick, eds. *Contemporary Issues in Decision Making*. Amsterdam: Elsevier, 261–270.

Merkhofer, M. 1984. "Comparative Analysis of Formal Decision-Making Approaches." In V. T. Covello, J. Menkes, and J. Mumpower, eds. *Risk Evaluation and Management*. New York: Plenum Press, 183–220.

———. 1987. "Quantifying Judgmental Uncertainty: Methodology, Experiences, Insights." *IEEE Transactions on Systems, Man and Cybernetics*, SMC–17, 741–752.

Meyer-Abich, K. M. 1989. "Von der Wohlstandsgesellschaft zur Risikogesellschaft. Die gesellschaftliche Bewertung industriewirtschaftlicher Risiken." *Aus Politik und Zeitgeschichte* 36:31–42.

Mitchell, J. K. 1990. "Human Dimensions of Environmental Hazards: Complexity, Disparity, and the Search for Guidance." In A. Kirby, ed. *Nothing to Fear: Risks and Hazards in American Society*. Tucson: University of Arizona Press, 131–175.

Mitchell, R. C. 1980. "How 'Soft', 'Deep', Versus 'Left'? Present Constituencies in the Environmental Movement for Certain World Views." *Natural Resources* 20(2):345–358.

Morgan, M. G. 1990. "Choosing and Managing Technology-Induced Risks." In T. S. Glickman and M. Gough, eds. *Readings in Risk*. Washington, DC: Resources for the Future, 5–15.

Morgan, M. G., P. Slovic, I. Nair, D. Geisler, D. MacGregor, B. Fischhoff, D. Lincoln, and K. Florig. 1985. "Powerline Frequency Electric and Magnetic Fields: A Pilot Study of Risk Perception." *Risk Analysis* 5(2):139–149.

Morone, J. G., and E. J. Woodhouse. 1986. *Averting Catastrophe*. Berkeley: University of California Press.

Mosleh, A., V. M. Bier, and G. Apostolakis. 1988. "A Critique of Current Practice for Use of Expert Opinion in Probability Assessment." *Reliability Engineering and System Safety* 20:63–85.

Münch, R. 1982. *Basale Soziologie: Soziologie der Politik*. Opladen: Westdeutscher Verlag.

Mydans, S. 1989. "Runaway Freight Train Derails, Killing Three." *New York Times*, May 13, 8.

Nagel, E. 1961. *The Structure of Science: Problems in the Logic of Scientific Explanations*. New York: Harcourt, Brace and World.

Nelkin, D. 1971. "Scientists in an Environmental Controversy." *Science Studies* 1:245–261.

———. 1982. "Blunders in the Business of Risk." *Nature* 298:775–776.

———. 1985. *The Language of Risk*. Beverly Hills, CA: Sage Publications.

————. ed. 1979. *Controversy: Politics of Technical Decisions*. Beverly Hills, CA: Sage Publications.

Nelkin, D., and M. Pollack. 1981. *The Atom Besieged*. Cambridge, MA: MIT Press.

Newcomb, M. D. 1986. "Nuclear Attitudes and Reactions: Associations with Depression, Drug Use and Quality of Life." *Journal of Personality and Social Psychology* 50(5):906–920.

Nichols, E., and A. Wildavsky. 1987. "Regulating by the Numbers: Probabilistic Risk Assessment and Nuclear Power." Presented at the Annual Meeting of the American Sociological Association, Chicago, August.

Nowotny, H. 1979. *Kernenergie: Gefahr oder Notwendigkeit*. Frankfurt am Main: Suhrkamp Verlag.

Nowotny, H., and R. Eisikovic. 1990. *Enstehung, Wahrnehmung und Umgang mit Risiken*. Bern: Schweizerischer Wissenschaftsrat.

NRC (National Research Council, Committee on the Institutional Means for Assessment of Risks to Public Health). 1983. *Risk Assessment in the Federal Government: Managing the Process*. Washington, DC: National Academy Press.

NRC (National Research Council, Committee on Risk Perception and Communication). 1989. *Improving Risk Communication*. Washington, DC: National Academy Press.

NRC (Nuclear Regulatory Commission). 1975. *The Reactor Safety Study: An Assessment of Accidental Risks on US Commercial Nuclear Power Plants*. NUREG–74/104, WASH 1400. Washington, DC: Government Printing Office.

NSF (National Science Foundation). 1979. *Addition of a Risk Analysis Function to the Activities of the Division of Policy Research and Analysis in the Directorate for Scientific, Technological, and International Affairs* (STIA). AD/STIA Bulletin No. 79–7.

Offenbacher, E. L., and P. Slovic. 1989. "Societal Risk from a Thermodynamic Perspective." In J. J. Bonin and D. E. Stevenson, eds. *Risk Assessment in Setting National Priorities*. New York: Plenum Press, 119–134.

Olson, M. 1965. *The Logic of Collective Action*. Cambridge, MA: Harvard University Press.

O'Riordan, T. 1983. "The Cognitive and Political Dimension of Risk Analysis." *Environmental Psychology* 3:345–354.

O'Riordan, T., and S. Rayner. 1990. "Chasing a Spectre: Risk Management for Global Environmental Change." In R. E. Kasperson, K. Dow, D. Golding, and J. X. Kasperson, eds. *Understanding Global Environmental Change: The Contribution of Risk Analysis and Management*. Worcester, MA: The Earth Transformed Program, Clark University, 45–62.

O'Riordan, T., and B. Wynne. 1987. "Regulating Environmental Risks: A Comparative Perspective." In P. R. Kleindorfer and H. C. Kunreuther, eds. *Insuring and Managing Hazardous Risks: From Seveso to Bhopal and Beyond*. Berlin: Springer-Verlag, 389–410.

Ottoboni, M. A. 1984. *The Dose Makes the Poison: A Plain-Language Guide to Toxicology*. Berkeley, CA: Vincente Books.

Otway, H. 1980. "Perception and Acceptance of Environmental Risk." *Zeitschrift für Umweltpolitik* 2:593–616.

————. 1987. "Experts, Risk Communication and Democracy." *Risk Analysis* 7(2):125–129.

Otway, H., and J. J. Cohen. 1975. *Revealed Preferences: Comments on the Starr Benefit-Risk Relationships*. RM–76–80. Laxenberg, Austria: International Institute for Applied Systems Analysis.

Otway, H., and R. Erdman. 1969. "Reactor Siting and Design from a Risk Viewpoint." *Nuclear Engineering and Design* 12:365–376.

Otway, H., and M. Fishbein. 1977. *Public Attitudes and Decision Making*. Research Memorandum 77–54. Laxenburg, Austria: International Institute for Applied Systems Analysis.

Otway, H., D. Maurer, and K. Thomas. 1978. "Nuclear Power: The Question of Public Acceptance." *Futures* 10:109–118.

Otway, H., and R. Misenta. 1980. "Some Human Performance Paradoxes of Nuclear Operations." *Futures* 12:340–357.

Otway, H., and P. Pahner. 1976. "Risk Assessment." *Futures* 8(2):210–222.

Otway, H., and J. Ravetz. 1984. "On the Regulation of Technologies: Examining the Linear Model." *Futures* 16:217–232.

Otway, H., and K. Thomas. 1982. "Reflections on Risk Perception and Policy." *Risk Analysis* 2(2):69–82.

Otway, H., and D. von Winterfeldt. 1982. "Beyond Acceptable Risk: On the Social Acceptability of Technologies." *Policy Sciences* 14(3):247–256.

Otway, H., and B. Wynne. 1989. "Risk Communication: Paradigm and Paradox." *Risk Analysis* 9(2):141–145.

Pacey, A. 1990. *Technology in World Civilization*. Oxford: Blackwell.

Palmlund, I. 1989. "The Case of Estrogens: An Inquiry into Societal Risk Evaluation." Unpublished doctoral dissertation, Clark University.

Parsons, T. E. 1951. *The Social System*. Glencoe: Free Press.

————. 1963. "On the Concept of Political Power." *Proceedings of the American Philosophical Society* 17:352–403.

Parsons, T. E., and E. A. Shils. 1951. *Toward a General Theory of Action*. Cambridge, Eng.: Cambridge University Press.

Parsons, T. E., and N. Smelser. 1956. *Economy and Society*. Glencoe: Free Press.

Paté-Cornell, M. E. 1990. "Organizational Aspects of Engineering System Safety: The Case of Offshore Platforms." *Science* 250 (Nov. 30):1210–1217.

Paté-Cornell, M. E. and R. G. Bea. 1992. "Management Errors and System Reliability: A Probabilistic Approach and Application to Offshore Platforms." *Risk Analysis* 12(1):1–18.

Payne, J. W., J. R. Bettman, and E. J. Johnson. 1990. "The Adaptive Decision Maker: Effort and Accuracy in Choice." In R. M. Hogarth, ed. *Insights in Decision Making: A Tribute to Hillel Einhorn*. Chicago: University of Chicago Press, 129–153.

Peelle, E., and R. Ellis. 1987. "Beyond the 'Not-in-My-Backyard' Impasse." *Forum for Applied Research and Public Policy* (Fall):68–77.

Peltu, M. 1988. "Media Reporting of Risk Information: Uncertainties and the Future." In H. Jungermann, R. E. Kasperson, and P. M. Wiedemann, eds. *Risk Communication*, Jülich, Ger.: Research Center KFA, 11–32.

Perrow, C. 1984. *Normal Accidents: Living with High-Risk Technologies*. New York: Basic Books.

————. 1986. "The Habit of Courting Disaster." *The Nation* 243 (October 11):1.

Perusse, M. 1980. "Dimensions of Perception and Recognition of Danger." Unpublished doctoral dissertation, University of Aston, Birmingham, England.

Peters, H. P. 1990. "Risiko-Kommunikation: Kernenergie." In H. Jungermann, B. Rohrmann, and P. M. Wiedemann, eds. *Risiko-Konzepte, Risiko-Konflikte, Risiko-Kommunikation*. Monograph Series of the Research Center Jülich, Vol. 3. Jülich, Ger.: Research Center, 59–148.

————. 1991. "Warner oder Angstmacher? Thema Risikokommunikation." In K. Mertens, S. J. Schmidt, and S. Weischenberg, eds. *Funkkolleg 'Medien und Kommunikation' Konstruktionen von Wirklichkeit*. Studienbrief 9. Weinheim and Basel: Beltz, 74–108.

Peters, H. P., G. Albrecht, L. Hennen, and H. U. Stegelmann. 1987. *Reactions of the German Population to the Chernobyl Accident: Results of a Survey*. Jülich, Ger.: Nuclear Research Center.

Peterson, J. S. 1988. "Perception vs. Reality of Radiological Impact: The Goiania Model." *Nuclear News* 31(14):84–90.

Plough, A., and S. Krimsky. 1987. "The Emergence of Risk Communication Studies: Social and Political Context." *Science, Technology, and Human Values* 12(3–4):4–10.

Polanyi, M. 1958. *Personal Knowledge*. London: Routledge and Kegan Paul.

Pollatsek, A., and A. Tversky. 1970. "A Theory of Risk." *Journal of Mathematical Psychology* 7:540–553.

Popper, F. J. 1983. "LP/HC and LULUs: The Political Uses of Risk Analysis in Land-Use Planning." *Risk Analysis* 3(4):255–263.

Popper, K. R. 1959. *The Logic of Scientific Discovery*. New York: Harper and Row.

Portney, K. E. 1991. *Siting Hazardous Waste Treatment Facilities: The NIMBY Syndrome*. Westport, CT: Auburn House.

Portney, P. R., A. M. Freeman III, R. H. Haveman, H. M. Peskin, E. P. Seskin, and V. K. Smith. 1978. *Current Issues in U.S. Environmental Policy*. Baltimore: Johns Hopkins University Press for Resources for the Future.

President's Commission on the Accident at Three Mile Island. 1979. *The Need for Change: The Legacy of Three Mile Island*. Washington, DC: Government Printing Office.

Primack, J. 1975. "Nuclear Reactor Safety: An Introduction to the Issues." *Bulletin of the Atomic Scientists* 31(7):15–17.

Raiffa, H. 1982. *The Art and Science of Negotiation*. Cambridge, MA: Harvard University Press.

Rappaport, R. A. 1988. "Toward Postmodern Risk Analysis." *Risk Analysis* 8(2):189–191.

Ravetz, J. R. 1971. *Scientific Knowledge and Its Social Problems*. Oxford: Oxford University Press.

————. 1977. *The Acceptability of Risks*. London: Council for Science and Society.

————. 1986. "Usable Knowledge, Usable Ignorance." In W. C. Clark and R. E. Munn, eds. *Sustainable Development of the Biosphere*. Cambridge, Eng.: Cambridge University Press, 415–430.

————. 1990. *The Merger of Knowledge with Power*. New York: Mansell.

Ravetz, J. R., S. Macgill, and S. O. Funtowicz. 1986. "Disasters Bring the Technological Wizards to Heel." *Guardian*, May 19.

Raymond, C. A. 1985. "Risk in the Press: Conflicting Journalistic Ideologies." In D. Nelkin, ed. *The Language of Risk*. Beverly Hills, CA: Sage Publications, 97–133.

Rayner, S. 1979. "The Classification and Dynamics of Sectarian Organizations." Unpublished doctoral dissertation, University of London.

———. 1982. "The Perception of Time and Space in Egalitarian Sects." In M. Douglas, ed. *Essays in the Sociology of Perception*. London: Routledge and Kegan Paul.

———. 1984. "Disagreeing About Risk: The Institutional Cultures of Risk Management and Planning for Future Generations." In S. G. Hadden, ed. *Risk Analysis, Institutions, and Public Policy*. Port Washington: Associated Faculty Press, 150–178.

———. 1986a. "Management of Radiation Hazards in Hospitals." *Social Studies of Science* 16:4573–4591.

———. 1986b. "The Politics of Schism." In J. Law, ed. *Power, Action, and Belief*. London: Routledge and Kegan Paul.

———. 1987a. "Learning from the Blind Men and the Elephant." In V. T. Covello, L. Lave, A. Moghissi, and V. Uppuluri, eds. *Uncertainty in Risk Assessment, Risk Management and Decision Making*. New York: Plenum Press.

———. 1987b. "Risk and Relativism in Science for Policy." In B. B. Johnson and V. T. Covello, eds. *The Social and Cultural Construction of Risk*. Dordrecht: Reidel, 5–23.

———. 1988a. "Muddling Through Metaphors to Maturity: A Commentary on Kasperson et al., The Social Amplification of Risk." *Risk Analysis* 8(2):201–204.

———. 1988b. "Risk Communication in the Search for a Global Climate Management Strategy." In H. Jungermann et al., eds. *Risk Communication*. Jülich, Ger.: Research Center.

———. 1988c. "The Rules that Keep Us Equal." In J. Flanagan and S. Rayner, eds. *Rules, Decisions, and Inequality in Egalitarian Societies*. Avebury: Farnborough.

———. 1990. *Risk in Cultural Perspective: Acting Under Uncertainty*. Norwell, MA: Kluwer.

———. 1991. "A Cultural Perspective on the Structure and Implementation of Global Environmental Agreements." *Evaluation Review* 15(1):75–102.

Rayner, S., and R. Cantor. 1987. "How Fair Is Safe Enough? The Cultural Approach to Societal Technology Choice." *Risk Analysis* 7(1):3–13.

Rayner, S., and L. Rickert. 1988. "Perception of Risk: The Social Context of Public Concern over Non-ionizing Radiation." In M. Repacholi, ed. *Non-ionizing Radiation*. London: International Radiation Protection Association Publications.

Renn, O. 1981. *Man, Technology, and Risk*. Report of the Research Center Jülich. Jül-Spez–115. Jülich, Ger.: Research Center.

———. 1983. "Technology, Risk, and Public Perception." *Angewandte Systemanalyse/Applied Systems Analysis* 4(2):50–65.

———. 1985. "Risk Analysis—Scope and Limitations." In H. Otway and M. Peltu, eds. *Regulating Industrial Risks: Science, Hazards and Public Protection*. London: Butterworths, 111–127.

————. 1989a. "Risikowahrnehmung—Psychologische Determinanten bei der intuitiven Erfassung und Bewertung von technischen Risiken." In G. Hosemann, ed. *Risiko in der Industriegesellschaft*. Nürnberg: Universitätsbibliothek, 167–192.

————. 1989b. "Risk Communication in the Community: European Lessons from the Seveso Directive." *Journal of the Air Pollution Control Association* 40(9):1301–1308.

————. 1990. "Risk Perception and Risk Management: A Review." *Risk Abstracts* 7(1):1–9; 7(2):1–9.

————. 1991a. "Risikokommunikation: Bedingungen und Probleme eines rationalen Diskurses über die Akzeptabilität von Risiken." In J. Schneider, ed. *Risiko und Sicherheit technischer Systeme. Auf der Suche nach neuen Ansätzen.* Basel: Birkhäuser, 193–209.

————. 1991b. "Risk Communication and the Social Amplification of Risk." In R. E. Kasperson and P.J.M. Stallen, eds. *Communicating Risks to the Public: International Perspectives*. Dordrecht: Kluwer Academic Publishers, 287–324.

————. 1991c. "Die gesellschaftliche Erfahrung und Bewertung von Risiken: Eine Ortsbestimmung." *Schweizerische Zeitschrift für Soziologie* 3:307–355.

————. 1992. "Risk Communication: Towards a Rational Dialogue with the Public." *Journal of Hazardous Materials* 29:465–519.

Renn, O., W. Burns, J. X. Kasperson, R. E. Kasperson, and P. Slovic. Forthcoming. "The Social Amplification of Risk: Theoretical Foundations and Empirical Applications." *Journal of Social Issues*.

Renn, O., and J. Kals. 1990. "Technische Risikoanalyse und unternehmerisches Handeln." In M. Schüz, ed. *Risiko und Wagnis: Die Herausforderung der industriellen Welt*. Vol. 1. Pfullingen, Ger.: Neske, 60–80.

Renn, O., and E. Swaton. 1984. "Psychological and Sociological Approaches to Study Risk Perception." *Environment International* 10:557–575.

Renn, O., T. Webler, and B. Johnson. 1991. "Citizen Participation for Hazard Management." *Risk—Issues in Health and Safety* 3:12–22.

Reynolds, P. D. 1971. *A Primer in Theory Construction*. New York: Bobbs-Merrill.

Rip, A. 1985. "Experts in Public Arenas." In H. Otway and M. Peltu, eds. *Regulating Industrial Risks: Science, Hazards and Public Protection*. London: Butterworths, 94–110.

————. 1986. "Controversies as Informal Technology Assessment." *Knowledge* 8(December):349–371.

————. 1988. "Should Social Amplification of Risk Be Counteracted?" *Risk Analysis* 8(2):193–197.

————. 1991. "The Danger Culture of Industrial Society." In R. E. Kasperson and P.J.M. Stallen, eds. *Communicating Risks to the Public: International Perspectives*. Dordrecht: Kluwer.

Robertson, L. 1987. "Injury Prevention: Limits to Self-Protective Behavior." In N. Weinstein, ed. *Taking Care*. Cambridge, Eng.: Cambridge University Press.

Rochlin, G. I. 1987. "High-Tech, Low-Tech, and No-Tech: Complexity, Technology and Organization in U.S. Naval Flight Operations at Sea." Report based on ONR Contract N00014-86-0312. Berkeley: Institute of Government Studies, University of California.

Rochlin, G. I., T. R. La Porte, and K. H. Roberts. 1987. "The Self-Designing High-Reliability Organization: Aircraft Carrier Flight Operations at Sea." *Naval War College Review* 40(4):76–90.

Rogovin, M., and G. T. Frampton, Jr. 1980. *Three Mile Island:A Report to the Commissioners and to the Public.* Washington, DC: U.S. Nuclear Regulatory Commission, Special Inquiry Group.

Rohrmann, B. 1991. "Perception and Evaluation of Risks: A Cross-Cultural Comparison." Unpublished manuscript, University of Mannheim.

Rosa, E. A. 1988. "NAMBY PAMBY and NIMBY PIMBY: Public Issues in the Siting of Hazardous Waste Facilities." *Forum for Applied Research and Public Policy* 3:114.

Rosa, E. A., and W. R. Freudenburg. 1984. "Nuclear Power at the Crossroads." In W. R. Freudenburg and E. A. Rosa, eds. *Public Reactions to Nuclear Power: Are There Critical Masses?* Boulder, CO: American Association for the Advancement of Science/Westview Press, 3–37.

―――. Forthcoming. "The Historical Development of Public Reactions to Nuclear Power: Implications for Nuclear Waste Policy." In R. E. Dunlap and M. E. Kraft, eds. *The Public and Nuclear Waste: The Socio-Political Dimensions of Repository Siting.* Durham, NC: Duke University Press.

Rosa, E. A., and R. Kleinhesselink. 1989. "A Comparative Analysis of Risk Perceptions in Japan and the United States." Paper presented at the Annual Meeting of the Society for Risk Analysis, San Francisco, October.

Rosa, E. A., G. E. Machlis, and K. M. Keating. 1988. "Energy and Society." *Annual Review of Sociology* 14:149–172.

Ross, L. D. 1977. "The Intuitive Psychologist and His Shortcomings: Distortions in the Attribution Process." In L. Berkowitz, ed. *Advances in Experimental Social Psychology.* Vol. 10. New York: Random House, 173–220.

Rowe, W. D. 1977. *An Anatomy of Risk.* New York: Wiley.

Royal Society, Study Group on Risk. 1983. *Risk Assessment: A Study Group Report.* London: Royal Society.

Rozelle, M. A. 1982. "The Incorporation of Public Values into Public Policy." Unpublished doctoral dissertation, Arizona State University.

Rubinstein, E. 1979. "The Accident that Shouldn't Have Happened: A Narrative Account of What Is Believed to Have Occurred, Based on Reports from Many Experts." *IEEE Spectrum* 16(11):33–42.

Rucht, D. 1990. "Campaigns, Skirmishes and Battles: Anti-Nuclear Movements in the USA, France and West Germany." *Industrial Crisis Quarterly* 4:193–222.

Ruckelshaus, W. D. 1987. "Communicating About Risk." In J. C. Davies, V. T. Covello, and F. W. Allen, eds. *Risk Communication.* Washington, DC: Conservation Foundation.

Russell, M. 1986. "Science in the Use of Risk Management." Presented at the Winter Toxicology Forum, Washington, DC, February.

Rycroft, R. W., J. L. Regens, and T. Dietz. 1987. "Acquiring and Utilizing Scientific and Technical Information to Identify Environmental Risks." *Science, Technology and Human Values* 12:125–130.

Samuelson, W., and R. Zeckhauser. 1988. "Status Quo Bias in Decision Making." *Journal of Risk and Uncertainty* 1:7–59.

Sandman, P. M. 1987. "Risk Communication: Facing Public Outrage." *EPA Journal* 13(9):21–22.

Sandman, P. M., N. D. Weinstein, and M. L. Klotz. 1987. "Public Response to the Risk from Geological Radon." *Journal of Communication* 37:93–108.

Sapolsky, H. M., ed. 1986. *Consuming Fears: The Politics of Product Risks.* New York: Basic Books.

Sattath, S., and A. Tversky. 1977. "Additive Similarity Trees." *Psychometrika* 42:319–345.

Saxe, J. G. 1868. *The Poems.* Boston: Osgood.

Schelling, T. C. 1984. *Choice and Consequence.* Cambridge, MA: Harvard University Press.

Scheuch, E. K. 1986. "Kontroverse um Energie—ein echter oder ein Stellvertreterstreit." In H. Michaelis, ed. *Existenzfrage Energie.* Düsseldorf: Econ Verlag, 279–293.

Schnaiberg, A. 1986. "The Role of Experts and Mediators in the Channeling of Distributional Conflicts." In A. Schnaiberg, N. Watts, and K. Zimmermann, eds. *Distributional Conflicts in Environmental-Resource Policy.* Aldershot: Gower, 348–362.

Schoemaker, P. 1982. "The Expected Utility Model: Its Variants, Purposes, Evidence and Limitations." *Journal of Economic Literature* 30:529–563.

Schön, D. A. 1983. *The Reflective Practitioner.* New York: Basic Books.

Schön, D. A., and C. Argyris. 1978. *Organizational Learning: A Theory of Action Perspective.* New York: Addison-Wesley.

Schot, J. 1991. "Constructive Technology Assessment: The Case of Clean Technology." *Science, Technology, and Human Values* 18(2):113–132.

Schumm, W. 1986. "Die Risikoproduktion kapitalistischer Industriegesellschaften. Zur These von der Risikogesellschaft." In R. Erd, O. Jacobi, and W. Schumm, eds. *Strukturwandel in der Industriegesellschaft.* Frankfurt am Main: Luchterhand, 236–261.

Schwarz, M., and M. Thompson. 1990. *Divided We Stand: Redefining Politics, Technology, and Social Choice.* Philadelphia: University of Pennsylvania Press.

Schwing, R. C., and W. A. Albers, eds. 1980. *Societal Risk Assessment: How Safe Is Safe Enough?* New York: Plenum Press.

Schwing, R. C., and D. B. Kamerud. 1987. "The Distribution of Risks: Vehicle Occupant Fatalities and Time of the Week." *Risk Analysis* 8(1):127–133.

Sellers, W. 1970. "The Language of Theories." Reprinted in Baruch A. Brody, ed. *Readings in the Philosophy of Science.* Englewood Cliffs, NJ: Prentice-Hall.

Sen, A. K. 1977. "Rational Fools: A Critique of the Behavioral Foundations of Economic Theory." *Philosophy and Public Affairs* 6:317–344.

Sewell, W.R.D. 1971. "Environmental Perceptions and Attitudes of Engineers and Public Health Officials." *Environment and Behavior* 3(1):23–59.

Shapere, D. 1977. "Scientific Theories and Their Domains." In F. Suppe, ed. *The Structure of Scientific Theories.* Urbana: University of Illinois Press.

Shapiro, S. 1987. "The Social Control of Impersonal Trust." *American Journal of Sociology* 93(3):623–658.

———. 1990. "Collaring the Crime, Not the Criminal: Reconsidering the Concept of White-Collar Crime." *American Sociological Review* 55(3):346–365.

Shepard, R. N., and P. Arabie. 1979. "Additive Clustering: Representation of Similarities as Combinations of Discrete Overlapping Properties." *Psychological Review* 86:87–123.

Short, J. F., Jr. 1984. "The Social Fabric at Risk: Toward the Social Transformation of Risk Analysis." *American Sociological Review* 49:711–725.

———. 1989. "On Defining, Describing, and Explaining Elephants (and Reactions to Them): Hazards, Disasters, and Risk Analysis." *International Journal of Mass Emergencies and Disasters* 7(3):397–418.

Shrader-Frechette, K. S. 1984. "Risk-Cost-Benefit Methodology and Equal Protection." In V. T. Covello, J. Menkes, and J. Mumpower, eds. *Risk Evaluation and Management.* New York: Plenum Press, 275–296.

———. 1985. *Risk Analysis and Scientific Method: Methodological and Ethical Problems with Evaluating Social Hazards.* Boston: Reidel.

———. 1991. *Risk and Rationality: Philosophical Foundations for Populist Reforms.* Berkeley, CA: University of California Press.

Sieber, J. E. 1974. "Effects of Decision Importance on Ability to Generate Warranted Subjective Uncertainty." *Journal of Personality and Social Psychology* 30(5):688–694.

Simon, H. A. 1955. "A Behavioral Model of Rational Choice." *Quarterly Journal of Economics* 69:99–118.

———. 1976. *Administrative Behavior: A Study of Decision-Making Processes in Administrative Organizations.* 3rd ed. New York: Basic Books.

Skolnick, J. 1969. "Why Cops Behave as They Do." In S. Dinitz, R. R. Dynes, and A. C. Clarke, eds. *Deviance: Studies in the Process of Stigmatization and Societal Reaction.* New York: Oxford University Press, 40–47.

Slovic, P. 1967. "The Relative Influence of Probabilities and Payoffs upon Perceived Risk of a Gamble." *Psychonomic Science* 9(4):223–224.

———. 1972. "Limitations of the Mind of Man: Implications for Decision Making in the Nuclear Age." In H. Otway, ed. *Risk vs. Benefit.* LA–4860-MS. Los Alamos: Los Alamos Scientific Laboratory, 41–49.

———. 1987. "Perception of Risk." *Science* 236:280–285.

Slovic, P., B. Fischhoff, and S. Lichtenstein. 1976. "Cognitive Processes and Societal Risk Taking." In J. S. Carroll and J. W. Payne, eds. *Cognition and Social Behavior.* Potomac, MD: Erlbaum, 165–184.

———. 1978. "Accident Probabilities in Seat Belt Usage: A Psychological Perspective." *Accident Analysis and Prevention* 10:281–285.

———. 1979. "Rating the Risks." *Environment* 21(3):14–20, 36–39.

———. 1981. "Perceived Risk: Psychological Factors and Social Implications." *Proceedings of the Royal Society of London.* A. 376:17–34.

———. 1984. "Perception and Acceptability of Risk from Energy Systems." In W. R. Freudenburg and E. A. Rosa, eds. *Public Reactions to Nuclear Power: Are There Critical Masses?* Boulder, CO: American Association for the Advancement of Science/Westview Press, 115–135.

———. 1985. "Characterizing Perceived Risk." In R. W. Kates, C. Hohenemser, and J. X. Kasperson, eds. *Perilous Progress: Managing the Hazards of Technology.* Boulder, CO: Westview Press.

Slovic, P., B. Fischhoff, S. Lichtenstein, B. Corrigan, and B. Combs. 1977. "Preference for Insuring Against Probable Small Losses: Insurance Implications." *Journal of Risk and Insurance* 44(2):237–258.

Slovic, P., J. H. Flynn, and M. Layman. 1991. "Perceived Risk, Trust, and the Politics of Nuclear Waste." *Science* 254:1603–1607.

Slovic, P., N. N. Kraus, H. Lappe, H. Letzel, and T. Malmfors. 1989. "Risk Perception of Prescription Drugs: Report on a Survey in Sweden." *Pharmaceutical Medicine* 4:43–65.

Slovic, P., N. N. Kraus, H. Lappe, and M. Major. 1991. "Risk Perception of Prescription Drugs: Report on a Survey in Canada." *Canadian Journal of Public Health* 82:S15–S20.

Slovic, P., H. Kunreuther, and G. White. 1974. "Decision Processes, Rationality and Adjustment to Natural Hazards." In G. F. White, ed. *Natural Hazards, Local, National and Global.* New York: Oxford University Press, 187–205.

Slovic, P., M. Layman, N. Kraus, J. Chalmers, G. Gesell, and J. Flynn. 1991. "Perceived Risk, Stigma, and Potential Economic Impacts of a High-Level Nuclear Waste Repository in Nevada." *Risk Analysis* 11(4): 683–696.

Slovic, P., and S. Lichtenstein. 1983. "Preference Reversals." *American Economic Review* 83:596–605.

Slovic, P., S. Lichtenstein, and W. Edwards. 1965. Boredom-Induced Changes in Preferences Among Bets." *American Journal of Psychology* 78:208–217.

Slovic, P., S. Lichtenstein, and B. Fischhoff. 1984. "Modeling the Societal Impact of Fatal Accidents." *Management Science* 30:464–474.

Slovic, P., D. MacGregor, and N. N. Kraus. 1987. "Perception of Risk from Automobile Safety Defects." *Accident Analysis and Prevention* 19:359–373.

Smith, N. K. 1963. *Immanuel Kant's Critique of Pure Reason.* London: Macmillan.

Smith, V. K. 1986. "A Conceptual Overview of the Foundations of Benefit-Cost Analysis." In J. D. Bentkover, V. T. Covello, and J. Mumpower, eds. *Benefits Assessment: The State of the Art.* Dordrecht: Reidel, 13–34.

Smith, V. K., W. M. Desvousges, A. Fisher, and F. R. Johnson. 1988. "Learning About Radon's Risk." *Journal of Risk and Uncertainty* 1(June):233–258.

Soderstrom, E. J., J. H. Sorensen, E. D. Copenhaver, and S. A. Carnes. 1984. "Risk Perception in an Interest Group Context: An Examination of the TMI Restart Issue." *Risk Analysis* 4(3):231–244.

Spangler, M. B. 1982. "The Role of Interdisciplinary Analysis in Bridging the Gap Between the Technical and Human Sides of Risk Assessment." *Risk Analysis* 2(2):101–104.

Sperber, D. 1982. "Apparently Irrational Beliefs." In M. Hollis and S. Lukes, eds. *Rationality and Relativism.* Oxford: Blackwell, 149–180.

SRA (Society for Risk Analysis). 1985. *RISK Newsletter* 5(2):2.

———. 1990. *Membership Directory, 1990.* MacLean, VA: Society for Risk Analysis.

———. 1991. *RISK Newsletter* 11(1):1, 12.

Stallings, R. A. 1987. "Organizational Change and the Sociology of Disaster." In R. R. Dynes, B. de Marchi, and C. Pelanda, eds. *Sociology of Disasters.* Milan: Franco Angeli, 240–257.

———. 1990. "Media Discourse and the Social Construction of Risk." *Social Problems* 37:80–95.

Starr, C. 1969. "Social Benefit Versus Technological Risk: What Is Our Society Willing to Pay for Safety?" *Science* 165:1232–1238.

Starr, C., R. Rudman, and C. Whipple. 1976. "Philosophical Basis for Risk Analysis." *Annual Review of Energy* 1:629–662.

Sternberg, R. J. 1991. "Beyond IQ: A Triarchic Theory of Human Intelligence." Presentation at the Annual Meeting of the American Association for the Advancement of Science, Washington, DC, February 17, 1991.

Stevens, S. S. 1958. "Problems and Methods of Psychophysics." *Psychological Bulletin* 55:177–196.

Strathern, A. 1971. *The Rope of Moka*. Cambridge, Eng.: Cambridge University Press.

Strauss, A. 1969. *Mirrors and Masks: The Search for Identity*. San Francisco: Sociology Press.

Styan, J. L. 1965. *The Dramatic Experience*. Cambridge, Eng.: Cambridge University Press.

Suppe, F., ed. 1977. *The Structure of Scientific Theories*. Urbana: University of Illinois Press.

Svenson, O. 1981. "Are We All Less Risky and More Skillful Than Our Fellow Drivers?" *Acta Psychologica* 47:143–148.

———. 1988. "Mental Models of Risk, Communication, and Action: Reflections on Social Amplification of Risk." *Risk Analysis* 8(2):199–200.

Szalay, L. B., and J. Deese. 1978. *Subjective Meaning and Culture: An Assessment Through Word Associations*. Hillsdale, NJ: Erlbaum.

Tamuz, M. 1990. "When Close Calls Count: Enhancing Organizational Learning About Risks." Presented at the Annual Meeting of the Society for Risk Analysis, New Orleans, October.

Teigen, K. H., W. Brun, and P. Slovic. 1988. "Societal Risks as Seen by a Norwegian Public." *Journal of Behavioral Decision Making* 1:111–130.

Thomas, K., D. Maurer, M. Fishbein, H. J. Otway, R. Hinkle, and D. A. Simpson. 1980. *Comparative Study of Public Beliefs About Five Energy Systems*. International Institute for Applied Systems Analysis (IIASA), Research Report 80–15. Laxenburg, Austria: IIASA.

Thomas, K., E. Swaton, M. Fishbein, and H. J. Otway. 1980. "Nuclear Energy: The Accuracy of Policy Makers' Perceptions of Public Beliefs." *Behavioral Science* 25:332–344.

Thompson, M. 1980a. *An Outline of the Cultural Theory of Risk*. Working Paper of the International Institute for Applied Systems Analysis (IIASA), WP–80–177. Laxenburg, Austria: IIASA.

Thompson, M. 1980b. "Aesthetics of Risk: Culture or Context." In R. C. Schwing and W. A. Albers, eds. *Societal Risk Assessment: How Safe is Safe Enough?* New York: Plenum Press.

———. 1982a. "A Three Dimensional Model." In M. Douglas, ed. *Essays in the Sociology of Perception*. London: Routledge and Kegan Paul.

———. 1982b. "The Problem of the Centre." In M. Douglas, ed. *Essays in the Sociology of Perception*. London: Routledge and Kegan Paul.

———. 1983. "Postscript." In H. Kunreuther and J. Linnerooth, eds. *Risk Analysis and Decision Processes*. Berlin: Springer-Verlag.

———. 1991. "Plural Rationalities: The Rudiments of a Practical Science of the

Inchoate." In J. A. Hansen, ed. *Environmental Concerns: An Interdisciplinary Exercise*. London: Elsevier, 241–254.

Thompson, M., R. Ellis, and A. Wildavsky. 1990. *Cultural Theory*. Boulder, CO: Westview Press.

Thompson, M., and M. Warburton. 1985. "Decision Making Under Contradictory Certainties." *Journal of Applied Systems Analysis* 12:3–34.

Thompson, M., M. Warburton, and T. Hatley. 1986. *Uncertainty on a Himalayan Scale*. Milton Ash, UK: Ethnographica.

Thompson, M., and A. Wildavsky. 1982. "A Proposal to Create a Cultural Theory of Risk." In H. C. Kunreuther and E. V. Ley, eds. *The Risk Analysis Controversy: An Institutional Perspective*. New York: Springer-Verlag, 145–161.

Tierney, K. J. 1989. "Improving Theory and Research on Hazard Mitigation: Political Economy and Organizational Perspectives." *Mass Emergencies and Disasters* 7(3):367–396.

Toulmin, S. 1982. *The Return to Cosmology*. Berkeley: University of California Press.

Tucker, L. R. 1964. "The Extension of Factor Analysis to Three-Dimensional Matrices." In N. Frederiksen and H. Gulliksen, eds. *Contributions to Mathematical Psychology*. New York: Holt, Rinehart and Winston, 109–127.

Tunstall, J. 1962. *The Fishermen*. London: MacGibbon and Lee.

Turner, V. 1974. *Dramas, Fields, and Metaphors: Symbolic Action in Human Society*. Ithaca, NY: Cornell University Press.

———. 1982. *From Ritual to Theater: The Human Seriousness of Play*. New York: Performing Arts Journal Publication.

Tversky, A. 1972. "Elimination by Aspects: A Theory of Choice." *Psychological Review* 79:281–299.

Tversky, A., and D. Kahneman. 1973. "Availability: A Heuristic for Judging Frequency and Probability." *Cognitive Psychology* 4:207–232.

———. 1974. "Judgment Under Uncertainty: Heuristics and Biases." *Science* 185:1124–1131.

Tversky, A., S. Sattath, and P. Slovic. 1988. "Contingent Weighting in Judgment and Choice." *Psychological Review* 95:371–384.

United Church of Christ, Commission for Racial Justice. 1987. *Toxic Wastes and Race in the United States: A National Report on the Racial and Socio-Economic Characteristics of Communities Surrounding Hazardous Waste Sites*. New York: United Church of Christ.

U.S. Congress. House. Committee on Science and Technology. 1979. *Authorizing Appropriations to the National Science Foundation*. House Report 96–61. Washington, DC: Government Printing Office.

U.S. Environmental Protection Agency. 1987. *Unfinished Business*. Washington, DC: EPA.

———. 1990. *Reducing Risk*. Washington, DC: EPA.

Vaughan, D. 1989. "Regulating Risk: Implications of the Challenger Accident." *Law and Policy* 11(3):330–349.

———. 1990. "Autonomy, Interdependence, and Social Control: NASA and the Space Shuttle Challenger." *Administrative Science Quarterly* 35(June):225–257.

Viscusi, W. K. 1983. *Risk by Choice*. Cambridge, MA: Harvard University Press.

Vlek, C.A.J., and P.J.M. Stallen. 1980. "Rational and Personal Aspects of Risk." *Acta Psychologica* 45:273–300.

———. 1981. "Judging Risks and Benefits in the Small and in the Large." *Organizational Behavior and Human Performance* 28:235–271.

von Winterfeldt, D. 1987. "Value Tree Analysis: An Introduction and an Application to Offshore Oil Drilling." In P. Kleindorfer and H. Kunreuther, eds. *Insuring and Managing Hazardous Risks: From Seveso to Bhopal and Beyond*. New York: Springer-Verlag, 349–377.

von Winterfeldt, D., and W. Edwards. 1984. "Patterns of Conflict About Risky Technologies." *Risk Analysis* 4(1):55–68.

———. 1986. *Decision Analysis and Behavioral Research*. New York: Cambridge University Press.

von Winterfeldt, D., R. J. John, and K. Borcherding. 1981. "Cognitive Components of Risk Ratings." *Risk Analysis* 1(4): 277–287.

Wagner-Pacifici, R. E. 1986. *The Moro Morality Play: Terrorism as Social Drama*. Chicago: University of Chicago Press.

Wald, M. L. 1989. "U.S. Will Start Over on Planning for Nevada Nuclear Waste Dump." *New York Times*, November 29, 1, 6.

Waldrop, M. M. 1990. "Hubble Hubris: A Case of 'Certified' Blindness." *Science* 250:1333.

Waller, R. A., and V. T. Covello, eds. 1984. *Low Probability/High Consequence Risk Analysis*. New York: Plenum Press.

Walsh, E. J. 1981. "Resource Mobilization and Citizen Protest in Communities Around Three Mile Island." *Social Problems* 29:1–21.

Wartofsky, M. W. 1986. "Risk, Relativism, and Rationality." In V. T. Covello, J. Menkes, and J. Mumpower, eds. *Risk Evaluation and Management*. New York: Plenum Press, 131–153.

Watts, N.S.J. 1987. "Mobilisierungspotential und gesellschaftspolitische Bedeutung der neuen sozialen Bewegungen." In R. Roth and D. Rucht, eds. *Neue soziale Bewegungen in der Bundesrepublik Deutschland*. Frankfurt: Campus, 47–67.

Weinberg, A. 1972. "Science and Trans-Science." *Minerva* 10(2):209–222.

Weinstein, N. 1984. "Why It Won't Happen to Me." *Health Psychology* 3(5):431–457.

———. 1987. "Unrealistic Optimism About Susceptibility to Health Problems: Conclusions from a Community-Wide Sample." *Journal of Behavioral Medicine* 10(5):481–500.

———., ed. 1987. *Taking Care: Understanding and Encouraging Self-Protective Behavior*. Cambridge, Eng.: Cambridge University Press.

———. 1988. "The Precaution-Adoption Process." *Health Psychology* 7(4):355–386.

Weinstein, N., M. L. Klotz, and P. M. Sandman. 1988. "Optimistic Biases in Public Perceptions of the Risk from Radon." *American Journal of Public Health* 78(7):796–800.

Weiss, M. S. 1967. "Rebirth in the Airborne." *Trans-action* 4(6):23–26.

Whelan, E. 1985. *Toxic Terror*. Ottawa, IL: Jameson.

Whipple, C. 1985. "Opportunities for the Social Sciences in Risk Analysis—An Engineer's Viewpoint." In V. T. Covello, J. L. Mumpower, P.J.M. Stallen, and V.R.R. Uppuluri, eds. *Environmental Impact Assessment, Technological Assessment, and Risk Analysis: Contributions from the Psychological and Decision Sciences.* Berlin: Springer-Verlag, 91–103.

———. 1988. "Acceptable Risk." In C. C. Travis, ed. *Carcinogen Risk Assessment.* New York: Plenum Press, 157–170.

Whipple, C., and V. T. Covello, eds. 1985. *Risk Analysis in the Private Sector.* New York: Plenum Press.

White, G. F. 1953. *Human Adjustments to Floods.* Department of Geography Research Paper No. 29. Chicago: University of Chicago.

———. 1961. "The Choice of Use in Resource Management." *Natural Resources Journal* 1(March):23–40.

White, G. F., and J. E. Haas. 1975. *Assessment of Research on Natural Hazards.* Cambridge, MA: MIT Press.

Whitehead, A. N. 1947. *Science and the Modern World. Lowell Lectures, 1925.* New York: Macmillan.

Wildavsky, A. 1979. "No Risk Is the Highest Risk of All." *American Scientist* 67(January-February):32–37.

Wildavsky, A., and K. Dake. 1990. "Theories of Risk Perception: Who Fears What and Why?" *Daedalus* 119(4):41–60.

Williams, A., and A. Lund. 1988. "Mandatory Seat Belt Use Laws and Occupant Crash Protection in the United States: Present Status and Future Prospects." In J. Graham, ed. *Preventing Automobile Injury: New Findings from Evaluation Research.* Dover, MA: Auburn House.

Wilson, R. 1975. "The Costs of Safety." *New Scientist* 68:274–275.

Wittgenstein, L. 1953. *Philosophical Investigations.* Oxford: Blackwell.

Wolff, C. 1990. "Exxon Admits a Year of Breakdowns in S. I. Oil Spill." *New York Times,* January 10.

Woolgar, S. 1981. "Interests and Explanation in the Social Study of Science." *Social Studies of Science* 11:365–394.

Wundt, W. 1883. "Über psychologische methoden." *Philosophische Studien* 1:1–38.

Wynne, B. 1975. "The Rhetoric of Consensus Politics: A Critical Review of Technology Assessment." *Research Policy* 4:1–52.

———. 1980. "Technology, Risk, and Participation: On the Social Treatment of Uncertainty." In J. Conrad, ed. *Society, Technology, and Risk.* New York: Academic Press, 167–202.

———. 1982a. "Institutional Mythologies and Dual Societies in the Management of Risk." In E. Ley and H. Kunreuther, eds. *Risk Assessment: An Institutional Approach.* New York: Springer-Verlag, 127–143.

———. 1982b. *Rationality and Ritual: The Windscale Inquiry and Nuclear Decisions in Britain.* Chalfont St. Giles: British Society for the History of Science.

———. 1983. "Redefining the Issues of Risk and Public Acceptance—The Social Viability of Technology." *Futures* 15:13–32.

———. 1984a. "Public Perceptions of Risk." In J. Surrey, ed. *The Urban Transportation of Irradiated Fuel.* London: Macmillan, 246–259.

———. 1984b. "The Institutional Context of Science, Models and Policy: The IIASA Energy Study." *Policy Sciences* 17(3):277–320.

———. 1985. "From Public Perception of Risk to Cultural Theory of Technology."

In V. T. Covello, J. L. Mumpower, P.J.M. Stallen, and V.R.R. Uppuluri, eds. *Environmental Impact Assessment, Technology Assessment, and Risk Analysis: Contributions from the Psychological and Decision Sciences.* New York: Springer-Verlag, 849–875.

———. 1986. "Public Perceptions of Nuclear Risks: Technological Treadmill or Institutional Development?" In L. E. Roberts et al., eds. *Nuclear Power and Public Acceptance.* Norwich, UK: University of East Anglia.

———. 1987. "Risk Perception, Decision Analysis and the Public Acceptance Problem." In B. Wynne, ed. *Risk Assessment and Hazardous Waste Management: Implementation and the Dialectics of Credibility.* London: Springer-Verlag.

———. 1989a. "Building Public Concern into Risk Management." In J. Brown, ed. *Environmental Threats: Perception, Analysis, and Management.* London: Belhaven, 119–132.

———. 1989b. "Frameworks of Rationality in Risk Management—Towards the Testing of Naive Sociology." In J. Brown, ed. *Environmental Threats: Perception, Analysis, and Management.* London: Belhaven, 33–45.

———. 1989c. "Sheepfarming After Chernobyl: A Case Study in Communicating Scientific Information." *Environment* 31(2):10–15, 33–39.

———. 1991a. "After Chernobyl: Science Made Too Simple?" *New Scientist* 26:44–46.

———. 1991b. "Public Understanding and the Management of Science." In D. Hague, ed. *The Management of Science.* London: Macmillan.

———. Forthcoming. "Misunderstood Misunderstanding: Social Identities and Public Uptake of Science. *Public Understanding of Science.*

Young, O. 1989. *International Cooperation.* Ithaca, NY: Cornell University Press.

Zald, M. N. 1988. "Looking Backward to Look Forward: Reflections on the Past and Future of the Resource Mobilization Research Program." Manuscript for Workshop on Frontiers of Social Movement Theory, Ann Arbor, June 7–10, 1988, University Of Michigan.

Zeckhauser, R. J., and W. K. Viscusi. 1990. "Risk Within Reason." *Science* 248:559–564.

Ziman, J. M. 1968. *Public Knowledge: An Essay Concerning the Social Dimension of Science.* London: Cambridge University Press.

Index

About the Editors and Contributors

WILLIAM R. FREUDENBURG, a Professor of Rural Sociology at the University of Wisconsin-Madison, has devoted some fifteen years to the study of social responses to controversial technologies and technological risks. He has contributed several dozen papers to social science journals on the social impacts of coal, oil shale, nuclear power, and other forms of energy development. His books include *Public Reactions to Nuclear Power: Are There Critical Masses?* and *Paradoxes of Western Energy Development*, both published in a series by the American Association for the Advancement of Science.

SILVIO O. FUNTOWICZ and JEROME R. RAVETZ are co-Directors of the Research Methods Consultancy in London. They collaborate on research and consultancy in the management of uncertainty and quality assurance of scientific information, and also on the analysis of scientific practice in the risk and environmental fields. Dr. Ravetz formerly taught the History and Philosophy of Science at the University of Leeds. Mr. Funtowicz is a Consultant for the European Community Joint Research Centre in Ispra, Italy. They are co-authors of the recently published *Uncertainty and Quality in Science for Policy*.

DOMINIC GOLDING is a Fellow in the Center for Risk Management at Resources for the Future. He received his Ph.D. in Geography from Clark University, where his research focused on occupational hazards and the social issues of risk assessment and risk management, especially with regard to nuclear power. His current interests include the history and development

of risk research, environmental equity, risk communication, and the evaluation of risk burdens in individual communities. Dr. Golding is the author
of *The Differential Susceptibility of Workers to Occupational Hazards: A
Comparison of Policy in Sweden, Britain, and the United States*, co-author
of *A Model Emergency Response Plan for Nuclear Power Plants*, and co-
editor of *Preparing for Nuclear Power Plant Accidents: Selected Papers*.

ROGER E. KASPERSON is Professor of Government and Geography at
Clark University. He has written widely on issues of technological hazards,
risk communication, radioactive wastes, global environmental change, and
the ethical and policy issues of risk management. For the past ten years,
Professor Kasperson has directed a series of research projects, funded by
the National Science Foundation, the Russell Sage Foundation, and the
United Nations University. He is co-author or co-editor of many books
including: *Equity Issues in Radioactive Waste Management; Nuclear Risk
Analysis in Comparative Perspective; Corporate Management of Health and
Safety Hazards: A Comparison of Current Practice; Understanding Global
Environmental Change: The Contributions of Risk Analysis and Risk Man-
agement*; and *Communicating Risks to the Public*.

SHELDON KRIMSKY is Professor of Urban and Environmental Policy at
Tufts University. Professor Krimsky's research has focused on the social
and ethical impacts of science and technology. He is the author of numerous
papers on the social and regulatory aspects of science. Among the books
he has authored and co-authored are *Genetic Alchemy: The Social History
of the Recombinant DNA Controversy; Environmental Hazards: Communicating Risks as a Social Process*; and *Biotechnics and Society: The Rise
of Industrial Genetics*. His current research examines the environmental
applications of biotechnology.

HOWARD KUNREUTHER is the Meshulam Riklis Professor in Practice
of Creative Management, Professor of Decision Sciences and Public Policy
& Management, as well as Director of the Wharton Risk and Decision
Processes Center at the University of Pennsylvania. His current research is
concerned with the role of insurance compensation, incentive mechanisms,
and regulation as policy tools for dealing with technological and natural
hazards. He is author and co-author of numerous scientific papers, books,
and monographs concerned with risk and policy analysis, decision processes,
and protection against low-probability high-consequence events.

HARRY OTWAY is Science Advisor on the executive staff of the Director
of the Los Alamos National Laboratory. He is also co-chair of a joint

community/laboratory working group to address community health concerns. He was formerly head of technology assessment for the Commission of the European Communities at Ispra, Italy, and leader of a risk research project at the International Institute for Applied Systems Analysis at Vienna, Austria. He has more than 120 publications, primarily on the social aspects of technological risk.

INGAR PALMLUND works as consultant, researcher, and writer. She has held senior positions in the Swedish Civil Service as Executive Director of the Swedish Council for Environmental Information and as Deputy Director General of Statskontoret, the Swedish equivalent of the Office of Management and Budget. She is presently a Visiting Scholar in the Department of Urban and Environmental Policy at Tufts University.

STEVE RAYNER is a Senior Researcher and Program Manager for Global Environmental Policy Analysis at Battelle, Pacific Northwest Laboratories in Washington, DC. He has published extensively in the areas of culture and social organization, risk analysis, and global environmental change.

ORTWIN RENN is Associate Professor for Environment, Technology, and Society and a senior investigator in the Hazard Assessment Group, at the Center for Technology, Environment, and Development, Clark University, Worcester, Massachusetts. Prior to joining Clark, he directed a research unit for technology assessment at the largest government research center in the Federal Republic of Germany (National Research Center KFA, Jülich). Renn has published seven books and more than fifty articles in journals and books.

PAUL SLOVIC is President of Decision Research in Eugene, Oregon, and Professor of Psychology at the University of Oregon. His current research examines perceptions of nuclear power, the dynamics of risk and trust, intuitive toxicology, and the development of methods for evaluating improvements and damages to the environment. Dr. Slovic is one of the leading contributors to research on public perceptions of risk, a subject about which he has written and lectured extensively. In addition to examining the subject in numerous journal articles, he is co-author of *Acceptable Risk*. Dr. Slovic is past president of the Society for Risk Analysis and a recipient of the society's 1991 Distinguished Contribution Award.

DETLOF VON WINTERFELDT is a Decision and Risk Analyst at the Institute for Safety and Systems Management, University of California at Los Angeles. His research and professional activities combine theoretical

ent, experimental studies, and applications. He has contributed to
etical developments in multiattribute utility analysis, as well as to
iputerization of multiattribute utility techniques. In addition, he
ted many experimental studies to test new procedures for improving
on making and risk communication. His current research interests are
e foundation and practice of decision analysis as applied to risk man-
nent and risk communication. He is the author of many articles and
orts on these topics, and co-author of *Decision Analysis and Behavioral
:search*.

CHRIS WHIPPLE is Vice President and Director, Western Operations of
Clement International Corporation. He directs Clement's San Francisco and
Seattle offices, in which the major activity is conducting applied risk as-
sessments for both private clients and government agencies. Before joining
Clement, he spent 16 years at the Electric Power Research Institute (EPRI)
working on risk assessment, management, regulation, and communication.
He currently serves on the panel of the Waste Isolation Pilot Plant of the
National Academy of Science Board on Radioactive Waste Management,
and on the editorial boards of *Risk Analysis* and *The Environmental Professional*. He is a past president of the Society for Risk Analysis and received
the society's outstanding service award.

BRIAN WYNNE is Reader in Science Studies and Research Director of the
Centre for the Study of Environmental Change at Lancaster University. He
has published extensively in the risk, science, and public policy fields, and
has authored two books, *Rationality and Ritual: The Windscale Inquiry
and Nuclear Decisions in Britain* and *Risk Management and Hazardous
Wastes*. He is currently jointly editing a book on the public understanding
of science.